FIREWEED

In the series *Critical Perspectives on the Past,*

edited by

Susan Porter Benson, Stephen Brier,

and Roy Rosenzweig

GERDA LERNER

FIREWEED

A Political Autobiography

TEMPLE UNIVERSITY PRESS PHILADELPHIA

Temple University Press, Philadelphia 19122

Published 2002

Printed in the United States of America

∞ The paper in this publication meets the requirements of the
American National Standard for Information Sciences—
Permanence of Paper for Printed Library Materials, ANSI Z39.48-1984

Frontispiece by Maurice Constant

LIBRARY OF CONGRESS CATALOGING-IN-PUBLICATION DATA
Lerner, Gerda, 1920–
Fireweed : a political autobiography / Gerda Lerner.
p. cm — (Critical perspectives on the past)
Includes bibliographical references.
ISBN 1-56639-889-4 (alk. paper)
1. Lerner, Gerda 1920– 2. Women historians—United States—Biography.
3. Women—United States—Biography. 4. Feminism—United States—History–20th century.
I. Title. II. Series.

E175.5.L47 A3 2002
973.91'092—dc21
[B]   2001054248

In memory of my parents,

Ilona (Ili) (1897–1948) and Robert Kronstein (1888–1953)

This book is dedicated to all those who in dark times

kept their integrity,

refused conformity,

and never lost hope in the strength of democracy

1. *(Epilobium angustifolium)* An ubiquitous pioneer on disturbed soil by roadsides and fire clearings in the forest.

A. E. Porsild *Rocky Mountain Wildflowers of Canada* (1979)

2. The common name alludes to its quick growth in areas devastated by fire, the pink magenta flowers brightening the fire-blackened land. During World War II the plant grew in large numbers in bombed and burnt-over areas of London.

John E. Klimas and James A. Cunningham
Wildflowers of Eastern America (1974)

3. According to a Native American legend, every fireweed plant is the soul of a tree that was burned in a forest fire.

CONTENTS

CONTENTS

Photograph gallery follows page 216

A NOTE ON USAGE

In order to protect their privacy, I have altered the names of some of the people in this narrative; in other cases I have used first names only.

Everything in this story is true, to the best of my knowledge and memory. Obviously, memory is subjective and fallible. I have tried to support memory with some historical research and evidence. I have also tried to indicate throughout where I am dealing with memory and where I am interpreting the past from a later vantage point.

In letters written long ago, I have retained the original spellings and grammar.

INTRODUCTION

When I think of writing about my life, it has to do with ordering, finding a form, even though one knows precisely the pretense of such an effort, its artifice. As a historian working on the lives of others one begins with the search for documents, the ordered remnants of personal life. Documents exist; they certify their own existence. But the rest is selected, the quilt a person has left of her life, something randomly or purposefully salvaged from the daily destruction. Those letters not consigned to fire; those ideas rescued from trash; those photos not given away or finally left to rot in some moldy basement. The historian starts with these, and the temptation is great to regard them as life itself, vested with significance simply because of their survival.

To write one's life, simply to sort out the clutter, to discern enough design to make a pattern—or is it to find meaning? A meaning beyond the event that extends to others, something that says not only, this happened to me, but this is the meaning of what happened to me. A questionable enterprise, to be sure, for it is a process that ends with one's own life, finite, and inevitably subjective and biased. One keeps reordering the past in the light of one's current insights and so what one sets down are not the facts, but a story. An explanatory myth at worst, an entertaining tale at best.

It need not be a dishonorable enterprise; one can strive for truth without having the illusion that one can find it. One can play with various forms in the hope that when the right one appears, it will be perceived as right. I would like to tell the stories and find the pattern that reaches from the past toward the future.

There is one more reason for doing this—our connection with and responsibility toward the dead. As we live on and grow older, the dead stay forever young. No one can remember them older than they were at the time of their death and so we seem, in our own aging, to be marching farther and farther away from them. Yet their immortality lies within us— as long as there are persons living who remember the dead, the dead live on. That is a hopeful thought, the thought embodied in the concept of the resurrection. For the dead do not live on unchanged; they are alive and transformed because they live in the transformed memory of the living. The living select what to remember, and what they select is what had meaning for them in their relationship with the dead person. If the living change, the memory of the dead within them also changes—that is natural and that is good. It is akin to the process of reinterpreting historical events from the point of view of the living present. It follows the example of some primitive tribes who plant the bones of their dead ancestors in the floor of their houses and who, when they move to new abodes, carry the bones of the ancestors with them.

At the moment of their transformation we swallow the dead; they become parts of us, the living, in a way they never were when they were alive. We now own them as material out of which we make our own life, the way the mushroom appropriates the rotten wood of the tree out of which it continues to grow. The dead have left us and they have entered us to be transformed and become immortal. Well, as immortal as we are ourselves, no more and no less. We are giving them the added space of our own lifetime and perhaps we can, as we ourselves are remembered, pass them on to yet another generation. To swallow the past and transform it is to accept it. It is to find balance, perhaps serenity.

What I have chosen to write is a partial autobiography, one that ends in 1958, at the time when I began my life as a historian. This new phase started with a few part-time courses taken at the New School for Social Research, then developed into a B.A. at the New School and my entry into graduate school at Columbia University in 1963. In 1966, I graduated with an M.A. and a Ph.D. from this institution, and ever since 1963 I have been a practicing historian. My specialty, the history of women, did not exist as a field of study when I began my career. I started out as an embattled outsider and in thirty-six years of steady effort have been an agent in the transformation of traditional history. My career has brought me rewarding work, professional recognition, acclaim and many public honors. All the books I have written since that time have been immediately published and have found a wide readership. Today, Women's History is taught at most academic institutions in this country and is an internationally recognized field of study. I consider myself fortunate to have been a participant and a leader in an intellectual revolution that gave women their history and moved them into the center of intellectual discourse.

In the past decades I have been frequently interviewed and questioned about my life and my development as a historian. I have been urged to write the story of "my brilliant career." Yet I have chosen here to tell not the end of the story, but what went before. My academic career is an open book. But I have been silent about my political past during the years of my academic success. And such silence, for all its complex reasons, distorts the truth. Now I would like to set the record straight. That is why I have written a political, a partial, autobiography—to explain the roads I have taken, the world in which I lived, the choices I have made in that world. The students I have taught, the audiences who have applauded my lectures, the readers who have enjoyed my books, are entitled to know how I became the person they knew and honored. I do not want to end my life within a closet of my own making.

The quest for living an honest life, a conscious life, has driven me since my adolescence. This enterprise is a part of it. But essentially, whatever the consequences, I must do this because I am a creative writer. I write to find out what I know. I write to give form to chaos. And then I must let go, let the work make it on its own, for better or worse.

Long ago, late at night in a New York winter, as my husband Carl and I left after a dinner party, I fell down the icy stoop of the brownstone and landed on my back. People came running to help me, and even as I felt the piercing pain rushing into my brain, I sensed my toes and said, "My back is not broken; I can feel my toes."

"You'll describe your own funeral," Carl said disgustedly as he helped me to my feet. That's about it. I probably will.

I

BEGINNINGS

[1]

THE FIRST THINGS I can think of are the breaks, the fissures. I've had too many—destruction, loss, then new beginnings. But every lifetime has losses. I think I have long taken mine too seriously, with a heaviness inappropriate to actuality. Mine were always experienced against a background of uncertainty about human relations, an anticipation of betrayal, abandonment and withdrawal of love, which marked my early childhood and have stayed with me most of my life. This, then, seems to be the place where to begin.

I grew up in a comfortable bourgeois household in Vienna in the 1920s. According to my grandmother's anecdote, my first life experiences were close to disastrous. At the time of my birth, the Viennese were suffering from severe food shortages in the wake of World War I. My mother was unable to nurse me. Whether this was due to her lack of good nutrition or for other reasons I do not know, but I have been told that she would not give up trying. Nursing her first baby meant a great deal to her; in her inexperience and stubbornness she refused to see that the infant was close to dehydration and starvation. According to family legend, Father's mother saved me by insisting that my mother turn me over to a wet nurse for proper nursing. Another anecdote has it that my father, just recently released from the Imperial Austro-Hungarian Army, in which he had served as a medical officer, used his uniform coat to cover bottles of milk he had obtained at black-market prices from farmers in the nearby countryside, so that his baby could be fed from a bottle. It is quite likely that from the very first weeks of my life I was confused about the availability of food and love, and confused about who my nurturing mother was: mother, father, grandmother or wet nurse.

Family anecdotes and old photos confirm that the ensuing five years were pleasant, comfortable and secure. The puny infant grew into a sturdy child. She was carefully dressed, well nourished, taken for airings in the city's parks or in the sizeable back garden of the house we lived in.

I have few memories of this period. On the whole, I experienced these as the good years, when I was pampered, fondled and approved of, when I was the center of my small world. In fact, these were the years when my parents' marriage was undergoing a severe crisis, which had started shortly after my birth.

They had married for love, when he was still in the military and she was barely twenty. She came from a merchant family in Budapest, the eldest of three daughters. Her father was a crude and noisily vulgar, self-made man, who at the time my father came on the scene was in one of his wealthy periods. There had been others, when he went bankrupt and disappeared out of town, leaving his timid wife to deal with the creditors and wait until he sent for the family. They had lived in Trieste, and they now lived again in relative splendor in Budapest. When my father, the young officer, asked my mother's father for her hand in marriage, the old man inquired as to his income. My father told him he hoped to buy a pharmacy eventually, but that meanwhile he would take a job. "With what you can earn," the old man mocked him, "you should be able to pay for my daughter's silk stockings." And so he refused to give his permission to the marriage. But it was true love. She took to bed, refused to eat, until finally the old man relented. Better yet, he gave her a fine dowry, tied up in an ironclad contract to her advantage, and a nice wedding.

Ili (Ilona) and Robert began married life in Vienna, where, with the help of his wife's dowry, he purchased a pharmacy in the fashionable First District. Ili was happy; she had escaped her father and with him her confined, unsatisfying life. She had painted as a young girl, but had been discouraged by her father's contempt and mockery. She read voraciously and wanted an artistic and literary life. She had done volunteer work with poor children, and she had notions about woman's emancipation—she thought eventually she would like to work. Meanwhile she hoped to have a fashionable salon, where talented people would meet for good conversation.

My father was struggling to make a success of his business and, quite possibly, he considered her social ambitions extravagant. He fully expected that with the birth of their first baby she would settle down to domesticity and a family-focused life. After the first year of marriage he informed Ili that they would move into an apartment in his mother's house, and no protest on her part could stop him. He was extremely devoted to his mother, "the good son" of three remaining sons (one had died in a mountaineering accident that was rumored to be a suicide). My father regarded his mother as the model of the dedicated housewife and visited her every day of his life. He saw no good reason why this housing arrangement would not be advantageous and pleasant. But it was a disaster from which the marriage never recovered.

An anecdote my mother used to tell me illustrates the earliest manifestations of her conflict with her mother-in-law. It seems that my mother was an avid fan of Henrik Ibsen's work. After my birth and while she was still lodged in a private sanitorium for a week of post-delivery care, as was the custom of the day for women of her class, she announced to my father that she wished to call the baby Hedda, in honor of Hedda Gabler, an Ibsen character. He objected that such a foreign-sounding name was wrong for a Viennese girl and would cause her life-long embarrassment. My mother agreed to compromise on Hedwig. But the next day he came back to the sanitorium and told her the baby could not be named Hedwig. Mama objects to it, he explained, because she has a cousin by that name who is a thoroughly unpleasant person, and she does not wish to be reminded of her.

"You mean to tell me I cannot name my first child without your mother's interference," Ili exclaimed.

"Approval," he said, trying to calm her down, "not interference. Surely there is no need to create conflict in the family."

They argued for quite a while; then my mother lost patience. "If I can't name my own child, then let chance name her. I'm going to open this magazine, and the first name I see, that will be it."

She opened the magazine on a dancer named Gerda, so that became my name. With Hedwig as my middle name, a middle name I intensely disliked, never used and dropped as soon as I was able to do so.

My mother's persistence can be seen in the fact that my sister, born five and a half years later, was named Nora, after the Ibsen character, without any apparent objections.

Five years into the marriage, Grandmama had more important battles to fight than those over the naming of daughters. She had by then decided that my mother was not a fit wife to her son; moreover, she considered her an unfit mother.

From "rescuing the baby from starvation" on, everything Grandmama did was for the sake of seeing that her son's children had a "proper" upbringing, which she was certain my mother could not and would not provide.

Grandmama's standards were set by a childhood defined by economic need and strict discipline. Born in Breslau, a city in present-day Slovakia that was then a part of the German Reich, she was the eldest daughter of twelve children, ten boys and two girls. The family struggled for lower middle-class status, and the eldest daughter was charged with much of the incessant labor of cooking, baking, sewing and mending for the large brood. She also must have acquired the habit of command over her flock of younger siblings. Early marriage brought her to Vienna, where she soon was in charge of a household of four sons, an adopted daughter and her husband's apprentices, much in the manner of a medieval merchant's wife. My father's father was a wine merchant; his extensive cellar and storerooms began in the basement of his house and were tunneled under the garden. His office thus was a part of the house, and one can only surmise that Grandmama meddled into his affairs with the same determination with which she kept track of her sons' wives and children. Grandfather died before I was born and was reverently held up as a model husband by Grandmama through a ritualized inventory of anecdotes, which I early suspected she had invented.

Had Grandmama been fair to her beautiful young daughter-in-law, she would have noticed that she, too, had been raised by a German-born mother whose cultural background was much like her own. Mother's mother came from Reichenberg, now also in Slovakia, and was proficient in all the domestic arts, as befitted a proper Jewish German girl. But Grandmother Goldie, whom we always simply called "Goldie," omitting the familial title, was a shy, gentle soul who sought only to please those around her. Like Grandmama, she was constantly occupied with "handiwork" and produced knitted and crocheted objects, together with fine-stitch embroidery, sufficient to furnish more households than her three daughters could supply. But my mother had early rejected her own mother's model of domesticity, and instead had chosen to do "serious" work—painting, writing, book-binding, home-decorating—always, of course, as an unpaid amateur. What was puzzling was that Grandmama was perfectly willing to accept the fact that her other daughters-in-law were not full-time housewives and mothers— one was an opera singer, another a pharmacist—and both were welcome family members and regular visitors in Grandmama's home. Only my mother was the outcast, the enemy. I suspect that Grandmama's quarrel with my mother was based less on objective issues than simply on the clash of two strong personalities.

Since the naming incident, my mother had refused to give the older woman deference, and that may have been the sin that could never be forgiven.

As I remember her, Grandmama was a matriarch whose splendid intelligence and energy were entirely devoted to tyrannizing the household and any family members within her reach. She fully expected to win every battle she entered. In her own way, so did my mother. Thus, the war between these two women dragged on for twenty or more years; neither of them could win it or let go of it.

We moved into my grandmother's house when I was a baby and stayed there until we left Vienna. It was the only place of my childhood, a three-story apartment house on a quiet residential street on which each house had a large back garden with old trees. The two ground-floor apartments were rented out. My grandmother lived on the first floor, and we lived on the second. A superintendent lived with his family in a tiny apartment in the basement. Our apartment, like grandmother's, was ample and beautiful, with a living room—we called it a salon—large enough to have four windows fronting the street. There was a large formal dining room, three bedrooms, a study and two half-enclosed porches. One of these served as a breakfast-sitting room; the other was attached to the kitchen. These porches faced each other at right angles to the apartment at either end. Since my grandmother's sitting porch, on which she spent most of her day, was underneath our kitchen porch, she could watch most of what went on in our apartment. All of our visitors had to pass her door in order to reach ours, and she made it her business to be closely observant of every detail of our lives. This was the world of my early childhood, bounded by rooms, balconies and garden, circumscribed by concepts of childrearing derived from German middle-class culture and devastated by continual conflict.

IN THE "GOOD YEARS" before I was five, I was unconscious of the raging domestic battles and accepted as perfectly natural my daily ceremonious visit to Grandmama. She usually received visitors while seated at the head of a heavy, dark walnut table in her living room, which was situated underneath our salon. She sewed by hand, white on white, with incredibly fine stitches hardly visible to the naked eye, and prided herself on being able to patch sheets so that one could not notice the patches. No matter how humble and domestic grandmother's occupations, she always dressed like a lady and wore gold and diamond rings on her bony, heavy-veined hands. She seemed to the child like a queen sitting on a throne, and one approached her with a mixture of fear and awe. The child was expected to curtsy upon entering the room, kiss Grandmama's cheek, receive a pat on the shoulder or the head and answer each of the questions rapidly put to her. "Sit down," Grandmama would start, "don't fidget. What did you do this morning? What did you eat for lunch? Was your mother home for lunch? Have you been an obedient child? Did you have your daily walk?" And so on.

Mercifully, *Tante* Emma would interrupt this interrogation and remind Grandmama that the child probably wanted some cookies and milk. Grandmama was a fine cook and took great pride in her hospitality. "A cookie and milk" was more likely to be a full meal during which *Tante* Emma would usually find something pleasant to talk about. Diminutive and very kind, *Tante* Emma, grandmother's adopted daughter, devoted her life to being the old lady's constant companion. One learned later that she was a spinster, which explained her traditional role in the family as unpaid retainer, devoted servant/acolyte and long-suffering recipient of the old lady's frustrations and bad temper. But the child thought of her as the good fairy in the fairy tales, plump, jolly and always up to something nice. She was a person of great goodness who treated a child as a child and never made any demands in return, and so she became one of the few reliable anchors of my childhood. It was because of her that the ceremonious and inquisitorial visits with Grandmama were made tolerable, even pleasant. Grandmama's apartment, with its dark furniture and heavy velvet drapes, its perennial smell of mothballs and food, its aura of old age, stuffiness and censure, stood in contrast with the bright, modern apartment that represented Mother's domain. Sooner or later I would have to choose between these two worlds

My earliest memories are of being bad. My governess and I shared a small room in which, each evening, a black iron coal stove gave off a friendly light as a background for my nightly sponge bath in a basin of warm water. By morning, the stove was black and cold, and the room was nearly as cold as the outdoors, for my father was convinced that our good health depended on sleeping with open windows, summer or winter. At the time of my first memory, I was nude, waiting for my Fräulein, who was filling the washbasin in the kitchen. While she was out of the room I did something I knew was forbidden: I opened the bottom drawer of the big wardrobe, which held Fräulein's clothing. There was nothing remarkable in it, and I tried quickly to close it, as I heard her footsteps in the hall. The drawer stuck and I could not budge it. In confusion and fear I backed up against the wall near the stove, too upset even to realize I was touching the hot stove and getting burned. "That's your punishment for being bad," Fräulein said, smearing Vaseline on the red marks on my buttocks, which now hurt fiercely. Yes, I deserved it and it served me right, I felt as I cried in pain and shame.

There were, in my world, many rules and regulations, and the child learned them unquestioningly; still, she learned badness together with obedience. The rules were arbitrary and often senseless, and one followed them simply because adults had the power and the will to punish. From the incident with the drawer I learned that badness is immediately followed by punishment; that hot coal stoves burn when you touch them; and that, if you are going to be bad, you'd better be sure not to get caught.

Other badness was more complex and more damaging. My little room connected with a door to the room that was then my parents' bedroom. Sometimes at night I was awakened by my parents' voices, arguing. I could not understand what was said, but it frightened me and I called out. Then one of them would come to my room and comfort me in a low, even-toned voice and assure me that I had been frightened by nothing more serious than a dream. But there were other times when I heard their voices when I did not cry out, but instead tiptoed to the door and pressed my ear against it. Sometimes I could understand what they were saying. Once I heard myself referred to—the child. My mother's voice: "I'll never give up the child."

My father's: "Mama can take care of her." (I knew this meant Grandmama.)

"Never. Never."

I ran back to bed and buried my head under the pillow. I did not want to hear more of these terrible words. Sometimes later, Fräulein caught me listening at the door. *"Der Horcher an der Wand hört seine eigene Schand,"* she immediately quoted the appropriate adage. Fräulein was always full of adages. He who listens at the wall, hears talk of his own disgrace. I blushed to the roots of my hair. Of course, my father wanted to get rid of me because of my badness and give me to Grandmama, who was strict. But Mother wouldn't give me up, never.

How much later it was that I found out my mother was pregnant I do not know. She made me listen to something by pressing my ear against her round, hard belly, saying it would be my little brother and wasn't it lovely that we would now have a little brother with whom I could play. "Where is the little brother now," I wanted to know.

"In Mummy's stomach, where you used to be before you were born." This kind of silliness could be dismissed as the nonsense parents say to children, when they don't want to tell them the real truth. That the stork would bring baby brother from the store, as Fräulein told me, made much better sense. "But I'll always love my little girl," said Mother, hugging me against her funny big belly.

I was five and a half years old when my sister was born. I had waited long and intently for baby brother, and then they said there would be no baby brother, but a nice baby sister who could play with me much better than any brother could. Wasn't that nice? No, it wasn't, especially since Mother was gone somewhere and Fräulein said she would be leaving soon, too, now that baby was here, because there would be a nanny for the baby. The nanny would be nice, and she would take care of me and wash me and take me for walks and do everything for me that Fräulein had done. And then Mother came home with a blanket bundle carried by a nurse in a stiff white uniform with a blue veil on her head. Mother looked funny and went straight to bed. And when the child asked to see the baby, she was shown a glimpse of something tiny and wrinkly and red inside the blanket, and the tiny thing opened up its mouth and screamed so loudly it sounded worse than howling cats.

"The baby is not too well," said the nurse, "and you mustn't come near it. Baby needs to sleep now, and you be a good girl and play quietly. And let Mother rest."

And that's how everything changed and became absolutely horrible. My room had been taken away and Father now slept in it. Mother was alone in the parents' bedroom, mostly lying still in her big bed, often crying; she was very sick. The new children's room, which I now shared with baby and Nanny, was a large, sunny corner room next to my mother's. But I was not allowed to go into Mother's room, unless she called me, which she didn't, because of her sickness.

Baby sister was also very sick. She lived in a basket cradle with a curtain all around it, and I must never never come near baby's bed because of her sickness. Baby cried all the time she was awake, sometimes whimpery and sometimes angry-shrill. She had boils full of pus all over her body and looked like the gruesome toad from the fairy tale. The doctor came each morning, and I was sent out of the room. "Just be good and make no noise." I sat under the piano in the salon and sometimes behind the big upholstered chair in the library. The library adjoined the salon on the one side, the children's room on the other. Its huge book-filled shelves muffled the sounds from the children's room, and as I watched the comings and goings of various people I understood very little of what was happening. Nanny carrying basins and pails from the room to the kitchen and, on returning, carrying clean towels and a tray; Father and the baby doctor coming out of the room looking worried. The maid going in and coming out with a pail full of disgusting, yellow-red liquid. Sometimes I crept close to the door that led to the children's room and took up my old habit of listening at walls, more guilty than ever, but I heard nothing said about myself. Everyone seemed to have forgotten my existence.

Each day, the baby doctor took a sharp knife and opened up one of the baby's boils, drained out the pus and changed the dressing. The next day he went on to the next boil—it all had a funny name, furunculosis, and maybe baby sister would die. Nanny believed in scientific explanations and was unstinting in her description. She even brought me in to show me "poor baby." Baby sister, when you removed the pretty lace-edged blanket from her crib, was a mummy doll wrapped in yellow bandages (they were soaked in some sort of yellow cream to promote healing), and the only thing living about her was an always angry red monkey face. "And now go out to the porch and play. I have to get some food into poor baby."

Clearly, everyone was a liar. They had promised me a baby brother to play with, and instead they had brought some crazy sick baby who screamed all the time and would never play with anybody. The best thing would be if she died. I thought dying meant going away, out of my life.

But then they kept talking about how *Mutti* would die, too. Mitzi, the cook, and Nanny talked about it all the time and forgot I was there to hear it. And Father talked about it sometime, mostly to admonish me to play quietly and not to cry and not to ask for food and not to ask for *Mutti*.

Another doctor with a grey beard came every day to see *Mutti* and to cut things on her. Then Nanny would be running into *Mutti's* room carrying trays and towels and would emerge from the room with pails full of blood and pus. One time I sneaked into the open door while the doctor was there and saw him bending over Mother's breast and pressing on it; pus came out and Mother screamed and I screamed. Father carried me out angrily and pushed me into the kitchen. "Can't you mind . . . "

"Her milk turned bad," said Mitzi, "and she gave it to the baby." Which made *Mutti* into some kind of wicked witch, poisoning her baby, but I didn't care because she never called for me and had forgotten me. This went on for weeks, perhaps months. At a time when antibiotics were unknown, women did indeed die of puerperal fever and mastitis, and babies died of birth-related infections, and the only cure known was drainage and salves and hot compresses and rest. And healthy little girls, caught in such a family tragedy, were the last thing anyone had time to worry about.

So I became bad, worse than ever before. Sometimes they forgot to give me a meal and I screamed and whined; at other times I would refuse to eat what was set before me. When I was ordered out of a room, I stalled, and when I was carried out I kicked and bit and clawed. I cried for Fräulein, who had after all taken care of me for three years and who had abandoned me as well. I did not like

Nanny, and she did not like me. One day when I acted up, she slapped me across the face and then again across the rump. After that I was afraid of Nanny and was very good with her and very obedient, for I had never been slapped before.

Mother was out of danger first. The doctor came only twice a week and he no longer cut her, and then he stopped coming altogether and Mother, still quite weak, sat up in a chair with a warm blanket around her shoulders. And sometimes, she would let me come into her room and play on the rug near her chair, and then it seemed almost like old times.

The baby improved, too, after sixty-four boils had been cut—Nanny supplied the number with pride, as some sort of achievement. The day came when baby could be out of bandages. Nanny unwrapped her with great care (I had noticed, all during these weeks, the patient care she gave the baby; no slapping the baby when she cried). Long coils of yellow wrapping trailed to the floor. It was like one of those surprise gift balls you unwrap and in the center there is a tiny doll. Nanny collected the bandages in the pail and went out to get warm water for the baby's bath. "Stay here," she said to me in a friendly tone. "Be a good girl and mind the baby."

No crying now. I bent over the crib and there, lying on a white flannel blanket, was the prettiest small creature with perfect arms and hands and legs and toes, all waving in the air. Her skin was pink, but it had marks where the boils had been. As I looked at this transformation in wonder, a sort of awe came over me. I had never really seen a baby. I picked up the rattle tied to the crib and held it where the baby could see, and I watched as her dark eyes turned to it. She had lots of black hair, and her face was pink and relaxed; she no longer looked like an angry monkey. Suddenly, as her eyes focused on the rattle, she smiled and became so beautiful, so marvelous—

I suddenly understood that I loved this baby and was sorry for her because of all the marks on her skin and the pain. I'll take care of you, I pledged silently. I'm your big sister, and I'm so glad you're not dead.

"The baby smiled at me," I told Nanny when she came into the room. "I made her smile."

And I thought, now everything will be good again, the way it was. And maybe better.

I WAS WRONG about that. It never again was the way it had been; that is inevitable when a new baby comes into the family. That classical drama, the dethronement of the first-born, was irreversible, but it was made much worse in our situation by the complex undercurrent of what the birth of that child meant to our parents. The story was told to me by my mother when I was in my early teens, and since it is a story that does not much accrue to her credit, I have no doubt as to its truth. She told it in a number of versions, one of which made her seem more of a victim; another made her seem more active and aggressive in her drive for self-realization. Regardless, the facts, as closely as I can gather, were that she was greatly disappointed in her situation and miserably unhappy in her marriage in the years of my early childhood. In this mood, she had a brief affair, which my father discovered. She asked for a divorce, but my father insisted that if she went ahead with it, he would keep "the child." (Click, click went my memory— "Mama will take the child"). Anyway, according to prevailing law, she would lose the child, being the "guilty party." Having no means of support and not wanting to lose her child, she gave up the idea of a divorce. Perhaps there was a genuine reconciliation—despite my mother's various bitter accounts of what was done to her, I know that my father deeply loved her and continued to love her all her life, and in a way she loved him, too. They could not live together harmoniously, and they could not live apart. After the reconciliation, life resumed normally, and in due course my sister was born. They must have hoped that this new birth would bring a strengthened marriage, but the severe stresses of the first months of desperate illness of both mother and baby must have strained their relationship beyond endurance. They had separate bedrooms after the birth of my sister, and several years later they drew up a legal contract. I do not know exactly under what circumstances this astonishing document was drawn up. I saw it as a teenager, and I knew from my own experience that they lived by it the rest of their lives. The contract provided that husband and wife agreed to maintain joint residence and the appearances of a conventional marriage, with both carrying out the responsibilities of raising their children, but that they would each be free to have their own lives, as long as they were discreet in their conduct. My mother was specifically granted several months of vacation time away from home each year. Her dowry, which had been placed in my father's business and which formed the bulk of his business capital, would stay so invested, but in turn my father had to support her "in proper style" and set aside the interest from this investment of her capital for her own use. These latter provisions had been stipulated by her father when he had settled the dowry on her.

I have long sought to comprehend what went into the making of a document so much closer to a marriage contract among feudal clans than to a financial settlement of an emancipated modern couple. Obviously, the proper upbringing of the children was a main concern of my father, as was the keeping up of appearances. My mother's version of my father's motives was that he wanted propriety more than anything else. This may be true, but it was not the whole truth, for my father was a truly good man. His later actions, especially in the Hitler years and the years of her terminal illness, belie such a version and leave no doubt that he truly loved her. Most likely he hoped that by tying her to him and to the children, he would bring about the change he hoped for so desperately, that she would become a respectable and reliable wife and mother.

But what about her—how could she have agreed to and abided by such a humiliating contract? She always explained that she did it for the sake of the children, because she did not want to lose the children and knew she would have to in case of a divorce. For the many years when I was her loyal, partisan defender, I believed this explanation and accepted as my due the burden of guilt it put upon me for wrecking my mother's life. She also said that since she was unschooled and untrained, she had no choice; she could not make a living alone. I no longer believe either of these explanations is sufficient. Even in her own circle, there was her younger sister Manci, at that very time studying to be a doctor. A few years later Manci divorced her first husband and lived an independent life, supporting herself and her mother. Sometimes in those years, there ensued a bitter quarrel between these two sisters having to do with money, and to the end of their lives they barely saw each other. I've often puzzled over the connection between my mother's attitude toward money and dependency and that quarrel with her independent sister. Since all the participants are dead, I will never know.

As for my mother, the contract gave her a kind of power. She firmly believed that at any time, if she withdrew her dowry from my father's business, he would be ruined. Even as a teenager, I could see this myth for an illusion, for by then my father was quite well-to-do and could have easily weathered the withdrawal of her dowry from his business, but to her this fond illusion offered a surrogate for the power to be self-defined and self-supporting. It seems to me most likely that my mother was afraid of becoming independent, that she liked what the contract gave her—comfortable support and some freedom without all the responsibilities of independence.

All of which the six year old did not know, but still she felt its reverberations. The room arrangement: "Mother's room" was redecorated soon after her recovery, in a modern style, its brick red, woven curtains covering one full wall, its fireplace lined with jet black tiles, a desk and tubular steel chair transforming the bedroom into a studio-sitting room. Now her room was marked off from the rest of the apartment in a distinctive and private way. The children were not permitted into her room, except by her invitation. If one wanted to see one's mother, one did not just knock at the door; one had to make an appointment. When one was invited to the room, one was treated quite formally as an adult, which was delightful. One might be offered a cup of tea with milk, and Mother would talk about things no one else ever talked of to a child. She might take down a book from the shelves above her bed, and we might together look at pictures of paintings. She might read some poetry; she might tell a story. Time in her room was a special, treasured treat.

Father's room was in the small study adjoining; the connecting door to Mother's room was locked. Father's room became crowded and ugly; he permitted no one to make it neat. Papers and magazines were stacked high on the floor and on the cluttered desk. Father welcomed early morning romps in his bed; he was quite open to children's visits, but he was not in the room very often, as he left early and came home late.

The geography of the apartment reflected the strange structure of the family's life. The salon, a huge formal living room with grand piano, upholstered furniture and Persian rugs, was used mostly for social gatherings and for the chamber music evenings that were regular monthly events. The library adjoining it at one end was a comforting place where I could sit and read and even occasionally chance to meet a parent. The dining room, which adjoined the salon at the opposite end, was furnished with heavy carved walnut chairs with upright backs that looked appropriate to an English castle. This was the stage on which family dinners were enacted. According to Central European custom, the main meal of the day was a late lunch over which Father presided. At the dining table, children were cautioned not to speak unless spoken to. To me, these ceremonious meals seemed quite early to be scenes of warfare. The battlefield of the dining table became the stage for my earliest rebellion: refusal to eat what was offered, bad table manners, incessant teasing of my little sister, boisterous explosions of chattering alternating with surly withdrawal. The punishments for these infractions were endless and tedious, and also quite ineffective.

Nothing was ever again as it had been, and the most obvious sign of this was Mother's withdrawal. She spent less and less time at home and with the children; and she transformed herself into a fashionable lady, quite remote from the woman she was at home. The fashionable lady inhabited "Mommy's city," a mysterious region where she met her friends. Sometimes, in the early years, her women friends came to visit her at home of an evening—lovely creatures, mostly younger than she was, artists, dancers, writers. They drank tea in her room and smoked cigarettes, chatting long into the night in ways that seemed mysterious and attractive, but which totally excluded the coarse world of bumbling children with dirty socks and scruffy clothes, forever hungry for sweets and noisily concerned with school and soccer games. The daily care of the children was given over to a governess, and Mother kept her supervising of that care to a minimum. The spontaneous invitations for visits to her room and her always unscheduled appearances in the children's room were infrequent, much longed-for treats. Her unavailability was the predominant theme of those years and so the child, frequently disappointed and rebuffed, finally transferred allegiance to the governess.

The governess who followed upon Nanny with the iron hands was a kind, intelligent, warm person who stayed for five years. We called her Bebe—she was a true substitute mother for all that time, the one person about whom all memories are good and warming. She was fun; she loved children; she played games and taught skills and was always available, satisfying the greed of even this neediest of all children. She was, in fact, a trained kindergarten teacher and was studying to become a child psychologist. Bebe, if she could have stayed another five years, might have set everything to rights, acting as buffer, mediator, mother surrogate.

She made of the children's room a safe refuge, an island in that sea of warfare, where everything was bright and joyous and serene. This room was beautifully decorated with stenciled wallpaper on which horses ran through stylized gardens and fields of brown and yellow and green. The same colors and motifs appeared on the storage wall with its closets and chest-of-drawers and toy shelves, on the custom-made tiles of the large woodstove, on the scatter rugs and curtains. My bed and that of my sister, Nora, stood head to foot along one wall, opposite the storage wall. At night, Bebe pulled out a folding bed and slept beside us. There was a round table with four chairs and a cheery yellow lamp, which was the place where friendly meals, games and homework were centered.

And more and more, little sister made her presence felt. Once recovered, she quickly made up for lost ground and became a bright, funny toddler who had a gift for making herself liked by everyone. Perhaps because of the embattled start of her life, she managed to make Father and Mother focus on her. On walks, they each held her hand; they admired her and praised her and repeated with pride the "cute things" she was saying. Perhaps even this late it is the dethroned child in me remembering things in that way; perhaps none of it happened like that, and my anger and jealousy are still coloring my perceptions. But that is how I remember it. I also remember that I enjoyed little sister quite a lot and played with her, bossed her around and took pride in teaching her.

The way she really affected my life is evident in my self-definition. When we were alone or with Bebe, I was boisterous and confident, but when we were with the parents or with their friends, I was constantly aware of my shortcomings compared to Nora. Nora had friendliness and charm, two qualities I felt I lacked and which I relinquished to her, as though there were only a limited quantity of these properties available to be distributed among us. If there was a party in the salon, the two of us would be summoned to come in for a while. We entered, dressed in identical clothing—a fact which always mortified me—she was two, when I was almost eight. She would run into the room and spin around in the center of a circle of adults and everyone would admire her and laugh at her antics. More likely than not, when I followed her into the room, I'd trip over something or bump into a person or a piece of furniture. She was cute and girlish, while I was bumbling and surly, and the more I noticed her effect on others, the more I became confirmed in my role of tomboy and rebel.

I tried to make myself into someone as different as possible from that little sister, giving up the competition in which I should have engaged, because of that great age difference between us and because of that pitiful start she had had. Perhaps I would have lost out anyway, but I now believe it would have been far better to compete than to do what I did, which was a form of giving up a whole side of my being.

Nora manipulated the adults around her with pleasantry and charm; I defied them and caused them to confront me. She avoided conflict by tears and sickness; I courted it and intensified it by stubbornness and angry will. All during her childhood she refused to acknowledge the battlefield on which she was reared, while I was in an unending search for comprehension of it and then for mastery. This is not to make a judgement that she was wrong and I was right or the other way around—it is just to say how it was.

Bebe understood me; she seemed to be capable of loving me "just the same." But when I was a little over ten, Bebe left, and the void of that loss was not healed for a long time. She told us she was leaving because she wanted to continue her studies at the university. In fact, as I soon found out by worming the story out of the cook and my aunt Emma, she was fired by Mother, who had become convinced that Bebe was trying to take over her children. I heard that explanation in the first few days after she left, while I was still hysterical with weeping over her departure. Click, click—I immediately connected this loss with my own badness.

On Bebe's days off my mother took care of us, giving us our supper and bath. But over the years, these occasions, which I had earlier anxiously awaited and enjoyed, no longer pleased me. I was disagreeable with Mother, impatient with the small ways in which she did things differently from Bebe. Once, during the bath, when I had again defied my mother, she stormed out of the room, saying it seemed I loved Bebe more than I did her. "I do," I shouted after her, "I certainly do—Bebe IS my mother." Now that came back to haunt me—I concluded that this incident had caused Bebe's departure.

I moped and cried for weeks after she had left, refused to let my mother come near me and presented a perfect spectacle of a disturbed child. Bebe came to visit and tried to convince me to accept what had happened in good grace. I could not do that.

It was the second serious loss of love and security and it was one, I vowed, I would never suffer again. At age ten, I decided to depend emotionally on no one. I had said the truth when I called Bebe my mother, she had been that for five years, and now I would try to make it without a mother, without a father. Just on my own.

In those years I read stories of expeditions to the Antarctic. My hero became Captain Amundsen, discoverer of the South Pole. I got a brown leather sailor's cap with CAPTAIN AMUNDSEN written on the band. I wore it incessantly and refused to take it off, even for meals. It was cold where I was, and white and lonely. Like my hero, I had few resources left; all I had was the will to survive.

[2]

I WAS LIVING ALONE on the South Pole, dreaming heroic dreams. Down below the real world was far less heroic. Two years earlier, when I was still in elementary school, I had learned that I was a misfit, a freak, an outcast. Always was and always would be.

My father programmed me for it, by making rules that prevented my easy contact with most children my age. I was to socialize only with children who came from suitable families. That excluded three quarters of my classmates on account of their father's hopelessly lower-class occupations. Since my father did not think it suitable for me to develop friendships with boys, that left only a few eligible girls at public school. Though I tried, I failed to win their approval.

In my building there was only one other child, the superintendent's little daughter, Mitzi, and she was not allowed to play ball with me because her parents carried out the garbage and washed the stairs. In the park, Governess and I saw "nice" children who also were there with governesses, and for the hour each day we spent there I could toss a ball, run hoops and play catch with them, while the nannies chatted on the park bench. But then we said goodbye, and the next day there was a different girl with a governess. Sometimes the same girl came back a few times. But I made no friend.

Each day on the way to school, the children from the orphan asylum passed us, walking in two groups, boys and girls separately. They had to walk two by two, with a teacher in front and a big boy or girl monitor in the rear. They all wore black clothes and black shoes. They giggled and pushed each other and pointed fingers at the children who came to school from homes with parents. They lived in a big orphan asylum some streets away, behind a black iron fence and a row of tall trees. I imagined they must have a fine time there, all together.

"Can I invite two orphan girls to come play with me?" I asked my father. "They're Jewish."

"Of course not. That would not be allowed. They must stay in the orphan asylum."

"Maybe I can go there to play?"

"You should be grateful you have a father and mother and a nice home and a sweet baby sister."

I looked at my father hard. I understood he wasn't going to let me have a friend. If I were an orphan, I could live in a big house with lots of children and have all the friends I wanted. I'd just as soon be an orphan, I thought.

Since my father prevented me from forming friendships with girls, I had to make do with the playmates he approved—my cousins and the children of his business partners, all boys. Boys were all right if my father knew their parents. So I played boys' games—soccer, trapper and Indian, handball, marbles. I built hideouts and climbed trees, ran races, read adventure stories like *Robinson Crusoe* and the tales of Karl May about Winnetou, the Indian chief, and Old Shatterhand, his white companion. I read the sagas of Greeks and Romans, of heroic Vikings and knights and noble warriors. I identified with adventurers, warriors and the male heroes of the books I read. I never had a female heroine. When I put on my Captain Amundsen cap and removed myself to the world of heroism, I accepted the fact I would never be a nice, pleasant, "good girl," the kind of child adults liked.

For a time, I took flight in magic. I believed in the truth of fairy tales, in the power of wishing, in the magic by which the unpopular third son, the unloved stepdaughter suddenly emerge to recognition and approval. These were the years when I regularly prayed, because prayer was a sort of magic, and if you did it right, who knew but that you would get your rewards. And I observed meticulously a set of self-imposed routines designed to safeguard me from unseen evil and from known dangers.

On my way to school each morning I took care to avoid stepping on any cracks in the pavement—a sure way of bringing on bad luck. I made certain to hop up on each front step I passed on the way. When I saw a black cat, I crossed the street to avoid it crossing my path. When I saw a dark-colored horse, a nun or a beggar I would spit to my right side to avoid bad luck, but on the rare occasions when the horse was white, the day was saved. White horses were good omens.

But there weren't too many such lucky days. The daily trip to school had become an ordeal. The three roughest, dirtiest boys in my class lived on my street. Franz, the meanest of them, was the son of the super of the corner building. Each morning and afternoon, he and his friends entertained themselves by harassing me. Sometimes they merely walked on the other side of the street, pointing at me, chanting, "Candlestick, Candlestick"—a sneering reference to my long, thin legs in the hated white knee stockings. At other times, they ran ahead of me, stopped suddenly and contrived to bump into me, forcing me to walk in the gutter. Some days they tore my schoolbag away and used it as a ball, scattering my books. If I ran, they ran faster. If I hid out and waited until they had gone ahead, they would pounce on me at the next corner, hollering. One day I cried out, finally exasperated, "What do you want?"

"Your lunch," said Franz.

From then on, each day I gave Franz my two crisp rolls with butter and jam and my nice red apple in exchange for a dry slice of black bread, which was his lunch. We got free milk at school, so it wasn't too bad, and I thought I had struck a pretty good bargain. But after a few weeks of truce Franz resumed his teasing. I began to hate him and fear him and hate myself for giving up my good lunch as a tribute. I did not say anything about it at home, because I was afraid they'd make me walk to school with the governess. That would have been utterly humiliating and led to worse teasing.

At night, I cried and put curses on Franz. I wished he would break a leg; I wished he would get the measles. But his health was excellent. Still, he often was in trouble in school. He was always dirty; his hair was unkempt; his shoes were scuffed and often unlaced. The teacher would make him come up front, beside the blackboard, where there was a little washstand with a basin and pitcher, and she would make him wash his face and hands while the rest of us giggled and pointed. Then she lectured him about being clean and neat. I rejoiced at his humiliation and did not see any connection between it and his bullying me.

Two other boys in class teased girls by pushing their hair into the inkwell or smearing their skirts with chalk. The girls who got teased that way screeched and formed little clusters against the boys, then ran off giggling, not too displeased. When it happened to me I fought and raged, then suddenly gave up when I saw I was getting nowhere. Boys did not like girls who fought back, and girls did not like me. I had a bad time going to school, and yet I loved school. I was smart and always knew the answers and the teacher favored me and that, I thought, was why the children did not like me. "Teacher's pet," the boys chanted when they passed me. So it was, so it would be.

Then Nancy Morgan came to our school, accompanied by her governess. "Stand up, class." We always stood in polite greeting when teacher or strangers came to class, and now we could observe the newcomer while teacher wrote her name in the class book. She was elegantly dressed in what we would have considered Sunday clothes, and she wore no apron to protect her dress the way we all did. Her thin legs were bare except for short white socks and black patent-leather sandals.

"Sit down, children. This is Nancy Morgan, your new classmate from England." Teacher pronounced it "None-tze," the name being as unfamiliar to her as it was to us, and the class exploded into laughter and imitations of sneezing. We got a stern lecture on courtesy toward strangers, but I barely heard it, I was so fascinated with the girl. Had I been in her place the children's laughter would have brought me to tears or noisy protest. But Nancy simply stood in front of us, regarding us with a haughty expression. "My name is Nancy," she said in a pleasant voice, slurring her vowels and endings and correcting the teacher's pronunciation. "I must say you are much more rude than English children."

I admired her from that moment on. What courage, what coolness . . . In the following weeks Nancy made no effort to be friends with anyone and frequently expressed her opinion that Viennese boys and girls were frightfully rude. Her attitude encouraged me; once she got to know me she would realize that I was well mannered and that we could be friends.

I approached her during lunch hour in the schoolyard. Nancy was leaning against the fence; her lunch consisted of dainty triangles of white bread filled with meat and lettuce. "I don't feel like playing," I announced, fishing Franz's black bread out of my lunchbox.

Nancy watched me disdainfully. "How can you eat this dry?"

"Oh, I drink water. And we have school milk."

"I drink chocolate," said Nancy.

"I like chocolate, too. We get it for parties and on Sunday. Cook makes it with whipped cream."

"Cook . . . I bet. Why are you telling stories?"

"What?" I noticed the way Nancy watched me eat my dry bread. "This is not my lunch," I explained. "We exchange lunches."

Nancy wiped her fingers with a napkin and brought out a fat yellow pear, which she examined closely before deciding on the proper place for biting into it.

If I told her my story, she'd understand, and maybe we'd walk home from school together. The boys who laughed at her harassed me. But then, watching the way she took little round bites out of her pear so as to make a neat pattern discouraged me. Better to change the subject. "I like your coat," I offered timidly.

It was spectacular, a small version of a coachman's coat, with a cape at the shoulders and a flare at the hips, made of orange wool and trimmed at the collar and cuffs with brown velvet. Nancy always kept it in her seat and took it out into the yard with her. "I liked it the first time I saw you in it." I touched the sleeve to feel the soft fuzz of the wool.

"Keep your dirty hands off it."

"My hands aren't dirty—" But Nancy had already snatched the sleeve away. "What I can't stand is people bragging and telling lies," she said, and walked away. I felt worse than when Franz hit me; my chest turned to stone. No tears this time.

To make it worse, sewing class was next. I hated sewing. All year I'd been struggling with the stiff white cotton fabric that we were supposed to make into an apron. Now I attacked it furiously. In no time at all the fabric was black from my sweaty hands; the needle kept sticking; the thread broke. The stitches looked drunk. I balled the material in my lap.

"Can't you do it?" asked my seat mate, Trudi Vodraschka. When it came to sewing, Trudi was always helpful. Her stitches were even; her fabric stayed white; none of her needles ever broke. Trudi indicated that she would thread the needle for me. I reached for my thread and scissors.

Trudi nudged me. She had her own scissors in her hand and was snipping the air with them. Her hand advanced toward the opening of the desk in front of us. She nudged me again. There, contrary to regulations, Nancy's beautiful orange coat lay folded on the seat. All the coats were supposed to be hung on the coat rack at the back of the room. Trudi's scissors, snapping like jaws, came closer and closer to the bunched-up fabric . . . Gently, they began to explore the fabric, now catching an edge of it, now circling a velvet-covered button. Suddenly, my own scissors moved as if of themselves.

"Come on," Trudi whispered. I felt tight in my chest again, excited. Trudi's arm and mine were side by side, our scissors playing with the forbidden fabric. I raised my head and watched the teacher. She was busy with Matilda, who had come up to her desk to ask a question.

Trudi's knees poked mine. I could hear Nancy's sneering voice in the playground. It was easy now to press the blades together, once, twice, to feel the delicious softness of the wool under the connecting scissors. Trudi withdrew her hand and picked up her sewing, but first she nudged the coat slightly so that the three clearly visible cuts were covered by a fold of fabric. I put my hands on my desk and got busy threading my needle.

"Was you scared?" Trudi whispered.

I shook my head.

"I wasn't either." Trudi grinned.

The tightness in my chest had vanished. It occurred to me that I was now like the poor kids, Trudi, Mitzi, Franz and his friends, who did forbidden things without being scared and got away with it.

Once away from school, though, I worried. I worried so much I could barely eat. I tried to think of what to say to my father. I contemplated being sick and staying out of school for a few days. But I went the next day and was relieved to find that Nancy was not in school. During recess Trudi jumped rope with me. I thought maybe Nancy would never come back.

But in the middle of the afternoon session the classroom door opened and Nancy's governess came in, pushing Nancy before her. She stretched her hand out dramatically. "Turn around, Nancy. Show the teacher."

Nancy pivoted and revealed three cuts in the coat, just below the cape.

"Look at what these children did. A two-hundred-shilling coat ruined. What kind of a school is this?"

The teacher was silent, looking pained. "If a child must be given such an expensive coat," she finally said somewhat sharply, "she should not be permitted to wear it to school. However . . . Kindly step outside, Miss. Nancy, go to your seat."

"We shall insist on compensation. And punishment." The woman retreated.

"I'm shocked," said the teacher. "That anyone should deliberately want to hurt a classmate . . . And to destroy something beautiful. But perhaps it was an accident. All right now, who did it?"

It was absolutely quiet. My heart was pounding furiously. Now Trudi and I would have to face the music.

In a way it had been an accident. We'd just been fooling around with the scissors. No, I had meant to do it. I had done wrong and Trudi had done wrong, and now we would both have to be punished. That was the way it was in my world—there was order and there were rules, and if you disobeyed the rules and they caught you, you had to confess and apologize and take your punishment. I tried not to think of what my parents would say; I tried to think of how I would have to get up out of my seat—but then there was Trudi's foot nudging me. She was afraid to go first; she wants to make sure we get up together . . .

"It takes no courage, children, to hurt someone behind her back. But it does take courage to admit a mistake. I repeat, who did this?"

My knees seemed funny. I did not want to go first, but if I did Trudi would get her courage. Face the music together . . . I raised my hand.

"You?" One thing I had not expected was that teacher would be sad. Angry, yes, but sad . . . I got to my feet, feeling all eyes on me.

"You mean to tell me you cut Nancy's coat? A good student like you—what made you do this, child?"

I nodded in dumb silence. I waited and waited for Trudi's voice.

"Was it a dare?" the teacher asked. "Did anyone tell you to do this?"

The teacher likes me, I thought, she's the only one here who likes me and now she won't like me anymore.

The teacher walked over to the bench where Trudi and I sat, standing just behind us. "Trudi Vodraschka," she said suddenly, "did you have anything to do with this?"

Trudi jumped up. "No," she whispered.

"Come, come now, the truth. Both of you were playing with the scissors, the coat was lying right there—"

I knew the teacher was trying to help me. Still, I was not surprised at what I heard next.

"I always get blamed. I didn't do nothing. Just because I sit next to her I can't help it."

I faced the teacher. The sad look on her face hurt so, I no longer could think at all. "I'm sorry, I'm sorry." Then the tears came.

Everything blurred after that. Waiting in the principal's office until they called home, crying, people trying to console me, cold compresses on my forehead. In the end it was almost like being sick. There was a grand confession at home, which felt good because everything came out at once, the rebuffs, Trudi, Nancy. Still, I managed not to mention Franz.

Mother made a phone call to Nancy's parents, and they arranged that we would have the coat repaired. Father muttered about people making a mountain out of a molehill; Nancy should've been punished for having the coat on the seat instead of hanging it up as the other children did. Cook served ham gelatin, as she did when one had a fever, and I offered to pay for the repair out of my pocket money and birthday money. Everyone was surprisingly understanding.

"You will not be punished," my father explained, "because you've been honest. Honesty is its own reward."

There was something crazy about this. If an honest confession wiped out wrongdoing, then anyone could do whatever they wanted.

"I hope you learned your lesson from this," Father said. "A Trudi Vodraschka is not the kind of person you should choose for a friend. I've tried to explain that to you before."

"Trudi's father beats her when she does something wrong. She told me. So maybe that's why she couldn't admit it. If I were beaten—"

"Trudi can't pick her parents, but you can pick your friends. I expect you to have nothing more to do with this girl."

"Yes, Father." As I said it I knew I did not mean to obey this rule, now or ever. I didn't want to live in the kind of world my father described, where people were judged according to their fathers' income. Trudi had been mean to me, but so had rich Nancy. What was wrong with me was that I was afraid to break the rules. Yet those who did got away with it. By lying, Trudi escaped a beating. By bullying me, Franz got a good lunch. Well, no more. From now on I would make my own rules.

The next day Trudi requested to be given another seat. She didn't want to sit near me anymore for fear I'd get her into trouble again. Well, I didn't want to be near Trudi either, because she was a snitch. The girl who was moved next to me was a timid goody-goody. I decided to hate her and have nothing to do with her. I was through trying to make friends.

There was another piece of business I had to attend to. The following morning on my way to school I waited at the corner for Franz. He came, kicking an empty box along the gutter. I called him and he crossed the street.

"So?" He stood in front of me, his unkempt hair rising like a brush out of his low forehead. His stance was that of someone ready either to ward off a blow or to bolt, even as he glared at me to try and scare me.

"I don't like your lunch," I said. "I'll keep my own from now on." I had rehearsed that sentence and it was, after all, not so hard to say it. Now he would try to hit me. I was ready for that and wondered how he would do it, with his fist or with his school bag. I figured if Trudi could stand her father hitting her, I could stand Franz hitting me. The odor of his clothes, cabbage and poverty came up against me and I suddenly knew that Franz's father must be beating him, too. There was a wall behind me and I braced my back against it. So we all get beaten, I thought.

"Oh yeah . . ." He was shifting his weight from one foot to the other. "You just watch out—I'll get you . . ."

Suddenly I was not thinking at all. Without realizing it I pushed against his chest with both my hands. "If you ever bother me again, I'll kill you . . . That's all. I got a poison needle my mother gave me—you just get stung with them once and—wham."

He jumped back. "You crazy."

There was fear in his eyes. I advanced on him again, first stuffing my fist into my pocket, then whipping it out smartly, as though it now held a powerful weapon.

Now he really jumped back. "Okay, okay—I don't like them sissy rolls anyway."

My hands dropped to my side. "Boy, are you nuts," Franz said respectfully. Then, spitting exactly in front of his shoe, he spun around and kicked a pebble in the gutter so hard it hit the house across the street and returned halfway before he kicked it again, this time ahead of him so that he had an honorable excuse for leaving.

I watched him as he made his way, erratically zigzagging back and forth in pursuit of his pebble. I could handle him; I could be as mean as he was. No little person would bully me, from now on; I'd just stand up and fight them. And no adult would bully me, either; I'd just lie to them. This was the real world, which did not have rules like our family did. In the real world the poor stuck together and the rich stuck together, and those in the middle had to find their own way. I had tried to fit into one group and into the other; now I would make it on my own.

It wasn't even hard, once you stopped believing what they told you. I hitched up my school bag and began to walk toward school, carefully stepping on every crack I could see in the pavement. Nothing happens when you do that, I thought. That was all lies, too. Nothing happens at all.

AT THE AGE OF TEN, I moved from elementary school with its pleasures and torments to a world in which education was taken seriously. Central-European children of that day were educationally sorted and put on two vastly different tracks: the larger group continued in public middle school, which might lead to a terminal diploma at age fourteen or to entry into a technical school; those who aspired to a university education were put into *Gymnasium,* an eight-year school that, depending on the type chosen, might include rigorous training in Latin, Greek and mathematics. At age eighteen *Gymnasium* students had to pass a week-long examination before an outside commission, the Matura, which gave them access to university training.

I entered a private *Gymnasium* for girls, run by a Jewish director. It offered the standard "classical" curriculum, with heavy emphasis on history and literature in Latin, German and French, and some math and sciences. Going to *Gymnasium* was a distinct step upwards toward adulthood and separated me from my little sister, who had not yet entered elementary school. There were after-school sports activities in my school, and so I managed to spend less and less time at home. But the fact that I still had a governess at home, who treated me no differently than she treated five-year-old Nora, made me continue at home in the role of the rebellious, angry child.

It was during this time I tried to find an ally in God. This was not simple, for religion, like everything else in my family, was a battleground of conflicting interpretations. My mother never went to synagogue and showed no interest in religion. Grandmama kept all the holidays in the traditional way; on these occasions all the family gathered in her home. All except my mother. Jewish holidays, then, became for me the symbol of "father's world," and whatever religious meaning they might have had for me was wiped out by Grandmama's iron rules about "appropriate" behavior, by food rituals, by the self-congratulatory community of brothers who met here and nowhere else and hurried through their prayers because they needed to complete them before they could get at their food. I sat at the foot of the table with the "children"—us four cousins—and watched the grownups as though they were actors on a stage performing a play they did not understand.

I felt much more involved with the ritual and symbols of that omnipresent God of the Catholics in whose land I lived. In Austria at that time, Catholicism was the state religion. After 1934, we lived in a virtual theocracy and religion became a compulsory part of public education. But in the days of my earlier childhood, the church was merely culturally dominant. I do not remember a day when there was not the sound of church bells ringing regularly, a comforting, pleasant sound that became a part of one's consciousness, like the rising and setting of the sun. The major church holidays, including a number of saint's days, were official holidays, and no child could escape the pervasiveness of Catholic ritual during Easter, Pentecost and Christmas. To add to my confusion, my family, like many assimilated Jewish families, celebrated Christmas with a decorated tree and with gifts. I was never offered an explanation for this practice, so I accepted it as normal, until I learned that other Jewish children celebrated Chanukka, but not Christmas. Actually, I loved Christmas; I loved the Christ child. The attractive mythology of the saints, the Virgin Mary, the guardian angels came to me not just through the surrounding culture, but through the works of art that decorated the walls of my home, reproductions of Renaissance paintings that my mother brought home from her various trips to Italy. I spent much time looking at art books in our library and there, too, Catholic symbols became synonymous with beauty and perfection. During the holidays, the music of the Mass was everywhere. The undecorated, plain interior of the synagogue in which the only music was the chant of the Cantor could not compare with these Catholic seductions.

My confusion of allegiances came to a crisis point because of one of my governesses. There had been a number of governesses after Bebe had left us, most of them staying only a short time. I disliked them on principle, but there was one I hated. She had a pointed nose, sharp elbows, skin that looked like dried parchment and she was a religious fanatic. She prayed on her knees, morning and night, said the rosary several times each day and punished me frequently and cruelly. She must have disliked me as much as I disliked her. One of her favorite punishments was to make me kneel in the corner of the room on dry lentils and peas scattered on the floor. I was to stay with my face close to the wall and contemplate my mean nature. This was painful and humiliating and it sent me into noisy rages. Fräulein subscribed to *The Little Church Messenger* and read it aloud to my sister and me. It was a frightening paper, illustrated with crudely drawn pictures of the tortures of the saints and the tortures of souls in hell. Fräulein talked a lot about hell and how to stay out of it. One important way to stay out of hell was to become a good Catholic. My sister was too small for conversion, but I was just the right age for Fräulein's project, and she began to take me along to evening services at the neighborhood church, while cook kept an eye on Nora.

The church was dark and smelled smoky. All one could see on entering was the white stone bowl of holy water and the brightly lit altar in the distance. Fräulein dipped her bony forefinger in the bowl, then made a cross sign on her forehead, touched her lips and made a cross sign over her chest. I was fascinated. "Do the same," she whispered.

No, I can't do that. My God will strike me dead. Never kneel, never make the cross sign. I stretched my hand in the direction of the basin; then, bone dry, I waved the finger in the direction of my hair. Coward ... She pulled me along impatiently, after making her curtsey in the aisle, toward the altar beneath columns with their pictures too dark to be seen, past the side altar with its tray of candles, some lit, some half-burned, some blinking.

The candles held my eyes. In *The Little Church Messenger*, it said that candles meant prayer and hope—you light a candle and your prayer gets answered. Angels hold candles as they stand on tufts of white cotton clouds at the feet of the Virgin. At the side altar the Virgin stood serenely in her blue plaster robe, the folds of her garment making her look taller than any human. The Virgin's pretty face had a faraway look, as if she were listening to something way up in the stars. The Virgin seemed kind and understanding. I felt tempted to light a candle to the Virgin, but it never came to that.

On the way home, Fräulein was animated and unusually talkative. She praised me for being good and quiet in the church and, as usual, admonished me not to tell my parents about it, because they might not understand. It was because I was Jewish that God had told her he wanted her to save my soul. The Jews had killed Christ and for that sin they all would burn in hell, but the innocent children might be saved. If my soul were saved I might go to heaven after I departed this earth and sit with the Virgin and God and all the angels. Fräulein speculated on whether God would assign me a guardian angel even before I was properly saved. Perhaps, if I prayed the prayer she had taught me, Our Father thou art in Heaven, each night . . . It was all fascinating, even entertaining, for a few weeks, but then I began to find her church gloomy and her admonitions irritating. It was just another set of rules she was putting on top of all the rules I already had to contend with. More and more I felt uneasy about going to her church; my God might not like it and might punish me in ways quite unforeseen.

Before All Saints' Day Fräulein grew quite agitated and urged me more fervently to pray and plan to go to confession. On All Saints' Day, the souls of the dead awaken and haunt the sinners. She threatened me with ghosts, with devils and unredeemed sinners in long white nightshirts coming to my bed to get me. *The Little Church Messenger* had appropriately scary pictures of nasty devils sticking pitchforks into naked sinners. That evening I refused to go to the church with her. Her nose and dry cheeks got flushed and her voice was shrill with exasperation. "You'll end up in hell . . ."

"I'm not going to church anymore, it's awful." But I was really frightened. Enough so that I did what I had never done before—I told my mother about Fräulein dragging me to church and threatening me with hell.

"Why didn't you tell me sooner?" Mother was really upset. "That's a terrible thing for her to do."

I noticed that she didn't for a moment doubt my story. I was touched by that as much as by her obvious concern. Really, why had I not told her sooner? "Fräulein said not to."

Mother hugged me and held me close. "From now on you must tell me everything. I won't let you be abused and mistreated."

"Everything?"

"You must, darling. Promise me." She was near crying. "I'll take care of you."

"I will, I promise." She had never before seemed so close, so warm. She held me to her and I, too, began to cry, and suddenly it seemed she was my true guardian angel.

She proved it by sending Fräulein away. Right then, by the end of the week. Fräulein's nose was red and as she packed her things I stood watching her, thinking she might still put a curse on me. But she was strangely meek and mute and muttered about needing a reference.

I felt pleased with myself for having fixed Fräulein. Having turned away from false gods, I now turned my attention to the God of Israel. I enrolled in Sabbath school and went to youth services. I said my *Sh'ma Yisroel* each night three times for good measure (in the fairy tales, all magical spells were repeated three times for effectiveness). I tried my best to believe in being a Jew and to find allegiance to this group to which birth had assigned me.

Once weekly, according to state law, the Jewish children had to leave their classroom and gather with children from other classes for the obligatory religion lesson given to us by a visiting Rabbi. Meanwhile the others had their catechism from the local priest. When we came back to our class we tried to blend in with the others, but it never worked; we were the Jews, those who had to leave the room when catechism was taught. Our school Rabbi had a black beard and was a fanatical Zionist. He talked seldom of God, but always of the return to the land of Israel. On the map it was a thin strip of yellow, the same color as the other British possessions in Africa and Asia, and it always made me think it was a desert place, all sand and camels. Why would anyone want to live there?

There are a few things I remember from synagogue—Purim celebrations, when I vied with the other girls to play Queen Esther; *Simchas Torah,* when we paraded through the building and the garden waving little white-and-blue flags, the flags of Zionism. I remember the awesome sound of the Shofar on Rosh Hashanah. I remember the sound of Hebrew, which I loved, and the few moments of the Saturday service when there was *a cappella* singing.

Women sat upstairs in the synagogue, their seating arrangement reflecting the rank of their husbands. The Rabbi's wife and two daughters, one of them a girl my age, sat front and center, and next to them sat the wives of the wealthier members of the congregation. I always thought, perhaps unjustly, that each row represented a level of income—the farther back you sat, the poorer you were. Those in the last rows could neither see the Torah nor the Rabbi or Cantor officiating; they could just barely hear what went on.

Upstairs and downstairs were in sharp contrast: the men below were wrapped in their white prayer shawls, swaying over their books, each man chanting knowledgeably and partaking of the service in his own way, while upstairs the fashionably dressed women in their large hats could barely follow the service in the Hebrew prayer book, most of them orienting themselves only by knowing the major chants and prayers. It was fascinating to watch the men come up when called to read a portion of the Torah, and I admired the way they knew not only the Hebrew but the appropriate intonation. But each Sabbath, when the *Shammes* read out loud the money contributions made by each member of the congregation, and those who had made large donations were called up to read from the Torah, I was disgusted. How many times did I question the Rabbi about this practice, which I thought was despicable? Did God care only about money? Was a Jew judged by the size of his donation? Yes, it appeared that a Jew expressed his devotion in terms of benevolence. Why, my own family, said the Rabbi, was among the big donors. Did I notice the window near the altar with my family's name discreetly set in a corner medallion? It meant they had contributed this window; that should make me proud. Did I realize that my uncle, who had so unfortunately died in a mountaineering accident, had been the very man who installed all the lights in the synagogue? All of this was supposed to lend some sort of glory to my family. I could not agree.

I had become intrigued by the poor. True, my contact with them was limited, but I made up for my inexperience with what I learned from books. I had begun to read social fiction at school. Maxim Gorki's *The Mother* impressed me deeply. Gerhart Hauptmann's *The Weavers* we read at school, the way we read the classics—each pupil taking a turn at reading a part out loud. Hauptmann's play depicted the desperate poverty of nineteenth-century weavers engaged in home industries. I identified with its characters and tried to locate people like them on my daily walk from school.

My walk to school took a half hour each way and gave me considerable freedom from the constant adult supervision at home and at school. I could choose from several routes. One led through fine old residential districts, where each house stood fenced and shielded from the street by an ample front garden. Sometimes one could glimpse a well-dressed child and its governess behind the fence or watch a delivery truck pull up at the kitchen entrance. Recently, instead of enjoying the pleasant sights of this daily walk, I had taken to going the long way, along streetcar tracks on streets lined with tenement flats, which abutted the residential district. Here I saw an entirely different life from the kind I knew. There were no trees or gardens, but littered empty lots and the driveways of small factory buildings. In the distance, sometimes one could get a glimpse of the Danube Canal with its grey embankment and busy bridges. Fat women in loose housedresses and broken-down shoes pushed their baby carriages along the side-walk. Groups of children played unsupervised in the street and in the garbage-strewn lots, noisy, poorly dressed and full of boisterous energy. There were people in every doorway, on every stoop. I loved the excitement of it and the variety of sights and sounds; even the slight tension I experienced, as people would glance at me as an outsider who definitely did not belong here, felt good. I noticed none of the suffering and drama the books described; on the contrary, life here seemed loose and exuberant, as if the poor did not know they were poor. Even the sounds enchanted me.

Every Viennese middle-class child learned to be fluent in High German and in Viennese dialect, the language of servants and storekeepers. But children like me seldom had a chance to use dialect. The dialect spoken in the streets was different— full-bodied, coarse, intensely expressive. I loved to hear it and practiced it silent-ly, as I swung my schoolbag in time with my steps. If anyone had spoken to me, I would have known how to answer them in their own language. But people just ignored me. Still, these daily walks meant something to me I could not then quite define. I was broadening my vision—the life I led was not necessarily the best and most desirable. There were other worlds out there, and some day I would know them.

These daily walks had been going on for some time. I was in my thirteenth year, shooting up in height, skinny and perpetually ravenous, especially for sweet and starchy foods. On my way home each day I had formed the habit of stopping at a bakery so I could munch on a sweet roll as I walked home. Each day I made the required visit at Grandmama's apartment, and recently I had begun to time my visit so I arrived as she sat down to midday dinner, the main meal of the day. My grandmother was an excellent cook who baked her own bread and made her own noodles. I had fallen into the habit of eating a full meal with her before going upstairs to sit down at our own dinner. From time to time Grandmama would wonder out loud why my mother could not manage to feed her children properly ("The child is thin as a rail . . ."). I managed to ignore these jabs at my mother, since I was quite accustomed to them. Still, they made me a little self-conscious about feeding at my grandmother's trough.

One day, having enjoyed a particularly delicious meal at Grandmama's, I just could not finish my second meal upstairs. My parents were concerned—was I coming down with something? Rather than have my temperature taken, I explained that I had already eaten downstairs. Father seemed amused by this, but Mother was furious.

"How long has this been going on?" she demanded as soon as we were alone. "What do you eat for breakfast? What do you eat in school?"

I recounted each item and confessed my trips to the bakery. Mother added it up: I was eating breakfast, school lunch, a snack on the way home, two dinners, afternoon snack and supper—at least seven meals. How could I be such a glutton? People were going hungry all over the world and I was stuffing myself that way. What would this lead to? Mother, at that time, was on one of her health-food regimes, after spending a long vacation at a health farm where they seemed to live mostly on grated carrots and apples. She had lifelong weight and allergy problems and believed strongly in the merits of a scientifically balanced diet. Usually the starving peasants of China were brought up to me only when I did *not* eat (Think of all the food you waste, the starving peasants of China would gladly live on your leftovers). Strangely, this time I did not defend myself, as I might have, by pointing out that my growing body seemed to need all that food. Mother made me feel horrible. "I just like Grandmother's cooking," I said lamely, instantly making everything worse.

What I really meant was, I liked eating at a table where I was the focus of interest, where my talking was encouraged, where there was no obvious hostility making the air thick and the food choking. Mother understood that meaning quite clearly. "The first place you go to with your news, your stories from school, is your grandmother. As if you didn't have a mother . . ."

I protested vehemently; I didn't agree with Grandmother on most things, I didn't share her values. I just liked her food.

"If that's true," said my mother, tears gathering in her eyes, "you've let yourself become corrupted. You can be bought for a meal."

The charge hit home so hard I, too, began to cry. The politics of food . . . It was true, I had turned myself into some kind of monster, stuffing myself with food in order to get attention and love. In the warring camp in which I lived, the main rule was that one must choose and bear the consequences. I knew that much, and I had chosen badly. I would change, I promised, I would change. From now on I would come straight home from school and eat my meals *in my own home.* Now I had chosen *right,* and Mother rewarded me instantly with the generous hugging and kissing that alternated so capriciously with her long periods of aloof absent-mindedness. She squeezed me to her ample breasts and I felt enveloped, bathed in milky infancy. She squeezed body and bones of the love-starved, rebellious youngster and there was true feeling in her unrestrained, excessive gesture. I had chosen food and she would give me love—as it turned out, more love than I could bear.

The incident was a turning point for her as it was for me. She had understood instinctively that she was coming close to losing her daughter to the other side. That threat pierced her self-absorption, and from then on she made her claims to me actively. I had intruded upon her with my extreme actions, no longer willing to be merely a pawn. I was making trouble.

We cried and hugged and kissed. "This is your home," she said over and over again. "Not downstairs."

I agreed. From now on I would eat my meals in my own home. Ground rules . . . But something sharp, ugly and keen kept on inside my stubborn head. All it meant was that from then on I would sit at our dining table as her ally, on her side in the battle. That's all she wanted. It wasn't my home any more than was my grandmother's living room.

I downed that voice and threw myself into trusting my mother, embracing her cause. She could seduce people that way, whenever she wanted to, and she certainly wanted me on her side. I became her loyal and devoted follower.

This was made easier for me because my relationship with my father was already conflict-ridden. My father had taught me how to lie. My lying began in small ways and then, once in practice, it got so that most of what I said to him was never quite true. When I was honest I was usually scolded for being "contrary" and obstreperous. When I seemingly submitted and lied, I was treated as a good girl.

Ever since that time I have known about the strength of the powerless to check those in power. I have never believed those versions of history and those representations of reality that present the world from the point of view of the powerful. My childhood taught me the wisdom and effectiveness of resistance and the necessity of skepticism toward the values of those who made the rules. What I learned about politics, I learned at home. And soon, the politics of the dining table would become the politics of the street.

MEANWHILE, life went on and I was preparing for my bat mitzvah. I studied the Hebrew Bible carefully. Like all children, I had questions I did not know how to ask. Why was God so vengeful, so lacking in pity? How could he select one people to be his chosen people? Did that not mean he damned the others? If that was so, no wonder the Catholics were so preoccupied with hating the Jews ... Anti-Semitism was all around us; it was an accepted part of life, so that one could not really imagine a world without it. It seemed to me that our synagogue was held together more by fear of anti-Semitism than by anything else. We had to stick together because THEY hated us. We had to stick together because we were surrounded by enemies. We had to show we were proud of our faith. We had to be good to show our enemies that Jews were good.

Every time I went to synagogue it bothered me that I had to sit in the women's gallery. Not that I understood it to have any symbolic meaning or that I connected it with the position of women in Jewish life; it simply annoyed me that I could not see the services as well as the men. It made me notice that I was not being taught the same as the boys my age. We were a modern congregation that allowed girls to be bat mitzvahed, but for quite inexplicable reasons the girls had to wait until age fourteen, while the boys were confirmed at age thirteen. The ritual meant that one was accepted as an adult member of the Jewish community. Clearly, girls were considered to be less mature than boys, a judgement that was obviously counter-factual and made no sense. Still, I was enrolled in the youth group studying for bat mitzvah.

I cannot say exactly when my doubts became stronger than my belief in prayer and my desire for belonging, but I know there were months when I studied Hebrew and attended services and doubted so strongly I despaired of finding answers. My doubts focused on the hypocrisy and injustice I observed within our congregation. The incident that became decisive for me focused on a slight, emaciated woman, whom we called the "egg woman." She and her family, a skinny husband and two sickly looking children, made their living by selling eggs to members of the Jewish community. They came to our home once a week, delivering eggs, always standing in the doorway of the kitchen as though they were beggars. Sometimes they would leave with packages of food and some of our old clothes. My grandmother considered them her protégés and regularly mentioned how kind it was of the congregation to give them charity and a chance to earn a living. On Shabbat and on the High Holy Days I saw the family in the synagogue, and once I noticed the little girl was wearing one of my cast-off, outgrown dresses. They had no assigned seats and stood on the stairway, where they could not see any of the service. Why, if the congregation was so charitable, could they not be given a seat in the temple? Because the seats are sold to people who can afford them, my grandmother explained. Doesn't God care for the poor? To this there was no answer.

Then one day the egg woman came alone, and Grandmother told me her husband and both children were sick with TB. Grandmother worried out loud about whether it was wise to continue buying from her; she might be a carrier of infection.

Eggs have shells, my kind Aunt Emma pointed out quietly; they cannot be contaminated. But on another day when the egg woman came, my grandmother railed and shouted at her, because two of the eggs had not been fresh; she demanded to have these eggs replaced. The woman protested; she had no way of knowing what the eggs were like inside, but my grandmother insisted. The egg woman began to cry; her children were sick; she needed every penny. I stood by helplessly while this drama played out, and my grandmother finally relented, with a stern warning to the woman. I ran out of the room, struck dumb by the violence of my anger. The skin-and-bones woman pleading with my grandmother over a few pennies—if that was Jewish charity, if that was what God approved, then I had to get out.

Yet I continued my bat mitzvah preparation, trying to fight down my distaste and reasoning down my doubts with common sense. Maybe this was just my grandmother, not the whole congregation. Surely, God was not running each synagogue, only human beings were ... But my doubts persisted, and I stopped praying. Once that happened, it was as it had been with stepping on the cracks—if you stop believing, the magic goes. And with no magic, there was nothing left to hold me. I wanted to leave the synagogue because I needed to leave my father's and my grandmother's world. So, a few weeks before the event and with preparation for a big party already underway, I announced that I would not be bat mitzvahed, because I no longer believed in it.

My mother supported me; she thought I had a right to make up my own mind. But my father responded by asking me to go through with the ceremony, for grandmother's sake. Afterwards I could do what I wanted.

"What would Grandmama get out of it, knowing I don't believe in it?"

"Don't tell her," said my father.

I could not do that. I had too much respect for what religion meant to believers to pretend to be one when I no longer was. Besides, I was still superstitious. If, after all, there was a God, hypocrisy would be punished.

Hypocrisy, but not unbelief? Arguments had no impact on me. But it was my kind and loving Aunt Emma who truly pushed me over the edge. She was, of all of them, the most upset by my announcement. She argued with me first on religious grounds, then by making me feel guilty for hurting Grandmama and finally on opportunistic grounds. "Think of all the gifts you'll be getting," she said, "just for going through this little ceremony."

For the gifts—never. She thinks everyone and everything can be bought. This was the best person I knew in Grandmother's world, the kindest, most humane person, and if she could reason like this, then I must get out, once and for all.

I stopped going to synagogue; I stopped going to Bible study, and I was not bat mitzvahed. I have not been an observant Jew since; I have been an agnostic. Anti-Semitic experiences and the holocaust and persecution have not made me change my mind. I consider myself a Jew belonging to the Jewish community, the Jewish tradition, sharing a common fate. I do not believe that fate is inextricably linked with religion.

The decision not be bat mitzvahed was truly my coming of age, my ceremony of confirmation. I expressed it by reading myself out of the emptiness of the family tradition. I could not belong there. The community I had tried to find among my age-mates and my co-religionists had disillusioned me. Maybe there never would be a community for me. But if it came to a choice I would take my place at the side of the egg woman rather than at the side of my grandmother. That much I understood, and the political avalanche that began to engulf me then simply confirmed my decision and strengthened it. By the time I was fourteen, I had become a political person.

[3]

BIRTHDAYS WERE BIG EVENTS in my family. I've probably been ruined for life by the first birthday Bebe made for me, my seventh, which became the standard against which all my future birthday celebrations would be measured. When I awoke that morning in my green and yellow room, I was surrounded by pink, white and blue balloons bumping up against the ceiling and transforming the room into a fairyland. Crinkly white crepe streamers coming down from the ceiling made a tent around my bed. Gifts were hidden and had to be searched for; all the meals were special treats with my favorite dishes. In the afternoon my two cousins came with more gifts, and we had a party with ice cream and cake. Birthdays remained special in our family—days of truce between Father and Mother, when they spoke as in one voice and smiled in pleasure and celebration.

My father's birthday, which was on February 15, was celebrated upstairs and downstairs. We usually had a late afternoon reception in our apartment at which Grandmama and *Tante* Emma made their rare appearance, after which everybody moved downstairs to my grandmother's for an elaborate meal. It was a family tradition that children's gifts should be handmade, and in this year, 1934, we had as usual spent weeks in preparation. Nora and I had covered sheets of brown wrapping paper with a flour-and-water paste, which we colored and then imprinted with swirls, dots and lines made with nails, combs, wire brushes and a variety of small objects. The then-current governess, whose face and name I have forgotten, was big on finger-painted paper and never tired of showing us how various useless objects could be transformed into things of beauty by applying this paper to them. Book covers, picture frames, notebooks, various containers—there was no end to it. My project was a wastepaper basket, which I aimed to cover inside and out. Fräulein believed that regularity of design was essential to beauty; she encouraged us to experiment until we found a design we liked and then to repeat it in a pattern. I had chosen yellow and orange as my colors, bright favorites that, I thought, would make even an aluminum waste basket look good. But since it was for a man, the pattern should be masculine and so I experimented with dark brown on the bright background.

For some days now, the talk at the dinner table had been only of politics. My mother was disturbed by the government of Chancellor Dollfuss, who had come to power in 1933. She said he represented the clerical party; they were reactionary and secretly anti-Semitic; they did not believe in the rights of working people and tried to foist their religious ideas on everyone. That the last point was true I could tell from my own experience: since Dollfuss had come to power, there was a crucifix in every classroom, and public school children had to attend religious instruction at school once a week. My mother objected to all of this, and she also spoke strongly about the rights of trade unions. Such talk always led to arguments. Although my father was himself against Dollfuss—he had always voted Social Democratic and was a strong supporter of our Socialist city administration—it irked him to hear my mother defend the unions. As an employer he was not enthusiastic about unions, and he inevitably ended the argument by telling my mother she didn't know what she was talking about—she had never worked a day in her life. Also, it appeared she had done something foolish—she had voted Communist in the last election, the only Communist vote in our district. It was a protest vote, Mother explained, because the Social Democrats weren't doing enough to stop the clericals. As far as Father was concerned, she had only helped the clericals with her throw-away vote by weakening the Social Democrats. At age thirteen, I had no opinion on this subject, but I enjoyed the discussions.

I knew about the Social Democrats in concrete ways. Austria had been, since 1918, a parliamentary democracy. In many of the provinces, the clerical party was strong and it had grown ever stronger in the year since Hitler had come to power in Germany. But Vienna, the largest city in Austria, where nearly one-third of the Austrian population lived, had long had a Social-Democratic majority. In elementary school, I was taught about the good things the Social Democrats of

Vienna had done: each Viennese baby was provided with a free layette at birth; each child got free milk in school, free inoculations and dental care. There was no religious indoctrination in school, and children were encouraged to question their teachers and practice democratic self-government. But the greatest, the proudest achievement of the Viennese Social Democrats was their building, at government expense, of huge complexes of apartment houses for workers, available at cheap rent. These workers' homes were the pride of Vienna, and every foreign visitor was taken to see the largest and most beautiful of them, Karl Marx Hof. The workers' houses were modern, the buildings painted in bright pastel colors; many apartments had balconies, and all of them had luxury features such as modern bathrooms, wooden floors and laundry rooms with electric washing machines in the basements. Each block of houses had space for a nursery school and a kindergarten. The buildings were spaced far enough apart so that each window had a view of lawns and trees. Such luxuries, at rents working people could afford, were unheard of at the time. The housing projects became symbols of proud achievement for the Social Democrats, and of a waste of public money for the right-wing parties. Marx Hof was quite near my home; I had, on various afternoon walks, admired its playgrounds and the beautiful statue of a naked youth that stood in front of the center building.

I had another quite personal association with the Social-Democratic city government. Our garden was separated by a brick wall from the large garden of a Socialist Workers' Home, which was the last house on the street where I lived. In the corner of our garden stood an oak tree, which I regularly climbed to a level from which I could look into the adjoining gardens. The tree was my hideout, my secret place. I did not know just what a "Socialist Workers' Home" might be, but from my lookout I had observed a number of family picnics and parties, which were held in that garden. There would be tables with picnic food, a red flag planted somewhere near the house, children playing and sometimes music and singing. I watched these festive occasions with envy and figured out that this was a place where Social Democrats and their families went to have a good time.

I did not know then the larger political picture against which the events of February 1934 played out. Ever since Adolf Hitler had seized power in Germany in 1933, the independence of Austria was threatened. Hitler's avowed aim was to incorporate all German-speaking countries into a greater Germany. In Austria, a constantly growing Nazi movement sympathized with Hitler and worked to accomplish his aims. On the other hand, the two major parties pledged to Austrian independence, the Social Democrats (SPÖ) and the Austrian People's Party (ÖVP), were fighting each other in Parliament and in the streets. Each party had bands of armed defenders—the Social Democrats had their *Schutzbund* (Defense Corps), and the clerical party had its *Heimwehr* (Home Defenders). There had been armed clashes between these groups during strikes or public demonstrations ever since 1927. But after Hitler's rise to power, the government of Engelbert Dollfuss openly turned against democracy. Dollfuss governed by "emergency decrees" and first ended freedom of the press, then proceeded to abolish jury trials and to suspend the right of assembly. Early in February 1934, the government raided Socialist Workers' Homes and the headquarters of the SPÖ. Arrests of leaders of the *Schutzbund* in the provinces followed quickly. The *Heimwehr* announced that it would end parliamentary democracy very soon and proceeded to an armed uprising in Linz, the capitol of Upper Austria. The headquarters of the SPÖ in Linz were raided, some of the leaders were arrested and the *Heimwehr* demanded that the *Schutzbund* hand over its weapons. Instead, the Linzer *Schutzbund* offered armed resistance, and fighting broke out all over the province.

On Sunday, the 11th of February, trade union and *Schutzbund* leaders in Vienna were being arrested. The SPÖ still hesitated to call for armed resistance, but by Monday morning word of the fighting in Linz had reached the Viennese workers. Spontaneously, and against the advice of their party leadership, they called for a general strike.

On that day, the 12th of February, three days before my father's birthday, Fräulein, Nora and I were sitting in our room, working on our birthday gifts for Father, when suddenly there came rapid, explosive sounds from outside, like dry peas popping into a pot, only much louder, interrupted every so often by a louder boom. Mother rushed into the room. "Are you all right?"

We were. "What's happening?"

"It sounds like machine-gun fire," my mother said in a strange voice.

"Holy Mary, Mother of God, protect us," intoned Fräulein, "it must be those reds."

"Is there a war?" I asked, not knowing what a war might be like, but knowing the rapid-fire noise frightened me.

"You're safe here," said Mother. "Whatever it is, it's far away, so it won't hurt us."

Then came more staccato noises, pop pop, which froze us in fright. "That IS machine-gun fire," Fräulein asserted. "We should go in the basement to be safe. God knows what'll happen."

"I'm sure that won't be necessary," Mother said. "This is a long ways off."

The door was flung open and, without bothering with the customary knock,

Mitzi, the cook, burst into the room, her hair disheveled and her face red. "I was just at the grocer, Ma'am, and he says there's a revolution. They're fighting in Marx Hof and down in Heiligenstadt. I picked up an extra bottle of milk, just in case. He says there may be a general strike and no lights and he closed up his store. All the other stores are closing, too. Holy Mother and all the Saints, have mercy on us." "Mary, Mother of God, protect us sinners."

"That's enough," said my mother. "It's a good thing you got the milk, Mitzi. Why don't you go in the kitchen and put it away." Just then the phone rang.

It was Father, glad to know the telephone company was still working. There was a general strike in progress and he wanted us to get candles out and fill all the tubs with water. We must all stay indoors, for safety.

Mother asked, should we go in the basement, and told him about the machine-gun fire.

Father did not think we were in any danger. If there was fighting in Marx Hof, it was at least two kilometers away from us. Anyway, this was just a minor skirmish, probably across the river in Floridsdorf, in the workers' district. He said he had orders to go on emergency service, which meant he must keep the pharmacy open and stay at his post. But he'd try to call us every two hours, as long as he could.

Filling the bathtub and washtubs and hunting up candles to put into every room in the house kept us busy, so we got used to the steady crackling noise and the occasional booms. Then the lights went out and the phone went dead and we sat around the children's table by the light of a candle and my mother told wonderful stories, so tightly woven and full of surprises we did not have time to let in the fear. That's the way she was when things were serious—she had courage and she would not let children be frightened. We sat in the dark room with the flickering candle and Fräulein stopped her praying and my mother made magic.

We ate in the dark that night and went to sleep to the sounds outside, which did not slacken but pierced our dreams. And they were still there when Nora and I woke, and all the soothing words that came from the adults around us did not change their assault.

As we sat in our room, trying to pretend everything was normal, we heard trucks roaring by our house and screeching to a stop at the end of the street. I managed to lean out the window and see police trucks in front of the Workers' Home, but Fräulein hauled me back and yanked the window shut. Soon after that we heard shooting quite close by.

"Why are they shooting in the Workers' Home?" I asked first Fräulein, then Mother. They had no answer. The trucks roared past our house again, going in the opposite direction. I wanted to run out to the garden, to my tree, and see for myself what had happened. But there was no way I could escape from the watchful adults determined to keep me inside.

They could stop me from running outside, but they could not stop me from imagining what was happening out there. It was as though a strange presence had taken hold of our lives and everything normal seemed perverted by it. I kept thinking of the dragon of the fairy tales who invaded towns and took over the lives of the inhabitants. That dragon had come and entered our lives, and I struggled with my inadequate understanding to learn what I could about it, its demands and fierce habits.

It is sixty-seven years since that day in February, and the children of Europe and Asia have lived through so much worse than these comparatively simple days of civil war, fought with machine guns and a couple of howitzers. When the children of Guernica were bombarded in their market square in broad daylight, the world still noticed and marked it as an unprecedented atrocity. The children of London knew nightly bombardments, compared to which the hand-to-hand street-fighting in Vienna in 1934 looked like child's play. Jewish children all over Europe experienced horrors beyond words, torn away from their parents. And the children of Hiroshima and Nagasaki were torched alive in that hungry furnace, their silent screams beyond description and image. But for me, it all began that day, and it marked my life forever. And the brave, desperate and hopeless resistance of Austrian workers against fascism was the warning signal of the disasters to come, of the dark night descending over Europe.

The next day was much like the day before, except that late in the afternoon the lights went on again and the telephone was working. "The general strike is broken," my mother explained, close to tears. The radio was on again, and my mother kept close to it. The radio played endless Strauss waltzes and military marches and every so often the announcer came on and reported that the minor skirmishes in the suburbs were now under control of the brave forces of *Heimwehr* and police and that in most of the city order had been restored. Father came home in time for dinner, and as we sat eating there was a sudden fierce boom that shook the walls.

"That's artillery," my father said in a shaky voice. "What on earth—"

"Maybe we should go down to the basement?"

Father looked worried as the booming noise continued. "Howitzers, closer than Floridsdorf—it must be Marx Hof . . ."

"There are women and children in there," my mother whispered, "how can they do that?"

Father turned on the radio, but there was nothing but dance music.

The sounds stopped as suddenly as they had begun, and Father got his usual voice back and said, "That should end that." Only there was no relief in his voice and no promise of anything. He went downstairs to comfort Grandmother, and when he came back he seemed more like himself again.

"What's happening?" I asked, as I had asked several times that day, but I got no answer.

"Nothing to worry about, we'll take care of you."

The radio announcer said the workers in Hernals had given up their weapons and all that remained of the unrest were small pockets of resistance. Then the machine-gun noises began again and went on for more than an hour, and I concluded that the radio was lying and that Father knew nothing, no more than I did.

The next day, the only source of real information was Mitzi, who was seldom to be found in the kitchen. She ran any number of errands to various stores and always came back full of stories, some true, some rumors, some inventions. The butcher had a nephew in the *Heimwehr,* and he said there was a regular war going on in Floridsdorf and that's where the machine-gun fire was coming from. The workers had barricaded themselves in the housing projects and were armed to the teeth. The reds were trying to take the radio station. The grocer had heard from the truck driver that there was fighting in the provinces, in Linz and Salzburg and Carynthia. It was a regular revolution. The neighbor down the street had worse to tell. The police had been tipped off about the workers' club just behind us. Well, it was hard to believe, but that place was an arsenal . . . The police had raided it and there'd been some fighting. The neighbor saw two dead men lying in the yard just before the ambulances came and picked them up . . .

"But the artillery," Fräulein persisted, treating Mitzi with new respect as a purveyor of important information. Mitzi did not disappoint her.

"They've got it set up on Hohe Warte, pointing at Marx Hof. The police gave them an ultimatum to surrender. What we heard was nothing, just shooting in the air to scare them. They'll surrender soon, just watch."

"Nobody in their right mind would hold out against cannons like that," said Fräulein. "After all, it's just a stucco building, not a concrete bunker."

"What's a concrete bunker?" I asked.

Never mind.

Hohe Warte was a beautiful, hilly district not far from us where rich people lived in fancy villas. My cousin Rudi lived there, and every so often we took an afternoon walk to visit him. I always admired the huge garden sloping downhill, with its old trees and espaliered fruit trees and the neat vegetable garden behind the house. If you stood at the back door of Rudi's house you could not see the end of his garden; it was that big. Near his house there was a place where on holidays they gave fireworks and people came to see the view, which extended downhill to Marx Hof and beyond to the Danube Canal and even farther than that, to Floridsdorf and the hills of the Vienna woods.

"On Hohe Warte?" I asked in horror, picturing the place. "Is that where the cannons are—where we usually see the fireworks?"

"Right," said Mitzi importantly. "They got real fireworks to watch this time."

If you stood up on that hill you could see the laundry hanging out on the balconies in Marx Hof and the geraniums people kept in pots. I could not imagine what it must be like in those apartments with machine guns and howitzers blasting into them.

In the room next door my father and mother were having an argument.

"You can't be serious," Mother was saying. "Not at this time."

"It's my birthday," said Father.

"To give a party while they're murdering women and children next door to us . . ."

"Don't dramatize. There's no point making things worse than they are. The police are trying to restore order, that's all."

"I won't be part of it," Mother said. "This is the limit."

"Very well, we'll have it at Mama's. One must celebrate the seasons as they come. If not we'll be giving in to anarchy."

"I can't believe you'd really do that."

I had forgotten all about the birthday tomorrow. If it were my birthday, would I want a party? Certainly not. It was horrible to think of it while the shooting went on.

"No, I won't be a part of this," Mother shouted. "I won't have anything to do with it."

"Suit yourself," Father said in an icy tone.

That afternoon, I tried to finish my birthday gift for Father. The paper with its bright orange background and the regular swirling patterns in muted shades of brown looked different now. The orange seemed to me like fire, fire shooting from the howitzers into the balconies and windows of the housing projects. I took the brush and dipped it deep into the darkest brown and without thinking, without knowing why, I made a huge, dark-brown cross over the entire paper. That was better, but still it was wrong. The cross was wrong, the cross was for Christians. I turned the cross into something inside a dark brown circle, a circle of darkness, and then the dark spots began to be everywhere, covering most of the original, covering all of the orderly shapes—

"For goodness sakes, what are you doing?" Fräulein arrested my furious brush by holding my arm, holding tight, pinching. "You've spoiled your gift. Look what you've done—it was so pretty and now it's ugly. Ugly."

I wrenched my arm free, spattering paint wherever it would go. "That's right," I muttered. "Just as ugly as out there."

THE NEXT DAY, just as she had promised, Mother did not prepare anything for the birthday dinner and the party and stayed in her room all morning.

By late afternoon, Grandmama had cooked the dinner and fixed up her living room the way she did for the High Holy Days. The table with its gleaming silverware, the shiny candle holders and the *Meissen* china looked beautiful and festive, but outside the rumbling of guns continued. Grandmama had ordered the Venetian blinds to be drawn and the heavy draperies closed. Around six the guests started arriving. Each of the relatives as they came in shook hands with Father or pressed dry kisses on his cheek and pushed their gift packages in his hands.

"I'll open it later, thank you, you really shouldn't have . . ." Father put the packages on the heavy dark credenza.

"My, what a big lady you've become." Uncle Hans, puffing his eternal cigar, patted me on the head as though I were a horse. I pretended not to hear. I was worrying about when they would notice that Mother was not here, when they would ask and one would have to explain . . . But just then Mother came in quietly, dressed in her most fashionable dress and smoking a cigarette in a long silver holder. She nodded greetings to all the uncles and began to talk to one of the aunts, standing in a corner of the room, as though she had just happened to pass through and stopped a moment. I was relieved that now there would be no scene, and at the same time, I was bitterly disappointed that Mother had come, after all.

Everyone turned to the door when Uncle Richard made his entrance, followed by his wife and son. Uncle Richard was a banker, the richest man in the family, Grandmama's favorite and everyone's darling. He brought a very small package tied with a silver string.

"Maybe a diamond ring," Father laughed, pumping his brother's hand.

"Could be, could be. You'll see." Uncle Richard turned toward the uncles, who formed a ring around him and talked politics. "Nothing to worry about," he assured them all. "The sooner we get rid of that useless bunch of parliamentarians, the better. Dollfuss is showing some muscle and energy, at last. He'll be able to stand up to Hitler."

"That clown," Uncle Hugo exclaimed. "He'll be out before the year is up."

"Don't count on it," Father said seriously. "More likely he'll be on some military adventure."

"Well, let's hear the news before we eat," Uncle Richard commanded. He couldn't stand anyone contradicting him.

To this day, I can still hear the radio announcer's voice:

—entered the Marx Hof at 5:45 PM tonight. Without food, light or heat since Monday, the rebels finally gave up resistance to the combined forces of police, *Heimwehr* and Army. Our brave executive forces immediately took command of the situation, arresting the red leaders and confiscating the guns in apartments and on the roofs. It is reported that herewith the last resistance in the suburbs has ceased. You have just heard the official government newscast. We will resume normal programming shortly.

"So it's all over," said Uncle Hugo sadly.

"Let's eat," Father invited.

There was a lot of shuffling and moving of chairs until each found his seat, identified by the small place card at the foot of the wine glasses. Grandmama, who as always sat at the head of the table, rapped a spoon against her glass. The silver against the crystal made a sharp, bell-like sound.

"My dear ones, dear family." She stood up for her little speech, looking diminutive yet forceful in her black velvet dress with the lace collar and the fine old gold brooch. Her bright blue eyes in her lined face were clear and sharp as always, looking from one to the other around the table.

"Let's not forget what brought us here tonight—to celebrate our beloved Robert's birthday. These have been trying times for all of us, but now order has been restored and we must take the good as it comes our way. Let's all join in saying, Happy Birthday, Robert!" Happy Birthday.

All the voices were swimming in a bright chorus with the light and the silver and in the midst of it came another blast of artillery that made the walls dance and the glasses tinkle. The guests gasped, and Father said, that's nothing, and everybody stopped drinking and looked at the crystal chandelier which was swaying above the table. Father got up and said, that's just a mopping-up operation and Uncle Richard said, hear, hear, and drank his wine down in a gulp. I tried to catch Mother's eyes and saw that she was crying. Suddenly she said so loudly that everyone turned to her: "You heard the radio—all resistance has ceased." And then she laughed with her lips only, more a silent shriek than a laugh, and the tears continued down her cheeks.

"No point getting hysterical," Uncle Richard responded firmly.

Grandmama cleared her throat and rang for the cook. "Let's have the soup." But her hands were trembling.

"Excuse me," Uncle Hugo interrupted in some embarrassment. "Where did you park your cars?"

"Why downstairs, in front of the house . . ."

"Exactly," he continued gravely. "I think we better go and move them. Disperse them. The neighbors might not like the idea of us having a party tonight—excuse me."

Several of the uncles rose and left the room. "Not all at once," Uncle Richard called after them.

I sat in front of my plate with a lump in my throat big enough to choke me. What would happen now to the children in Marx Hof? How many of them had been wounded or even killed? I could barely hold back the tears.

Uncle Richard told a joke and everyone laughed loudly. Father walked around the table, pouring wine from a bottle wrapped in a white napkin. On his face was, firmly set, the smile he used with his customers in the store. As he came to me, he bent forward and whispered in my ear. "Do you have to spoil my party?"

I said nothing, frozen and hard like a block of ice. In this moment everything changed irrevocably. I would never trust the government again—they were murderers and liars. The radio announcers were liars. The newspapers lied. And my family, my father's family, were cowards and hypocrites. As for my father—I now knew I hated him.

[4]

MUCH OF WHAT THEN HAPPENED has been washed out of my memory by worse horrors. And yet, there is only one experience of defeat; all the rest is variation. When the guns stopped and the triumphant news bulletins alternated with martial music hour after hour and the red flags disappeared from windows and the red ribbons from lapels, when the signs with the word "Socialist" were painted over and the wall newspapers were only those of the right-wing parties, one could feel a wind blowing sharply around the corner. A young person could get a whiff of something sick and decaying, a new smell, the smell of fear. Defeat means becoming invisible, becoming silenced, speechless, unspeakable. It would happen again and then again, but it was never as forceful and terrifying as that first time. Adults suddenly became frightened, appearing to the young person as though they had reverted to childhood, exposed in their helplessness. Adults, when truly frightened, retreated into customized masked behavior. They seemed to draw strength from that, as though ritualized behavior were the skeleton that held up their identity. A young person, suddenly, violently catapulted from childhood into adulthood, had still enough of the child's cold, discerning eye to see through adult pretense. What a young person learned in those first days was important: that superior forces can wipe out dedicated radicals as well as moderates; that adults are more concerned with survival than with heroics ("adults are cowards" was the way this young person put it). And that despair is the worst cancer there is.

After the defeat of Social Democracy in February 1934, we lived in Austria under a relatively mild but pervasive dictatorship of the right. Chancellor Dollfuss outlawed all political parties with the exception of his own party, which, re-emerging as the "Fatherland Front," became the foundation of this newly created "Christian state." After the abolition of parliament and democracy, citizens were virtually represented through trade and guild associations, formed on a medieval model. The leadership of the former left-wing parties and of trade unions was in internment camps and jails, while many former Nazi party members had sought refuge in Germany. From there they organized and financed an underground Nazi movement, which carried out a war of terrorism and violence inside Austria. Their campaign culminated in the failed putsch attempt in July 1934, during which Chancellor Dollfuss was assassinated. His successor, Kurt von Schuschnigg, carried forward the domestic policy of clerical fascism and Dollfuss's foreign policy of relying on Mussolini to protect Austria's independence from Germany. With the defeat of the *Schutzbund,* the *Heimwehr* became a kind of legal militia. Democratic rights and institutions were dismantled, among them the free milk program for schoolchildren, free kindergartens and religious freedom. Catholicism became the official religion of the state. In short order, the public housing projects were cleared of former Socialists, and loyal supporters of the new regime were given preference as renters.

At home, there were small changes. My mother was more subdued and even she, usually so unconcerned with the opinions of others, curbed her tongue and seldom ventured a statement on a political subject. During that summer we purged our library of "red" books. I don't quite remember who initiated that purge, but I recall piles of Social-Democratic magazines, pamphlets, travel descriptions of Soviet Russia and a few outright Marxist books being put in cardboard boxes and later discreetly placed among the storage boxes in the attic. We were not quite seasoned enough in those days to consider attic storage a dangerous solution, nor did we purge Gorki, Turgenev and Tolstoi (we would soon learn that all Russian names were suspect). Our library was large, and Anatole France, Emile Zola and Romain Rolland remained to hold up the standard of social justice.

At my *Gymnasium* the changes were quite noticeable. Our teachers and the principal were frightened. Overtly, the events out in the streets had not affected our lives and the subjects we studied. And yet, quite obviously, they had. Self-censorship had become a pervasive reality; no one dared to speak freely and spontaneously on any subject that might have political overtones. I remember the sense of it, like an odor, which hit me suddenly one day when I suppressed a comment

I had wanted to make in literature class. I never spoke to other students about it, but I wondered if they experienced it too. Lying to adults was something I had long practiced at home, but school had up to then been a place of relative mental freedom. That was never again to be the case.

I knew too much, and my curiosity about the forbidden was unquenchable. People had been killed in the February fighting; some had escaped and were in hiding; some had fled the country. I heard whispers and rumors of people arrested. Of my own acquaintances there was only one, the brother of a girlfriend, who had been in the Marx Hof fighting and had been arrested. He was nineteen, a first-year medical student, a tall, quiet boy. Possibly because of his middle-class family, he got off relatively easy with a one-year sentence. Because I knew him, I made pictures of him in jail in my mind, mobilizing my sense of guilt and personal failure. I felt ashamed to be a silent witness, sitting in comfort and safety, while others resisted with whatever they had. There was something I should be doing, I believed, but I did nothing.

Why I should have taken that burden of guilt on me from then forward, I cannot explain. In the days after the fighting I remember feeling rage at my helplessness. I knew no one with whom I could have spoken about this, but I was already looking for such a person. One of the lessons to be learned out of defeat was that there always are such persons around somewhere. The line of resisters is never quite severed. Meanwhile I looked for answers in books. Vera Figner's *Autobiography* remained in our library, unpurged. She was one of the Narodniki, Russian revolutionaries involved in the assassination attempt against the Czar in the 1880s, arrested, tried, condemned to life in Siberian prisons. She actually served twenty-two years and was liberated by the 1918 revolution. I read Gorki's *Mother;* I read B. Traven's romantic novels about South American revolutionaries. I made pictures in my mind of prisons, of torture, of brave, dedicated fighters in underground movements. I waited, keeping my eyes and ears open.

My father employed over twenty people in his pharmacy and in a pharmaceutical laboratory. One of these, a woman pharmacist in her forties, had been with him for over fifteen years. She was a very small person who barely could look over the counter as she dispensed medicines, and she was crippled, walking with a swinging, wide-hipped gait, like my Aunt Klari. This woman, whom I will call Edith Brandhofer, had been arrested. My father said she had confessed in open court to being a Communist and to having been involved in the fighting, and so she was sentenced to one and a half years in jail. My father was shocked at her confession, not so much, he said, because she had been an activist—he respected that—but because she had never told him she was a Communist. He felt she should have come out openly with that and taken the consequences. My mother argued her side, saying she was probably afraid she'd lose her job. "I wouldn't have fired her," said my father in an injured tone. "Who else would hire her, the way she's crippled."

"That's fine of you," said my mother, "but I suppose she couldn't take the risk." I was surprised at my father and more surprised at Frau *Magistra* Brandhofer's revelations—she did not fit my literary notions of what a Communist was or looked like. Where did she get the courage to take part in the fighting? And how could she stand jail? I eagerly waited for every crumb of information concerning her that my father could provide. What amazed me even more was his mentioning, quite casually, that of course, he was paying her salary while she was in jail.

"To whom do you pay it?" my mother asked.

"Directly to her sister. She's got a serious heart condition and is quite dependent on the money."

"Isn't that risky?" My mother seemed as amazed by his action as I was.

"Probably a little, but she's been my employee for fifteen years and a good one. Her politics are her business, not mine." It was the first and only political act my father ever committed. Typically, he saw it only as a humanitarian gesture, but it must have taken a lot of courage. As he knew quite well, the prudent thing would have been to fire her the day of her arrest. Instead he sent word to her that her job was awaiting her return and kept up his self-imposed financial support of her sister.

So I had two prisoners of my acquaintance, for whose release I could wait. And soon I found an activity that made me feel less useless and guilty. In the small, private *Gymnasium* I attended, we had a lending library of a few hundred volumes, which was run by a student volunteer. The post became available, and I volunteered to fill it, thinking it would give me a chance to influence the other students' choice of books. I scanned the library holdings for any books with a remotely political or democratic message and, to my delight, found it well stocked with Dickens, Anatole France and a few of my Russian favorites. There were even some Ilya Ehrenburg novels and the clearly subversive poems of Bertolt Brecht. I determined to spread these "political" books as widely as possible. I made it my business to read a lot of innocuous, entertaining novels and classical fiction. When a student came to borrow a book, I would engage her in a literary discussion and offer some suggestions of a light novel. On her second time around, I would suggest one of the political books. This scheme of "political edu-cation" worked well and gave me a reputation of being a literary connoisseur. While I romanticized this activity into some connection with "the underground," I really ran no risk at all. The message I was spreading was too diffuse to be of any practical value. And yet, it strikes me now, as I write this, that I chose this, my first political activity, with the same direction and pragmatism that has been typical of my entire life: I acted so as to spread ideas.

Subtly, but decisively, the days of February severed my childhood from my adolescence. After the Marx Hof battle my father had lost all authority over me. I identified him with the government, which was, in fact, quite unfair. But for me the decisive fact was that he acquiesced to conditions as they were, and then, gradually, appeared to justify them as the "lesser evil." It may be that in reality the opposite was happening: I was in rebellion against my father and equated the authoritarian government with him in order better to free myself from him. The authority he and Grandmama represented had become intolerable to me. I could not have expressed it then in the shorthand now available. But the fact is that at the age of fourteen the personal became political for me.

Where to take such rebellion was as yet an unanswerable question. In the chaotic and impassioned way of adolescents, I moved simultaneously in several directions and wavered between several answers. In the years between fourteen and seventeen, my relationship to my mother grew in depth and intensity. If in my early childhood she had ignored and neglected me, she now accepted and almost courted me. It probably was part of her struggle in the marriage, but I was at the time not aware of that possibility. Certainly, she tried to make sure I would become like her, not like my grandmother, and she used all her charm and seduc-tiveness to win me over. In those years my mother spent much of her time with me and treated me entirely as an adult. There is nothing more appealing to ado-lescents than to be so treated by adults they love and admire.

She was a beautiful woman, exotic, different. Her hair was utterly straight, black, and always cropped short; her skin was olive, her dark eyes intense and often dreamy. She dressed so as to accentuate her Hungarian type of beauty, wearing embroidered peasant blouses or mandarin-collared silk shirts, which she belted at the waist with some tasseled cord or a looped metal belt. She was a large woman, ample of breast and hips, but rather than feeling self-conscious about that, she emphasized it. At a time when Viennese ladies wore dresses and high-heeled shoes, she wore silk pants or long peasant skirts, which flowed to the floor, and open-toed sandals, which made her look like a gypsy. She liked that look and emphasized it with dangling silver earrings and large rings, which she wore on several fingers of her elegant thin hands. I was fascinated by her appearance, her style, her proud individuality. Sometimes she would tease me about looking so totally different from her, with my light brown hair, blue eyes, fair complexion and rail-thin body. I experienced such comments as a condemnation of my awkwardness, my bumbling transition from tomboy to adolescent. "But inside," she would insist as though she were reading my mind, "inside we're alike, you and I."

I was invited to tea in her room, and we spent hours discussing art, literature and, above all, creativity. If my father's ideal was respectability, my mother's was creativity. Creativity meant beauty, spontaneity, improvisation, play. One did what one felt like doing, never mind the consequences. One did not have to plan, keep to schedules, have a goal—one could simply live and breathe and enjoy and create beauty. To live the life of a creative genius—that was the highest ideal. My mother spent most of her time in a circle of young and poor artists and writers, who gathered in her studio. She adopted them if they fitted her standard of talent, treated them to meals and cigarettes, lent them money. I was allowed to come visit in my mother's studio and to partake of their discussions, which quite dumbfounded me with their profundity, total seriousness and abstractness. It was all heady stuff and I felt immensely gratified when some of my literary judgements, based on my high-school readings, were taken seriously enough to be criticized and disproven. I quickly learned that what would get me approval was a sharply critical, almost cynical attitude toward whatever was under discussion. I also learned that I could, if I tried, be considered clever by intellectuals, and so I read avidly, thought deeply and tried to produce cynical bon mots. Still, my life-long love of art comes from this adolescent experience, as does my writing. In this respect, my mother achieved what she wanted and did me much good. She fostered my creativity and gave me an alternate model to that of the middle-class housewife and homemaker.

I treasured and admired my mother's artistic talent and wanted to see her realize it fully. In later years, as I grew more politically active, I grew more critical of her. It seemed to me then that she wasted her time and energy on a lot of people who flattered her and exploited her generosity to them. I wanted her to live with the focused intensity of a Van Gogh, a Cezanne. I had no understanding of why such a choice seemed impossible to her at that time.

My mother's lifestyle was designed to be shocking to bourgeois sensibilities. She had a succession of boyfriends, usually younger than herself, writers or artists. She saw them mostly at her studio, but on occasion brought them home and treated them as guests. Certainly, my father was more discreet and for a long time carefully kept me from any knowledge of his private life, while my mother openly and defiantly involved me in it. My father "kept" a mistress in her own apartment, with whom he spent most of his evenings. This woman, about the age of my mother and far less attractive than she, seemed to be quite a conventional lady, tastefully dressed, soft-spoken and intelligent. I met her on the few occasions when she attended chamber music evenings at our house and when I later learned who she was, I was shocked only at how she did not fit my stereotypical image of a mistress, which was based on literature.

The kinds of arrangements that existed in my family were, in fact, quite widespread among the Viennese middle class. The only difference was the openness that existed about them in my family, which was entirely due to my mother. This, again, is something I learned to understand and appreciate only later in life.

The father–mother polarities were expressed in different values, different styles, different goals. All during the years of my adolescence I experienced them as actual polarities, like north and south, which coerced me into choices. If I accepted the one, I must reject the other. I lived in my mother's orbit as an awestruck outsider. With my father and the rest of the family, on the other hand, I tried to avoid conflict, restricted myself to platitudes and guarded my tongue. In short, I was secretive, sullen and cunning, a kind of person I did not like at all.

IN SCHOOL, in the daily stiff routine upheld by its skeleton of unbending regulations, I felt secure and strong. I learned with ease, had a fine memory and could, even by giving only a small part of my attention to the teacher, answer most questions when they unexpectedly came my way. There I enjoyed a favored position as the best student in class; I felt a kind of power in the way I could fend off the teachers or anticipate the questions they would ask. And sometimes, though rarely, I was carried away by the imagery of a poem, the challenge of some idea. But there were bad times, too.

Math class. A male teacher, tall, skinny, dour. He had a rasping, unpleasant voice and a monotonous manner of speaking. At the beginning of the hour he filled the blackboard with small, precise formulas or with endless equations. Then came a period when we had to copy what he had written on the blackboard, while he paced the floor between the rows of seats. Often, he made us try to solve the examples while he watched us. I tried to follow the steps he had outlined but usually got confused, trying to think of a simpler or different way of doing it. Why

always *x* and *y?* Why not sometimes *bb* or *ch* or *mongoose* and *mustard?* I never
seemed to understand that I was just to learn the process by rote and apply it. The
teacher came near my bench and bent over me. His right hand lay over my shoulder as he scribbled some correction on my paper. His left hand swiftly and strongly squeezed my breast. "Carry on," he said sternly, straightening and moving on
to the next pupil. I felt awful. There was no way of protesting such behavior; I
did not even have a word for it—that was simply the way that teacher was. All I
knew was I hated math—it was my only "bad" subject. I never could learn it or
like it and cannot to this day.

Marta entered my class in the middle of the year; it was in the fourth grade
of our eight-grade *Gymnasium.* She was small, fair-haired and pale, with a long
nose, heavy knitted brows and a look of keen intelligence in her eyes. She was a
student from Yugoslavia and soon let us know that she had been expelled from
all the high schools of her country for political activities forbidden by her government. She had a way of holding herself in control, of keeping her own coun-
sel and steering her own course that made an enormous impression on me. Like
me, she was clumsy in gym, but unlike me she made no effort to improve, but
treated the subject with supreme disdain. She spoke six languages fluently and
was an excellent student. As far as the teachers knew she had learned her lesson
and stayed clear of any troublemaking.

In my eagerness for and fear of political involvement, she was a fascinating
figure to me, and I sought her out and questioned her persistently about her experiences. It took some time before she trusted me, but then she seemed quite
pleased to have an admiring audience, and before long we became close friends.
How much of our friendship was based on her desire to convert me politically I
cannot say, but I know we trusted each other and had long, deeply serious discussions about everything and anything, from philosophy, religion and art to the
state of the world and the need for revolution. It seemed to me that Marta was
absolutely fearless and I idolized her for that. She was also brash, domineering,
opinionated and rigid, but I did not notice at the time and it would probably not
have mattered to me anyway, for she was my guide, my mentor, my heroine. I
admired the way she had freed herself from any emotional involvement with her
parents, whom she regarded as hopeless reactionaries, the way she disdained the
obsession of other teenagers with clothes, boys and dancing. She lived with a
young aunt who seemed to care little about her comings and goings. I was deeply
impressed with Marta's gutsy defiance of governmental, parental and police
authority when, a few months after settling in Vienna, she made contact with

political students who were engaged in mysterious underground work. Before long, Marta saw to it that my own political development was deepened by showing me the underground newspaper she regularly read.

There was a jail sentence of six months to a year for being caught with that paper, and I did not lightly make the decision to read and distribute it. After months of agonizing and soul-searching, I was probably shamed into it more by Marta's example than by anything else. I also somehow expected that this action, however small it was in the general scheme of things, would inevitably alter and strengthen me.

I can see the paper in front of me now and feel its weight in my hand. It was tissue-paper thin, smaller than the usual tabloid, printed solidly so as to get the utmost out of each risky square inch of paper. Sometimes it came with a false cover page, some innocuous-looking technical journal, which when opened to the inside pages contained forbidden news. I knew then it was a Communist paper, printed abroad and smuggled into the country. Column after tightly printed column brought news from every part of the globe, mostly terrible news of fascism, terror, repression, torture, but also news of riots, resistance, strikes.

Marta gave me the paper at school and I usually brought it home folded inside my bra or under my blouse. I would read it in bed, huddled under the covers and using a flashlight. Drawing on my reading of Maxim Gorki and Vera Figner, I pictured the printing of the paper, a secretive, romantic endeavor involving terrible risks for a handful of brave revolutionaries. Then the passing of it, hand to hand, across the border, in a lunch basket, a shopping bag, a briefcase. The very existence of the paper meant the existence of a network and I, by holding it against my body, by reading it in my comfortable, warm bed, was a part of that network. A tiny, humble part, but the connection was real.

The paper was always full of horror stories about Nazi Germany. Long before the international, mainstream press took notice, the stories of terror and torture in German police stations, jails and concentration camps were reported in gruesome detail and with considerable accuracy in the underground press. I read these stories in bed, keeping myself awake with horror pictures and dozing off to nightmares. Yet I committed the news in the paper to memory as though I were building a wall, putting brick upon brick, before I passed it on. I understood I was to pass it on, not destroy it after reading it, and so I did, but I was very much afraid for as long as the paper was in my possession. To leave it in a public place at school, such as a toilet or on a bench, was far too dangerous. I contrived to leave it on park benches, on doorsteps, in stores. My fingers were wet and sweaty when

I handled it and my heart would thump every time I heard a noise. It took me a long time to learn to stay cool, when I was full of fear. Yet handling the paper reduced the general mood of defeatism that had so oppressed me. I felt myself coming closer to the movement, that unknown band of political resisters out there; I felt myself becoming stronger and not so easily overwhelmed. I did not get there easily and spent many months vacillating, unable to involve myself because of fear.

BEFORE LONG Marta saw to it that my political involvement was deepened by getting me into a practical project to help some of the victims of the February fighting. The project was organized by Red Aid, which I took to be some sort of Red Cross for illegal political fighters and their families. A group of high-school and university students had taken responsibility for raising money to help support the families of imprisoned or exiled fighters. Marta had taken on a family and now induced me to do the same.

Theoretically, I was supposed to raise five to ten shillings a week for my family through the contributions of others, which would have enlarged the circle of sympathizers. In practice I supplied the money myself from what I earned by tutoring and doing small jobs for family members. I was far too scared to ask anyone else to take part in this enterprise.

The experience of being an illegal welfare worker did nothing to strengthen either my courage or my political understanding. Once a month, late in the afternoon, I went into a tenement house in a neighboring district, not too far from a park in which I had played as a child. I climbed up four flights of stairs, suppressing my nausea at the stale smell of cabbage and Lysol, and visited with a dispirited mother of three who seemed to hold me personally responsible for all the ills that had befallen her. She was always dissatisfied with the money I was bringing her, but the sum had been fixed by my contact person, Marie, who insisted that it was a matter of political significance that I not give any more to my family than she had allotted them. Any surplus was to be given to her and would go into "the fund," which served the ever-increasing numbers of needy politicals. I could bring old clothes, some toys for the children and books for the teenage boy; that was all.

The mother treated me as though I were a city welfare worker; the oldest boy was sullen and refused to talk to me, and my efforts at making friends with the runny-nosed toddler and the sallow-faced baby were equally unsuccessful. I understood only too well what separated us—not only my good clothes and well-soled shoes and the fact I was bringing them money, but my apprehension and lack of commitment, which I was certain they sensed and resented. Had Marta been in my place, she would have been accepted by this woman and her children. In fact, so would my mother. She would at once have seated herself at the kitchen table and begun to draw the baby or put on some kind of funny show for the toddler. But I was self-conscious and miserable in this role. I was apprehensive, as I came out of the tenement in the falling dusk, that someone might wonder what I was doing there. I looked over my shoulder to see if I was being followed. I never was, of course, but my anxiety was real.

A HALF HOUR LATER, as I entered my warm, comfortable apartment, the contrast was overwhelming. Once again, I switched roles and became the dutiful schoolgirl, who was told when to practice the piano and when to sit down to supper. I did my homework, teased my sister, fended off my father's questions and sneaked extra time in the toilet to read a chapter in some novel or other.

At night, sometimes, when there was chamber music being played, I sat in the elegant music room, serving as a page-turner for my piano teacher when she played the Schumann Piano Quintet, and felt the only happiness and freedom I had felt all day. At such a moment, all the heavy, contradictory roles fell away from me and I could be absorbed in something great and grand, something beyond me, beyond fear and need and uncertainty.

I considered myself a failure as a "political worker," but I kept it up dutifully for several years. Still, there was another element in all of this, one I have long been unable to see but which now, in the telling, is assuming more and more importance. I lived a strange, split life at home, forever battling to maintain a foothold of privacy and dignity for myself in the constant parental warfare. I deeply, desperately longed to escape this kind of life, even as I began to be drawn more and more into my mother's orbit. During most of my waking hours I was treated as a child, subject to rules and formal discipline, supervised by parents, relatives, governess, maid and teachers. I was a precocious adolescent, in need of a private existence. As I searched for that, there were two ways open to me—to become my mother's confederate, her friend and acolyte, or to lead a secret political life. I chose to do both. My secret lives, the life with my mother, which I kept strictly from father and grandmother, and my political life, which I kept strictly from everyone, allowed me to find a territory of my own. What a desperate choice it now seems . . . Still, this was what it took for me to become an adult. Defining myself as an outsider and moving toward danger the way the swimmer moves toward the breaking wave—these two tendencies shaped my character and being. By the time of my actual independence, that stance had become so natural and essential to me, I was totally unconscious of it.

During the twelve years I went to school in Austria, the government changed three times, not the way presidents and parties succeed one another peacefully in a democracy, but with violence and turmoil. This meant changes in the flag, the national anthem, the required school curriculum, the official holidays. It was as though one were living each time in a different country, and yet one had never moved at all. Such instability either makes one turn away from politics entirely and escape into a private world or makes one a committed political partisan. During my adolescence politics became central to my existence, an integral aspect of my self-expression, a major aspect of my intellectual life.

For me, adolescence was also a time of sexual exploration and a time for trying out friendships with people of vastly different values and beliefs. As with politics, my experiences in these areas were excessive, turbulent and intense.

In *Gymnasium,* I developed friendships with a few classmates, which were in effect experiments in normalcy. The girls came mostly from wealthy homes, were traditional in their upbringing and were concerned with beauty, ballroom dancing, gossip and boys. For a short time I belonged to a club called the Ladybugs, the purpose of which I have forgotten. I tried "going out" with one or another of the brothers of these girls, but their interests were so different from mine that usually the first attempt was the last. These middle-class girls offered no attraction to me intellectually, and usually their response to me was that I was stuck-up, difficult and not much fun. All of which was undoubtedly true.

For a short time I developed a friendship with an older schoolmate and her brother, both of whom seemed to me to embody decadent sophistication. Dolly and Georges (he used the French pronunciation) were the children of wealthy Jewish parents, the kind who usually would snub me because my parents were not as rich as theirs. Their father owned one of the two biggest department stores in Vienna. They lived in a sumptuous villa in a far "better" district than the one in which I lived. What attracted me to these two was that they were not the least bit snobbish; on the contrary, they went out of their way to disparage their parents' wealth and to disavow their parents' values. They considered themselves modern, in contrast to their parents'—all our parents'—hopelessly traditional ways. They avidly embraced all things American, including clothing, films and above all jazz.

They had an extensive collection of jazz records and never missed an American film. For quite a while I shared their enthusiasms and became knowledgeable about Louis Armstrong, Duke Ellington and Ella Fitzgerette, to whom we listened by the hour, smoking British cigarettes in half-darkened rooms.

Dolly's face was full of contrasts: the eyes deep-set and intelligent, the nose too broad, the nostrils flaring and the mouth like an angry scar. Although in action her vivacity and expressiveness were attractive, her looks repelled people at first glance. Dolly made no effort to please. Her flapper dress style and extreme combinations of colors and textures seemed designed to shock others and to express her contempt for traditional standards of beauty. I admired her spunky defiance of convention and tried to uglify myself in her image, much to my mother's dismay. My friendship with Dolly also set up a conflict with the political ideas and practices represented by Marta. Marta looked upon Dolly with disgust and pushed me to choose between them. For Marta there were always these absolute choices—one could not embrace two such divergent views of the world. In the end it was Georges who helped me make the choice, by his lazy and somewhat bored flirtation with me, which escalated far too quickly to suit my taste into the assumption that I owed it to him and our "friendship" to have sex. He regarded my virginity as ludicrous and contemptible and offered to relieve me of it as a sort of charity. Did I realize I was hanging on to the antiquated values of the parents? At the rate I was going I might never be able to free myself and become an adult. I admitted the logic of his argument, but I did not find him attractive enough even for kissing. The idea of anything more was revolting to me and so I began to avoid him and Dolly.

The following summer I fell seriously in love with an unattainable man. I was spending several weeks of a boring, enforced vacation in Marienbad, where Grandmama was taking the cure. This was a part of my parents' bargain—my mother was free to spend four weeks away from us during the summer and we children spent those weeks wherever father's mother spent her vacation. We were accompanied by our governess, but this summer there was no governess and it was assumed I was old enough to take care of myself between meals, which always were taken at the hotel where we stayed. The spa routine demanded that one take an hour-long promenade in the morning to the sounds of a "Kur-Orchestra," which played a program of light music in an open-air pavilion. Those taking the cure walked along sipping the beneficial waters, while observing each other and the current fashions. I was walking with somebody's young child, a boy I had offered to take out for the morning just to have something to do, since I was bored and restless and hated the entire routine. I saw the man coming toward me, sipping the water from his mug, and instantly fell in love with him, the way I had read about it in the great novels of world literature. There was no question about it—this was the man. He was old, I thought—well, at the least, mature—and looked like the film star Raymond Massey, tall, dark, very manly and romantic.

Incredibly, he spoke to me, asking if this was my little brother. We exchanged a few words and he asked me to meet him again the next day. I did and shortly was drawn into what for me was a serious love affair and for him was probably no more than a vacation diversion. He was forty-two, married and the father of two daughters, a small-town banker in Czechoslovakia; I was fourteen and despite my intellectual sophistication incredibly naive. He was honorable, or perhaps simply smart enough to keep our heavily erotic relationship just short of making him legally culpable of the seduction of a minor. He was an intellectual of sorts, very well read, and we talked endlessly of literature, creativity and love, sounding and probably feeling like characters out of Thomas Mann or Herman Hesse. The very hopelessness of the situation charged it with energy and passion; I felt myself to be involved in a serious, tragic love affair in which I could only expect loss. But at this stage of life, even to experience love's loss was to experience love, the real thing. We managed to extend this affair for over two years by the exchange of brief, secretive and passionate letters and by meeting the following year in the summer. Years later, the thought first occurred to me he may have been a dirty bastard using me to get his kicks, but I don't believe he was. It was just not that simple. I certainly got as much as, if not more than, I gave. At the very least, it kept me safe for a while from emotional involvements with boys my own age, who would have been less considerate and protective of me than he was. I ended the affair when I outgrew it and I have never regretted having it.

During the years of this relationship I was also drawn to an entirely different sort of intellectual guru, whose influence on me outlasted most of my other early infatuations. Karl Kraus, the greatest satirist in the German language and, as his admirers thought, the greatest German-speaking writer and poet of the century, had a circle of fanatically devoted followers. In his eclectic magazine, *Die Fackel (The Torch),* which appeared whenever the spirit moved him, he mercilessly satirized militarism, authoritarianism, bureaucracies and above all the debasement and misuse of the German language. Like all Kraus followers, I read every word of the master, from his twelve volumes of poetry, the decades of issues of his magazine and his books of aphorisms and epigrams to his monumental pacifist "play for a Martian theater," *Die Letzten Tage der Menschheit (The Last Days of Mankind).*

Kraus, who had fearlessly attacked the protofascist right wing since 1928, for reasons that seemed quite insufficient to me then and now endorsed the government of Dollfuss after the suppression of democracy in 1934. Most of his followers abandoned him over this seeming betrayal of his lifelong commitments, but it was just at that time that I first came into contact with his work and, perversely, despite my opposite political convictions, I fell totally under his spell. I attended every one of his lectures and his brilliant one-man readings of Shakespeare plays and Offenbach operettas—unforgettable performances to all who heard them—and immersed myself in his work and thought. It was his mastery of the language, his poetic talent and force, his reverence for the word that enraptured me and made me forgive and forget his reactionary politics. To this day I consider myself a Kraus disciple; my lifelong devotion to language derives from his impact on me, which is reflected in all my writing. Even then, the two disparate sides of my being, the writer and the political person, were beginning to emerge and somehow I managed to absorb the contradictions and encompass the tensions between them.

I was fifteen when I at last found a group of young people to whom I could relate without reservations. They were somewhat older than I, university students, politically active and dedicated to revolutionary change, as I was. They were also enthusiastic hikers, mountaineers and skiers. Belonging to this group, I could at last end my great romance with the older man, who as it happened was also a Kraus disciple. That fact certainly had strengthened my attachment to him. About the time I ended my relationship with him, in 1936, Karl Kraus died. I attended his funeral and wept as though a close friend had died. A phase of my adolescence had ended.

I met Bobby, a medical student, who a year later became my boyfriend, in this youth group. He was a wiry, combative intellectual whose aggressiveness hid a gentle disposition and great kindness. Bobby's head was small in proportion to his body. His long nose, thick lips and receding chin made him look like the Nazi caricature of the Jew, a fact only accentuated by his last name, which was Jerusalem. Bobby Jerusalem carried his extraordinary ugliness as a sort of badge. It made him one of the outcasts, the handicapped of this earth, and I understood after a time that, while he loved me for my mind and my person, he also needed me because I was good-looking, and he would always need the affirmative love of a good-looking woman. Strangely, this made for a firm bond between us, a bond that on my part was based more on friendship than on love, but in my innocence of love I did not know the difference. He needed me and I needed someone to make me feel needed. When it turned out that my father vehemently opposed the relationship, mainly because Bobby was unattractive and shorter than I by at least an inch, my determination to carry this love affair into permanence became strengthened.

Bobby's older brother, Fritz, a handsome fellow, was a genuine hero, a Communist who had served time in jail after 1934 and then gone to Spain with the International Brigade. I met him after he got out of jail and saw him later in France, after my emigration, and both of us understood that had he been available I would have preferred him to Bobby, but he was always either married or paired with one talented woman or another. Besides, considering the kind of political life he led, he certainly could not be bothered with admiring teenagers. He looked deeply into my eyes and said with great firmness, "Bobby needs you; you are good for him." And that affirmed what I knew and became a sort of pledge of my allegiance. What more could I ask of life than a good man, a good friend who loved me more than I loved him and who needed me?

WITH BOBBY I entered the world of student politics, of late-night debates over fine points of theory, of friendships and comradeship. We read Marx and Engels, Bebel and Anatole France; we devoured the novels of Nexö and Sholokov and spent long evenings reciting and discussing the poetry of Mayakovski, Beaudelaire and Bertolt Brecht, a heady mix of styles.

In 1939 my father arranged for me to spend a six-week summer vacation in England in the hope of separating me from Bobby. Instead, the trip only strengthened my political commitment. I traveled as part of a student-exchange program and stayed with a London family with several teenage daughters. I was very excited about traveling alone, meeting English girls and learning firsthand how an ordinary English family lived. I was met at the train station by the mother of the family and learned that they lived in a suburb of London, about one hour by train from the center. The three blond teenage daughters greeted me without much enthusiasm and quickly lost interest in me when my poor English made conversation difficult. Dinner consisted of a thin vegetable soup and soda crackers with watercress and cucumber and I retired early to my attic room, hungry and wondering how the rest of the trip would work out. The next morning I awoke, to my horror, to the sounds of the Horst-Wessel song the daughters were playing on their record player. When I questioned why they would play this Nazi song, I was informed that they thought the German Nazis were just great and that their father was very active in the Moseley party, which worked in England to improve relations between England and Germany. I told them I was Jewish and did not think much of the German Nazis. They shrugged and said, to each his own, and after that barely talked to me. My father had paid for my room and board in advance and it looked like I'd be stuck in a fascist English home for the next six weeks. The family's attitude toward me wavered between disapproval and indifference, and the meals did not improve either. I bought a weekly rail pass and left the house each morning to spend the whole day exploring the sights of London, coming home as late as possible.

On the train that first week, a grey-haired woman sat opposite me, reading the *Daily Worker*. She looked like an ordinary housewife, carrying a shopping bag and wearing the inevitable sensible shoes British women seemed to prefer to the fashionable footwear of Viennese ladies. I asked her if I might look at the paper, since I had never seen anyone read it out in the open. We got into conversation and she quickly elicited my sad story from me. By the time we reached London, she had invited me for dinner at her house the next day and drawn up instructions for finding her place.

When I got there the next day, I was astonished to find this Communist woman living in typical middle-class propriety in a small house in a row of identical houses; the inevitable tiny front yard filled with roses and the backyard overflowing with flowers and vegetables. Marjorie explained that gardening was her father's hobby; he was a retired policeman and spent most of his day with his flowers. A retired policeman whose daughter read the Communist newspaper . . . My astonishment knew no bounds, especially after I met the white-haired gentleman, who greeted me in a very friendly manner. Marjorie had prepared a veritable feast, a beef stew, fresh lettuce from the garden and a home-baked apple pie. After dinner she allowed me to spend as long as I wanted in front of her bookshelves, which held a library of radical and Marxist books the likes of which I had never seen before. Marjorie and her father invited me to come back any time and I enjoyed several feasts of good food, warm hospitality and radical politics. Marjorie suggested a solution for my problem with the fascist family—if I could get my father to give me the necessary funds, she knew of a great Socialist Youth camp that was then in session in Wales. She was certain I would enjoy it.

I PHONED MY FATHER and explained the situation, without going into too much detail on the politics of my new friends. Amazingly, he agreed to transfer the necessary funds to me. Within a week I left the fascist family and was on my way to the summer camp in Wales. This turned out to be a great experience for me. The camp was run by J. B. S. Haldane, the eminent biochemist, and his wife, Helen. Both were highly respected for their pioneering work in genetics; they were also somewhat notorious as active pacifists and as having recently and publicly joined the Communist Party. The respected position these radical intellectuals held in English society was something I had never encountered in Austria and I easily succumbed to their charm, their stimulating conversation and their simple and generous kindness to the young people from many different countries they had gathered around them. I spent four exciting weeks there, taking part in demonstrations for the Spanish Republican Army, engaging in endless discussions and spending the evenings around the campfire singing left-wing songs in several languages. I buddied up with a young Oxford student who made it his business to convert me to Marxism the proper way, which consisted of my reading of Marxist classics followed by hours of his explicating and discussing the readings with me in true Oxford fashion. I was especially carried away by Frederick Engels's *Origin of the Family, Private Property and the State* and his book on the peasant wars. Marx's *Eighteenth Brumaire of Louis Napoleon* dazzled me with its approach to social history, which made a long-gone society come alive in a way school history books never did. I swallowed the Marxist classics, which were in England so readily and openly available, the way a thirsty person swallows a cool drink. And I got an entirely new view of myself in a community of young people who looked upon me as a bit of a heroine for having survived youth in a fascist country and having shown some spirit of resistance. I returned from England not only with increased self-confidence and a stronger commitment than ever to my friendship with Bobby and to our common political work, but also with a new interest in Marxist thought.

THESE WERE THE YEARS when a radio consisted of five to eight different instruments carefully connected by wires. The radio in our home had a short-wave dial and after long and patient fiddling interrupted constantly by crackling or humming noises, one could hear the main radio stations of the various European capitals. Our phonograph was a hand-cranked model that played 78 rpm records, the only kind then available. I remember one evening being alone in our salon, the formal sitting room reserved for entertaining guests. First I played a record, which to me had a strange, almost exotic sound. It was Sophie

Tucker singing "My Yiddische Mamme." It was, I thought, schmaltzy and somewhat ludicrous; still, the deep sincerity of her interpretation involved me emotionally in her sentimental reminiscences of home and childhood. Our salon was furnished in Biedermeier style, with settees upholstered in striped damask and gilt-edged end tables with fluted legs. There were porcelain figurines of shepherds and shepherdesses on the tables, which I hated and often felt tempted to smash to the floor. An elaborate, gilded mirror above the settee reflected the colorful Persian rug and the polished parquet floor. All of it, in its bourgeois solidity, was as far from Sophie Tucker's voice and sentiment as it was possible to be. Somehow, that pleased me. Next I pulled out two records Marta had lent me, one by a radical folksinger who sang in Berlin dialect of hunger, unemployment and the coming revolution, the other Bertolt Brecht's *Threepenny Opera,* a work I greatly admired.

Finally, toward ten o'clock, I turned on the short-wave radio and tuned in Radio Moscow. A brief newscast in German gave the kind of news I would never get in the official press—of strikes and workers' resistance, of fascist terror in Germany, of Dimitroff's heroic defense in the Reichstag trial. At the end of the broadcast, they played the "International," the Communist anthem. I sprang to my feet and stood at attention, giving the clenched-fist salute.

Listening to these forbidden sounds in my own home in the absence of my parents, in the very formal room I associated with all the discipline and good manners I hated, was thrilling to me. As I flicked off the radio and returned to my own reality, I felt some kind of power connecting me with the great moving forces in the world "outside." I was a part of something bigger than myself, bigger than the constraints of my daily life. I could overcome my fear and the limitations of my overprotected upbringing; I might even become heroic, as other political people had. I, who was an outsider everywhere, could belong. Here was my hope, my escape.

[5]

T HE YEAR 1937 was one long period of waiting for the axe to fall. It was
only a question of time before the Nazis would invade Austria or before
they would engineer a political putsch. Now that Italy was an Axis partner of Germany, such an event seemed ever more likely. The support for *Anschluss*
(the incorporation of Austria into Germany) was growing steadily in the
provinces; urban discontent seemed to consolidate more and more into pro-Nazi
sentiment and an explosive anti-Semitism.

Like many of my countrymen and women, I began to experience that sense of
panic, fear and helplessness that was to characterize the next years for all of us. I
thought I knew what was coming. Like Cassandra, I knew the worst that could
happen and felt a sense of urgency to convey it to those near me in order to save
them and myself. I provoked political discussions at the dinner table; I tried to
engage my father and uncles in debates about the advisability of emigration, about
the need to make contingency plans in case of an *Anschluss*. No one would listen,
no one would hear. My father had made his own contingency plans much earlier
and in a more practical manner than I could conceive of: after Hitler's rise to power
he had, in 1933, established a pharmacy in Liechtenstein, the tiny principality
lying along the Rhine River between Germany, Austria and Switzerland. He had
had to overcome the resistance of the eight practicing physicians in Liechtenstein,
who were in the habit of concocting and selling their own remedies, and he had

had to engage in an educational campaign to show the local peasants the advantages of buying medicine in a specialized store. It had taken him four years of losses to make the enterprise mildly profitable, but he regarded it more as an investment against the remote possibility of having to leave Austria. He surely needed no advice from a teenage daughter. Everyone in the family drew on the experiences of our numerous relatives in Germany, who had lived for years under the Nazi regime without any harm coming to them. Unpleasantness, yes, and injustice and unfairness, but the German relatives all had had time to make careful plans for their emigration. Aunt Ida, the widow of my grandmother's brother Alfred, a banker, had just recently arrived in Vienna with her daughter. They were planning to emigrate to the United States.

If I ventured to mention my mother's relatives, her sister Klari and Klari's husband, Dr. Alexander Mueller, a renowned psychoanalyst, who had quite recently arrived penniless from Berlin, it was pointed out to me that they were stateless persons—the unfortunate consequence of his having been a prisoner of war in Russia after World War I while his hometown was assigned to another country in the peace treaty. Once freed from Russian imprisonment he returned home to find himself a stateless person. Such persons had no rights any government had to respect and unfortunately Klari, by marrying him, had lost her own citizenship and acquired his bad status. An unfortunate and exceptional case.

The uncles were likely to end such discussions by instructing me that family fathers had to make responsible decisions, not like carefree students, who could run from one country to the other without giving it much thought, having no dependents to consider.

Their instruction was wasted on me, as my information was wasted on them. But I could not give up my campaign of enlightenment, in which I told them news I had culled from the underground paper, ascribing it as coming from one or another student who was reading the foreign press. I was "political," and I felt incredibly vulnerable. Since my family had no idea of my political work and contacts, they saw no need for my special protection. What if the Nazis came and I needed to leave the country? I could not imagine my family ever agreeing to that. Worse—by my staying in my home, I was endangering them, not only myself. Still, life went on quite as usual.

Life as usual, in 1937, meant frequent bomb and terror attacks by Austrian Nazis. Movie theaters and railway stations were favorite targets. In February a band of Nazi youth exploded a smoke bomb in the main synagogue of Vienna, then rampaged through a shopping district, smashing the windows of stores owned by Jews.

The police, among whom were many underground Nazis, were slow to apprehend the culprits in these attacks. If any were caught, the courts showed them great leniency. If they were sentenced to prison, they were often given amnesty or parole. Yet former trade unionists engaged in peaceful demonstrations or in passing out leaflets were arrested promptly and jailed for long periods.

My father reported a very unpleasant incident. A young man, posing as a customer, had forced his way behind the counter at the pharmacy and demanded that my father open the locked cupboard containing the drug supplies. He did not seem to be armed, and Father thought he might have been an addict, so he tried to talk to him quietly in order to persuade him to leave. He would not, of course, open the cupboard. When other employees came to my father's rescue, the young man ran out the back door, shouting, "You'll pay for this, you filthy Jew." "Bad enough he's an addict," my father commented, "but an anti-Semite, too." Yet he regarded the incident as unimportant, something that could happen to any pharmacist in the course of doing business.

In the streets, the markets and the stores, the white knee socks, the symbol of underground Nazis, were more and more in evidence. Chancellor Kurt von Schuschnigg had outlawed the Nazi Party after his predecessor's assassination by Nazis, and he governed Austria as a dictator. He pursued the same policies as Dollfuss had, hoping to preserve the independence of Austria by relying on Italy's intervention. But in the years 1936–38, when the underground Nazi Party engaged in constant terrorist attacks financed by the "Austrian Legion" in Germany, Schuschnigg steadfastly refused all offers by Social Democrats on the left and monarchists on the right to form an anti-Nazi coalition.

Once a year, in February, my school arranged a skiing vacation to an alpine hut, where we slept on straw mattresses under the supervision of the gym teachers, and ate our meals on trestle tables. We spent all day walking up one mountain or another, carrying our skis on our shoulders and then skiing down through woods and on open slopes in descents that could take as much as three hours. It was exhilarating, and for that week all thoughts of politics, danger and fear were banished.

Returning from the trip on February 12, 1938, I took the streetcar home from the railroad station. Since I carried my rucksack and skis, I had to stand on the rear platform. At several streetcar stops I noticed newsboys hawking "Extras." Clusters of people around the tobacconists' stores were reading the newspapers on display there. A choking panic took hold of me. The peace of the mountains was still with me; I did not want to break into it with what I sensed could be only bad news. At one of the stops, a newsboy reached up to the passengers on the platform with his papers. Now one was in my hands. "Schuschnigg at Berchtesgaden with Hitler" screamed the headline.

"At last," a stout man exclaimed next to me, grinning broadly.

The conductor came out on the platform and, at the next stop, shouted to a man standing there with a newspaper, "What's up?"

"Schuschnigg is negotiating with Hitler," the man replied.

"Good luck," someone standing next to me said bitterly.

"Sellout," the conductor muttered, and he angrily pushed into the interior of the car. Like most of the transportation workers he was probably a Socialist and a union man. A young man with a cap pushed past him as he left the car. "The beginning of the end," he said gravely.

A middle-aged woman carrying two overfilled shopping bags set them down next to me and crossed herself. "Holy Mother of God protect us. It's all over," she said to no one in particular. She picked up her bags, descended the steps and briskly walked away.

It's all over, I thought, and my eyes filled with tears. I tried to keep control of my face as the streetcar moved on. Don't show any reaction, don't get into any arguments. It was the beginning of the end all right. My throat felt tight, as though breathing had become hazardous. Drops of sweat ran along my face and neck into my collar. I was afraid. I was terribly afraid.

The government-controlled press did not inform Austrians of what had happened at Berchtesgaden, but historians have since established the sequence of events. Schuschnigg had been lured to Berchtesgaden by the false promise that Hitler would guarantee the independence of Austria if Schuschnigg would agree to put some Austrian Nazis in his cabinet. Once in Hitler's mountain stronghold, Chancellor Schuschnigg was treated like a prisoner, not like a visiting head of state. Hitler bullied and threatened him, showing him German Army plans for the invasion of Austria. He was told that at that very moment German troops were massed at the Austrian frontier.

Presented by Hitler with a list of eleven demands for concessions, he negotiated as best he could, but ended up agreeing that the Ministry of Security and the Ministry of Interior would be given to a prominent Nazi, Dr. Seiss-Inquart; that amnesty would be granted to convicted Nazi terrorists; and that the Fatherland Front would accept Nazis to membership. In exchange, Hitler promised to guarantee Austria's independence and to cease his support for Austrian Nazis. Schuschnigg agreed further to try to persuade President Miklas to appoint Nazis to the Ministries of Education, War and Justice.

On Schuschnigg's return, President Miklas resisted these concessions, but finally gave in when told of German troop "maneuvers" at Austria's frontier. The Cabinet agreed to the terms a few days later. By the 18th of February Seiss-Inquart controlled the national police and Guido Schmidt, a Nazi, controlled foreign policy. Thirty-thousand men in the Austrian Legion, illegal Nazis who had found asylum in Germany, returned to Austria, and two thousand Nazis jailed for terrorist activities were freed. But, in a small gesture of defiance, Schuschnigg also released jailed leftists.[1]

The ominous Nazi infiltration of key government posts was a clear signal of what was to come: either forced annexation or a "peaceful" takeover of the government, not by German but by Austrian Nazis. Only a miracle—or foreign opinion—could help Austria now.

Hitler's speech before the *Reichstag* on Sunday, February 20, signaled his intentions unequivocally. The speech was broadcast by Radio Austria. Ignoring the promises he had made at Berchtesgaden, Hitler did not pledge Austrian independence, but declared that the suffering of German "co-racials," persecuted because they wanted unity with Germany, was a condition he found intolerable. Here, in this veiled reference to the illegality of Austrian Nazis, was the pretext he would use for invading Austria. In orchestrated response, Nazi demonstrations broke out in all the Austrian provinces.

On Thursday, February 24, Schuschnigg spoke in Vienna. He made no comments on Hitler's speech, but detailed the economic gains made by the Austrian state since 1918. "Austria shall remain free and for this we will fight to the death," he declared.

Austrian Nazis responded to this defiant statement of independence by staging raucous demonstrations in Vienna and in all the provinces. In Graz, twenty-thousand Nazis occupied the square in front of *Rathaus,* where Schuschnigg's speech was being broadcast, shouting so loudly that the speech could not be heard. They ended their rally by singing the Horst-Wessel song. But this time, their fervor was met with resistance. Thirty-thousand workers and pro-Schuschnigg forces paraded through Graz and chased the Nazis from the *Rathaus* square.

The workers of Vienna responded equally strongly. Leaders of the government-sanctioned trade union movement, many of them still secretly loyal to the Social Democratic Party (SPÖ) even after four years of clerical fascism, met and declared

---

1. G. E. R. Gedye, *Betrayal in Central Europe: Austria and Czechoslovakia: The Fallen Bastions* (New York: Harper & Bros., 1939), 229.

their willingness to fight against the *Anschluss* with arms, if necessary.[2] But there was no reply from the government to this offer.

Rumors were flying wildly. Schuschnigg would recognize the SPÖ and arm the workers. The Monarchist Party would be made legal; they would invite Kaiser Otto to return and assume the Hapsburg throne, thus thwarting Hitler's ambitions. Britain, France and Czechoslovakia would come to the defense of Austrian independence. Mussolini would mass troops at the Italian border and threaten an invasion if Hitler took Austria.

None of this happened. But Schuschnigg was desperately looking for allies and as he did, the iron reign of dictatorship loosened. The time of democratic struggle could be measured in days. It was short, passionate and doomed.

On March 4, in great secrecy, Schuschnigg met with shop stewards of the fourteen biggest firms, many of them underground members of the SPÖ. They pledged him their full support, including armed resistance, if he would agree to some concessions: freedom to express Socialist and trade-union ideas; freely elected, not appointed, trade union representatives; restoration of workers' sports and cultural organizations; a free labor press and an end to police espionage. The Chancellor agreed to negotiate these demands promptly.

On March 7, Schuschnigg met with a small trade union delegation and, in principle, agreed to their demands. He appointed two officials to negotiate further details.[3]

In the next few days the streets and plazas in the city were choked with spontaneous demonstrations by Nazi and Schuschnigg supporters. Traffic and business were paralyzed. The Inner City resounded to the chorus of competing slogans. Nazis demonstrated each night in front of the German tourist office, a place they had elevated to a symbol of unification. But their shouts and speakers now had to compete with Fatherland Front rallies near the Opera.

I MET MARIE, my underground contact, as usual, once a month in the city market. Both of us carried shopping baskets from which vegetables and paper bags protruded. Marie was a stout woman of undefinable age, wearing a kerchief on her head, a long skirt, a hand-knit sweater and sturdy shoes with black woollen stockings. She looked like a typical Viennese working-class housewife, anyone's

2. Ibid., 230.
3. Ibid., 256–58.

grandmother. In repose, as she stood in front of a vegetable stand, ostensibly comparing the quality and prices of several kinds of onions, she looked tired, even a little dull. When I greeted her and we started to walk away in conversation, her face became lively, her eyes sparkled with intelligent alertness and her broad face lit up with a smile, which showed her crooked, misshapen teeth.

"It's happening," she said joyously. "He's been meeting with the trade union comrades and promised to make the party legal again. The units in the factories are coming out of hiding. By Sunday we'll have free speech and assembly rights, and then we'll show those Nazis—"

"It'll take more than street demonstrations . . ."

"Once we can come out in the open again, the workers will show what they can do. Our comrades came out of jail and started right in organizing. There may be a general strike. Look what our folks did in Graz, even without legality . . ."

"What if Hitler marches in?"

"Schuschnigg will have to arm the workers. And many of us still have the weapons from February [1934]. We'll fight, and the rich will have to join us. I heard there's a lot of unrest in the Army; they want to fight, not give in."

"I sure hope you're right," I said lamely. "The students are running away as fast as they can. At least those who have contacts outside." As we paused at a fruit stand, she slipped a paper bag into my shopping bag. The newspaper.

"Here, take these apples I bought." The money I had collected was in the bag.

Marie turned away from the vendor and we kept on walking slowly among the stalls, talking softly. "Students are unreliable allies," Marie commented. "In the end it all depends on the workers. But listen, if things go wrong, I want you to stop working for us and we can't meet either. They'll be after the Jews first. So if you need to get out of the country, try and contact me. Maybe I can help get you across. But only in a real emergency. Get it?"

I nodded. We had earlier agreed on a procedure by which I could contact her in an emergency at the place where she worked.

"But Marie, if I'm out of contact—" The thought of never seeing her again really frightened me.

"You'll manage," she said in the tone of a wise old aunt. "You've been fine up to now, you'll do fine. Just don't panic. Anyway, things are going our way and we'll beat the shit out of the bastards. I gotta go now, so take care."

She turned abruptly and disappeared among the crowd of shoppers. I bought some carrots at the vegetable stand in front of me. Look natural, I thought, don't panic. How come Marie was never scared?

On March 9, at a Fatherland Front rally in Innsbruck, a stronghold of Austrian Nazis, Schuschnigg dropped his bombshell. "We must know whether the people of Austria approve of the path we propose to take," he declared. He had therefore decided to hold a plebiscite on the following Sunday, March 12. The question to be answered by the Austrian people was: "Are you for an independent, a Christian, German and united Austria?"[4] He urged an all-out effort to mobilize for a strong, a unanimous YES vote.

"Better late than never" was the general opinion. Schuschnigg's bold, long-delayed action mobilized citizen action. Hope sprouted like grass after a sudden rain. At last there was something people could do to show their belief in Austrian independence. A strong YES vote would show the world what Austrians really wanted. The democracies would speak out and Hitler would have to stop his threats and bullying.

In the next few days it seemed all of Vienna was out in the streets. Out of nowhere, Austrian flags with the crooked cross of the Fatherland Front appeared in apartment windows and storefronts. The same insignia blossomed forth in thousands of lapels. On every empty wall the YES slogan appeared in black and red paint. Miraculously, the metal three-arrow badge of the SPÖ was visible in lapels and on walls, something that had not been seen since February 1934. Suddenly there appeared thousands of SPÖ leaflets, urging a YES vote.

On Friday I skipped school and demonstrated in the Inner City. On the *Freiung,* a square in front of a church, the market women had closed up shop, put their knitted shawls over their heads and joined their strong voices with those of the crowd—the taxi drivers, the porters, the students and the young apprentices. Hurling insults at a distant *Führer,* they shook their fists at a few unlucky Nazis who ventured near them, shouting their slogans. The market women did not mind who stood next to them as long as they shouted the right slogans. The well-dressed ladies did not mind, either, rubbing shoulders with shop girls and maids, waiters and clerks. Here and there, a gentleman with a leather briefcase, a coffee-house journalist, a civil servant could be seen in the crowd. The vast majority of the demonstrators were in favor of independence.

At first they just stood there and waited, taking courage from their ever-increasing numbers and feeling their anxiety, their fear, turning to outrage. Some of them knew the right words, others responded, and in the end they all chanted

4. Ibid., 265–71.

together. Their shouts, erupting from one group and being answered by another, merged into a continuous roar, like waves crashing into the seashore. "Yes for Austria!" "Red-white-red till we are dead!" "Freedom, Austria!" "Down with the *Anschluss!*" "Freedom!" They shouted for Schuschnigg and for the red-white-red and for a freedom they were supposed to have forgotten. Most of all, it was just being there, bearing witness. Here is Vienna, here is Austria. "Red-white-red till we are dead!"

The next day, Saturday, March 11, was bright and sunny. Again the crowds appeared out of nowhere and shouted their slogans. Only this time, there were no Nazis parading. We thought, with a sense of triumph, that we had scared them off. Only one more day to the plebiscite and they'd be finished.

They had, in fact, been ordered by their party leaders to stay off the streets. While we were still out shouting ourselves hoarse, Hitler had served Schuschnigg with an ultimatum. Unless the plebiscite was called off, Hitler would invade Austria. Schuschnigg stalled until the early afternoon, then was faced with a further ultimatum that required him to resign. At three P.M. he offered his resignation to President Miklas, who promptly refused it. Now a final German ultimatum was delivered: not only must Schuschnigg's resignation be accepted, but President Miklas must appoint a cabinet made up entirely of Nazis. German troops stood ready with marching orders at the Austrian border.

Around four P.M., Nazi demonstrators suddenly appeared in the Inner City. "Give up," they shouted. "The Germans are coming." Rumors began to fly and the peaceful demonstration started to turn ugly. People decided to go home so they could stay close to the radio.

At seven o'clock in the evening, Radio Austria stopped its broadcast. There was a special announcement; then Chancellor Schuschnigg's voice was heard:

Austrian men and Austrian women: this day has placed us in a tragic and decisive situation . . . President Miklas asks me to tell the people of Austria that we have yielded to force, since we are not prepared in this terrible situation to shed blood. We decided to order the troops to offer no resistance. So I take my leave of the Austrian people, with the German word of farewell, uttered from the depths of my heart—God protect Austria *{Gott schuetze Oesterreich}.*[5]

5. Ibid., 2.

And, for the last time, the sweet sound of Haydn's national anthem followed in full measure. "Be blessed, Austria, my fatherland, my earth, my home."

It had ended. Betrayed by delayed resistance, by a government too conservative to grant democratic freedoms and treat its working population as allies, forgotten by Western democracies bent on appeasement, nine hundred years of independent statehood had ended. The Austrian flag was lowered and the swastika flag run up.

A few hours later, the deserted streets were taken over by open trucks full of Nazi youths holding flaming torches over their heads. Truck after truck roared down the streets with the impact of tanks. Squads of motorcycles added to the noise and frenzy. The chants and shouts of their *SIEG HEIL, SIEG HEIL* rent the night like machine-gun blasts. They took over the squares, the Inner City, the public spaces. The roaring of their motorized columns expressed their fury and exaltation. Drunk with beer and triumph, they showed the world that their time had come. They were the victors . . .

On March 12, 1938, German troops occupied Austria, meeting no resistance and greeted enthusiastically by millions of wildly cheering Austrians. The day was bright and clear, and from early morning on the sun shone warmly, gilding streets and houses and upturned faces with a festive glow. The thousands of flags, black swastika on a brilliant red ground, fluttered from windows, from streetlight poles and from church steeples, cheerfully, triumphantly turning the entire city into one spectacular parade. The gayety of the flags, their apparent unanimity, was mirrored in the faces of the people in the street. Their lapel pins sporting their newly acquired convictions spoke as triumphantly as the flags whipping in the wind. The streets were theirs, undisputed. Power pushed up from the pavement. The houses were theirs, the offices and the emblems of past glory—ministries, palaces, Hofburg and Ring. The airwaves were theirs, blaring march tunes, turning anticipation into parade. The Catholic Archbishop, Cardinal Dr. Innitzer, explaining that he wished to avoid violence, welcomed the entry of German troops into Austria. A few days later, church bells would ring in the triumphant arrival of the *Führer,* and on the following Sunday all churches would offer a special service of thanks for the "liberation of the homeland through our *Führer* Adolf Hitler." Meanwhile, *Heil Hitler* greetings and choruses praising his name would have to suffice.

The crowds fervently shouting for a free and independent Austria just days ago seemed to have vanished. Clearly, large numbers among them had decided to join the victorious conquerors. Emblematic of this mass conversion and betrayal was the action of Dr. Karl Renner, former Speaker of Parliament and former head of the Social Democratic Party, who publicly welcomed the *Anschluss*.

Children in white shirts and shoes polished to mirror brightness lined up in columns along the streets to await the arrival of German troops. Each child had a small swastika flag on a stick; the waving butterfly patterns of these small flags added to the air of festivity and carnival. What a victory! Not a shot had been fired to accomplish the joining of the small remnant of what had once been the Hapsburg Empire to the Greater German Reich. What an omen of future conquests . . .

Shop girls and salesmen stood in front of their shuttered stores; housewives in their Sunday best flocked to the squares, aglow with anticipation. The young men and the middle-aged seemed all to have kept their Nazi uniforms ready in their closets, for suddenly there they were, in brown shirts and black, booted, officious, massed in open trucks or strutting in formation.

For the rest of us, it was a funeral, made more obscene by the way sky and sun seemed to favor the victors. We sat behind drawn blinds, afraid to show a sign of life, afraid to venture out into the streets or public spaces. We could turn the radio off and for a time escape into the dignity of familiar surroundings. We could try to calm one another with hopeful predictions, but there was no escaping the knowledge that a pit had opened before us and we stood on its edge.

The first few days after the *Anschluss,* including the day of Hitler's triumphant entry into Vienna, were one long festivity for the vast majority of joyous Austrians and days of mourning and fear for the remnant. Within hours of the Nazi takeover a wave of arrests swept over Vienna and all the provinces. All prominent leaders of the Fatherland Front and the Schuschnigg regime, including the Chancellor himself, were immediately taken into "protective custody." Prominent monarchists were similarly treated. Many of them were jailed in the regular jails, often purposefully placed into cells with political enemies, to make their jail time more difficult. Some were sent to Dachau, a concentration camp, where they were tortured and killed. Among these was the beloved former Mayor of Vienna, Karl Seitz. Thousands of former Social Democrats, elected officials of the Republic, trade union leaders, journalists and intellectuals were arrested during the first few nights. They were treated more harshly, many of them severely beaten in police stations and hastily improvised jails in schools and office buildings. Most of them ended up in Dachau or other German camps, but some were released without trials after a few weeks, having learned their lesson that only compliance with the Nazi regime could save them in the future. Historians have estimated the number of those arrested within the first two weeks of the *Anschluss* as between forty and seventy thousand.[6]

But the worst treatment, spontaneously improvised rituals of humiliation, was reserved for Austria's Jews. Gangs of armed Nazis terrorized pedestrians by suddenly forming a chain across a busy sidewalk and rounding up everyone who did not have a swastika displayed or who did not give the *Heil Hitler* salute. They would then pull out anyone they identified as a Jew, especially middle-class people or those who "looked Jewish." These unfortunates would then be forced to remove the oil-paint graffiti of the previous weeks, the crooked cross of the Fatherland Front and the ubiquitous slogan "Red-white-red unto our death" from pavements or walls with toothbrushes and strong lye, to the amusement of crowds of bystanders. This happened to my mother and other people I knew. Other "cleaning squads" of Jews gathered in street raids were marched into SS barracks and made to clean the toilets with their bare hands. Groups of elderly Jews were forced out of coffeehouses and marched up and down the street, then forced to do knee bends until they collapsed. In one of the largest synagogues, SS men and civilians with Nazi insignia forced the men to use their prayer shawls to wash the floors and toilet bowls in local SS headquarters. Wherever such spectacles were organized, crowds of onlookers cheered, laughed and showed their approval.

Raids on Jewish homes and businesses, followed by theft of property by Nazi gangs, began almost immediately and became commonplace despite their illegality. In small stores and businesses the owners were forced to stand by helplessly while neighbors and passersby were invited to help themselves to their goods and supplies. In larger businesses such raids were organized by formal raiding parties, often with the participation of the police, who "confiscated" valuables and property under the cloak of some trumped-up charge, such as "unpatriotic activity." These spontaneous expropriations and thefts became so widespread that by the end of April the Nazi government issued a number of edicts designed to halt the "wild" expropriations and put the process of expropriation and "planned Aryanization" under official control.

RELATIVES CAME IN PAIRS and in family units to Grandmother's house, some to say goodbye just before they were leaving, others to test out their plans for

6. Herbert Rosenkranz, *Verfolgung und Selbstbehauptung: Die Juden in Oesterreich, 1938–1945* (Wien: Herold, 1978), 21. See also Fritz Molden, *Fires in the Night: The Sacrifice and Significance of the Austrian Resistance, 1938–1945,* trans. from the German by Harry Zohn (Boulder: Westview Press, 1989). Molden estimates that seventy-five thousand people were arrested in Austria during the six weeks following the *Anschluss*. Molden, 4.

escape. Some were gone already, and one did not hear from them, because it might endanger those left behind. The *Herr Generaldirektor* uncle had a nervous collapse. He never left his darkened bedroom and talked only of suicide. His wife, a fluttery, vain little person who had always been preoccupied mainly with clothes, hairdos and gossip suddenly took hold of the family and took steps toward emigration. They would end up in England, including the suicidal uncle, who would live to a ripe old age.

The foreign students left, one by one. Marta had already left in February, returning to her native Yugoslavia, whose local fascism seemed to her less threatening than the German variety. Several of our friends among the medical students returned to their homelands. They gave us their home addresses and promised fervently to help us, each and every one, with contacts, organized support and a place to sleep, once we got out. They were leaving, not deserting us, they said. And it was true. But to us who were left behind it felt like desertion. Only later, when one really understood that we were all doomed, would each person who escaped make us feel good, as though a piece of ourselves had escaped with them. They would be able to carry on the struggle. They would remember . . .

In the first week after the *Anschluss,* Father came home from work in the early afternoon, which was contrary to his usual work routine. He looked very upset and spent a long time talking with Mother behind closed doors. He made a few phone calls and shut himself up in his room. Then he asked Nora, Mother and me to come into his room, which seemed very crowded with all of us sitting on the single chair and on his bed. He closed the door firmly and spoke almost in a whisper. He had bad news.

Early that afternoon he had had a phone call from a business acquaintance, a man he had known for many years as a Nazi sympathizer. The man was now a Nazi Party member and he told my Father it was risky for him to make this phone call. He had seen Father's name on a list of people to be arrested within the next few days. "If I were you, Herr Kronstein," he said, "I'd get out at once." And he hung up.

Could the man be believed? Was this just another empty threat to instill fear? Father thought the man was honest. There were a number of reasons why Father might be on an arrest list. It could be something as silly as his argument with the intruder who wanted drugs. It could be because of Magistra Brandhofer and the fact that he had paid her wages while she was in jail. It could have something to do with his brother Richard, the banker in Switzerland. At any rate, Father thought he should take this seriously. Fortunately, he had been traveling to Liechtenstein once a month for the past four years, which was noted in his passport. It was toward the end of the month anyway, and he could legitimately make a business trip to Liechtenstein, as he did each month about this time. If no one came to arrest him, he would come back in a week. The main thing was that this conversation had to stay within these four walls. "It's a secret," he said, looking sternly at us children.

Mother cried softly; for once she did not argue.

"You and the children will be quite safe. This is still a country governed by law. No one will hurt you."

"They could arrest you at the frontier," I said, thinking of the mass arrests made on the Czech frontier the night of the *Anschluss*. I had it on the tip of my tongue to suggest he cross the frontier illegally, as some of my student friends had done, but I did not say it. It would only worry him to know I knew about such things.

"They could there as well as here. If that's what they want, they'll do it. But I trust it will take them a few days before they get to me. And I'll be gone by then."

He turned to my mother. "I'll try to get residence permits for you and the children in Liechtenstein," he said. "Just in case." He tried hard to appear calm. "If anyone asks where I am, say I'm on my usual business trip to Vaduz."

He left half an hour later, having said goodbye to his mother and Aunt Emma, which must have been even harder for him than it was to say goodbye to us. He carried only a small suitcase. And the next morning he phoned cheerfully from Vaduz, saying he had had no trouble whatever on the frontier.

That was lucky, for only a few days later the new emigration legislation for Jews was enacted, which assured that there would be no tourist or business travel for Austrian Jews and that only those with the required exit permits would be allowed to leave.

About a week later, early in the afternoon, the doorbell rang and before anyone could answer, fists hammered on the door. They were there—a group of SA men in uniform (I counted ten of them), armed with pistols and rubber truncheons. They stormed into the hallway; they wanted my father. Our explanation of his absence enraged them and they quickly searched the apartment to see if he were hiding somewhere. Then they pushed each of us into a separate room before we could say a word to each other. I learned only later, after they had gone, what happened to the others. They took my twelve-year old sister into the dining room, one man pushing her, the other sticking a pistol in her ribs.

"Where's your father?" they yelled.

"He went away," she cried, "to his business in Vaduz."

They let go of her and told her to stay in that room. They did the same thing to my mother, but used no weapons. She tried her best to calm them down, pleading with them to let her stay with her little girl.

"He's gone abroad and taken his money," the SA man in charge concluded. "Pigs . . . We'll find the evidence, if it takes all day."

Two other men argued with our cook, Mitzi, in the kitchen. How could she go on working for these Jewish pigs? Did she have no pride? She said she needed the job. They assured her she'd find better jobs easily, now that Hitler had taken over.

As for me, one SA man had shoved me into the salon, the room with the grand piano, the beautiful damask couches, the Persian rugs. "Jesus," he exclaimed when he took it all in. "That's how the rich live—just take a look at that . . ." He was swarthy, dark-haired, not at all the ideal Nazi type, with heavy shoulders and strong arms, the kind of fellow who spends a lot of time improving his athletic prowess. I was afraid to be alone in the room with him; I was worried about Nora, what they might be doing to her . . .

He turned his attention from the room to me. The way he looked at me frightened me more. "What's a girl like you doing here? You the governess?" My light-brown hair, blue eyes and light coloring had made him mistake me for an "Aryan."

"I'm the daughter of the house," I said.

"Of course, a Jewish pig . . ." he blustered. "Where's your father's money hidden?"

They swarmed over the place like locusts. Doors, cupboards, drawers were flung open, their contents dumped on the floor. Some of the men stabbed the sofa and chair cushions with their knives, presumably to find hidden treasure. They took the pictures off the wall and slashed their backing. In the study, one fellow was trying on my father's wristwatch, while another stuffed some jewelry into his pockets.

They noticed me watching them. "Give her a receipt," the leader ordered. "We're confiscating valuables." The point was they were not stealing. A few months later such fine distinctions would no longer be made.

Still, one fellow was pocketing silver spoons, no receipt. My mother stood with her back against a wall, hugging Nora, who had finally been released from her room. She watched the systematic destruction of our home in silence, her eyes signaling me to equal acquiescence. She was worried I would act up.

She need not have worried. I was so relieved that this raid had nothing to do with my politics, I was willing to let it all happen without resistance. There were so many of them; they were armed; and anyway, law and power were on their side. Thank God *Vati* is abroad, I kept thinking. Thank God he is not here. From the remarks passed between the men it was clear they were trying to find some evidence that my father had taken money and valuables—known as *valuta*—abroad on his trip. To do so was not only a crime, but it was a capital crime. If they could find withdrawal slips from the bank, empty jewelry cases, a locked box with nothing inside—that would do it. Hidden valuables or money would also show "evidence" of the sort they were seeking. "Jewish Businessman Smuggles *Valuta* to Switzerland," the headlines would scream. They might even try to extradite him.

"The books," the gang leader suddenly exclaimed. "I bet there's money hidden in the books."

There was a wall of books reaching from floor to ceiling in our library. He eyed them suspiciously. What else were so many books good for, if not to hide money?

"You there," he shouted at me. "Get up on that stepladder and hand down the books."

I moved slowly. "Which ones do you want?"

"Start on the top shelf on the left."

I handed down the first three books. He arranged three of his men in a row and ordered them to shake the books and riffle through them. When they had shaken down the books, they threw them on the floor, which soon became cluttered with piles of discarded, half-open books. He ordered the other men to other rooms, where they kept up their search and destruction. I handed the books down one at a time, as each of the men had his hands free. I figured they would soon get tired of this fruitless search.

"Move over to the other side. Let's start from the right."

In memory, it has always seemed to me this book search lasted hours. There were over a thousand books in our library. But it could not have lasted that long. All I remember is that stretching up for the books, bending down to hand them on and seeing them desecrated, violated, destroyed in front of my eyes was painful to both my body and my soul. I had my period that day and was beginning to have heavy cramps. My arms ached and slowly rage began to build up, coming from my belly into my chest, so that I could hardly breathe. I began to take two books at a time, letting them fall to the floor if the men were not ready, forcing the men to bend down and pick them up. The gang leader was no longer supervising; he had moved on to other pursuits. We were halfway down one of the bookcases already.

Suddenly, without any conscious thought coming to me, I picked up as many books as I could hold between outstretched hands and threw them to the floor in front of the SA men. They exploded like a shot and the men jumped back.

"Watch out, girl!"

"Sorry, they fell out of my hands." I tried to look as innocent as possible and carefully handed down a few more singles.

The leader came back into the room. "There's nothing in them books," one of the three reported to him.

"That's enough," he agreed. "Let's go downstairs."

They all filed out. "We'll be back," the leader promised.

For an instant, I felt wildly triumphant. My tiny gesture of defiance had worked, enough to make the bullies retreat. More, it had restored me to myself. Then reason returned and I realized that I had taken a large, possibly dangerous risk—and for what? To make me feel better, to overcome helplessness and humiliation. Was this the way to survive under terror?

I did not have time for contemplation, for the gang had trooped downstairs and, to my horror, they were banging against Grandmother's door. I rushed down after them to give what moral support I could. I was there through it all, but I cannot remember whether Nora and Mother were there.

When the SA men burst into the apartment, tiny *Tante* Emma confronted them bravely. She herself was Catholic, although she had a Jewish mother, and perhaps it was this that gave her a sense of entitlement to lawful and civil behavior. Or more likely, she was simply protecting her adopted mother, to whom she was totally devoted.

"By what authority are you here? We've done nothing wrong, this is our home—" They simply pushed her aside.

"She is an old woman," *Tante* Emma protested, "she has a bad heart . . . Don't upset her." Grandmother was, as usual, seated at the head of her dark, solid oak table in the dining room. She wore her black dress with the white lace collar, and her thin white hair was neatly combed back in a tight bun. Her light blue eyes, hard as marbles, glared at the intruders, but she did not speak.

"We're investigating smuggled *valuta,*" the gang leader said as though forced to justify himself. "Your son skipped the country with money and valuables. Just cooperate and nobody's going to hurt you."

Grandmother greeted this with stony silence, but her bony wrists began

knocking against the table as her hands trembled. The scene, as it had been enacted upstairs, was now repeated—the threats, the questioning, the search, the
destruction—but the SA men seemed somewhat subdued in the presence of these
two elderly women.

Then one of them, in his systematic search of the room, came upon the two
glass-front cabinets. He whistled. "Wow, just take a look at that . . ."

One of the cabinets was filled with candy boxes, some full, some empty. It was
customary in Vienna for visitors and guests to bring flowers and candy, and my
Grandmother, a notorious hoarder, kept these offerings for months at a time before
surrendering a box of chocolates to be eaten by the family. The sons sometimes teased
her, saying that, out of thriftiness, she served only spoiled candy. *Tante* Emma tried
to explain this to the raiding party, apologizing for an old woman's peculiar foibles.

They let it go, but the second cabinet was more serious. It contained various
glass objects and at least six empty jewelry boxes. "Now we've got it," the leader
exclaimed. "Where's the jewelry?"

Tante Emma explained that Grandmother had given the jewelry as gifts to
family members for weddings and birthdays. Thrifty as she was, she always kept
back the boxes, which might come in handy another time. It sounded like a lame
excuse even to me.

"A likely story," the SA man exclaimed with heavy irony. He ordered his men
to take the boxes in evidence.

Things were going badly. This ludicrous piece of "evidence" could mean serious trouble. The men continued their search. Suddenly, there was a shout from a
back room, which had twenty years earlier been the "smoking room" for
Grandfather but now stood largely unused. One of the men, as he tapped along a
wall, had heard a dull sound. "A safe, this must be a safe." All of them ran into
the room except one, who stayed behind to guard Grandmother.

"Do you have a safe?" one of the men asked *Tante* Emma.

"No." She pointed to the wallpaper that covered the entire room from floor
to ceiling. "Do you see a safe?"

But they persisted in tapping the wall and finally cut open the wallpaper with
a knife. And there it was, black, metal and ominous—a safe, covered over by wallpaper.

"Why, I had no idea that was there." *Tante* Emma sounded genuinely surprised,
and also frightened. "Mama, did you know—when was that room papered?"

"Twenty years ago," Grandmother answered firmly.

But they had found what they wanted. They went for tools and in a short while had broken the door: the safe was empty. Like the empty jewelry boxes, it was just the kind of proof they wanted. They wrenched it out of the wall and took it away as "evidence." And renewed their search of the other rooms, encouraged by their success.

Tante Emma, whose explanations had been disregarded, now seemed to give up. She went to the kitchen and after a few minutes carried a tray with a cup of tea and some biscuits to Grandmother. "Here, take your afternoon tea, Mama."

The young SA man detailed to guarding her turned his back to the table and looked out the window. He was a gangly youth, barely past his teens, with straight blond hair falling onto his forehead. The domestic scene seemed to embarrass him.

Grandmother's hands shook badly, but she managed to drink some of the tea, then pushed the tray away. The sounds of search and destroy hit her ears harshly. She was a meticulous housekeeper, fanatically orderly, keeping everything in its right place. Preserving her possessions and preventing waste and disorder were her governing creed, her gospel. What was going on in her home that day was beyond her comprehension.

Tante Emma left the room to see what damage was being done elsewhere. The young SA man turned back toward Grandmama and with some lingering sense of propriety, possibly moved by a remnant of pity at her trembling hands, he reached for the tray.

"You're finished with that, let me take it away," he said politely, carrying the tray to the sideboard, which we called a credenza, and setting it down.

Grandmama's eyes flared; she shouted her outrage as though she were addressing her servant: "The tray doesn't belong on the credenza, take it out in the kitchen where it belongs."

"Yes, Ma'am," the young SA man responded, as though she were his own grandmother, and he meekly carried the tray out.

That the gang left a few minutes later must have been mere coincidence, but it seemed to me then, as it does now, that it was Grandmother's defiance that made them go. Out of such small triumphs in the face of increasing disaster did we fashion the skills and strength we needed for survival.

OUTSIDE, THINGS WERE GETTING WORSE day by day. In the streets, open season on Jews was granted to anyone with a Nazi insignia in his lapel. Jewish businesses were forced to close their doors; Jews were dismissed from their jobs and official positions; the university was closed to Jewish students and faculty within six weeks of the *Anschluss*. The legal and administrative regulations to justify these excesses were soon enacted. Violent anti-Semitism came naturally to Austrians who had a long history of anti-Semitic political parties and movements. The Germans had to be educated in violent anti-Semitism; the Austrians erupted with it spontaneously. Within weeks of the *Anschluss* the situation of Jews in Austria was far worse than was that of Jews in Germany five years after the Nazi takeover.[7]

A Jewish orphanage was closed, the orphans thrown out and the building turned into a Nazi barracks. All government employees were forced to take a loyalty oath to Hitler; those unwilling to do so were summarily dismissed. By the end of April a decree of the Education Department assured that all school and university sessions would open and close with the students and faculty giving the Hitler salute. Everywhere, former Nazi sympathizers and "illegal" Nazis now emerged proudly with new power and status. In the private school I attended, which had many Jewish teachers and a Jewish director, many of the gentile teachers turned out to have been underground members of the Nazi Party. The Jewish director was replaced by one of these Nazis before the end of the school term.

During these months, the persecution and daily harassment of Jews increased. Destitute families doubled up in apartments and many people never left their homes for fear of arrest during the random street raids, which were a daily occurrence. The number of Jewish suicides increased from five in January to over a hundred during each month of that summer. In our circle, each family had its own horror stories; everyone had heard of some acquaintance who had committed suicide rather than be taken to jail. This was long before the "final solution," long before any of these persecutions were cloaked under the mantle of legality. The Austrian treatment of Jews was improvised on the spot; its versatility, ingenuity and brutality were then unprecedented.

BOBBY AND I talked of getting married. Bobby had been hard hit in the past weeks. It was his misfortune to be faced with his final exams during the early weeks of the Nazi occupation. In Austria, after medical students had completed their course work, they did their internships and residencies, and only after that stood for their exams. Bobby had completed all the requirements; all he now needed to do

7. Ibid., 31–38.

was to pass eighteen exams, one in each medical specialty. These exams were arranged by difficulty and, presumably, by their importance to the practice of medicine. Thus, Anatomy came first, then Internal Medicine, and so on. The last two exams, Ophthalmology and Pharmacology, were considered easy. During these terrible weeks Bobby had passed sixteen of his exams and only the last two remained when, by decree, the university was closed to Jews. He was forced to leave without his M.D. degree. This turned out to be a catastrophe for him and delayed his entry into the profession by more than ten years. Fortunately, we did not know this then and thought that in the United States he would be given a chance to complete his exams and get his degree. At any rate, his emigration was just a matter of weeks or months. He and his parents had applied early for their U.S. visas, with his rich aunts in Florida acting as their sponsors. It was now only a matter of waiting for his quota number to come up and he would leave for the U.S.A.

Bobby had persuaded his aunts to act as my sponsors, too, although they opposed the idea. They did not want him to be burdened with a dependent when his own future was so insecure. Besides, they had first to give affidavits to Bobby's sister, her husband and several other blood relatives. He felt strongly that once we were married they would look on the situation differently and would help not only me but my family. The other good reason for marriage was that, once he was in the U.S.A., it would put me on a priority list for my immigration quota. Getting a "better" quota number was a life-and-death matter in those days and I was lucky even to be able to consider the possibility.

Bobby's loyalty and friendship were touching and supportive and our relationship had over the last three years developed into a solid affair, marred only by the constant subterfuge and hiding we had to practice due to my still living at home and being supervised like a child. We were lovers, friends, comrades in the antifascist fight. He expressed his love and need of me constantly and passionately and I felt certain I loved him as well as he loved me. But marriage was not something we would normally have considered at this time. We were such good friends, we took for granted that our relationship would be long-lived and permanent. But neither of us was ready for marriage. He had to get his medical degree first and I had to go to the university and train for a career. That is what we would have done under normal circumstances. But these were crisis times.

The helpless and persecuted cannot act according to their own wishes and desires; they have to learn to do what is needed. Bobby had to go to America as soon as his visa was approved, regardless of his concern for me; I had to marry him to save myself and the rest of my family. Since my father was out of the country and since I doubted he would approve our plan, we would have to wait until May, after my eighteenth birthday, when I could get married without parental permission.

It did not work out as we had planned.

THE NEXT TIME THEY CAME, less than a month after the first raid, they came "officially," armed with a warrant. It was the regular police who arrived; just three policemen, polite, officious and efficient. They came with a warrant for the arrest of my father; since he was not here and we "claimed" he was still abroad, they decided to take his wife and eldest daughter. "Maybe it'll persuade him to come home," they opined. They had orders to seal up the apartment. What was to be done with the child, with Nora?

Tante Emma volunteered to keep her and the police seemed to think that was a good solution. Generously, they allowed her to take a few clothes and her school bag downstairs. Our maid had left weeks ago, seeing the handwriting on the wall. Now the policemen taped our front door shut and put a sign and seal on it to show it was official.

Mother looked terrible; her hair was disheveled; her eyes went from Nora to me in desperation. She reached for Nora to give her a last hug, but the policemen were getting impatient.

"We'll be home soon," I called to Nora. "Don't cry; we'll be all right."

They walked us down the stairs and put us in the rear of an open truck. The superintendent of our building stood outside with her little girl, watching with open disapproval. "What are you taking the girl for?" she asked the police. "A disgrace, that's what it is, a disgrace . . ." She left unsaid whose disgrace it was. The police ignored her.

"Thank you, Frau Polatscheck," said my mother. In the neighboring doors and windows curious faces appeared, some impassive, some lusting for a spectacle. Two of the policemen manned our truck; the other drove a regular police car.

Mother grabbed the railing with both hands, tossed her head back and stood tall. "Don't let them see you cry," she said with her old magnificent spirit. "Don't let them break you."

"Don't worry," I cried. *"Mutti,* darling . . ."

The ride in the open car seemed endless, a gift of grace. Evening over the streets, dimming the raucous displays of conquest, the everpresent swastika flags. We passed through the old city, the buildings stooped with history, the church bells echoing. A store closing its doors, the salesgirls hurrying home to uncooked suppers, a beggar leaning against a wall, a woman pushing a baby carriage. Somewhere behind them the Vienna Woods, the grey river, the vineyards on the hillsides. Life, beautiful life, and we must leave it, to be shut up with fear and terror. We must learn to be braver than we are; we must learn to survive.

My mother put her arm around my shoulder. She showed me that she would be strong; she would rally all her strength to survive.

"Don't you worry about me," I said. "Just in case we're separated."

"We're not going to be separated."

"Bobby will get a lawyer for us," I assured my mother. "He'll know what to do."

We passed the police station and drove toward the Quai. My heart sank. They were going to take us to Gestapo headquarters. Did my mother notice? Did she understand what that meant?

We pulled up in front of the Hotel Metropole, which had been requisitioned as Gestapo headquarters. It was in an old baroque building near the center of the city. On the lowest floors there were apartments, tenanted as usual. There was a radio on somewhere, playing symphonic music very loudly.

The stairway was carpeted, the stairs were of marble. The stuccoed ceilings were decorated with roses and tiny clusters of grapes. On each landing an SS man in black uniform with skull and crossbones insignia stood guard.

They took us to an upper floor and then separated us, one policeman walking off down the corridor with my mother, another holding me back and pushing me into a waiting room. Through the walls came the music.

I was worn out, hollow with excitement, hunger and fatigue. There was no chair in the room and I leaned against the wall. The policeman exchanged some papers with the SS guard and left me. Somewhere behind these doors were questions, examinations, maybe force. Images from the Black Book on Nazi terror flashed through my brain. I pushed them away. Don't anticipate, don't frighten yourself. Suddenly I identified the music—it was the last movement of Beethoven's Ninth Symphony. It seemed miraculous, impossible—the world reaching in to me, giving its best.

Freude, schöner Götterfunken . . .

Joy, spark of the Gods. There was joy in living; there would be joy again.

Oh, *Freunde . . .* Deaf Beethoven, a broken, disenchanted old man, sang to joy and friendship, to hope. That is what I must remember. That is what I must hold on to.

The dark door opened.

[6]

T HE CELL DOOR was made of steel, solid except for a small window at eye level. The steps and corridors were of steel as well, and every footstep echoed loudly. I do not remember how I got there or any of the preliminaries that must have taken place: registering, being fingerprinted, checking my clothes and the bundle of toiletries I had brought from home, getting my blanket, then being led upstairs and along the interior corridor unto which the cell doors opened. I remember being separated from my mother somewhere downstairs—they led her away and she turned back toward me, trying to look encouraging, but I saw that she was terrified and the tears stopped inside my head, hard rocks. We had tried to be brave as long as we were together, each for the other one's sake and now it all had hardened into that rock-like feeling behind the eyes and in the chest. Keys opened the lock on the cell door, and someone pushed me in and then the door clanged shut. I stumbled; a young girl grabbed my arm. Another got up from the only seat there was. "Sit down," the girl said. A third young woman moved aside to let me in.

The cell was just large enough for one person, crowded for two. Now we were four. A bunk with a straw sack on it hung suspended by chains from the wall; similarly suspended were a small table and the single seat. On the opposite side of the table, close to the door, was an open toilet without a seat. One of the girls now sat on it, using it as a chair. The left wall of the cell was about six feet away and bare. The single, double-barred window was about three feet square and so far up against the ceiling one could see nothing but a sliver of sky. The walls were concrete, painted grey. There were two straw bags spread on the floor, covering every inch of space. Every time one of us moved, she bumped into another person. The air was thick and smelly. I began to shiver, as though I had a fever.

"I'm Poldi," the girl said. "This is Lise and that one, on the floor, is Magda. She just came in this morning." At this, Magda began to sob noisily.

"Enough," Lise said. "You've been at it all day." She was small, brown-haired and rather pretty. She looked about my age, as did Poldi, who was blond, stocky, with freckles and ugly crooked teeth. Poldi spoke in heavy dialect and seemed inordinately cheerful. I tried to focus on the girls and not look at the cell anymore, but nothing in my body seemed to work as it should. I shivered.

"You missed supper, such as it is," Poldi explained. "Drink some water, then you won't feel so hungry." She poured some from a pitcher on the table into the single cup and offered it to me. I took a few sips and felt like gagging.

"So what's your name?"

"Gerda."

"And what are you in for?"

I shrugged. "They just came and took me and my mother." Lise and Poldi did not look Jewish and I was afraid to bring up the subject.

"What they do with your mother?"

"They took her away downstairs." At this I began to sob and sob, and nothing could stop me.

"That's what you get with all your dumb questions," Lise said. "Can't you wait a minute." She patted my shoulder. I just sat there sobbing.

Since I could not or would not talk they gave up on me after a while and one of them went to the bed and another slipped in at the foot of the bed and Magda stretched out on the straw sack on the floor, which left just a small space between her and the wall. It had grown dark outside but an electric light bulb was on, high up on the ceiling, and there were lights in the hall shining in through the eye opening in the door. I stretched out, still sobbing, and felt the hard canvass of the mattress against my cheek. It stank of sweat and dirt and the blanket they had given me and which I tried to wrap around me to stop my shaking and shivering smelled worse. My face nearly touched the wall and I held myself stiffly so as not to push against Magda, but after a while when she had cried herself to sleep she leaned against me and that felt warm. I stopped shivering and lay on my back, trying to collect myself and not wake the others. I was exhausted and could not sleep. The light was in my eyes, no matter how I turned, and there was constant noise, a variety of bad sounds out in the hall that I felt I'd rather not interpret. I was terrified. This was what I had feared and imagined for four years and now it had happened. All the nightmare pictures I had made in my head for all these years now came out and they were real, they were happening to me and I thought if I opened my mouth I would just scream and scream. I'm going to die here, I thought. I'm too young to die and I'll die here like an animal in a trap. For some reason the thought made me stop sobbing. I needed to think, keep my wits about me.

Someone stepped on me and over me. I sat bolt upright. It was Lise going to the toilet. Embarrassed to be watching her I turned toward the wall. I'm gonna die in a stinking toilet, I thought. Lise again stepped over me and crawled back into her bunk and I felt sorry for myself as I had never felt sorry before and the tears began again. It was comforting to cry and make myself feel like a baby, but there was no mother and no friend and there would be no one and somehow I got back that sense I'd had when I played Captain Amundsen on the South Pole. It was cold and dangerous and I was alone—all I could do was to try and be brave. To be brave I would have to stop myself from thinking terrible thoughts; I would have to stop listening to what was going on out in the hall. I would have to do what was needed to get out of this cell alive, whatever came after it. I would have to stop worrying about my mother; she would have to manage for herself.

I began to calm down. With new shrewdness I made use of the fact that the others were sleeping to go to the toilet in some sort of imagined privacy; then I crawled under my blanket, closed my eyes and fell asleep. In all the nights in jail thereafter I slept a full night's sleep.

They wake you up by pounding on the door with a stick, which sounds like tanks coming at you. There was a lot of shouting outside, all incomprehensible; then the door was flung open, the girls in the bunk jumped down, Magda sprang to her feet and everyone started dragging the straw sacks out.

"What're ya dawdling for?" a warden bawled at us. "Get going, we haven't got all day." I stumbled around trying to get shoes on my feet and barely made it before we were ordered out of the cell.

The prison was one of the regular Austrian civil prisons, six stories high with cells opening onto an interior enclosed courtyard. The two ground floors were closed off from our view and all we could see was two floors below and one above us. Now prisoners were moving along the walkways, slowing down as much as possible so as to make the most of the opportunity of looking at one another, greeting acquaintances, exchanging a few words. The wardens, on the other hand, tried to move us along as fast as possible to keep us from talking. The other floors were all occupied by men. On this first day I barely could take it all in and let myself be pushed toward the end of the corridor, which was a washroom with ten or more tin sinks lined up on both walls. There was only cold water and at each sink there was a small piece of yellow laundry soap. We had a very short time in which to wash and I was told by the experts not to waste time brushing my teeth here; that could be done in the cell. Some of the women tried to rinse out their underwear, but there was barely time for that. Later I learned to wash only one part of my body each day in rotation and to use the precious time for conversation instead. We were locked inside our cells day and night except for the few minutes in the washroom and the "time out." This hour in the open courtyard was something to which we were entitled by law once a day if the weather permitted, but we only got it a few times a week, at best. The civilian guards, still conscious of rules and regulations that had to be observed, explained that this was due to the terrific overcrowding in the jail in the past few months. They just didn't have the staff to let all of us out each day.

Once back in the cell we swung the bunk frame up against the wall and locked it, now giving us "free" floor space in our six-by-twelve-foot cell. A warden and prisoner-flunkey rolled a cart with food from open door to open door. We were supposed to line up against the left wall and wait. Poldi was the person nearest the door and used the time for animated exchanges of shouts and information with the other inmates.

Each person got a large mug with brownish hot liquid and a good-size chunk of black bread. Then the door was flung shut. I tried the so-called coffee and could not swallow it. Magda had not even touched it and pushed away her mug on the table.

"Drink it, both of you," Lise advised us. "The soup at lunch and dinner is worse and that's all you gonna get. And save some of your bread for the rest of the day. That's it and no more."

I watched Lise and Poldi measure out their morning ration of bread and put the rest away with the small pile of their belongings they kept on the single small shelf above the table. Magda's little bundle was on the floor in the far corner, but she was not saving her bread, she just kept chewing on it.

"She's afraid we're gonna steal it," Poldi said venomously. "Yesterday she was worried about her money and today it's the food. We don't steal, stupid, we're Socialists."

Magda stared at her in horror and backed off against the wall. She was older than the rest of us, perhaps twenty. Her hair was permanent-waved and her eyebrows had been plucked into the shape of a perfect arch. Although she looked disheveled now and pale with fear and crying, she obviously was a girl who spent a lot of time doing her make-up. Judging from her clothes and good shoes she was well-to-do, which was probably one reason for Poldi's antagonism toward her. Poldi and Lise were dressed like working-class girls. I was amazed that they would admit so freely to being Socialists.

Lise seemed to read my mind. "You and your big mouth," she scolded Poldi.

"What's the difference," Poldi replied. "We got nothing to lose. That's what we're here for. Anyway, she gets on my nerves, that fine lady with her bawling and complaining. We're all in the same boat here."

The flunkey came for the cups and spoons and Poldi got momentarily diverted. "We got to get chairs in here," she demanded. "This is a one-man cell and they're stuffing four of us in here and no place to sit all day long."

"You ain't the only one," the flunkey replied, surly.

"What's up?" One of the wardens got into the conversation.

Poldi repeated her demand, adding, "I know what the rules are—each gets a chair or something to sit on."

"Ah, the big-mouth red," the warden said in disgust. "You better stop telling me my business." She slammed the door shut and grumbled outside.

Still, a half hour later the flunkey opened the door and brought a small wooden stool. "All the luxuries of home."

We were ecstatic at this development and thanked and hugged Poldi. She immediately took the occasion to organize us into some discipline—each got a number and we would take turns sitting on bench, chair and toilet, with one still left to sit on the floor. After breakfast, tooth-brushing time, then toilet time, then storytelling.

It was bad enough when the others used the toilet in the small, unventilated space. When my turn came, I balked. Poldi and Lise were nice about it. "Just try, we've all had to get used to it."

But I couldn't perform and thinking of what might be the consequences of my excessive daintiness did not help either.

"We'll all turn around so you can have privacy."

"Drink a glass of water, sometimes that helps."

With so much camaraderie one could get used to anything. Or almost anything. After a few days I did get used to it and even managed to tolerate the comments and crude jokes and the strict rationing of toilet paper. There never was enough of anything and t.p. was considered an indulgence. We used it as our only paper for writing, making games and sometimes drawing, so it was precious indeed. "How do you know so much about the rules?" I asked Poldi, hoping to elicit her story.

She was glad to oblige. Anyway, storytelling was the morning's activity and we each had to take our turn. You could tell anything that came to mind, but first you had to tell about yourself and your family.

Poldi, now nineteen, had been here before. She was arrested after the 1934 uprising, together with her parents who had been February fighters. She had been caught with some leaflets her parents had given her to hide. Anyway, everyone in the building knew she was an active member of the Socialist Youth group. She got a year, but because of her age they let her out after six months. What actually happened was she got an ulcer from the stinking food and they had to put her in the hospital and that was too much trouble, so they finally let her out. This time they had just taken her together with her father for no special reason. Yeah, she still had the ulcer but it was okay as long as she ate regular.

"This slop?"

"You gotta eat it or you'll get an ulcer too," Poldi said emphatically.

Lise's story was somewhat similar. Her father was a streetcar conductor and very active in his trade union. They lived in a housing project and the whole family, father, mother and an uncle, were arrested in February after the fighting. Lise and her kid sister and brother stayed with neighbors, but the parents were out soon. This time the situation was a lot worse—her father was in jail somewhere, arrested for leading a demonstration at work against the *Anschluss*—Lise thought he'd get six months at least. And then a few weeks later she'd got caught painting slogans on a wall—"Free the prisoners" is what she'd written.

"They'll let you go with time served," Poldi predicted, "seeing you got no record."

Maybe, maybe not. Lise was more worried about her father, to whom she was very attached.

"Mine is no good," Poldi told us. "Even if he is a Socialist. He's always beating up on us—but not on me. No more."

Magda had little to tell and clearly did not feel like sharing much with the rest of us. She was a secretary in a nice office but had lost her job just a few weeks ago, when the new law against Jews came out. Then she'd been hauled in on one of these street actions—a gang of SA men made all the Jews they could round up scrub the pavement on their hands and knees. She'd taken off her good coat and put it on the sidewalk before starting to scrub and that so enraged one of the men that he arrested her and brought her in here. She had no idea what the charge was, but whatever it was it was a lie.

"It can't be a big deal," Lise thought. "Probably they're just trying to scare you."

Magda agreed. "I'm sure I'll get out today. They'll see it's just a mistake." We argued that awhile, but contrary to her despondency yesterday, Magda's optimism seemed unshakable today.

The lunchtime soup was up to Poldi's dire predictions. I forced myself but could barely get it down. "Why is it so salty?"

"That's not salt, that's bromide," Poldi enlightened me. "That's to keep us quiet. It's in the dinner stuff, too. There's nothing you can do but eat it."

"They're poisoning us . . ."

"You got the idea."

Now it was my turn for desperation. "Doesn't it make you dopey and forgetful?"

"Sure, you get sort of stupid and satisfied with everything," Poldi said unhelpfully. "That's why they give it to you. So we don't have any riots."

"That's terrible. I have to do something. I have to be alert and keep my memory or I can't take my exam when I get out."

"What exam?"

It was amazing to me that I could have forgotten about the exam for almost twenty-four hours. All year, it had been foremost on my mind and my first thought on entering the prison was that I simply had to get out in time for it. The *Matura,* the final exam after eight years of academic *Gymnasium* was the absolute prerequisite for a university education anywhere in Europe. With it, one could enter the university; without it, never. Students who failed one or another part of the *Matura* might retake it the following year, but that was their last chance. My exam was scheduled for May 29, five weeks away. I'd been preparing for it all year.

All the girls thought I would be out in plenty of time for it. It wasn't as though I were political or criminal or anything like that . . . But what if I lost my memory because of the bromide? Poldi thought if I would walk around vigorously after eating, the drug would have no effect. The way they did with the suicides they caught on time, let them walk it off. How did she know so much about the suicides? That question led to another of her jail horror stories, which entertained us for at least another hour.

I brooded over my problem all afternoon. At dinnertime, when the warden came in, I asked when I would get a hearing and tried to explain about my exam. She thought it was a great joke.

"You've just got here. Wait your turn." This set off Magda who tried to tell her how it was all a mistake in her case, but all she got in reply was the door being shut in her face. Now totally despondent, Magda crouched in a corner and did not say another word.

After the straw sacks had been handed out and the light turned on, our door was opened once again and the warden pushed in a girl. "Move over for her and manage the best you can," she said not unkindly. "I'll see can I get you another mattress."

"And where will we put it," Poldi screamed in outrage. "Hang it from the ceiling? We're overcrowded already, put her somewhere else." She banged on the door with her fists. "That's against regulations, you can't do that. You can't do that."

But they could and they did and the mattress for her never came. We stood around looking at her and what we saw frightened us.

She was small and skinny and could not have been older than twelve, though she looked like ten. She wore a thin, ragged cotton dress and a dirty shawl, the kind peasant girls wear, which she had placed over her head and shoulders and clasped tightly at the neck. Her black lace-up shoes were worn down, and her black cotton stockings marked her as a peasant girl more surely than anything else in her appearance. She looked terrified; the tears streaked down her cheeks. Every few minutes she wiped her nose with her shawl and sniffled loudly. We tried to find out her name and got incomprehensible gibberish.

"She's a Gypsy," Poldi guessed.

"A Slovak peasant."

"A Croat."

The girl backed off against the wall. "A Yid," she finally brought out.

"My God," I exclaimed, "she's talking Yiddish." I told her to slow down and finally managed to make something out of what she said. Her parents were street peddlers in the Jewish quarter in the second district, and they had all been arrested by the police. Apparently beaten, for she shielded her head with her arm and gestured blows. Her teeth were chattering. In her agitation, she accidentally touched Magda.

"Get away from me, you dirty Polack," Magda shouted. "I don't want to get your vermin."

"You cut that out," Poldi told her, offering the girl our only cup. She drank greedily. "I bet she hasn't eaten a thing."

The girl nodded and Poldi surveyed our meager stash of hoarded bread from this morning. "Let's all pitch in and give it to her."

Lise and I brought our last slices and placed them next to Poldi's on the table, but Magda refused. "I don't have to," she argued. "I want her out of here, the dirty thing. Anyway, I ate up all my bread."

Poldi slapped Magda in the face with the back of her hand and began to search through Magda's pile of things. "Ah, there you are—she's been hoarding . . ." She came up with a small crust of bread, which she added to the other pieces on the table. "You eat now," she told the girl gruffly as though she were an obstreperous kid sister.

The girl fell to at once, eating the way people do who are truly hungry. She seemed indifferent to the violence of feelings her entry in our cell had provoked and continued her silent, concentrated eating as though she were alone.

Magda made a careful circle around Poldi and inched up to the door. Suddenly she put her face against the window and began to scream. "Let me out of here, I'm innocent. I'm in here by mistake, let me out." She banged the door with both fists and both feet. Her voice and behavior were different from before; she seemed quite out of control and uncaring of any consequences.

"Stop it, you'll get us all in trouble," Poldi screamed at her, trying in vain to pull her back from the door.

Lise urged us all to the rear of the cell. "She's cracked," Lise shouted. "Let her be, they'll take care of her."

Even though my heart was pounding and my head seemed about to burst with tension, I knew it was good advice. We had to separate ourselves from Magda. I was so angry at her, I had to hold my hands against my body to keep from hitting her. The door was flung open.

"Shut up this minute," the warden commanded. "I'll put you in the rubber cell."

By now we were all screaming. The warden grabbed hold of Magda and pushed her outside, slamming her against the wall. Lise threw Magda's bundle after her.

"Take that child out of here," Poldi demanded. "You're not supposed to have children in here. Let her out, she's just a child."

When the door opened again, the girl tried to hide under the bunk. Two wardens pushed into our cell, slapping us aside to get at her. Finally they half-carried the girl out, her feet dragging limply along the floor. The slamming of the door was followed by a sudden, ominous silence.

IT IS SIXTY-THREE YEARS since these events happened. I have not been able to think of them, remember them or write about them in all these years, except for making a short story out of one small jail incident the year after I came to America. It was a "good" story, describing a positive incident in all that horror, the only positive incident that happened. The rest of it I could not deal with, and even as I am writing this I cannot deal with it. I remember most my feeling of deadly hatred for Magda at that moment, a feeling so violent and overpowering I have never experienced the like before or after. I would gladly have seen her dead. I did not care if she were put in the padded cell, beaten or killed. She had carelessly endangered us all; she had put herself outside of our fragile community of survival. What horrifies me about this memory to this day is how quickly and totally I came to such feelings of cruelty, violence and hatred. They were the other side of total helplessness, of profound, unalterable fear.

It was the same thing some nights later when a woman lost her mind and raved and screamed in an inhuman, possessed voice that echoed through the steel hive in which we were pinned down, each in our enclosure, like butterflies stuck on pins in display boxes. Her screaming made us conscious of what it was to be a prisoner, locked up in a tiny enclosure and utterly helpless, while her voice proclaimed that freedom in insanity was still freedom and death was a way out, a way to be chosen. She had passed into that realm where guards could not touch her; they could kill her but they could not touch her; her demented voice howled with that wild animal cry that dissolves steel cages and the jailers' power to punish. And what did I feel? I remember it clearly—I felt blank, poisonous hatred. I wanted only to get my hands on her and strangle her cries, to beat her, destroy her, because she was pulling me with her, tempting me to that place from which there was no turning back. And when they dragged her out of her cell and then suddenly her crying stopped, and we made pictures in our mind about the way in which they flung her, unconscious, into the padded cell in the basement, even then there was no pity. Only relief.

This was about survival and victims didn't survive. They could go mad or be beaten to death or starve and choose their own form of death, but if you wanted to survive you could not do it alone and you had to fight with all your strength to keep some sort of social contract. That is what I learned in jail, in the first forty-eight hours and the ensuing days and weeks, and it has marked all my life irrevocably. These hours, days, weeks and months in jail were the most important events of my life—they gave it a meaning and a shape I have ever since tried to comprehend. Perhaps if I had been thrown into a different cell, everything would have turned out differently. But I happened, quite by accident, to be thrown in with two women whose knowledge of how to survive was stronger and sounder than my own and whose politics had shaped their knowledge and ethics. I learned from them as I had to, very quickly and thoroughly, and it is to them I owe my survival as much as to anyone. I also owe to them those parts of me that are hard, bitter and frightening to other people.

Once the three of us were alone in that cell we brought some sort of order and rhythm into our lives. I ran a school—classes of the regular one-hour length in German, literature, history, math, French and geography. It was my way of fighting the bromide-induced mental lethargy and the prisoner's worst enemy, boredom. We had an hour of physical exercise each day and an hour of political discussion. It was a full day and a full program and through our contact with prisoners in the other cells our scheme spread to other cells on the floor and even to the men. Our "school" became a model for the rest of the prison. We had orderly times for "relaxation"—playing with cards made of toilet paper, chess sets made of chewed-up dried bread and dominoes made of twigs collected in the yard. We sang songs each day to cheer ourselves up. When, the second week of my stay in jail, my rations were cut in half—all Jews were put on half rations—Poldi and Lise shared their food evenly with me and I accepted. By then we knew each other as "politicals" of similar persuasion. We were humane and decent to each other and we would have done anything to help one another. And yet we could be monstrous to those who threatened our group survival.

This is not humane and certainly not good and I wish I could tell a tale of heroic survival in full humanity. Others have told such tales and maybe they are the truth and maybe they are half-lies. I would not know and nothing I know can help me to imagine such tales as reality. My children, as adults, have complained to me about their childhood having been "so serious." I suppose that is one of the marks I carried with me—I am "so serious" and nothing much has been able to shake that. Another mark I carried out with me was claustrophobia. I cannot be in a small enclosed space—a ship's cabin, an airplane toilet, a narrow room without view, even a small elevator—without feeling that panicky tightness of the jail.

There is a big difference between being a regular prisoner with a finite sentence to serve and being the kind of prisoner I was. Even Poldi and Lise with their complex political past could expect some sort of orderly progression of events—an examination, a trial, sentencing, a finite number of months that had to be served. I was, as it later turned out, a hostage for my father and the only purpose of keeping me and my mother locked up was to put pressure on him to return from abroad and be jailed himself. When this did not succeed and my father was blackmailed into signing away his business without compensation, we were released. But this I could not know at the time. I only knew that as a Jew there were no more rules or laws protecting me. Someone had grabbed me, stuffed me in this steel cell and thrown away the key. I might stay there forever, for all I knew. When there is that kind of perspective, total lawlessness, willful power on one side and abject powerlessness on the other, one can survive by either having hope or by settling with the likelihood of one's own death. I did both.

My hope focused on my *Matura* exam. To get out in time for that exam became my fixed idea, my obsession.

I began a systematic campaign to bring the situation to the attention of the guards, the prison authorities, the police, the Gestapo. Each time the door was opened, I recited my request for a hearing. I wrote petitions on toilet paper and handed them to the amused wardens. I formally and repeatedly requested an interview with the Chief Warden. What I accomplished was to have the guards mark me down as slightly crazy, but also to make them aware of my situation. There was never any response, no promise, no reply. I used my one-postcard-a-week mailing privilege to implore my friends on the outside to petition the school authorities to get me released. After a few weeks I changed my approach and asked just to be allowed to get out of jail under guard to take my exam. The guards considered this so unusual and crazy a request that they may very well have transmitted it to their supervisors—I later learned that it was part of my dossier. This campaign occupied a lot of my energy, attention and emotions; at the very least it had the effect of giving me hope and a goal.

I have good reason to believe that my release and that of my mother was at least hastened by my campaign. What I later learned was that, quite independently of me, the Nazi teachers in my school had started a campaign to get me released. As it happened, I was the only imprisoned student in the school. This was in the early months of the Nazi occupation of Austria and the old laws were still in effect. The final solution was years away. Thus my Nazi teachers were convinced that my case represented an aberration of justice, a simple mistake.

I was the best student in my class and had been selected for a part similar to the role of the valedictorian. In our school system a student could elect to do an honor's thesis in one subject, which usually meant a full year's work of research and writing. Few students chose to add this to the burdensome last year of preparation for the *Matura*. I had done so and had completed my thesis on the subject "The German Ballad through Five Centuries." It had already been approved and rated "excellent" by the supervising teacher of German Studies, who happened to be a devoted "illegal" Nazi, meaning that she had belonged to the Nazi Party for years before the *Anschluss*. This honor's thesis on a subject dear to her heart accrued much credit to her and it may be for this reason she involved herself in a campaign for my liberation. In a way, I was her "Exception Jew"—the one Jew who did not fit her stereotypical anti-Semitic ideas, the one Jew she knew intimately. She wrote in my behalf to the Board of Education, even the Gestapo. When I was finally released she told me all about these efforts and said, naively and with utter conviction: "If only Hitler had known what they did to you, it would never have happened."

I knew nothing of all this, as the days wore on in jail. The only change was for the worse. The cut in rations made us constantly hungry and hunger became a compulsive preoccupation. We talked of food, fantasized of food, dreamed of food. I struggled against headaches, racing pulse, dizziness, lethargy and forgetfulness. And death moved closer and closer.

Poldi had met a comrade during one of our "time out" periods in the yard, a woman in her twenties who had been caught running an illegal printing press. She expected a speedy trial with only two outcomes possible: concentration camp or a death sentence. The woman was trying to deal with this bravely and Poldi and Lise were the only comrades she knew in jail who could understand her ordeal. She did not know which outcome she hoped for, but Poldi knew and hoped for the death sentence. "They just kill you slowly in the camps," she pronounced with her usual uncanny wisdom in such matters. "It's just a slower death and on top of it you've got to work for them." To hear her and that woman talk in such terms, quite seriously and without any dramatics, was like entering the world of the dead. I listened to the words and to something else, vibrations of courage coming out of their simple faith in the immortality of their revolutionary cause. One day in the yard the woman moved close to us and pressed a kerchief into Poldi's hand. "I'm going tomorrow," she said quietly. "Keep that, as a remembrance."

"Austria?"

"No, Germany, I don't know where."

"Maybe it'll be one of those straight work camps," Poldi said encouragingly.

"They're OK."

"Maybe you'll be where my father is," Lise said. "Look for him." The woman nodded. She looked very pale and quite calm. "I'm dead already," she said, "so it can't get worse. You take care." We promised to take care, whatever that might mean. That night Poldi cried for the first time. And I thought of death and how one must choose. We all must die and we do not know when or how, but we can choose to live unafraid by being ready to die. I am dead already so it cannot be worse. This is the road of the heroes, and suddenly it seemed no longer unattainable but quite simple, quite wise. Everything people in power do to their victims is based on instilling fear and ultimately all of that fear comes down to fear of death. If one could learn to be ready for death, one could live unafraid, one would be free, as this woman was free.

I celebrated my eighteenth birthday in jail. I wanted to get out and take my exam and be able sometime to study at a university. I wanted to follow my boyfriend to America. I wanted to help my mother and sister get out of Nazi Germany. I really wanted to live. But to survive I had to become braver than I was and to do that I had to accept that I would die here. It was quite miraculous how calm and strong the will to live became, once one accepted death.

The notches on the wall that served as my personal calendar of imprisonment grew and grew. The Monday of my exam was only a few days away and nothing had changed. No response to my appeals, no interrogation, nothing. Whoever had shut me up in that cage had forgotten my existence. Even the guards showed some concern and told me not to give up hope. They might still let me out Saturday. Nobody ever was let out on Sunday. But Saturday passed and Sunday passed and Monday morning came with the usual jailhouse clatter and discomfort and noise. Nothing. Nobody said anything to me, as though they were hoping I did not know what day this was. Eight A.M., the start of the exam. It would go on until three in the afternoon with a one-hour break for lunch. The same the next day and on for four days. The last day was the oral exam; then it was over. And here I was, forgotten.

Right after breakfast, the warden opened the door and told me to come out. I reached for my bundle, but she said to leave it. Bad news, it meant I wasn't going "out." My heart started racing wildly with hope—perhaps they were after all going to let me go to the exam with a guard? No, that wasn't it. "You're going to the Gestapo," the warden said.

They took me in the prison van along the Quai and the Danube Canal to the Hotel Metropole, where our imprisonment had started five weeks ago. Then, we had just been briefly questioned and sent on to jail. Now, I worried about being interrogated by the Gestapo instead of by the police. This must mean they had found out about my political work. If that was so, then it was all over for me. Poldi had told us a number of horror stories of what went on in the padded cells they had installed in the basement, how they tortured you there and beat you and left you near dead. I tried not to make pictures in my head.

Gilded woodwork and crystal chandeliers . . . I ended up in some anteroom that still looked as it had when the Metropole was simply a hotel. One could imagine the waiters hurrying down the corridors with trolleys of room-service food and fancy drinks. I sat on a satin-covered, gilded chair. What an absurdity . . . Two hours passed, then another. No food, no drink; there was a guard outside the door. I had not had a chance to eat my breakfast bread; by one in the afternoon I was weak with hunger. Then the door opened and they brought my mother in. We hugged and cried and for a few minutes managed to whisper to each other, hoping no one would come into the room and separate us. She thought all of this was a good sign; we would be interrogated and freed. I told her about the exam and she thought it still might work out. If they let us out today, I could still take a part of it and maybe make up the day I missed some other way. I thought, she's trying to cheer me up.

"Whatever they ask you to sign, sign it," my mother said, "the lawyers can take care of it later."

I did not agree but I did not want to discourage her, so I just nodded.

The inner door opened and they called my mother away.

"*Mach's gut,*" she called from the door. Do it well.

A moment later I got called into another office. The man who confronted me was small in his black Gestapo uniform. He wore rimless glasses and looked more like a bookkeeper than a policeman. He offered me a chair and asked a few perfunctory questions, referring to the dossier he had in front of him. Where was my father? Did I know he had taken gold and money abroad, which was a capital offense?

My spirits rose. These questions meant he knew nothing about my politics. Yet suddenly his tone changed and he spoke quite sharply. "Take your glasses off." I thought he would hit me and hesitated, but then I did as he told me.

"Take your jacket off."

I felt sick with fear. Was he going to attack me, rape me? I froze. He repeated his order.

"I'll take nothing off," I said as firmly as I could. "You'll have to force me." I jumped up and stood with my back to the wall.

He looked at me angrily and I stared back at him, willing and ready to make him fight with me. Since he had a pistol in his belt, this was quite foolish, but I did not consider my odds at all.

"Oh, sit down," he said disgustedly. "You've seen too many movies."

"I've been arrested without reason and I've not been charged with anything. I've been in a stinking overcrowded cell for five weeks and been given half rations so I'm starved. They put bromide in the soup and the coffee to dope us up. Are there no laws left?"

"There are laws," he said. "Of course there are laws. I'm trying to get your case cleared up. So sit down and cooperate."

I sat down and put my glasses on. He pushed a cigarette case toward me and I took a cigarette. "I need some food," I said. "I haven't had anything since five o'clock yesterday."

"That's too bad. But we don't run a hotel here. You better answer my questions— I can send you back to jail, you know, or I can send you to Dachau."

"I don't care where you send me," I said, and I meant it, too. "I've been ask- ing for five weeks to be allowed to take my *Matura* exam and today is the day and here I am while the exam's going on. So I don't care."

He looked at his papers. "Ah, yes, you're the 'crazy one' with the exam." His voice was a little more relaxed and natural now. "You really care so much about it?"

"I do."

Again, he looked at his papers. "I see you did an essay on the German ballad. Now that's a strange topic for a Jew." This did not seem to call for a reply on my part. "What can you possibly understand about the spirit of the German ballad?"

"I've read German ballads all my life," I said. "I've studied them for two years. I probably know more about it than you do." I realized as soon as the words were out that being impertinent to this man was not smart, but by now I really did not care what happened after.

"Let's see," he said. "What ballads did you write on?"

I named four and he knew them all and had an opinion of their merit. I responded to him as though we were sitting in a living room having a friendly chat. "This subject," he said finally, "happens to be my special interest. I'm a high school teacher."

My eyes went to his black uniform, the SS insignia, the pistol. "Well," he said, "under more normal circumstances."

I took a chance and asked him a technical question that had interested me in my work on the ballads. He had an answer, and again for a few minutes we talked earnestly and interestedly as though we were in a different time, in a different place.

"You do seem to know your subject," he conceded.

"So you keep me here and I can't take my exam and I'll never get to the university," I said bitterly.

"Just wait here." He got up and left the room. I tried not to think, since the whole situation was crazy and utterly unreal. This could not be happening to me or anyone.

He came back with a cup of coffee and a roll on a plate. "Here."

The way prisoners do, I did not wait or hesitate, for the food might vanish. I ate and drank and he watched me not unkindly.

"I'm sorry you missed your exam," he said. "Such things happen. It's a big organization."

"Why don't you let us out," I cried. "My mother hasn't done anything either."

"We'll see." He closed his folder and pointed me to the door. Strangely, as I rose to go, he also rose and extended his hand, as though this were indeed a social occasion. I shook his hand and he passed me on to the guard. My mother was not here and I thought, the way this had gone, it was some kind of trick or a miracle, but surely it was not real.

I was pushed into the paddy wagon and driven, at dusk, to the Elizabeth street jail and handed over to my usual warden, who marched me down the iron corridors, the clanging door, the key. There were Poldi and Lise waiting, as I entered the cell.

"They didn't beat you?" Poldi exclaimed in surprise.

"No. But they'll keep me here till I rot." I was so dejected I could barely get my story out and only the amazement shown by Lise and Poldi made me see what had happened other than in the worst light. I had been lucky, running into the one halfway decent fellow in the Gestapo; it had been a wild fluke he shared my interest in the German ballad. But in the end, what did it matter. I had missed my exam and I was back here and again, they'd thrown away the key.

I passed the next days in hopeless despondency, no longer even bothering to mark their passage on my wall calendar. All of Poldi's cheering explanations and her hopeful interpretation of every portent and sign only had the effect of driving me deeper into despair. I had lost all hope and with it all nerve. It was as though in that wild abandoned dice game I had played with the Gestapo man I had shot all my reserves and now nothing was left.

On Monday, six days after I had been to the Gestapo, the door opened in the late afternoon and the warden called my name. "Come on, you're going."

I did not move.

"Take your bundle," the warden said impatiently. "You're going out."

"I don't believe you."

Poldi pressed my bundle in my hand. "Come on, it's real."

"They'll just send me to Dachau," I cried. "I'm not going."

I braced myself against the wall and sat down in the corner farthest from the door.

They actually had to carry me to the door and they half-dragged me out the corridor. Only when we had passed the first steel gate, the chief warden showed me a pass. "You're going free," she said. "Not a minute too soon—looks like you're losing your marbles."

"Damn," I said. "Damn, damn, why couldn't you have let me go last week when it mattered?"

And so, reluctantly I left jail. But first I was reunited with my mother in an official-looking police office, where we were given some papers to sign. I read them and was appalled—we agreed to leave Germany (Austria) at once and never return. Until such time as we were going to leave we agreed to report to our local police precinct once a week and explain why we were not yet gone. I wanted my mother not to sign this, but she already had. She urged me to sign right away and not make a fuss—they wouldn't let us out if we didn't sign, so why argue. I signed what was in fact an order of deportation and loss of citizenship without any due process or trial or cause. And then, only then, were we out on the street.

We took a streetcar home, and I felt terribly self-conscious in my smelly clothes, which hung from me like the clothes on a scarecrow. It seemed to me I had lost thirty pounds and everyone in the streetcar must be able to see we were just out of jail. Walking from the streetcar stop to our house seemed an exhausting task. We were both weak and holding on to each other.

Our apartment was closed and dark, so we went downstairs to Grandmama's where they greeted us with tears and great excitement. My sister was beside herself with joy.

"You're out just in time for the *Matura,*" said my Aunt Emma.

"That was last week."

"Not at all," she said. "They postponed it for a week because they had to find a new commission. An all-Nazi commission."

It was true. She showed me the official letter from school and the date was tomorrow, 8 A.M.

I will never know whether it was my Nazi teachers' appeal, my prison campaign or that crazy interview with the Gestapo man—here I was, free and just in time for the exam. I went the next day, a small celebrity among my teachers and classmates, and appeared before the Nazi examination commissioners, each with his or her Nazi Party pin in the lapel, and asked to be permitted to eat during the exam.

"Why such an outrageous request?"

"Because I was just let out of jail," I said, "and I've been systematically starved and doped with bromides. I'm too weak to take the exam if I can't have something to eat." It appeared the commissioners were familiar with my case and, after a brief consultation, granted my request. And so, feeling somewhat smug and triumphant in my puny display of political resistance, I munched on cheese sandwiches all the way through my four-day exam. And despite it all, I graduated magna cum laude and received the handshake of the super Nazi commissioner congratulating me on an exceptional achievement. It was a humorous grace note to a harsh reality. What had gone before was deadly serious and marked me for life. What would come after was much worse for all of us. And my promising academic career, that wonderful utopian goal toward which all my energy and hopes had gone during those weeks in jail, vanished in the storm that swept over Europe and over our lives. I would not get back to it for over twenty years.

[7]

I N JAIL, my mother had been brave. She had pulled time quietly without
lapsing into despair and she had not lost hope. She managed to make friends
with one of the guards and on my birthday the guard threw a package into
my cell—a gift from Ili. It was the best birthday gift I have ever received; nothing after it could match it. Out of the miserable short rations we received she had
saved up bread, chewed it until it was the consistency of clay and made chess figures for me. Poldi and Lise and I took turns playing them on an imaginary board
on the table and they helped to while away the hours and days, but more, they
spoke of her love for me, of her creativity and ingenuity. They were a lifeline she
threw out into the nothingness for me; it reached me and helped me through.

But when we came out of jail, when it looked as though the worst was over,
my mother collapsed. She took to her bed and lapsed into fits of weeping, into
abject passivity.

Our situation was absurd and dangerous. We were in fact under a deportation
order. Why this cruel punishment was imposed on us without a trial or any accusation of wrongdoing is unclear to me to this day. At that time in Austria, Jews
in general were not deprived of their citizenship rights and still had some sem-
blance of legal rights.

My father had, within a few months after his arrival in Liechtenstein, managed to get his residence permit extended to his entire family, which meant that

we actually had a place of refuge to which we could go. Although our arrest had put Father under terrific pressure to return to Austria, he had sensibly resisted it, realizing that it would only mean that he would be arrested and none of us would be able to escape. But the cost was high—while we were in jail he suffered a major heart attack and was only now recuperating. He did what he could by getting an "Aryan" lawyer in Vienna to represent him and wind up his business interests. The way I understood it, the best that could be hoped for was to sell his business outright at a halfway fair price; the alternative was to "aryanize" it by taking a Nazi business partner and hope that he would not ruin the business or keep all the profit. In either case the money could not be taken out of the country under the new laws. All emigrants were permitted to take was personal clothing and household goods and five dollars worth of cash per person. We hoped that once he was recovered, Father could run the pharmacy in Vaduz profitably enough to support us, which in fact he managed to do for several years. Father's flight, while it may have been the cause of our arrest and harassment, was also our lifesaver.

During the time we had spent in jail it had become more and more difficult for Jews to leave Austria. All borders in Europe and most other countries of the world were closed against refugees from Nazi persecution and only a lucky few had the connections and money to escape. In April approximately twenty-five thousand Viennese Jews applied to the U.S. consulate for immigration visas; at the time the quota number for immigrants from Austria was fixed at 1413 per year.[1] I had applied as early as March. Bobby had received his U.S. visa while I was in jail and had left immediately—a decision with which I was in total agreement, although it made my situation more difficult. Due to his urging them in person, Bobby's Florida relatives had at last agreed to give me an affidavit of support. Meanwhile, my father had started an application for all his family with the American Consul in Switzerland. But first we had to get out of Austria.

Despite our order of deportation we were unable to get the papers necessary to permit us to leave the country. The sale of my father's business was not something that could be accomplished in a few weeks. Yet until it was done, we could not expect to settle our tax liabilities, which was a prerequisite for getting all the necessary emigration permits. To hasten our departure we were ordered to report each Tuesday morning to the local police station. This turned out to be a refined

1. Herbert Rosenkranz, *Verfolgung und Selbstbehauptung: Die Juden in Österreich, 1938–1945* (Wien: Herold, 1978), 80.

form of torture. The first time we appeared, the sergeant interviewing us wanted to know what we were still doing here. My mother explained that we had been unable to get the papers necessary for leaving the country.

"Well, tell your husband to come home and take care of his business," the policeman grumbled.

"Yes, sir, I certainly will."

"We're not going to let you play games here. Two weeks should be plenty of time to get your papers. After that it's back to jail."

Mother collapsed in tears after that first visit. She swore she'd rather die than go through this again. I begged her to call the lawyer and have a conference and see what we could do to get the necessary exit papers. She promised, but did not do it.

I called the lawyer and he said I was too young to handle these complex business affairs. I agreed, but told him my mother was sick and seemed unable to handle anything. Meanwhile, on our third visit to the precinct, the desk officer got nasty. "Probably holding out jewels and money so they can live it up in Switzerland. You're supposed to be out of here—how you do it is your business. If you're not out by next week, we'll send you to Dachau, you Jewish pigs."

Grandmother was too old, my sister was too young, the uncles had left and one of them was hiding in his bedroom, apparently out of his mind. Mother would not and could not handle the problem—so I had to do what needed to be done.

Convincing the lawyer to deal with me was the least of my problems. He turned out to be a decent man, ashamed of what he had to do to save us; he was used to normal business dealings, not gangster politics.

The Nazis had enacted a number of bureaucratic regulations that made it exceedingly difficult for Jews, even the lucky few who had visas to other countries, to obtain the necessary exit permit. The would-be emigrant had to secure a document that testified to the fact that he had paid all taxes. This had to be verified and stamped by four different agencies and required the applicant to provide proof of birth, citizenship, legal residence. One had to secure a permit for emigration from the police department, a new passport from the passport division and a permit from the department in charge of emigration, and then one had to reapply to foreign consulates so that the visa could be affixed to the new documents.

Our lawyer had managed to free some of our savings accounts, which had been frozen by the police, permitting us to buy groceries. The maid had left; we were faced with the unaccustomed problem of feeding ourselves. Mother made a few futile forays into the kitchen and decided to live on tea and bread. I had never cooked a meal before and had no knowledge of the simplest domestic skills. I remember taking inventory of what was left in the kitchen and wondering how I would deal with all the staples. I began making farina for breakfast and thought, with some sugar, I produced a fairly edible product. Once having mastered this, I thought we could easily survive on Mother's tea and bread and my farina until I could take some cooking lessons from Grandmother. But Mother and Nora balked when I produced farina for the third or fourth dinner. We went out to a restaurant, which I considered a sinful and needless luxury. We needed to save all our money for what lay ahead of us. Over this we quarreled, displacing all the anxieties and fears and anger we were unable to express openly into fierce arguments over the food we would eat.

I remember to this day my anger against Ili and Nora for the fuss they made over the farina. I was trying to provide the best I could, and they were making impossible demands on me—that's how it seemed to me. Nora to this day remembers my being difficult, dictatorial and unpleasant. No doubt I was. I was quite overwhelmed by what needed to be done and I was very frightened. Nora was only twelve years old and she did not have to go to the police station every Tuesday. By then, the usual greeting was: "What, you're still here . . . Why don't you turn on the gas oven so we don't have to see you no more?" The police sergeant was not prescient about the gas ovens; he meant his invitation to us to commit suicide quite literally. By then, a number of our acquaintances had indeed committed suicide. This was long before the final solution, long before any of these persecutions were cloaked under the mantle of legality. The Austrian treatment of Jews was improvised on the spot; its versatility, ingenuity and brutality were then unprecedented.

Some of our friends had left, the lucky ones who could get a visa, a visa to anywhere. Some left for Britain, the women signing on as domestic workers; others left for Singapore or Hong Kong. For a few weeks, some Latin American countries admitted a few hundred refugees; then they closed their borders. In our circle of acquaintances we exchanged refugee information of this sort and stood in line endlessly at the various embassies hoping for a scrap of hopeful information. There were black-market prices quoted for some Latin American countries' visas, but the way one actually carried out such a transaction was quite mysterious to me and I doubted I would know how to do it. So I focused on getting us out as the first step, and then to America.

I stood in line day after day in some office or other, petitioning for this paper or that, and was told time and again, come back next week. Come back in two weeks. The paper is not available. You must go to yet another office. But the lines for the exit papers, lines for access to government offices, were the worst.

The long lines in the dimly lit stairwells of office buildings formed at dawn. Business was transacted only until noon; if one was not lucky enough to get in, one had to come back the next day. Place numbers in waiting lists were not recognized on succeeding days, so that applicants had to stand in line for many hours only to start all over again the next day. At each step of the way huge fees were extracted from the applicants. The system was so designed that after weeks of effort the relevant deadlines for the various papers expired so that one had to start anew. It was a devilishly refined form of torture and it functioned as it was intended, to make us feel as outcasts from the human race.

Office workers and other passersby taunted us and some spat in our direction. Sometimes, policemen or SA men would push everyone back, regardless of how long one had waited. Women fainted, old people collapsed. A Jewish veteran of World War I, pointing to his medals, appealed to get in ahead of others. The SA men in charge pulled the medal off his lapel and stamped on it. *"Saujud!"* After a few days on these lines people became abject, hopeless. We were afraid to talk, afraid even to look at each other. Much worse was to come, but then we did not yet have the images and concepts by which to visualize the lines waiting for deportation, the forced marches from the cattle cars. What I did not know then, what none of us in these lines knew then, was that this system and the following system of the pauperization and degradation of Viennese Jews was designed and directed personally by Adolf Eichmann, who used us as guinea pigs on whom to test out the bureaucratic methods by which he would later so successfully implement the "final solution."

By the middle of the summer I had lost all hope. It was like trying to fight your way out of a swamp and sinking in deeper with every step. They would ship us off to Dachau. A young man I knew had been sent there after being caught in a street police raid. A week later his parents had received a postcard: "If you wish to collect the ashes of your son N. L., present this card and *Reichsmark* fifteen at Gestapo headquarters."

One day, I said to my mother: "I can't stand it any more. Something's got to give." She tried to calm me. I went out to the hairdresser and had my hair shorn off to within an inch of my scalp. I'd accomplished something, at least.

Somehow my mother rallied and became closer to her old self. Not enough to take on any of the emigration problems or business negotiations, but enough to take care of daily needs. She decided we needed to move out of the apartment: she and Nora would move to a cheap pension with meals and I could accept the offer of my future mother-in-law, Bobby's mother, to stay with them. Ili began to take efficient practical steps with some of her old zest and initiative. She found an acquaintance with an Italian passport who agreed to take her fur coat over the border and keep it until we could get to Switzerland. "That's worth a lot," she rejoiced when the transaction had been completed. "You can live at least a year on a full-length mink coat."

She shipped out other things of use and began to pack the most indispensable of our books. Each week she sent some packages of them to my father, thus saving what to us seemed most precious and irreplaceable. I have some of these books to this day and am so glad she was able to save them. She then proceeded to sell whatever was valuable in our apartment, piece by piece, to antique dealers and private buyers, but we could get very little for these things, since thousands of other Jewish families were doing the same sort of selling.

Finally, she organized an open house sale. I remember little of that event, except that it was very painful. I had never lived any other place in my life, and now everything I had lived with and held dear was not sold, but virtually stolen. People from the neighborhood paid us twenty-five shillings and walked out with a Persian rug. Some years later they would no longer go through these fictitious sale transactions, but the way it was then, it was all done legally. We even wrote out receipts. Ten shillings for the antique clock, which I had always disliked while it hung in the salon, but which surely was worth thirty times that much. The son of the baker who had the store at the corner and from whom we bought bread every day walked out with a Meissen shepherd figurine, for which he offered us five shillings. A superintendent from one of the buildings on the street came and knocked down our already ridiculously low price for several chairs. His son who accompanied him and helped to carry the chairs home was in the SA uniform. We would have given him the chairs for free, if he had asked that—we were in no position to argue.

My mother now turned all her energy toward planning for our future. All kinds of crash courses had sprung up in the Jewish community and everyone was learning a trade. We all learned facial massage, manicure and hairdressing. Many of our women friends took sewing classes in preparation for having to earn a living in exile. My grandmother gave me regular cooking classes, which provided me with enough of a repertoire of nutritious meals that I would never have to experience the farina disaster again. Mother took up the sewing of leather gloves and belts, and all of us spent what time we could improving our English. It was in a way as it had been in jail—we were trying to kill time with activity and keep hope alive and all the while we were losing ground. We were coming to terms with a momentous upheaval in our lives: from having been privileged and sheltered and protected we were suddenly hounded, threatened and overwhelmed by the hatred of people ready and willing to see us dead.

Each week brought new anti-Semitic regulations and laws. The public parks, museums, buildings were closed to Jews. Signs went up all over the city, "No Jews or dogs allowed." The beautiful city I had loved all my life was defaced by swastika flags on every building and shop window. Many restaurants and cafes excluded Jews. The newspapers no longer printed anything but the official Nazi version of the news. On walls and public bulletin boards *Der Stürmer (The Stormtrooper),* an anti-Semitic propaganda sheet, appeared daily, setting forth its filth and hatred in coarse cartoons and grotesque caricatures so that even barely literate readers could be re-educated.

It became unpleasant and dangerous to leave the house. Downtown, gangs of SA men and hoodlums daily searched for Jews and staged rituals designed to publicly humiliate them. This was spontaneous anti-Semitism, not yet organized into the efficient death-machine it would later become, but as to terror, it was quite sufficient. One learned quickly how to make oneself inconspicuous, to blend into a crowd, to make no eye contact with anyone, to call no attention to oneself. It took daily courage to venture out and pretend one was still a person with some rights as a citizen or a human being.

For me, being a refugee began when I moved out of the apartment in which I had been raised and slept in the dark, small room Bobby had lived in since he was a teenager. His mother had kept it undisturbed, a sort of shrine to her youngest son after he had left. She, like most of us, had trouble accepting the new reality. Inviting me to live with them was an act of kindness by Bobby's parents who, after all, had to deal with their own impending migration to America. It was his mother's sisters in America who had furnished the affidavit of support on the basis of which Bobby got his U.S. visa. His parents and sister would be next and then it would be my turn. The idea of all of us being dependent on Bobby's relatives in the future seemed awful to me, but the first thing a refugee learns is never to refuse any possibility of getting help. My living with Bobby's family these months before emigration was a symbolic acceptance on their part that I would now be part of their family.

Yet I was little comfort to them. I found Bobby's father overbearing, pompous and insensitive. I was disturbed by the way his mother treated him as a minor deity. I was my usual arrogant self, anxious to assert my independence and to distance myself from too much familiarity and parental supervision. It was my first experience of living in other people's houses, a guest on sufferance, and I quickly knew I would always hate it. I regretted I had ever agreed to the arrangement, but there was no way of getting out of it without hurting my future in-laws' feelings.

To be helpless and without a foundation of rights and recognized status is a shattering experience. It is not only a matter of being suddenly de-classed; it is a matter of suddenly being a nonperson. A person without rights and citizenship is a person without self-definition. One does not dare think of the past, because memories make the present unbearably painful by comparison. The future is murky, a sea landscape in fog, offering a few discernable landmarks—Liechtenstein, America, marriage—but they have no meaning or shape. They were not chosen, they might vanish or never be reached. The refugee lives from day to day, from hour to hour and throws out lines across the fog: pipedreams, fantasies, bragging tales, long-range plans. All for nothing, for the only skill worth learning is adaptability. Learn to travel light is the basic refugee wisdom.

We had not yet learned that wisdom. On the contrary, the regulations concerning emigration taught us to invest all we could in our clothes and household goods, the only things we would be able to rescue. So, skimping on carfare and food, we drew whatever savings we could out of the bank and bought the most expensive clothes we could find. In particular, I acquired a light blue tweed greatcoat, which I dearly loved, because I never previously could have afforded it and because it seemed to me to express what I thought I still was, a young woman of impeccable taste and good breeding. I arrived in America in that coat and, since it was virtually indestructible, I wore it for years, marking myself off as an un-American oddity and unemployable wherever I went. Nobody believes you are poor when you wear clothes like that and in America, in order to get and keep the kind of low-grade jobs for which I was competing desperately, one had to blend in.

Refugees sleep on other people's couches and eagerly accept invitations to lunch or dinner. They are excessively polite and try to make themselves unobtrusively useful. Like poor relatives, they anticipate the wishes of their hosts, who expect, at the very least, sincere and frequent expressions of gratitude. I was not able or willing to offer any of this as I should have and instead offered my cheerful, optimistic activism as a way of showing my appreciation. I ran errands, cheered up the despondent, found useful information and hints for survival. That's another way of being a refugee and it was one more suited to my personality and inclinations.

Thoroughly exasperated and frustrated by my weeks of waiting on line in government offices, I suggested to the lawyer that we take some "unconventional steps," that is, that we bribe some people. The lawyer was shocked by such a suggestion but after a while, miraculously, papers began to move.

It was the end of August before we finally had all the papers together. We could actually leave . . . It is strange that so important an experience could ever be forgotten, but then my memory has been playing all kinds of tricks on me for decades, recalling useless trifles and forgetting the main events. I cannot remember anything about our actual leaving on September 9, 1938, Nora's thirteenth birthday, not what we wore, not how we said our goodbyes, not how it felt. I only remember sitting in the train as it was speeding across Austria and thinking that we would be arrested at the border and sent back to the police station in Döbling to be terrorized and humiliated. We would be discovered to have invalid papers; our passports were secretly marked; the agents were at this very moment preparing the papers necessary to arrest us. This I remember.

And for six decades, at irregular intervals and with slight variations, I dream the same nightmare. It always has to do with getting ready to leave and there is too much luggage; there are too many people trying to interfere with our leaving; there are too many unfinished tasks. Sometimes the luggage falls off the car or the cart or down the stairs and all the contents spill out and as I stuff it all in again, the train pulls out without me. Sometimes the taxi taking us to the train will be unable to find the station. Sometimes I wander for horrifying hours through unknown streets of unknown cities trying to find the place I am supposed to be going to, the place of escape and safety. I usually get there when it is too late. Or I arrive, having lost all the papers I need for admission. Nothing can be contained, nothing can be controlled and the hidden dread, the disaster is always there, always waiting. So, after all, I have not forgotten that departure. I just remember what I actually experienced, deep down, where experiences are real and forever.

We did cross that border without the slightest trouble and got off at the next stop, in Switzerland, and there was my father, with a car, waiting for us and the Swiss flag flew and the day was sunny and we were saved. And behind us and ahead of us, the unknown horrors lay in wait.

EXCEPT FOR THE MEDIEVAL CASTLE dominating the town from the mountainside, Vaduz, the capital of Liechtenstein, was in every way like a neat and pleasant Swiss village. The farmhouses bordering the main street each had huge smelly manure piles by the barn doors around which chickens gathered. Cows were herded through the streets on their way to and from their low-lying pastures and each spring, with some festivity and the blessings of the priest, the herds were driven to the alpine meadows where they spent the summer. Liechtenstein was three-quarters steep mountains, one-quarter lowlands bordering on the Rhine River, which separated it from Switzerland. It had a police force of eleven men who guarded the frontier posts against Austria and Germany. Because of the country's customs and diplomatic union with Switzerland there was no formal border check; one simply crossed the Rhine River bridge and one was in Switzerland. That is, if one had the proper papers. If not, one would undoubtedly be stopped by the border guards on the Swiss side. What we had was a temporary residence permit in Liechtenstein, which was renewed every other month. Such a permit entitled one to visit Switzerland for a few weeks at a time, but no more than that. The Swiss did not readily grant temporary residence to refugees.

The first few days in Vaduz we did not think of such matters; we only tried to comprehend that we had really been saved. Father had a small apartment on the main street, just above a bakery, and we settled in as though we were on vacation. Father had aged considerably and lost a lot of weight. His face was gaunt, transformed by deep wrinkles running from his cheeks to his chin; his eyes had a feverish intensity and seemed to have sunken into their sockets, and he walked like an old man. There was no question he was still quite ill. In the days before open heart surgery, a massive heart attack turned a person into an invalid whose life was always in danger. Even his voice had changed and he spoke more tentatively and softly, with less authority.

He had changed and everything else was different, too. I no longer was a schoolgirl, inhibited and frustrated by powerful parental authority. My father was a sick old man; I had for some time now taken care of my mother. It was I who would be making the leap into the unknown, which would offer hope and rescue to my family. Our constellation had profoundly shifted.

Still, my father maintained his old role of provider and breadwinner. He talked about that first, those early days, assuring us that the business was improving, that he earned enough to support us modestly, very modestly; fortunately the living was cheap in Vaduz. The main thing was to provide an education for Nora and he was sure he could do that. He had selected a school in the mountains near Lucerne where he felt she would get a good education and be safe for the next four years. As long as she was a boarding student in a Swiss school, she would be given a residence permit. We all agreed to that and within a few weeks we drove her to the school, which happened to be an extraordinary institution founded on Ghandian principles and known all over the world. Nora was happy there.

Father assumed, as a matter of course, that Mother and I were going to live with him in Vaduz. He had gone out of his way to make things comfortable for Mother and offered her a separate bedroom, which she could turn into a study. She tried it for a few weeks and made heroic efforts at housekeeping. She tried, she really tried.

Our accustomed roles as wealthy tourists on a vacation lasted for a few weeks. Despite our good clothes, we were quite poor and we certainly were not tourists. Keeping house in the small apartment, going to the few shops and sitting each afternoon in the single cafe on the square, we soon became aware of our actual condition. We were not Vaduz residents; we had no friends, no acquaintances. Our only entry to other people was as "the pharmacist's wife and daughter," which automatically made for social distance. Father made a point of the need for discretion—we were not to talk of being refugees; we were not to stress being Jewish. After all, we were there only on the sufferance of the authorities and our permits could always be revoked. Ili could not take her easel and paints out into the woods and meadows or go out at night without Father—such things were not done by respectable women in Vaduz and one had to fit in.

Fortunately I had to go to Zurich, where the nearest U.S. consulate was, to look after my U.S. immigration papers and to see if I could convince the Consul to give me a letter stating that I was in the process of getting a U.S. visa. With such a let- ter in hand I might even get a residence permit in Switzerland. Ili and I went to Zurich and planned to spend four to six weeks there to take care of that business. Before we left, Father had a serious talk with Mother to explain to her the stringent financial limits he had to set for us, since he had to continue paying for a half-empty apartment in Vaduz and had to hire a person to cook for him during our absence.

Ili was excited about being in Zurich. She thought, if she could get away to Zurich every two months, she might be able to continue as "Mr. Pharmacist's wife." But she was not a machine; she could not be expected to produce artistic work under these cramping, hideous conditions, without a soul to whom she could talk, without friends, without any kind of cultural stimulation. My thoughts, hearing her talk like this, were that she had not yet learned to accept her refugee status. She was still talking as though she were a woman with choices.

She was adaptable enough to find us a room in a working-class district of Zurich, somewhat cheaper than what our budget allowed. We would share the bathroom with the landlord and what we saved by getting such a cheap room we would be able to spend on such necessary luxuries as going to museums and attending lectures. I spent my usual hopeless hours at the U.S. embassy and was quite upset to find that the earliest possible date for my getting a visa was six months away. But Ili and I ran into conflict within our first few days at Zurich, once again over food. I suggested that we get an electric hot plate for our room; we'd make coffee in the morning and have it with a piece of bread and jam and get a cheap three-course meal at noon at the student cafeteria. We could eat dinner in our room, cheese, bread and a piece of fruit, which would leave us with just enough money to get a drink or a cup of coffee in a coffeehouse. We tried it for two days; then Ili rebelled. She could not and would not subsist on the rotten food served in the student restaurant.

"Leave it to me," she demanded. "Just for two days and I'll show you how to manage." We had the Spartan breakfast in our room. For lunch she took us to a good restaurant in the center of the city, where we sat pleasantly at a table covered with a white tablecloth and where, without embarrassment, she ordered soup and an extra order of bread, followed by a cup of coffee. She explained to the waiter that we were on a diet. Good enough for lunch, but when do we get a main meal? Late in the afternoon, dressed in her best clothes and fur coat, Ili marched me into one of the fanciest hotels in town. We sat in the lobby for at least an hour, reading all the foreign newspapers and acting like rich tourists. Then she took us into the bar, ordered a beer for herself and a glass of wine for me and asked the waiter to serve the hors d'oeuvre cart. It was loaded down with fancy salads, patés, smoked salmon, fish and various mayonnaise spreads, served with toast triangles and thin wafers. Ili filled up her plate and encouraged me to do the same; then, without the slightest qualms, she again asked for the cart a half an hour later and repeated the process. Meanwhile, we watched the bar scene, listened to the piano player and fell into the accustomed vacation roles.

"Now wasn't that better," my mother demanded. "At least you could sit in some comfort and enjoy the scene. You did like what you ate, didn't you?"

I had to admit it was better than the student cafeteria. But she couldn't do this every day.

"Just why not?" Mother asked. "There are lots of restaurants and hotels. We'll just make the rounds."

I balked at this, first arguing reasonably, then simply blustering. It was embarrassing, it was humiliating . . .

"That's in your head," she said. "I've as much right to eat in the Hotel Baur-au-Lac as I had last year."

Well, it meant only one thing—she was denying reality and she would persist in denying reality. "We're poor. Get it through your head. We're poor and we're refugees and we've got to learn to live with what we have."

"Bad enough I have to live in a room that smells of cabbage soup. I don't have to eat it, too."

The argument led nowhere and in the end we decided to split our money. She could eat wherever she wanted and I would do the same. And I'd thank her not to tell me about all the splendid meals she'd had . . .

It was, like most scenes between us, symbolic and heavy with unspoken issues. I was going to join the working class and like it, gritting my teeth and denying my past. I was going to blend into the environment into which I now had been thrown by fate. Ili was going to be herself and find a role that was expressive of her values—she was going to fight against giving up her standards. If she had to compromise, she would do it grudgingly and under protest. I was too young and too callow to see the strength and dignity of her position—all I could see was that she would make a bad refugee and that there would be trouble between us.

Yet we had a good couple of weeks, enjoying the excitement, beauty and cultural offerings of this great city. While we were there I buried myself for hours in the remarkable Social History Archives, reading whatever struck my fancy, dipping into this or that subject of labor history and recent political history. It was the first time in my life I experienced the serenity and joy of working day after day in a good archival collection. It seemed like a peaceful island full of treasures and wisdom and when I emerged from the building at closing time, I could for a little while believe that I was a university student, that I had a future that included books and knowledge. Then I ate my starchy dinner in some cheap restaurant and rode the streetcar back to the bare little room on the third floor of a tenement and took stock of my situation. I would never be a student, never go to the university, never be a specialist in linguistics and ancient languages as I had hoped to be. All that desperate struggle to get admitted to the *Matura* exam and thus secure my academic future had been for nothing. Reality, my good friend, once again had me by the throat.

Usually, at night, Ili had some kind of free entertainment lined up—a church concert, a lecture at the university, a film showing in some organization or other. She was marvelous at finding these treats and always insisted on ending the evening over a mocha at a good cafe. She also had made contacts with refugee organizations and found out that a certain Jewish committee would give refugees a small monthly stipend for living.

"You want to become a charity case," I cried in outrage. "How can you do such a thing? We don't need it, Father gives us enough to live on."

"Well," said my mother, "I might want to use it some day, when I find I can't stand living in Vaduz any longer."

Despite our disagreements we really had a good time together and sometimes I could talk to her about America and interest her in looking at American journals and films. Then, one day, two policemen came to our apartment with orders to take us to the police station.

"What have we done? Are you arresting us?" We hauled out our various permits, but the policemen were not interested in them. They were polite enough; they had their orders. We could argue everything out at the station.

It was toward evening. At the police station, which was not unlike the one in Vienna, we were kept waiting for a long time and then sharply interrogated as to our status. Citizens of what country? Passports? Residence permit? What were we doing here? When were we planning to leave?

We had a right to be in Zurich, where I was attending to my emigration papers. We had valid residence permits for Liechtenstein. The way we understood it these entitled us to come and go into Switzerland as we pleased.

That was not the understanding of the Swiss police. We had no valid papers for residence in Zurich and since we were not staying at a hotel we could not claim to be tourists. On and on. We asked them to check our status with the Liechtenstein authorities. They saw no reason to do that, since we were holders of German passports. They would just take us over the Austrian (then German) border and we could do what we wanted. They were under no obligation to take us to a place of our choice. We tried to explain that this would mean certain death for us, but they just laughed at such a preposterous claim. The Austrians were no barbarians; if we had committed no crime they would not harm us. Besides which, that wasn't the concern of the Swiss authorities. They had to do their job and that was all.

Meanwhile, over our protest, they stuffed us into a large jail cell for the night. With our past experience, we at once expected the worst. They might hold us for weeks; no one would know where we were. Father would not get suspicious that anything was wrong until the time of our scheduled arrival, which was ten days away. Or else they might in fact deport us to Austria. We were numb with fear.

It was difficult to talk our situation over, for the cell was very crowded. The two benches along the walls were already filled with women of all ages, some of them drunk. A large woman wrapped in many shawls had stretched out on the floor and was snoring peacefully. Mother whispered to me that most of these women seemed to be prostitutes. She was right and some of them were quite interested in our story, while several of them looked on us with disgust and suspicion. Refugees, probably living on taxpayers' charity—they wanted no part of us.

We had already heard enough stories about the Swiss attitude and actions toward refugees from Hitler to fear the worst. One of Ili's former friends, whom we had met in Zurich, had told us of refugees being rounded up and kept in detention camps. Several bus loads had indeed been shipped back into Germany. The much-vaunted hospitality and the usually generous refugee policy of the Swiss apparently did not apply to Jewish refugees. We had reason to fear the worst.

We sat close together and talked and cried. One of the prostitutes, a young woman with large fake eyelashes and a gorgeous head of dyed-red curls tried to reassure us. "Long as they keep you in this cell, you'll get out in the morning. This ain't the regular jail, just a police station holding cell." She offered us a cigarette, which we gratefully accepted. We did not sleep that night.

In the morning, a different detective interviewed us. We were permitted to phone Father and he got hold of the Mayor of Vaduz who vouched for us with the Swiss police. On the strength of that, they decided to return us to Liechtenstein, not to Austria. My mother wept with joy.

"We'll leave on the next train, Officer," she assured him.

"You will," he said sternly. "With an escort."

And so the two policemen drove us to our room, waited till we packed our belongings and then drove us to the train station. They got on the train with us, as though we were prisoners, waiting at the border crossing until my father drove us across the Liechtenstein border. We were told never to try this trick again—the only way we could get into Switzerland was with permission of the Swiss police, a valid permit in hand.

This incident, short and relatively harmless as it was, affected both Ili and me profoundly. We felt it was worse than what had happened in Austria—this was what the rest of our lives would be. There's no escaping the reality of being homeless and, for all practical purposes, stateless. There was no authority, no institution, no law to protect us. If the Swiss, who in our past experience and imagination had always been the models of humanitarianism and hospitality, could treat us like this, what was left? I concluded to stay in Liechtenstein until I had my American visa. Ili reacted differently. After a few days in Vaduz she made up her mind to live in France, on the Riviera, where living was cheap enough so that she could exist on my father's allowance. The French would recognize her Liechtenstein papers; they were a civilized race and would not act like the Swiss who were really hidden Nazis—one could see it in their faces . . . The French had a long tradition of being decent to refugees. Besides, there were strong refugee organizations in Paris. Nothing my father or I could say would change her mind. What it came down to, she finally admitted, was that living in Liechtenstein the way she would have to live was impossible for her. She could not survive it. She did not say that to Father, but he understood it and resigned himself. She would have to take whatever the consequences were; he was through trying to protect her. Or so he said.

My mother left shortly thereafter and, after a brief stay in Paris, settled first in Nice, then in Cagnes, a little village in the hills above Nice. She wrote happy letters with long and vivid descriptions of the beauty of the landscape, of the new friends she had made and of the paintings on which she was working.

After *Kristallnacht* and the pogroms, everyone in our family who had any means of escaping Germany did so without further hesitation. My cousin Willie escaped to England; my other cousin, Rudy, was enrolled, like my sister, in a Swiss school, which allowed him to stay in that country. Uncle Richard, the banker, who had long had residency in Switzerland, managed to bring Grandmother and *Tante* Emma to that country and they lived out the rest of their lives in the peace and quiet of Lucerne. My uncle Alfons, the insurance salesman, escaped to Shanghai, leaving his gentile wife behind in Vienna. My mother's sisters escaped to Holland, where, for a time, they thought themselves secure. Our family was incredibly lucky in having means of escape. The Czech, Hungarian and Yugoslav branches of the family were not so lucky and eighteen members of the family, cousins and uncles and aunts of my mother and father, later perished in the holocaust.

While I was impatiently waiting for my American visa, a friend of my father's, an attorney in Vaduz, asked him if I would be interested in serving as a governess to his children. I would have a nice room and full board and a small stipend, since as an alien without work permit they could not legally employ me. But it would be enough for pocket money. I would have one day a week off and of course I could go out at night to visit with my father. I met the family, three bright and lively children, two boys and a girl, ages four to ten, and the wife, who seemed very friendly and cheerful. Their house was large, with a beautiful garden and I had a nice room with a view of the mountains. I agreed to the deal, since it would help out my father and would make the time pass more quickly. I expected to be treated, as they had promised, as a member of the family.

From the beginning, I was told to address everyone by their first names and in that sense I was a member of the family. My duties were explained to me and I assumed they would be similar to those of the governesses in my home—that is, I would do no housework or cooking. But that was not my employers' expectation. As a "member of the family" I was expected to do whatever the lady of the house did, and she was a compulsive housewife who considered idleness sinful. I was in full charge of the children, their homework, their clothing, their lessons, their recreation. I bathed them and put them to bed and got up at night when one or the other of them awakened. In between I was instructed to follow the mother, Lizbeth, in her household activities and make myself useful. This turned out to include washing the stairs one day or polishing the silver the next. I had to help the maid in hanging up the wash on the long lines outdoors and help with the kitchen cleanup and the food preparation. When I protested that this was not work governesses usually did, I was told to be grateful I had found employment. This was the way Swiss girls were trained and it was astonishing my mother had not trained me better up to now. Even though I could see the advantages in learning housework thoroughly, I still felt, with a thirteen-hour workday, that Lizbeth was taking advantage of me.

According to the advanced working-class consciousness I had acquired in the years of discussions among my student friends and especially my talks with Marta, I should have strongly resisted this or quit my job. I once broached the subject with my father, hinting that I was overworked and taken advantage of, but his reaction was to praise me for helping him by supporting myself. It was help he really needed and he thought it might be good training for me for my future in America, where at the very least I would have to know how to keep house for a family on a limited budget. I heard what he really was saying: life is hard for all of us now and you must learn to adjust.

From what Bobby was writing, things were not going to be too easy in America, either. There had been years of a severe economic depression and there was much unemployment. Bobby had in his first months in the U.S.A. tried to get a job as a doctor, but he had by now found out that would be impossible. He would have to go back to medical school in America for at least a year and take all his exams over again in English. Under these circumstances, he counted himself lucky to have found a job as an orderly in a big Harlem hospital. He did not tell me how much he earned, but clearly it was very little. If he would have to go back to medical school, it meant I would have to support myself and him for several years. Whatever skills I could amass would be helpful. So I did nothing about my bad employment situation.

Then the lawyer took the occasion when his wife and the children were not in the house to make a pass at me in the hallway. I shook him off and threatened to tell his wife, which only seemed to amuse him. But he never tried it again.

Once more, I considered telling my father, but I was not sure he would believe me. Or if he did, it might upset him enough to bring on another heart attack. What was the point? It became clear to me that my boss had done this without much interest in me, simply out of boredom and to get what he considered his due—probably he thought it was part of my job. Obviously, from his response to my threat of telling his wife, such things had happened before and he was not afraid of his wife's reaction. Still, I found a way of hinting to Lizbeth that I'd just as soon not be left alone in the house with her husband. She picked up on it at once and fell into a flood of profanity.

Was he at it again? The sonofabitch, the filthy bastard, she'd had it out with him so many times . . .

Then, as though my complaint had authorized her, she unburdened herself to me, telling me the story of her miserable married life, his constant adulteries, his humiliation of her, his indifference to the children, the shame he was causing her. I ended up comforting her. We would be in alliance against him; this time he would not get away with it.

So I now really was a member of the family. Strangely, the incident improved my situation, not by lessening Lizbeth's demands on me, but by making me feel stronger, making me feel in the position of having something to give. Lizbeth was a neurotic, obsessive and miserably unhappy woman and I could be her friend and ally, instead of simply being an exploited domestic worker. This shift in our power relations made my work easier to bear; it was subtle, but decisive. I learned something from it that I would later use to help me understand the history of slavery and of exploited workers: the situation between them and their bosses could never be seen simply as a history of victimization. There always existed the possibility of some interaction, which could alter power relationships.

All within limits, though—the one who paid the wages would always have the upper hand. The limits of my relationship with Lizbeth became clear to me one night, when her husband was out of town on a business trip. She invited me to share a bottle of wine with her, after the children were asleep. We sat in her bedroom, on the double bed, sipped wine and told stories, and for a while it was really cozy and nice. The wine was getting to me and I felt a little hazy, so that it took me some time to understand that she had begun to fondle me and touch me in a way not unlike her husband. This was new to me; no woman had ever done this before. When I tried to get up, she pulled me back onto the bed and hugged me to her.

I finally managed to get free. "You're drunk, Lizbeth."

"No," she said. "I really like you. Don't you see how lonely I am."

"You're drunk."

I made it back to my room, cold sober now, feeling more violated than I ever had in my life. First he, then she—I was just an instrument for them with which to hurt each other. They could do whatever they wanted to me and I could do nothing. The respectable lawyer, my father's friend, and his respectable church-going wife, with me they felt neither shame nor constraint because I was a person without rights. I could do nothing; they trusted to that and they were right. Accusations would cause a scandal that would hurt my father, not them. Leaving their employment abruptly and without explanation would lead to the same.

I cried that night and I thought hard about reality, that reality I wanted my mother to face and that I had not yet quite learned to face myself. I thought about my options, made several plans and in the end discarded them all. It would go on as before until my visa came. As a refugee in Europe I was helpless; I would have to count myself lucky just to be alive and have a roof over my head. My hope for becoming a person with some rights and with dignity lay only in America. I was going to be an immigrant, not a refugee. An immigrant. A thin blade of grass, green as hope, cracked through the frozen ground.

[8]

I SAT IN THE TRAIN traversing the gentle landscape of Southern France. The nightmare of Nazi-occupied Austria, the difficult year in Liechtenstein—all that was behind me. I had said goodbye to my sister, who was safe in Switzerland, assuring her I would see her soon. Leave-taking from my father had been more peaceful than I had anticipated; he had mellowed in the last year after his heart attack. Now he even approved of my forthcoming marriage to Bobby, which turned out to be the lifesaver for the whole family. We parted in peace.

Looking back on it now, I can see how blessed it is that we do not know what the future holds. My father already sensed that he would never leave Europe and the grace with which he made my leave-taking easy was a blessing I could not then appreciate. It must have been terribly hard for him to let me go and give me that hope of reunion. Or perhaps, that early, he still believed that he, too, would make it. He always had an optimistic outlook on life. It was March 1939 and Europe was still at peace, although Hitler had taken over Czechoslovakia and no one believed he would stop there. I tried to think of what lay ahead of me—marriage, a new beginning in an unknown land where I knew not a soul except Bobby. It seemed unreal, yet I held on to it as something I must believe in, something as tangible as a rescuer's life raft.

The hills rode by, the pink houses, the old stone fences. Van Gogh's country, the tender landscape of Daudet and Maupassant. It did not seem real to me that such landscapes could still exist in this age of tyrants and refugees. I was worried about my mother. In France, she had to exist on the always precarious tolerance of visitors' visas, grudgingly extended to German refugees every few months. But then, I reassured myself, this was merely temporary. They would all get their U.S. visas soon. I was going to spend two weeks with her in Cagnes before my embarkation for America in Le Havre.

She was waiting at the station. In her loose dirndl skirt with her bare legs in sandals she looked like the Hungarian peasant woman her grandmother had been. Her black short hair glistened in the noon sun, her skin was tanned and her embrace was firm. "It's impossible," she cried. "You've grown more beautiful."

"Oh stop it." Her effusions about my looks always embarrassed me. I thought I was kind of neat-looking at best, but certainly not beautiful.

"Darling, you'll love it here. Wait till I show you around. There is so much to do I don't know where to begin."

"Let's begin with the luggage." We carried the two heavy suitcases to the bus stop, making a little joke of our strength. My two heavy packing-cases full of household goods had been shipped directly to the boat by the freight-handler.

"So how are you?" I asked.

"Gerda, the sun has cured me. I need the sun more than I need bread. I spend hours lying naked in my room, the windows wide open, the light flooding in. You must try it, it will restore you."

The bus took a steep winding road along the coast and it was more beautiful than the picture postcards: the lushness of vegetation, the profusion of roses, geraniums and hibiscus against the dark trees, cypress, eucalyptus and cedars; the houses in these unbelievable pastels. The riot of colors oppressed me.

"Are you happy here?" I asked my mother.

"It's a good place."

The bus stopped in the tiny village square, around which the houses grew like honeycombs up the sides of the hills. An old woman all in black passed us, carrying a long loaf of bread under her arm. *"Ah, bonjour, Madame, c'est votre fille qui est arrivée?"*

My mother beamed. *"Oui, oui, c'est ma fille, bien sur."*

The old woman nodded approvingly. She was the carpenter's mother, Ili explained, a sweet old lady who lived in that little pink house by the vineyard. Ili had painted her; she had also painted the *charcutier*, a wild-looking sort of man who raised white pigeons. They offered food in exchange, which worked out well. As we walked through the village she entertained me with anecdotes about the people we passed; she knew the children by name and knew the lineage and exploits of the various cats. My mother always belonged; she was never a tourist.

"Voila." We stopped at a lime-colored house with a heavy door. Inside, we ascended in total darkness, a chill of damp earth and old stone enveloping us. The steps felt smooth and familiar, as though I had trod them all my life. We came to her door suddenly; as Ili pushed it open I could not keep from exclaiming, so startling and pleasant was the warmth of the sunlight after the darkness of the passage. The one large room had the high ceilings, the tall windows, the tile floors typical of Mediterranean houses. But the colors were unusual: rose, blue and gold, pervading the room with the luminous glow, the serene silence of early Renaissance painting. I sat down, feeling suddenly very weary.

From a tiny kitchen my mother brought a tray of white bread, goat cheese and honey. "That's just about all I can offer you. We usually eat in the restaurant." Her coffee was strong and delicious and I concentrated on it.

"Have some fruit." There were apples and apricots in a wooden chopping bowl and a single orange, polished brightly. "The orange is just for color, we never eat it."

On a shelf the brushes and paints stood in open jars. "Where do you work?" I decided to ignore the "we."

"I've been doing a lot of sketching outdoors. I'll show you some other time, Gerda."

Behind the old-fashioned brass bed stood the usual stack of canvasses, large sketch pads and frames. I was thinking that I had never seen her room look so neat before. Ili was no housekeeper; when she painted she paid no attention to anything else. Everything was too neat. I felt certain she had not worked in quite some time.

"Maybe you'd like to take a nap," she suggested. I agreed like a child, giving in to my weariness and apprehension. For a while she sat on the bed beside me, stroking my hair, and it seemed good and simple. But she could not stop herself. "What do you think of this dreadful bed?" she asked me. "All those brass knobs and twists. We call it 'the iron mistress.'"

"I don't like it." I pushed her hand aside and sat up. "Suppose you tell me who 'we' is?"

"Oh, just Guy. Guy Blanchard." She found something to do by the table. "Very nice, French, fairly young. He writes."

I might have known. We had gone through this before and I cannot honestly say that I blamed her. She was not a woman who could live without a man. Still, I was deeply disappointed.

"Gerda, I promise you it won't cut into our short time together." She might have read my thoughts. "Sorry I came right out with it that way. I planned to tell you later, but then I thought you'd be happy hearing about it, knowing I'm not lonely. He's a fine, gentle boy. Nothing can interfere with our two weeks, Gerda, please believe me, darling." She looked down upon me with her fine, expressive eyes and all the brightness had left her face. She looked worried and I could tell from her swollen eyelids, her stained fingers, that she had again been sleeping far too little and smoking far too much. I felt as though a heavy stone had been placed once more in the habitual spot upon my chest. "I believe you, Mother." Then I turned to the wall and pretended sleep.

I awoke much later, in darkness. Ili sat by the window, a silent massive figure. Her eyes looked straight ahead; her hands lay in her lap in an ancient and weary gesture. She is getting old, I thought both with pity and malice, she sits like an old woman in front of a fire, only the fire has gone out. I jumped out of the bed with noise; I would have turned on the light, but I did not know where the light switch was. Still, I did not startle her.

She followed my movements with her eyes only. "You slept so beautifully," she said with tenderness. "I remembered all the old times . . . It's a blessing to have you here." She said this earnestly, without the slightest awareness that such a phrase would make me wince with embarrassment. She was given to making such banal, deeply felt statements in regard to me.

"Well, I'm starved," I cried like the teenager I had been a few centuries ago. "Do we eat?"

"Of course. You may want to wash. Go in the kitchen, you'll find a towel and soap." The way she said it, I felt reprimanded.

"You don't need a light," she said. "Besides, all I have is candles. I told you I live like a peasant. You'll have to adjust for the time you are here."

For an instant I felt as though she had read my face as I was sleeping. My hidden thoughts crawled out like cockroaches—pride, arrogance, fear. I felt helpless, then angry.

"Yes, Mother," I replied in a false tone of humility that I took to be very cutting. But Ili said nothing. I went into the kitchen as I had been bidden, stumbling against a table leg in the dark and cursing loudly.

AS I HAD FEARED, Guy Blanchard was waiting for us at the restaurant. The scene was familiar: my mother walking ahead of us into the low-ceilinged room, the few guests glancing at us without lifting their heads, the young man rising at one of the tables, a polite and meaningless smile on his face.

I had my party manners; I sparkled with false vivaciousness, praising everything. I found the table charmingly located, the food superb, the local wine quite unusual. From time to time Ili looked at me sharply, but I smiled as one does at one's hostess at a party.

Guy Blanchard was no better than I had expected. He looked very young, but he had none of the health and vigor of the young men of my circle. His face was pale, with colorless eyelashes and very light eyes that gave him a helpless, almost blind appearance. There was something fawning in his stooped shoulders, the beseeching gestures of his freckled hands as he passed the food between us, poured the wine and tried his utmost to behave like a man of the world. All through the dinner I tried to discover what Ili could possibly see in him.

His voice was expressive; he seemed to know that it was his best feature. "Tomorrow let's show Gerda the sunset. And the American house—"

"There is so little time." My mother appealed from one of us to the other, distributing her attention impartially. "It's all so unreal . . . Remember that ridiculous leather cap you used to wear, Gerda? It seems only yesterday. She was so crazy about it, Guy, she wanted to wear it to sleep. And now look at her. A young woman going to America, about to be married . . . It makes me feel old." She tossed back her head in a gesture of bravery, displaying her fine neck and shoulders.

"My goodness," the young man said, regarding her with his pale eyes. "It's hard to believe you have a grown daughter at all. You look more like sisters." He managed to give it just the right inflection of spontaneous surprise. She can't possibly fall for this, I thought, a line as old as the world. She'll laugh in his face.

But Ili lifted her hands to her forehead, smoothed back her hair and smiled with pleasure. "Do you really think so, Guy?"

I ate my *omelette soufflée* slowly, with deliberate effort, as though I were eating pieces of plaster, and they talked on, talked on and on. Working for his dinner, I thought. She's blind to it. Two weeks of this, fourteen such meals and she doesn't even care how I feel—

I pushed my plate away and the wine glass fell. The cheap red wine we had been drinking spilled on the tablecloth and on the young man. He jumped up, dabbing angrily at his front with his napkin. His face blossomed out in patches of pink.

"Just sprinkle a little salt on the stain," Ili said sharply, whether more annoyed with him or me I could not say. "And sit down please, don't spoil our reunion. *Garçon,* more wine." Her capable strong fingers set the disordered table to rights. Her face was turned toward the fire, overcast by purple and orange tongues of light. It would not work and now she knew it, too, but she would not give in. Her self-control was remarkable, yet she wasted her time and energy on this foolish young man, this defiant, angry daughter. What it cost her no one would know.

These thoughts came quite naturally, for I loved her, still loved her passionately. Yet with a watchful eye and an adding-machine mind I took notice, later, that she picked up the check. And that the young man had quite regained his composure despite his wine-stained pants and put his arm into hers as we left the restaurant.

"YOU'RE DECEIVING YOURSELF about this boy."

The argument raged for several days. I had made up my mind to save my mother from Guy Blanchard. If this went on, how could she keep her self-respect? What if something like this were to happen in America? I felt righteous and determined.

"There seems to be some confusion in our relationship." Ili spoke pensively, her forehead flecked with the shadows from the candlelight. "You seem to feel you are responsible for me. I'm the mother and you're the child."

"That's touching. When you have no other answer you always come back to that. I haven't been a child in a long time. Are you going to deny that it suited you that way? You wanted us to have a friendship of equals. Well, you can't have it both ways. Equals must be free to criticize, not just admire. Don't hide behind your motherhood now when I say something you don't want to hear."

"How clever you are—and how cruel."

I sat down at her feet, looking up into her face. "There is nothing I want less than to hurt you."

"Oh, I know," she said. "That's why you are so expert at it."

"Don't you see you're hurting me, too? We have so little time together before I go away . . . How do you think I feel finding you in this situation, this impossible fellow sponging on you—"

"Wait a minute, what are you saying? That's monstrous. I don't believe my ears."

"You pay for him," I cried violently, moving away from her touch. "I saw it myself."

"My poor child . . ." She hugged her arms around her as though she were freezing. "I hope you never fall in love with a man who doesn't have the price of his meal."

"This has nothing to do with love. He's hard up; he flatters you. And you fall for it."

"Strange," she said in a remote and impregnable tone. "He may not love me, but he treats me more kindly than you, who love me so much. If he lies to me, which is possible, at least he is charitable."

"Look," I continued, pressing my advantage, "if you should find me with someone altogether unsuitable, compromising myself, what would you—"

"Enough." She jumped up in great agitation. "Enough. I will not listen to another word." She stood beside the bed, clutching the brass headboard. The light of the candle did not reach there; in the twilight the brass gleamed and her white hands seemed like ornaments upon it, detached from her body, which was in the shadows. I suddenly felt frightened.

"I forbid you to speak of this again. Do you understand? If you must judge me, keep it to yourself." The dignity in her broken, tear-choked voice suddenly gripped me. I listened with a growing feeling of misery. If I could have taken back the harsh and bold words I had spoken I would have. But that is never possible. All that crusading fire, that youthful certainty ran out of me. I felt the tears coming into my eyes.

"It must be my fault," my mother was saying. "It's true. I did lean on you too much when you were too young for it. I didn't have the strength then. And I can't have it both ways. Equals, very well . . . But then you, too, must be honest with yourself. You're jealous, poor child. I was afraid it would happen that way, but I could not bring myself to part from you with a lie. Would that have been better? It's so easy to interfere in the lives of others, so easy to be judgmental. There is a hardness in you that frightens me."

"Come here," she demanded. "Look in my eyes. My poor baby, you are not fighting me only, you're fighting yourself. I've never tried to protect you from life and its errors. Can't you give me as much confidence?"

I cried in her arms, then. I apologized and took back my words. We were up most of the night talking and explaining, searching for the kind of happiness we had found in such intimacies before. But all the time a little devil was sitting behind my eyes, telling me it was useless. Time was against me; I would have to leave and she would stay as she was.

FOR A FEW DAYS everything was quiet. We spent our time in an uneasy threesome, each of us making great efforts at politeness. Perhaps after all we might manage to make the remaining days run out without further conflict. Already, like a miser, I was hoarding good memories toward the lean years. I was constantly aware of the impending separation. It would be years, not months; it might be forever. Ili lived in the present and always ignored the future. The past, we had quickly discovered, was both unpleasant and controversial. There always remained the faithful conversational standbys: the local population, art, the theater, America. We whipped those topics around morning, noon and night until I grew desperately tired of conversation. But Ili and Guy seemed unable to tolerate silence.

"You've changed," said my mother at least ten times a day. "You've become tough. Well, no wonder. Maybe it's a good thing for what's ahead." She said it as though it were some personal treason on my part. "One wouldn't know you're about to get married for all you talk about it."

True enough. I seldom thought about it and never talked about it. In fact, in this year, Bobby had become distant for me, like a ghost. The statement that I was going to get married to him had no reality. Now I made an effort, more to give substance to it than to share anything with my mother. What it amounted to was that I did not know how I felt about it. I did not know what marriage would be like after this long separation. If one were to judge by our relationship of the past, it would be reassuring to be married, to be secure in his love, his need for me, especially in this vast new country. He had always been a good friend and he had kept his promise to bring me to America. One could trust him, that was one of his main strengths. But it was also frightening to think of all the impending changes in my life, too many new undertakings all at once. Who would I turn to if things did not work out?

"So it's a good thing you've gotten a little tougher," my mother said encouragingly, intuitively responding to my unspoken fears. What it made me feel was how much I needed her to come and be with me, for intimacy, for support, for our real and great love for each other.

Like a travel agent, I turned the talk to the wonders of America. We were by then well versed in *Life* and *Reader's Digest*. Ili had subscribed for several months to the Paris edition of the *Herald Tribune* but had given it up as a hopeless endeavor, since no one could make any sense out of the newspaper language and those mysterious headlines.

"I'll learn and I'll teach you, once I'm in America," I promised. We decided on the spot to go to Nice for the afternoon and watch the tourists and the busy traffic.

A DAY LATER, lying on the beach and watching the delicate dance patterns of the seagulls above the water I felt sad and a little impatient. A few more days and my new life would start . . . Already, my attitude toward Guy Blanchard struck me as somewhat exaggerated. A perfectly ordinary young man who had an affair with a woman old enough to be his mother. But who was my mother instead. What of it . . . The seagulls swooped, circled and cried their hoarse cries. I wondered what New York would be like when I first saw it and would I find Bobby much changed . . .

Guy and my mother were talking in their usual fashion. To be alone, I went in for a swim. I enjoyed the choppy water, the struggle for breath, the force of the waves that tossed me and pulled me so that I had to use all my skill to fight them. I stayed out for a long time. When I came back I found Guy alone.

"Where is Ili?"

"Up at the house. Fixing something special for dinner."

I spread my towel and stretched out to dry, ignoring him.

"You do not like me." Guy put it somewhere between an accusation and a question.

I narrowed my eyes against the sun. "Right. Any reason why I should like you?"

"You mother and I—don't you believe that I love her and want to make her happy?" He used his elegant voice to great advantage. Only it made me laugh.

"How old are you, Guy?"

"Twenty-four."

"My mother is forty-two."

"I know that. I know that quite well." He wore a blue turtleneck sweater and white shorts, looking very French and much younger than twenty-four, yet his face was unblinking with a brashness I did not trust. "It is no argument at all. You must be much younger than nineteen if you have not yet learned that age has nothing to do with emotions. When two people are attracted to each other . . ." He looked at me in a cold, appraising way. *Touché.* It was not so long ago I myself had been in love with a man twice my age. The thought confused me. There was something in the way his eyes changed that increased my discomfort.

"Excuse me for presuming on our peculiar relationship," he said with precision. "I would like to ask you a personal question. Are you in love with that young man in America?"

"Of course," I answered. "Certainly."

Now he regarded me with an intensity that was unmistakable. "Then you're more complicated than I thought."

"I'll be going now. I'm dry."

"Wait," he insisted. "Are you afraid of me?"

"You must be crazy."

Suddenly his hand was on my arm. He had always been so polite and sub-servient that his gesture now caught me by surprise. Unexpectedly, his voice and his hand seemed to work together. "You don't understand yourself," he said insistently. "You're jealous, Gerda. That's what it is."

"Of you? Now I know you're crazy."

"No, no," Guy whispered softly. "You're jealous of your mother."

Words failed me. I tried to free my arm, but Guy had a strong grip and the struggle seemed to amuse him. He pinned me down with his other arm. "Let go of me. I'll shout."

"Spirited thing, aren't you? Full of fire. Go ahead, shout. Your mother will be very pleased at the scene."

"Dirty dog."

He forced his mouth on mine, pressing my arms and shoulders into the sand. I stopped myself from breathing, it was too revolting. I had enough sense to realize that struggle would only prolong it, so I just made myself dead.

He finally let go of me. I shuddered and walked away, knee-deep into the water. I bent down and threw water into my face with shaking hands. I was crying. I did not cry for love betrayed, for weakness or guilt. I cried for shame, shame for this man who did not have the decency of discretion, shame for my mother who had ended up with someone like this. Shame for myself, the girl, the child . . . That passionate adoration of my mother in my adolescence, that infatuation with her, her friends, these other men . . . Why had I not seen it then, whatever had made me idealize her, blind to her failings . . . The bitter, long-deferred pain had finally come to settle where it belonged.

Guy was waiting for me, now abject and worried. "I don't know what came over me; you must forgive me. Please—"

I stopped him with a gesture. "Just don't come near us while I'm around. Stay away, earn your meals elsewhere."

I stood on the beach for a long while, watching him climb up the hill to the village. He was gone; only the seagulls and I were left to share the sunset. It was slowly getting cool.

Now it was as it should have been from the beginning: between her and me; between myself and my childhood. By the time I started up the hill, the sun had disappeared.

IT WAS NIGHT IN THE ROOM except for the small pool made by the candles, one on the table, one on the chest, one on a chair beside the bed. The tile floor and plaster walls sent up a chill of dampness.

"Guy was here," Ili said at once. "He told me everything."

"Told you what?"

She puffed on her cigarette and smiled contemptuously. "You had an argument, he thinks he upset you. He is afraid he causes trouble between us."

I sat down at the table, which was laid for two. "I'm sorry it had to happen. Did he say anything else?"

"Forget it," she said. "You could not help it."

She began to serve the food, which was more carefully prepared than usual. Only after our plates had been filled and she was seated opposite me on the straight-backed chair did she answer my question. "He said a lot of things and most of them were lies. I sent him away myself. It is true he causes trouble." She said it quietly, with an air of sarcasm. I had prepared an elaborate explanation; her attitude deprived me of any chance to launch it.

"Will he come back after I'm gone?"

"That is none of your affair," said my mother.

"But it is. If it concerns you, it concerns me. You can't suddenly destroy what's between us."

"Gerda," she said in a tone of severity that frightened me, "you know very well that it's been destroyed already."

Another truth served out on a platter . . . Oh, for an end to this battle! I hated this room suddenly, the prison bareness of its huge walls, the hard contrast of its textures. I sat on the bed; there was no place else to sit and the brass knobs gleamed like evil eyes. On the table the one orange lay darkly in its bowl. "There's no use acting like I'm to blame, Mother. You sent him away but you're mad at me. I tried my best to fit into this situation here."

"You certainly did. That makes three of us who tried."

"Don't say that. Don't equate me with him. Maybe all these years didn't count with you, they were just wiped out when he appeared on the scene. Just don't put me on a level with him." My voice beat against the shadows of the room. "Do you know what really happened down at the beach? I wasn't going to tell you, but you might as well know."

As I told her she sat impassively, looking at me with eyes that veiled their disappointment. "I guessed as much and I'm not really interested. Your frankness, in my opinion, does you no credit."

I had shot my bolt and it had bounced off stupidly. "He's making a fool of you—"

"That is none of your affair," she repeated coldly.

We sat in silence. I wondered how many nights of such silence had given her this calmness. I wondered at her pride, which was so much greater than mine. My efforts at instructing her seemed suddenly contemptible. My judgment of her shriveled and wavered in the flickering candlelight. *"If he lies to me, at least he is charitable . . ."* I had not wanted to tell her about the beach, so help me, I had wanted to spare her. He, too, had said he was sorry.

"Mother, why am I saying these things? What am I doing?"

She sobbed, drawing me to her and cradled my head in her arms. "You're trying to destroy our relationship," she whispered. "You're rejecting me. That's what it is. You're young and you have to free yourself from me. I understand, I understand."

"But I love you so much . . ." In her embrace I felt warm and comforted. "Everything's all right now," I mumbled. "You forgive me, don't you? You'll come to America and we'll live together always. It'll be even better than it used to be . . ."

"You hush now," she crooned. "Hush . . . you're not to blame."

I DON'T THINK I WILL EVER FORGET the few remaining days. Like an island suspended in place and time they were filled with a quiet kind of happiness, different from any we had known in the past. We talked little; we walked along the shore, sometimes we swam great distances. We sat in the dunes, long afternoons, and watched the birds. In the evening my mother took out her sketch pad and, remembering the day's impressions, filled page after page with her sharp, expressive lines. I felt that already the passage from past to future had been bridged. Like the good fairy in the tales, my mother had equipped me, the adventurous child poised for a long and hazardous journey, with magic sources of strength in the face of danger. We never saw Guy nor did we mention him again.

ON THE LAST MORNING Ili was up before me, opening the shutters to let the sun wake me. She had washed and dressed and made up her face, but the powder could not hide the dark circles under her eyes. I rushed up and kissed her and made her laugh with some foolish joke. The bus was leaving at ten; she would come with me to Nice and take me to the train. I had saved my surprise until the last moment to make the farewell easier. Now I could not wait.

"Close your eyes," I cried and put the package in her lap. "You can look now."

She opened the large box and I could see that she was holding back the tears. "Oh, it's beautiful. It's so extravagant, darling, so beautiful . . ."

It was a large artists' paint box with oil and watercolors, something she had been wanting for a long time but had not been able to afford.

"It's an investment," I said. "You'll do a lot of designs with this, for fabrics and ties and wallpaper. When you come to America you'll sell them and we'll all be rich."

"Thank you," she said, walking over to the window. "The bus will be here soon."

"I'm all packed."

She stood against the yellow shutter looking heavy and middle-aged and making no effort to hide it. "I'm not going to America," she said.

"But of course you are."

She stopped me with a gesture. "Understand me, Gerda. I'm not going because I do not want to. You've grown up, my darling, and your life lies before you. Unfortunately, I've never been a normal kind of mother—I think it's too late for me to start now. No, I could not live with you and Bobby and help with the dishes. It would be hopeless. I could not learn to draw designs and fit my talent to the need of drawing ads for perfume or soap to make money. I can live here, just about, on the little money I've left. It would not be enough to live on over there. Besides, I don't want to. I'm tired of new places. That country never did appeal to me, anyway—I don't like their gaudy movies. Please, darling, don't look so horrified. I've known this for a long time."

"It's because of what happened with Guy—" I had not wanted this; it was inconceivable.

"Guy . . ." She laughed. "Maybe twenty years from now you will understand this. No, it's not because of him."

I just stared at her.

"Despite the appearances, I give myself over to very few illusions. But I don't have limitless resources of strength and warmth. Sometimes, you just need to be with another person. Sometimes, when you live without roots, you make your roots by setting up a home. Even if it's just a bare, cold room shared with a weak and confused young man with some talent. There is a price on everything, Gerda. There is a price on survival, too."

"My God . . ."

"I'm tired," she said. "I'm very tired from having lived a strenuous life. I don't mean to go under and I don't mean to lose myself. I will paint, my best work has not been done yet. I will survive—on my own terms."

The tiles of the floor were blue, pink and gold and the light from the window was rose-colored and gentle. My mother was dark and heavy, a peasant woman with an ancient face. I kissed her and cried, but it was like kissing a statue.

We walked down to the square together, carrying my suitcases, the way we had, long ago, carried the mattresses in prison. The bus pulled in and the cat on the stoop licked his paws. "I'm not coming to Nice either," said my mother. "No use prolonging this."

"Listen," I cried, "all of this is nonsense. The Consulate will send the visa and I will send the money and you will come to America, just as it was arranged. Bobby and I will stay out of your way if you want, you can have your own life. Do you hear?"

The flies buzzed in the baker's window. The bus driver came out of the restaurant, hitching up his pants.

"You must take care of yourself on the boat," she said. "And you must write, just the same, so I don't have to worry."

"Mother, I love you, I need you with me. Please, you think it over."

The bus driver lifted my suitcases into the trunk and came around the front to collect my ticket.

"You will come to America," I insisted.

She embraced me, then pushed me away. I climbed into the bus. I put my hand out the window and felt her fingers, strong and warm and hard with knowledge.

"God bless you," she said, like the women in prison.

"I'll see you in September," I lied. "I'm sure of it."

The bus started rolling and she let go of my hand.

"Au revoir in September."

She was shaking her head. All the long time while the bus was winding its way down the mountain road I could see her, back there in the little village square, strong and wise and dry-eyed, shaking her head. The delicate landscape of pastels and sunshine stood behind her like a horrible wild joke.

I never saw her again.

11

BECOMING AN
AMERICAN

[9]

I ARRIVED IN THE UNITED STATES in April 1939 after a terrible voyage of seasickness, loneliness and fearful anticipation. As the ship passed within sight of the Statue of Liberty, immigration officials processed all passengers in the large social room below deck. I waited and waited; the hours seemed to pass slowly and when my turn came and I was asked to step aside and wait some more, I became very frightened. Almost everyone had left the ship by now and still I was waiting with a handful of others. As the others were processed before me, I realized that we were the problem cases—some were handed their papers, others were led away in tears by an officer. I was sure now that something was terribly wrong—they would deny me entry; they would send me back.

The official who endlessly examined my papers questioned me closely about each of the six affidavits of support I had submitted. They had already been approved by the U.S. Consul in Switzerland, but apparently this official had the right to cancel the Consul's decision. Did I know any of these people who were sponsoring me? Who was this person, Bernard Jensen, who was my main sponsor but only had an income of fifty dollars a month?[1] No, I had no relatives here, except my father's second cousin who had not given me an affidavit. Bernard Jensen was my fiance and his relatives had given me an affidavit. On and on and

---

1. Bobby had changed his last name during his immigration process from Jerusalem to Jensen.

over the same ground again. Finally, a strange question—where did I expect to stay on my arrival?

I instantly became cautious; this was some kind of trap. I don't know; I expect my fiance will have made some sort of arrangement for me. Did I have hotel reservations? No.

Long pause and much shuffling of paper. Consultation among the two officials. I began to panic. Is something wrong, I asked. Are you saying I can't land?

"Did you ever hear of the Mann Act?" the official asked.

"No."

"You are eighteen years old?"

"I'll be nineteen next month. Why, what is the matter?"

"The Mann Act forbids the entry of unattached female minors into the U.S.A."

I did not understand anything about that law, but I understood they were making serious trouble. What did unattached mean? What were they worried about? "I'm meeting my fiance and his family, what's wrong with that?"

"I'm afraid you may have to go to Ellis Island," the official said. "We may have to deny you entry."

"You can't do that. I have no place to go. I was deported from Austria by the Nazis, they'll kill me if I come back. You can't do that—please, don't do that." He finally had me in tears.

"Well, just a minute, Miss. Don't get excited. I have to go by my regulations. Just wait."

I don't know if I was alone in that great hall or if there were others still waiting to be processed. It seemed to me I was alone at the end of the world—totally helpless and abandoned. I had no one to advise me, no Consul to whom I could appeal. If they sent me back to Austria, which is what I thought they would do, because I came with a German passport, I'd be sent straight to the concentration camp—the police had told me that often enough. In my German passport, with the swastika on the outside cover, my name was doubly underlined and I knew that was the signal for customs that I was a Jew and was to be jailed on reentry. Later, the Germans would attach the name Sarah and Israel to every Jewish person's passport, but when I traveled that was not yet done. As I sat there, I had no hope whatsoever that U.S. immigration officials would be merciful and let me stay. From all I knew, nothing had been done by the U.S. government to make any special allowances for Jewish refugees. To whom could I appeal? The Swiss Consul? The League of Nations? Truly, I felt doomed.

When the official came back, Bobby was with him, agitated and arguing. He shouted at me from across the table: "Don't worry, I'll get you out."

I was too afraid to move. The official sat down and addressed me sternly, like a schoolteacher. "Your cousins are here to take you home," he said. "Why didn't you tell me in the first place?"

What cousins? I kept my mouth shut. Bobby had worked out something, but what? "Joseph and Hilda," he said helpfully. "You know they live in New York."

"Oh, yes. I forgot." Joseph and Hilda were acquaintances from Vienna. I had no idea they lived in New York, but anyway—maybe there was some hope . . .

But it was clear the official did not believe us. He turned to Bobby. "I explained the Mann Act provisions to you, Mr. Jensen," he said sternly. "Violation thereof is a deportable offense. You claim to be engaged to this young lady. Very well, Immigration will require her to bring proof of marriage before we will grant her permission to stay."

"Certainly," said Bobby. "We plan to get married." He stood there as I remembered him, short, combative, ugly and utterly reliable. I felt so grateful to him for rescuing me, for having waited all this year for me.

"Step forward," the official said. "I will ask you to sign this paper, which specifies that you will submit proof of marriage to Immigration within one week of today. Failure to do so will mean immediate deportation." I signed without reading what he put in front of me. I would have signed anything.

They let me get off the ship; they did not send me to Ellis Island. Joseph and Hilda were waiting with my luggage; they shook hands and hugged me and Bobby thanked them warmly. "I thought they'd put her on Ellis Island," he said over and over again. "Without you they would have."

We walked to a taxicab together, but Joseph and Hilda excused themselves. "You two will want some time alone."

Perhaps, perhaps not. The seasickness seemed to come on me again, now that I stood on solid earth. Everything kept moving up toward me, pavement, taxi, luggage. I thought I'd get sick. Now that I was here I did not want to be here. Bobby pushed me into the cab. "You're just exhausted," he said. I cried most of the way.

BY THE TIME WE REACHED BROADWAY I began to feel a little more reasonable. Bobby was nervous, I could tell from the flood of words that were coming from him, endless comments on sights we were passing, chit-chat, anything so as not to have to really look at me, touch me, resume the contact we had lost on the day of my arrest, almost a year ago. That was the last time I saw him, for he had left while I was still in jail, promising to send for me. Which he had; which he did; for which I owed him gratitude for the rest of my life. Here I was and he did not know how to face me and I did not know what to say or do. So I learned a lot about Broadway.

We pulled up in front of a nondescript, shabby apartment building on West Ninety-Fifth Street. Bobby paid the cab driver and dragged my suitcases into the lobby. "Wait here," he said. "I'll get help with the big boxes." I had brought two boxes filled with household goods and two red featherbeds, the indispensable centerpiece of a European girl's dowry. Maybe if I could have unpacked those for customs, they would have let me right in. Anyway, Bobby disappeared and I sat down on my suitcases in the lobby.

"You must be Gerda," a young woman said to me in German. She had come down with the elevator and was holding the door open. "Come on, I'll take you upstairs. We've been waiting for you." She took my suitcases.

"Bobby said to wait," I protested.

"It's all right," she said firmly. "I'll show you the way. He'll come up when he's through."

In the elevator she introduced herself. "I'm Lilo." She was very pretty, about my age, energetic, with a cheerful smile.

"I'm Gerda," I said stupidly.

"I know."

"Yes, how did you?" The elevator stopped and Lilo dragged the suitcases out.

"Your picture," she said. "Bobby talks about you all the time." She opened a door with a key she had in her pocketbook and moved into the room ahead of me. "Here you are."

I saw a narrow room with a window at one end. There were a couch, two straight chairs near a table by the window and a small chest of drawers. My photo hung in a central place above the couch.

"We must become friends," said Lilo. "I also live in this building, as do our other friends. I got here a year ago, so I know how you feel. Bobby has told me so much about you."

Our friends. The key. I just wanted her out.

Bobby pushed the door open. "I put the boxes in the basement—hey, Lilo, I thought I told you—"

"I'm just going," she said perkily. "You two must have a lot to talk about. See you soon."

"She's a busybody," Bobby said, and at once he began to explain the housing arrangements to me, the amount of rent he paid, his salary, his work schedule and on and on.

He offered me food, which I declined. "I'm just exhausted, I'd like to go to sleep."

"The couch opens up to two beds," he explained helpfully, and he jumped up to demonstrate. "But listen, first we really must talk about tomorrow. I have to get up at 5 A.M. and go to work and I want to explain the geography of this place to you so you can get around." Very helpful, very kind. He had a map all prepared and spread it out on the floor. We crouched over it, peering at the gridiron lines of streets. "New York is such a convenient place, any child can find his way around it. The north-south streets are parallel and so are the east-west streets. Fifth Avenue is in the middle and each block the numbers change by the hundreds." I looked at the neat and helpful map of New York and I thought perhaps I could choke him right now. Perhaps just walk out and go—where?

The map offered endless possibilities of evasion. Bobby explained Manhattan geography, ever helpful. "All right," I interrupted. "What's with this Lilo?"

One thing about Bobby and me and our relationship, we did not lie to each other. He did not know how to do it and neither did I. He stopped chattering and I got it, straight between the eyes, as I had asked for it.

It was just an affair, nothing serious and it was over, but she was a bitch, she had to do this little act to show her power over him—it was the last thing he wanted to happen when I'd just arrived and—

"Are you in love with her?"

"Never. Look, it's been a year, I'm no saint."

"You're a bastard," I said. "It's been a year for me too and I managed—" He tried to touch me and I knocked his hand away. "Now what will I do . . ."

"Just ignore what happened," he said. "We can start from where we left off."

It seemed I had no choices. "What's this law the Immigration was citing?"

Bobby was glad to change the subject. "It's to prevent prostitution." He laughed, with some embarrassment. "They're afraid I imported you to become a prostitute."

"Oh . . . that's why he asked about my age. I'm in a fine fix. I must marry you, whether I feel like it or not."

"You don't feel like it now," Bobby said sadly. "I was afraid of that."

"What do you expect, with such a welcome."

"I want us to get married," Bobby said firmly, in the tone he used when he had long deliberated something and his mind was fixed. "Lilo means nothing in my life. You do. We'll make it work."

I felt incredibly weary suddenly, as though I had aged rapidly. I had to marry Bobby within the week, so we might as well try and make it work. "I want to go to sleep," I said. "Alone."

He was nothing if not accommodating. He prepared my bed, made tea for me and dimmed the light. The narrow room was noisy with the perpetual roar of West Side traffic. It was just another kind of jail cell. It was not what I had expected.

And so I feel the U.S. Immigration Service owes me, for a bad marriage. One and a half years of struggle and misery and a divorce. Still, seen in some perspective, it was not a bad price to pay for becoming an American.

THE NEXT YEAR AND A HALF was a period of transition and of incessant learning. First of all, being poor. It was different from the way we had been poor in Europe in the months right after our emigration, because there was always enough to eat, there was a decent apartment and if one really needed something desperately there were relatives with some money to whom one could appeal. In New York it was poverty without a fallback. Neither Bobby nor I had any idea of the resources New York City offered to the poor, such as employment services, counseling, retraining and temporary welfare. We were convinced, and rightly so, that our immigrant status obliged us to be self-supporting and that any contact with any agency whatsoever was dangerous to our status. Although we later learned that the Hebrew Immigrant Aid Society (HIAS) and Jewish welfare agencies helped thousands of refugees like us, we never contacted them. Suddenly, then, I was poor the way the poor are—without any reserve money in the bank, without any relatives to fall back on, without the network of support one usually has if one lives long in a community.

We could just about manage. Bobby's princely salary of fifty dollars a month with occasional overtime secured our room (fifteen dollars a month) and minimal food. He got a hot meal at the hospital at noon and usually managed to bring some leftovers home for me. Carfare for job-seeking was a big expense and I learned to save a nickel a day by first riding the subway to Times Square where the *New York Times* want ads were displayed on large billboards in the Times Building. I would note down all the openings and do all my midtown job applications on foot. I tried for every kind of work but did not get very far. My English was poor and my expensive, well-cut European clothes—the only clothes I had—marked me at once as a recent immigrant. Usually, the second question asked was my undoing. Where have you worked before? I truthfully answered, Nowhere in this country and I was a governess in Europe for a year. "Sorry, we need references." My try-outs at factory jobs were equally hopeless. I had never seen machinery, much less worked at it, and my finger skills have never been good. I was usually fired the first hour. After a few months of this I was so desperate for work, I tried housework. That, too, failed. I went out for a few day-work jobs, tried to follow all instructions and worked hard at scrubbing and cleaning. But usually by lunchtime the lady of the house would get suspicious of me and start questioning me about my past, previous experience, etcetera. When I answered truthfully, I was fired. "You wouldn't be happy in this kind of work, with your education."

It was not only that I was unskilled and obviously a recent immigrant. I lacked contacts and necessary advice. Everyone I knew was a refugee and those who had found work either had previous skills or had relatives who had helped them. It was also the Depression. I knew little about it, except that in every job line there were dozens of applicants. Employment agencies would not even take your application, if you could not show references and previous jobs.

It took six months of unemployment for me to learn to lie. A friend helped me to construct a phony life story and primed me on what questions to watch out for. Never admit to having anything but a high school education. Don't say you're a refugee; don't say you're Jewish. Get some phony reference letters; pretend you've been here two years. Don't ask any questions; don't volunteer any information.

During this period I was utterly dependent on Bobby, which made the problems of our marriage more intractable. Money was not ever an issue between us and he was always generous to the best of his ability, but it was simply that I could not have survived without him; therefore I tried as hard as I could to make our marriage work. There were short periods of happiness and good feelings, but mostly it was a work-and-expense-sharing partnership full of tensions.

I had moved into his life and his circle, which consisted of a group of German-speaking antifascist refugees, mostly under thirty, and an older group of German-Americans. The latter were our only tie to American life, for most of them had been in the country for decades or were native-born. What held the group together was its determination not to be confused with pro-Nazi Germans and its sense of responsibility for upholding German democracy in exile. It was a highly political circle. The older German-Americans had their hiking club, Nature Friends; their *Turnverband* and cultural clubs; their insurance circle and their trade unions. The recent young immigrants considered themselves temporary political exiles who expected to return to their homelands after fascism was destroyed. They spoke only German, read only German newspapers and lived in a European world transposed to uptown Manhattan.

I felt ill at ease with that group from the beginning. First of all, I balked at being defined as a German-American or a German exile and felt much more comfortable with the handful of Austrian exiles among this group. Then, as it happened, most of them were not Jewish—they were working-class political antifascists. What I perceived as being poor, they regarded with pride as being working class. In order to get along with them and not create conflict I had to suppress my own life experience and pretend to be a good proletarian. They had me convinced for many months that I was indeed unworthy of being accepted by them and would have to change my ways, my outlook and my convictions. The leaders of the youth group were genuine resistance heroes in Germany; they had been in jail; one had fought in Spain, others in the underground. I admired them and tried to win their friendship but never succeeded. Yet they accepted Bobby. He basked in the reflected glory of his brother, the Spanish veteran; his political understanding was considered impeccable; like the others he was comfortable in his role of political exile.

I HAD A DIFFERENT ATTITUDE toward America than these young people had. I had fallen in love with the country. I still remember that first day—Bobby worked at a hospital in Harlem and he had instructed me how to walk cross-town on 125th Street and meet him for lunch. I did that and had my first experience of seeing black people in a black part of town. I found it incredibly fascinating. I thought Blacks were the most beautiful and interesting people I had ever seen, and responded like an excited tourist to the liveliness, noise, diversity and strangeness of Harlem. I smiled at everybody and got many smiles in return, which fixed in my mind the impression that Blacks were much more outgoing and friendly than other people. I took this cross-town walk daily for many weeks, and in the summer of that year, when I took a training course at Sydenham Hospital to become an X-ray technician, I also worked in Harlem. Sydenham was virtually a black hospital and I stopped being a tourist and a romantic as I dealt with the injured, the sick, the disturbed, but I never lost my feeling for Harlem as a culture, a community. In my innocence of the forms of U.S. racism, I acted quite unself-consciously with Blacks and was perhaps for that reason readily accepted by them. I ate my lunches in the parks with black mothers and their children or with the homeless idlers on park benches and I never felt alienation or hostility or danger. These things have to be learned and they are learned by every white person in America. Today I could not do what I did then without self-consciousness.

My biggest treat in those months was a ten-cent ride on the upper deck of the Fifth Avenue bus from Washington Heights to Greenwich Village. It revealed New York as nothing else could and I loved all of it. I wanted to be a part of this city, this country, learn the language, cease being an outsider.

After months of fruitless searching for a job, I decided I had to acquire a marketable skill. Fortunately, my uncle Richard in Switzerland was willing and able to help me pay for my training with a gift of several hundred dollars. I decided to become an X-ray technician, an occupation that was always in demand and paid better than office or sales work.

I chose to take an X-ray training course at Sydenham Hospital in Harlem, mainly because it was cheaper than the other courses. The admissions director assured me that after three months of full-time training I would be able to pass the licensing exam and with it get a job. In fact, I found out after I had completed the training that I could not take the exam until I had another three months of hospital experience. I reluctantly did several months of unpaid volunteer work in another hospital in order to be able to pass the test. No sooner had I passed than I learned I was still unemployable because to get the license one had to have a full year's job experience. Obviously, I should have been better informed to begin with . . . Yet I loved the work and was proud of my new skills. As it turned out, I would have to wait several more years before the war opened up job opportunities for me in the medical field. Meanwhile, back to the job search for unskilled jobs.

As I struggled with the harsh reality of immigrant life, straining all my energies toward survival, toward making a success of my marriage and toward assimilating to my new culture, Europe kept pulling at me with a thousand strands.

Shortly after Germany invaded Czechoslovakia in May 1939, over the feeble and ineffectual protest of the Western powers, the Spanish civil war ended with Franco's victory. Defeated Loyalists swarmed across the French border, only to be arrested and placed in internment camps. I worried about my mother in Nice—once the French started interning some foreigners, it might not take them long to intern all foreigners.

My mother, meanwhile, had other concerns. Her young man had left her, taking a hundred dollars she had lent him. She had moved from the little village where I had last seen her to Nice, where there were many German and Austrian refugee artists. She was happy in her new apartment. My father came to visit her in May 1939 and she made plans with him about emigrating to England in case the situation in Europe got too dangerous for them. She assured me she was being realistic. She asked me to visit several people in New York who owed her money. She wanted me to take some of her pictures to New York galleries so she could secure an exhibit.

My father wrote in a different vein. He had serious health problems, which required a more restful lifestyle than he could now afford. The fact that he had to provide separate living arrangements for each member of the family put a great strain on his finances. He expected war to break out in Europe and felt it was essential for the family to leave Europe as soon as possible. The obstacles to emigration were enormous, but he worried most about his ability to support his family in a new land. He had finally decided that he would come to America, but only if he could be sure to support himself and his family. He had some medications on which he owned the patents and which he would try to market in the U.S.A. He, too, sent me lists of friends of his whom I should visit to secure outstanding small debts or other tangible favors.

It was clear from this correspondence that my parents had no idea of my actual situation. They thought I was comfortably married to a man who adequately supported me; his wealthy family would surely be interested in helping my family, if only I were nice enough to them; they thought I knew my way around, had numerous wealthy contacts and could, if only I wanted to, find sponsors for them, move the State Department to act more quickly and favorably on their behalf, and look after their various friends, acquaintances and contacts from Europe. They thought I had access to relief agencies, refugee support networks and the like.

I suppose I could and should have told them the truth in blunt terms: that I was living in poverty; that I had no way of personally contacting Bobby's relatives who lived in Florida; that Florida was as far from New York as Vienna was from London; that his relatives had already given twenty affidavits of support to various relatives and friends before our turn had come; that having given so many affidavits already, any they now might give would have little value in the eyes of the U.S. Consul; that I had no contact with refugee agencies and was afraid of them; that all the refugees I knew were young and poor. Possibly this might have helped, but I could not do it. I could not risk upsetting my father with his bad heart by bringing bad news. My mother needed above all to keep to a steady course and have some hope in the future—I could not see myself taking that away from her. Besides which, I needed to hold out some hope myself, for my mind and political sense told me that disaster was not far off.

As I piece this story together, the strands of it keep escaping me. I have letters in front of me, letters that passed between us and missed—coming too late, saying the inappropriate, lying, concealing out of a sense of love and a need to protect each other. I wrote cheerful letters, describing the attractions of New York City, talking in glowing terms of my happy married life and I ran as many of the distasteful errands my parents imposed on me as I could on my limited budget.

My mother, after a short visit to Nora and *Vati,* returned to Nice despite all good advice to the contrary. My father struggled on with serious health problems and spent the month of July in a sanitorium in Switzerland. All during that month events in Europe were heating up. War was in the air. Yet I continued to write to my mother as though everything were normal, as though the personal still mattered. On July 7, 1939, I wrote to her:

> What I'm doing now is living, nothing but catching life, learning, learning, not from books, but from actions, from making mistakes . . . seeking success, seeking friendship. I'm trying to let go of alien wrappings and to seek my own content. To find my true function. Up to now I have been a talented, multifaceted child. Now I feel I am becoming someone—either the great woman I am meant to be—or nothing. I'm taking risks, I'm gambling. My life is becoming a conscious life, everything is just beginning. We're strange, you and I. When we'll be a hundred, we'll still believe the world was created just this day. My dearest, my own—I'm very close to you.

In fact, I was frantic. With my limited contacts, I tried to secure affidavits and letters of support for them so that they might be classified as "immigrants" by the U.S. Consul in Zurich. With such a certification European governments were willing to give transit visas and even residence permits. U.S. consulates all over Europe were swamped with immigration applications, but they proceeded with infinite slowness on a business-as-usual policy while Europe was disintegrating. With the hindsight of half a century and with new documentation now available we can now say that this was a deliberate policy to discourage immigration. It was also arbitrarily carried out by the different Consuls in different countries. The U.S. Consul in Switzerland was known to go strictly by the book.

Securing an affidavit of support for my parents was only the first step in a seemingly endless bureaucratic process. The immigrant who had secured an affidavit of support acceptable to the U.S. Consul and who had passed a medical examination was then obliged to wait until his/her quota number came up. My mother was born in Hungary and therefore, according to immigration regulations, she fell under the Hungarian quota, while my father and sister, both born in Vienna, fell under the more favorable Austrian quota. The Hungarian quota had an eight-year waiting period on it. In July of 1939 we were mere amateurs at the immigration business. We still hoped that once I secured the proper affidavits, the U.S. Consul in Zurich would make allowances "to unite family members," as the law required.

I cannot think with anything but bitterness of the fact that the U.S. government under the presidency of Franklin Delano Roosevelt never did anything to change the racist and anti-Semitic quota system built into the 1924 Immigration Act. Had it done so, hundred of thousands of Jews might have been saved out of Europe, my mother among them. The fact that it could be done, with the stroke of a presidential pen, was shown when the Hungarian quota was suspended after the 1956 Hungarian rebellion in order to save anti-Communist Hungarians by the tens of thousands. None of this was done by the Roosevelt administration, except for the rescue of a thousand prominent intellectuals and artists. My mother was not famous enough to fall under that eligibility. I still have a thick folder in my files, filled with pleading letters I wrote to various people, including Mrs. Roosevelt, to ask them to intercede on behalf of my mother. I was turned down everywhere.

On August 21, 1939, my mother wrote from Nice:

Something drives me to work [on her painting] as though I had a warning. Hurry up. I'm not so young anymore, and have not accomplished anything yet . . . I will not come to America. I think, if there is no war, I will stay alone in France.

This serious focus on her work was new. I was happy about that, yet her almost weekly fluctuations in decisions about her future alarmed me. I expected her to make "reasonable" decisions, to be consistent, to be prudent. From where I was sitting, it seemed suicidal for her to stay in France, when she could be safe in neutral Liechtenstein. It immensely complicated the process of getting her immigration papers. Why was she so willful, so stubborn and unreasonable?

It was only six months since I had last seen my mother. Our visit had been so difficult, so full of good intentions badly carried out, so charged with misunderstandings and tensions, that I felt unable to free myself from its complexities. It was as though I were stuck in a bad nightmare and despite repeated efforts at awakening, I kept repeating the bad dream. I wanted, I needed desperately to straighten matters out between us, to make our relationship as close, as passionately intimate as it had been. Yet I seemed to see her in a new light, with an ever more critical eye. I was out of step with her needs, her despair, her efforts at finding the right direction. And she had no concept of my life in America, so that our letters, with all their old intense words of intimacy, were tragically out of touch. And from my distant vantage point I could see the clock ticking, the noose tightening. Europe was rushing to its doom.

AUGUST 23, 1939—HITLER AND STALIN SIGN "NON-AGGRESSION PACT."

Two days later I wrote to my mother:

Do you remember—on March 11, 1938 [the day of the *Anschluss*] I collapsed totally and could do nothing but cry, but then I did not cry for another year. This is the difference between earlier generations and ours: for us politics is life, for our lives depend on the form taken by our society. Probably this time, again, it's the way it was then—it's somewhat easier to stand it all when one is on the inside. It is easier to sleep with the gas mask next to one's bed than it is to sleep with the mental image of the one who sleeps with the gas mask. This sounds grotesque, but you and I know how true it is.

Five days later she wrote to me:

God give us strength to persevere. Send me an affidavit . . . At this moment the U.S. embassy here handles only the affairs of U.S. citizens. I tried to get a permit to visit Nora in Switzerland, but the border is closed. No telephone; telegrams are censored. The iron plate has been lowered, we are trapped. It is hopeless. Now my darling, I don't want you to worry about us. *Vati* and Nora are safe. Here in Nice it is more dangerous. An appeal was made to the population to urge those who do not urgently have to stay in Nice to evacuate the town and to move to the interior of the country. A lot of foreigners and emigrants have left. I won't, I'm not going to drive myself crazy. We are building a bomb shelter in our house. I have a gas mask and whatever happens to others will happen to me. Tomorrow I'll volunteer as a hospital aide, or maybe because of my languages I'll get assigned to office work. *There will be no war.* Everything was bearable until the Russian pact. That takes the last hope away. To the last minute I thought it was a trick, an error or maybe I don't understand it. Now, you can just lie down and despair.

In a letter written just a day after my mother's letter *Vati* informed me that he had secured a Swiss transit visa for her. She could now come to Vaduz and to safety, or she could stay in Nice. It must be her decision. He himself did not write for several weeks because he was still very ill. He needed five weeks of rest before he could go back to work.

SEPTEMBER 1, 1939—GERMANS INVADE POLAND FROM THE EAST; RUSSIANS INVADE POLAND FROM THE WEST. POLAND SURRENDERS.

SEPTEMBER 3, 1939—ENGLAND AND FRANCE DECLARE WAR ON GERMANY.

As my mother had said, the iron plate had been lowered. They were trapped, my family and all the others. With the fall of Czechoslovakia an entire branch of our family disappeared from view and many of them perished during the holocaust. My mother's sisters were in Holland. The Hungarian branch of the family seemed as yet relatively safe, since Hungary was an Axis partner. Some of the lucky ones of our Vienna relatives and friends were then in England—with the outbreak of the war they would, once again, be in direct danger. Looking at the daily changing map of Europe it seemed like an enormous trap in which my relatives and friends, my teachers, all the people I had loved and admired were rabbits around whom a huge net was being drawn, tighter and tighter. Thinking of them all, I felt frightened, hopeless. Nothing I could do would have the slightest impact on their lives and on their safety. I had to trust that they would act reasonably. Surely, my mother would leave Nice and seek safety in the interior of France. The French Army was strong and French defenses were supposedly secure against any attack.

Sixty years later and a continent away, I have asked myself and friends have asked me, What was my reaction to the Nazi-Soviet Non-Aggression Treaty? I pushed it aside at the time, too preoccupied with the fate of my parents and too panicked to attempt any interpretations. Instead I relied on the analysis that my experience had taught me to regard as a reliable predictor of the future. Ever since the Munich Agreement of 1938, it seemed clear to me that the European powers and Great Britain were not going to oppose Hitler's march across Europe. They expected him to march into the Soviet Union; obviously they hoped he would get bogged down in a long fight, which would weaken both fascism and Communism to the advantage of the big capitalist powers. This core belief of European antifascists was well grounded in the dismal foot-dragging of the former Allied powers in defense of the democratic government of Spain. This had been the testing ground, and democracy had caved in. Everything else followed from it: the signal to Hitler and the Axis powers was to proceed unhindered and to proceed eastward. I had no doubts about the accuracy of this analysis, even though I fervently hoped the democratic powers would see the error of appeasement in time. When the Hitler-Stalin Non-Aggression Pact was signed, it seemed to me a terrible but necessary step on the part of the Soviet Union to avoid or at least delay a German invasion. Sixty years later and with the information now available about the secret agreement between Stalin and Hitler to divide Poland between them, I no longer see it that way. Then, what preoccupied me most was a deep and painful conflict—I had become convinced that only war could stop Hitler from conquering Europe and so I wanted above all to see the Allies move against Hitler, to see the war begin that would eventually end the Hitler regime. Yet if this were to happen, my mother would be caught in the war. I think this personal conflict made me so judgemental and unforgiving toward her. At the time, that was the conflict I experienced and projected on my political judgment. The Nazi-Soviet pact was prolonging the period of uneasy peace. One part of me wanted that state of affairs to continue at all cost, just to save my mother. Another part of me wanted the conflict to begin.

In her next letter my mother wrote bravely of her intention to work in defense of the French. She tried to reassure me. "Be calm when you think of me. I have reached the point where nothing can happen to me. I can die, certainly. But you can do that only once. I ask myself, is reason still alive anywhere?"

OCTOBER 1939—ALL JEWS IN POLAND ARE ORDERED TO WEAR A YELLOW STAR AFFIXED TO THEIR CLOTHES.

Late in October, Ili's efforts at becoming a volunteer for the French war effort had apparently been thoroughly rebuffed. "Nobody here wants us or needs us," she wrote with a realism unusual for her. "I have to tell you that the situation is hopeless. I will not see you again. It's impossible to get out of this country now . . . what a terrible fate."

A letter from *Vati* written almost the same day was equally desperate. "I am stuck here in Liechtenstein. Since October 1 the Swiss require an entry visa; it took me three weeks to get it for one-time entry only. Now that I live all by myself in this tiny village, without family, friends or people close to me, I am sometimes close to despair." But his healthy optimism soon prevailed and he wrote about his plans for coming to America.

For several weeks, at this most crucial time, I was unable to write to them. My mother's letters took three to four weeks to reach me at a time when I was frantic for news, and when they did come they did not engage with the practical questions I so very much wanted answered. I could not write to disagree with her; I could not respond the way she seemed to want me to respond. I was out of touch, truly, and so I fell silent.

Early in November I was delighted to be able to forward the affidavits that Bobby's aunt and uncle had at last furnished to the Consul in Zurich. They were for the entire family—*Vati,* Ili and Nora—and with them, most likely, Ili could escape her bad Hungarian quota.

Bobby and I had improved our living conditions by moving into "a collective." Five of us—another couple and a single man—rented a three-bedroom, fifth-floor walkup apartment in a tenement on Broadway at 133rd Street. It was clean and had a magnificent view of the Hudson River from two windows. Another set of young people from our group lived in an adjoining apartment and we often pooled our resources for communal meals. This way, the few among us who were unemployed could be sure of food and shelter. Everyone was very enthusiastic about collective living and Bobby loved it because he and I were hardly ever alone, which made for less conflict. Despite our best intentions and earnest efforts our relationship was not working out well. We got on each other's nerves, found fault with each other, criticized, complained, quarreled. Our relationship in Vienna had worked because it was part-time and gave us a refuge from the pressures of school and family. Here we were totally thrown upon our own resources and dependent on each other for all support. It was all too intense. For Bobby, the friends in the youth group and his indulgent family offered some backup support. I had no one in this new country in whom I could confide. All my hopes and expectations were focused on making this marriage work, which was not a good way for making it happen. Bobby hoped and expected that living in a group would give me more support and make things better between us. Unfortunately, that did not happen.

EARLY IN 1940 I finally got a regular job. I learned about it through a young refugee woman I knew, who also briefed me on how to apply for it. It was a sales job in a fancy candy store owned by Jewish refugees from Vienna, who were opening a new branch on Fifth Avenue. For this branch, considering its elite clientele, they would hire only Protestant women with several years' experience. I got the job entirely by lying and bluffing, acquiring an impeccable Swiss life story and pretending to have had years of experience in the best Swiss candy store. I got away with it and learned how to be a success in America. Well, a modest success— forty-eight hours a week on my feet (in high heels) without a rest period for eighteen dollars a week . . . Still, it was a beginning.

After I started working I became more and more irritated with our collective living situation. I did not like the lack of privacy, the constant interference of everyone with everyone, which was rather worse than living in a large family. I liked least of all the fact that the men, after their work, were sitting in the living room, waiting for the women, who had also just returned from work, to get dinner ready. Anytime I said anything about it, I got a lecture on my bourgeois notions. One night, when I had had a particularly tiring time at work and my feet hurt, as they usually did, I got into a nasty argument with one of the men, who happened to be unemployed at the time and still expected me to fix his dinner. That night I told Bobby I wanted us to move out, I didn't care where. This became another source of conflict for us, but finally we did move out, when I threatened to leave without him.

We found a lovely two-room apartment in Queens and it looked for awhile as though the change would do us good. We fixed it up, our first real home, and began to act like a married couple, spending more time together and trying to enjoy activities that were not entirely political and collective. But it did not last.

APRIL 9, 1940—GERMANY INVADES DENMARK AND NORWAY.

APRIL 30, 1940—JAPAN JOINS AXIS POWERS.

MAY 10, 1940—GERMANY OCCUPIES BELGIUM, THE NETHERLANDS AND LUXEMBURG.

MAY 17, 1940—GERMANY INVADES FRANCE.

MAY 27, 1940—BRITISH EVACUATE DUNKIRK, LEAVING GERMANY IN CONTROL OF EUROPE.

JUNE 10, 1940—ITALY DECLARES WAR ON BRITAIN AND FRANCE.

JUNE 14, 1940—GERMANS OCCUPY PARIS; FRANCE SURRENDERS.

In the spring of 1940, when fascism and darkness had overwhelmed Europe and only the brave resistance of England under Nazi bombardment offered a glimmer of hope, we were back on the emigration seesaw. Ili could not get a permit to leave France for Zurich, where she had to pass the medical exam without which the U.S. Consul would not grant her a visa. He absolutely refused her request to let her take the exam in France. Her visa application in Zurich would have permitted her to immigrate as part of the family unit on the Austrian quota of the head of the family. Her failure to appear for the medical exam as required meant that she would have to start a new application at the U.S. consulate in Nice on her own, which meant I would have to get a new, separate affidavit for her from Bobby's relatives. And, most likely, it meant she would have to come under the Hungarian quota. A death sentence.

That spring, Father's condition worsened. He had a combination of heart and thyroid problems; by the end of April he had a second heart attack. He survived it and was then in the hospital in Lucerne, Switzerland. He had secured permission from the Swiss government to let mother come to Switzerland on the ground of his dangerous illness and his need of her to nurse him. He really seemed to want very much for her to come. In letter after letter he complained that she had not yet arrived and for the first time he questioned whether she really wanted to come. She in turn wrote to me that she had tried to get an exit permit for Switzerland, but that her appeal had twice been denied by the French military authorities. She had a permit to exit France to go to the U.S.A. only (valid for six months) but not to go to Switzerland. She could not tell this to *Vati* for fear of further upsetting him. (Why not, I asked myself. Why can she not tell him the truth if it is the truth?) She wrote: "You see this is a knot that cannot be untangled."

A few days later she wrote again, telling me how anxious she was to find work and earn money. There was, she had learned, a journal for music in New York; there must be one for art. Would I find it and give her information on possible employment opportunities for her? Could I try and arrange an exhibit for her?

The naivete of her plans for self-support, her way of loading her problems on me while refusing to take the steps she could have taken earlier to go to Switzerland and to safety, exasperated me. I remember feeling mounting frustration and finding no way of expressing my thoughts and emotions to her in a way she could understand. Her constant shifts of mood and attitude only added to the problem.

World events of this period are only obliquely reflected in the correspondence that passed between my mother and me. Two days after Hitler's invasion of

Holland she wrote me a letter obviously designed to calm me down. Father was improving and Nora was with him. She is praying that her sisters will be safe in Holland.

> We are alert and ready. Perhaps we will work, probably in factories. Everyone needs strong, healthy people. I can read and write five languages, can type and do stenography, I can draw and I can write. Cook and do women's work (even though I hate it); I can live on practically nothing, eat little and I don't smoke now. Everything is simplified, I'm not weighted down with possessions. And there is no fear . . . I won't let go. Don't worry . . . We will live to see a better world. I embrace you— there is deep peace in my heart. I have a firm confidence we will survive it all. Only you be calm . . . Life is burning bright. The intensity of it all seems to burst my skin. It is too much. In case I need it I have everything: money, car, caring friends. Don't fear for me.

The threads of my parents' different needs were pulling and drawing, attracting and repelling each other—a tangled web of conflicting interests and emotions. The letters tell one story, my memory another; the reconstructed facts from later stories tell yet another tale. While my father lay near death in the hospital in Switzerland and sent frantic appeals to Ili to come to him, he may have expressed his own need or he may have simply wanted to use the occasion to save her life by making her leave France. He had already then fallen in love with a woman in Liechtenstein, a widowed German Jewish refugee, whom he would later marry. Thus, making Ili come to Vaduz must have seemed like a mixed blessing to him, to say the least. I knew nothing of this relationship until years later. Had I known, it would have relieved me of much anxiety, but as usual my father was "protecting" me.

Ili, by her own account, dreaded going to Vaduz more than she dreaded the danger of her situation. Still, during my father's health crisis, she tried, every way she could, to come to Switzerland. Shortly after, she met the man with whom, by all later accounts, she had the most significant and positive of her many love relationships. Rudolf Ray (Rappaport) was a well-established artist who greatly and positively influenced her own painting. He was a Latvian by birth and had for many years lived and exhibited in Vienna and, after 1938, in Paris. He was successful, critically acclaimed; his work had been bought by several museums. He was now awaiting his visa to the United States.

In light of these facts, the correspondence I am now rereading is even more weird and more tangled. My mother fluctuated almost daily in her loyalties to the two men who then meant most to her in her life. My father, always traditional and totally loyal, did everything in his power to save Ili's life at the expense of postponing or possibly even thwarting his own happiness. And each time one or the other came to some "solution" that looked humanly possible, some bureaucrat in one or the other countries on whose existence they now depended— Liechtenstein, Switzerland, France, the U.S.A.—pulled a string, wrote notations on some record, cited an obscure law or regulation, and whatever they had come to decide in such agony and turmoil was rendered null and void. All of us were jerked around like puppets on invisible strings. Power and self-determination were nonexistent. That is what it means to be stateless, to be a refugee. Your life is out of your own control, in the hands of people to whom you are nothing but a cipher, a number.

IN THAT YEAR OF IMMIGRATION, adjustment and transition, time and money were equally in short supply. During my second summer in America I could look back and see how much I had learned, how much I had grown in survival skills, in self-confidence and in practical knowledge. But something else had begun that would increasingly become of importance in my life and would finally be my main focus and means of self-definition: I had begun to write.

I did not really think of it as writing at first, just as taking notes and jotting down observations, but soon I began to write short poems in English. They were simple and lacked any kind of craft, but they had a stark economy of expression and a certain feel for evoking images. I used a Brechtian style of verse, simply because I knew no other. It was my way of getting at English, of beginning to understand the structure of the language, the way its grammar differed from German, the way its simple syntax could be used to express complexity. English seemed clumsy to me at first, since I measured style by the precision of German syntax and the density of German prose. English seemed like the speech of children, straightforward, without refinement. I used it like that, artlessly placing the short words one next to the other. The longer words, the place names, the names of rivers seemed poetic to me—Virginia, Mississippi, Appalachia, Georgia . . . I explored the language by writing, moving from the simple to the more complex and getting a feel for the difference between the German in which I thought and the English in which I attempted to write.

VIRGINIA

Shady trees on soft green hills.
Orchards full of fruit.
Grey the sky.
In the dawn brown earth
and horse and cow.

At sunrise fields
carry long slim tobacco
slowly swaying
its leaves in the wind.

A child playing themes from Beethoven's Ninth reduced to C major and five notes—that was my entry into becoming an American writer.

THE YEAR 1938

On New Year's Eve, 1938 crawled into history.
For one place or another,
The between years ended.

The years between wars are merely pauses—
breathing spaces for the lost generations,
refueling stops for warriors and ideas.
The battle never stops, it knots and twists—
and the years between wars are the gathering
of the harvest ripened in battle
the forged young men and women of the future—
the years between are their universities of living.

Season of the future,
The years between wars are a time of sorting
clearing the timid from the brave.
The years between wars
are the smile of the century.[2]

2. These poems are printed here with permission of the author.

And yet, even these inept attempts gave me enormous satisfaction. I was acquiring both language and land in the process of setting these lines on paper. I took the building blocks of my infantile vocabulary and shaped them into towers, into houses, into walls—and so, gradually, I made them my own. Can barely speak, but I'm writing.

It went like that, in wild and disconnected swings from despair to hope. Thin sprouts of hope, feeble roots in the American soil began to grow and seek light and then, again, the darkness of our European fate would descend and blot it all out.

[10]

MAY 10, 1940—ALL GERMAN FOREIGNERS LIVING IN FRANCE MUST PRESENT
THEMSELVES TO THE AUTHORITIES FOR TRANSPORTATION TO DETENTION
CAMPS.

THE REFUGEES were herded into the nearly fifty camps established for this purpose in the countryside. My mother landed in the camp at Gurs in the Pyrenees.
I learned about my mother's internment from my father. I knew about Gurs only
that this camp had been used at the end of the Spanish civil war to intern fleeing
Spanish Republican refugees and members of the International Brigades. In fact
twenty thousand Spanish political prisoners had been interned in Gurs on a
muddy plain at the foot of the Pyrenees, surrounded by barbed wire, on which
they had gradually built primitive barracks that provided bare shelter. With the
outbreak of the war, the French allowed thousands of these men to escape the
camp by volunteering for labor service; thus only a few thousand were left by the
time the refugee women arrived.[1]

1. My reconstruction of the history of and conditions at Gurs are based on the following sources: Gabriele Mittag,
ed., *Gurs: Deutsche Emigrantinnen im franzoesischen Exil* (Berlin: Argon Verlag, 1990), especially the articles by
Mechthild Gilzmer and Gabriele Mittag; Lisa Fittko, *Mein Weg ueber die Pyrenaeen: Erinnerungen 1940–41*
(Muenchen: Carl Hanser Verlag, 1985); Charlotte Salomon, *Life or Theater? An Autobiographical Play,* trans. Leila
Vennewitz (New York: Viking Press, 1981); Hanna Schramm, *Menschen in Gurs: Erinnerungen an ein franzoesisches
Internierungslager (1940–1941)* (Worms: Verlag Georg Heintz, 1977).

I did not know when my mother arrived in Gurs nor did I hear anything directly from her while she was there. The postcards, letters and money I sent to Gurs were all returned. I followed the news in the papers and on the radio as though my life depended upon it, but I was cut off from my mother and her experience. All I knew was that my mother was now in a situation far worse than when we had been in the jail in Vienna and that, as the war proceeded and the Germans inexorably moved across Western Europe and France, she might end up in their hands once again. As it later turned out my mother was in Gurs perhaps no more than five to six weeks, but in my experience, my memory and my nightmares, that period seemed to last many months.

I have pieced together what she lived through from survivor literature. In May 1940, ten thousand women, rapidly gathered from all over France, were deposited in Gurs without adequate provisions for their existence. The selection criteria that determined their fate were rigidly bureaucratic: as long as a woman had no French citizenship she was assigned to Gurs. Alsatian nuns, Jews, Parisian prostitutes, antifascist refugees from all over Europe and suspected Nazi sympathizers from Alsace-Lorraine were all interned in the desolate barracks, each holding seventy to a hundred women. The three hundred barracks stood on muddy ground, each surrounded by a ditch in which the rainwater collected. Sections of twenty-four barracks were surrounded by barbed wire fences, thus separating prisoners from each other. The camp was guarded by French prison personnel and French soldiers, who generally regarded the prisoners as hated foreigners, traitors, enemies of the state. Their treatment of foreigners in the camps was a mixture of indifference, brutality and a quirky humanitarianism.

The barracks were unfurnished except for straw sacks; each prisoner was given a blanket, which often was infested with vermin. There was no heat and the prisoners suffered terribly from the cold. The latrines consisted of plain boards with cut-out holes mounted over steel drums; they were accessible only by means of steep wooden steps without railings, which elderly and sick women found very difficult to navigate. The latrines were constantly surrounded by long lines of waiting women. The water supply was totally inadequate and available only for a few hours each morning. The washing troughs, the kind used for feeding cattle, stood on open ground, exposing the women to the staring eyes of the male guards. The worst feature was the totally inadequate food supply, a starvation diet consisting of watery soup with half-cooked chickpeas and an inadequate supply of bread (200 grams a day). Prisoners were entitled to receive food packages, but these were usually raided by the guards before the prisoners received them.

Prisoners with money could supplement their meager rations with overpriced food sold in a canteen.

My mother was at Gurs at the same time as Hannah Arendt, Dora Benjamin (Walter's sister), the painters Lou Albert-Lasard and Charlotte Salomon and the wife of the writer Lion Feuchtwanger, Herta Liebknecht. Ili's cousin Lisa Fittko, who met her at Gurs, described her attitude and activities with respect. Ili had smuggled a box of paints into the camp and kept up her spirits and those of the other prisoners by giving painting classes. "She was the same person in Gurs that I had always known," wrote Lisa Fittko. "She had to know everything; understand everything. Dirt and hunger could not dampen her spirits and her sense of humor."[2] Lisa Fittko was a political prisoner whose German-born husband was on a Nazi death list. Lisa's resourcefulness and survival talents were extraordinary. My mother was totally apolitical, but from Lisa Fittko's memories of her and by her own account, her steadfast spirit gave her a sort of leadership position in her barracks and she lived through this horrifying experience with courage and dignity.

The armistice signed by France in June 1940 ceded the Northern part of France to German occupation, with the Southern part, the so-called Vichy government of Marshall Petain, remaining nominally free. Paragraph 19 of the armistice agreement established the obligation of the French government to surrender all "foreign political asylum seekers" to the Germans. The Petain regime, exceeding the requirements of this shameful paragraph, later interpreted it as an authorization to hand over all Jewish refugees within its borders, utilizing its own police forces for this purpose. The seventy thousand Jews deported from France to the extermination camps, beginning in March 1942, included women and children. This moral and political collapse of France lay still ahead at the time of which I am writing.

In the week before the armistice, as French troops were in retreat, the camp in Gurs emptied out. Somehow, the prisoners bribed or cajoled the guards to write them passes; others faked passes for themselves and their friends; still others were let go deliberately by guards who themselves felt their world was coming apart. There were those who fled because they had some outside connections or someone waiting for them. Charlotte Salomon was able to escape, because she was registered as nursing her ailing grandfather. Lisa Fittko fled to find her husband, who had been imprisoned in a detention camp for male "politicals." Those

2. Fittko, 43.

who had neither money nor connections stayed behind. Many of those who fled were later caught in the Petain government's collaboration with the Nazis in the deportation of foreign Jews, among them Charlotte Salomon.

My mother, who had neither money nor a place of refuge, still had the courage to flee. After weeks of being out of communication with her, I finally received the following letter. It was written the day of the signing of the French-German armistice and was addressed to *Vati,* Nora and me:

23/6/40 Gurs chez Mme. Lafitola

Since yesterday afternoon I am out of the camp and after long considera-tion I settled into a neighboring village in order to await in peace and security for further developments. The reason I am staying here: 1) I do not want to lose contact with the other women. There are some very smart people among them, the best one is a Mrs. D, the former owner of the Waldhotel in Vaduz. She was active in the big aid committees and works under American protection for the refugees. There is the possibility of an extraordinary transport and rescue mission to the U.S.A. This woman likes me a lot and at any rate, she is a very active, strong personality who always knows what is going on, very serious. I want to stay in touch with her. 2) It is almost impossible to go in the area of Biarritz. The trains and trucks are overfilled with refugees; there are no rooms to be had. I want to wait here to find out to which city the U.S. Consul will send my dossier. That's the place where I will go. Please find out at the U.S. con-sulate in Zurich whether my files can be processed in Bordeaux, Pau or Perpignan.

The most important thing is now to get food and lodging. More trans-portation is unthinkable, everything is incredibly expensive. As always, there are people, friends, who help me as much as they can. I was very pop-ular in the camp by bringing news and initiative to the women. I started a free drawing class for fashion drawings and further developed my special scheme for "Quick Method of Instruction," which I plan to utilize in America, if I should live to see it. I also did cosmetic facials and gave a course in it for 5 ladies. The nervous exhaustion, the uncertainty, the hor-rible tragic events I witnessed, the constant noise in the barracks and the isolation from all the world, all that came together and I collapsed, the moment I was outside. I arrived here yesterday in a procession that made the Jews' flight from Egypt look like a Cook's tour—we improvised knapsacks out of pink blankets, and out of bed rolls. I really collapsed, had a high fever alternating with chills, fainting, vomiting, diarrhea, the works. There was no doctor, but we had the old home remedies—hot water bottles to the feet, cold compresses and aspirin . . . And a bed, God, a bed in a tiny room for two, not for twenty, as before, just for two—that was a relief. Today I'm still in bed and my friend, who is sweet and devoted, moves around gently and is trying to clean up our unbelievable dirt. This woman has been my battle comrade since the day of my arrest. She recognized right away that if someone relieves me of housework and daily shit work, I am much better suited to mental work and to all the intrigues and persistent efforts necessary for myself and others in this situation. Only no dishes, no laundry, no mending of socks—better for me the running around, making connections, getting rooms where thousands of other people failed. Interesting, how this has happened to me over and over again in emigration—somebody always appeared to free me from daily chores. But that is only an aside.

Today is a wonderful day. I enjoy the quiet. We live in the tiniest room, when you stand up you touch the ceiling. Next to it is a barn. There, in a corner we can pee or do what you do in the toilet, since such an establishment does not exist here. We laugh a lot, between 2 fainting spells. We found a pump and after hours of attempting to clean ourselves we found a trough where we put our laundry to soak. Tomorrow we will wash, that is Stella will wash because I am too weak and can't walk 3 steps. But tomorrow I will have to go to the police and to find out all the news. Our landlady has 3 children of her own and 5 adopted ones. All of them have already spied out the corner where we hid our treasure, one banana and the cheese that we acquired by using all our remaining charm and sex appeal and humor. The blond angel, 3 years old, went to our treasure chest and stole the banana. It was gone. I feel like Chaplin in *Gold Rush,* just missing out on my banana treat. But the little scamp was cute, all the same. Because it is Sunday her mother wiped her face with the corner of a dishcloth and decorated her with a sky-blue bow.—I've been considering for an hour whether, after all, I should not wash, try to wash, because we think this is a hopeless endeavor. This filth won't be conquered soon. Perhaps after another 24 hours in bed I'll try again with cleanser, turpentine and yellow soap.— You see, given half a chance, my sense of humor returns. In the last few days I almost lost it. Now let me give you a list of women of our acquaintance I met in camp . . .

I have paid the room in advance for a month, have some cheese, margarine, one can of sardines, soap, onions, $1/2$ kg. of sugar, some figs and 100 frcs. There is no aid committee here. That's another reason I want to stay close to the women from the camp; they just have to help me. If it comes to the worst, I'll rent out my bed part time . . . The money Richard sent me in Mai got lost. Stella can knit children's jackets for the peasant women in exchange for food, but my skill at cosmetics is not much in demand here. The same with my talent for analyzing the art of the Old Masters. We'll find something and I can survive for 14 days. [Then follows a list of possibilities for her rescue—a friend with a car, an Englishwoman in an artist's colony, various people to whom she sent letters to send food. A list of art galleries in New York City that Gerda should contact so they can give her a letter saying she will have an art exhibit there.] Please send me journals and books, I have not had anything to read in months. And I really long for chocolate and jams. My motto is: Life begins tomorrow. Often you think you can't go on, and then it goes on anyway. Nora, think about that beautiful saying: What does not kill us makes us stronger . . . Thank God that my sisters are well. Are they still at home? Now I'm very optimistic because my friend is at the door, beaming. She got some butter.

Children, stay well and write and love me as I love you.

[An Appendix to Father] I just want to say that with all my gallows humor my situation is desperate. In a few days I will be penniless . . . There is no one here who will lend any money . . . The Red Cross is supposed to come here. Please do what you can. I'm trying everything. The situation is serious, very serious. Please have confidence in me. I'll certainly make it; I found resources of strength that surprise me. And I wait to collapse until I'm safe.

On July 7, my mother wrote me a letter from Nice. She was hungry, she was penniless. Silence from Switzerland. She described her flight from Gurs, the horrendous prices charged for space on a truck, the need to lay in supplies of food. Yet: "I made no mistakes. I saved everything, my pictures, my luggage, and I kept myself from accidents, through concentration and intuition."

I received her letters and desperate appeals in a state of despair. In July I lost my job and was myself on the edge of destitution. My marriage was breaking up;

I had no idea how I would live two weeks or a month from then. My father's letters continued in a tone of reassurance. He had sent Mother sufficient money for her to live on. He was sorry to hear about my losing the job and did not want me to worry about the family. Immigration to the U.S.A. was delayed, again, this time because the U.S. government had halted all immigration procedures until new regulations could be enacted. He was, nevertheless, still hopeful.

It was typical of my father to be aware of my situation and to try to be protective of me, even when he actually could do nothing. Yet, at the time, I was emotionally much more entangled with my mother than I was with him.

She and I had parted so badly and the letters had only aggravated the misunderstandings and gaps in comprehension that our different fates imposed on us. It was not going to be possible to express with any kind of adequacy the deep abiding love between us, the empathy and sharing for which we both longed so deeply. The only stable support I had in this new country was no longer supportive—I knew I had to leave Bobby and make it on my own. I was frightened, I needed a mother, a friend, someone to encourage and support me.

August 1940. My mother writes: "Send food. Send money. Do something. A friend is sharing her tea with me. I have nothing, no hope."

I am breaking up my marriage; I have no idea how I'm going to live but I know I cannot go on this way. I'm killing my mother, I think. I cannot help her. I cannot help myself. Nevertheless, I tried to share my experience with her, hoping it might distract her from her own situation:

August 9, 1940
The best thing that happened to me: I have begun to write and in English and I managed to write two very fine poems. A composer friend of mine, Richard, at once set them to music and they will be used by our group's chorus. People who have read them think they're excellent. I remind myself a little of Roswitha Bitterlich [an Austrian primitive painter] insofar as the miracle has come over me and I first write my poems and then I look up the words in the dictionary—and lo and behold, they fit. I'm well, I'm really well.

Western Europe was now firmly in Nazi hands. The invasion of Britain seemed not just a nightmare, but a realistic possibility. I wanted to be in Europe, to be part of the fight, to resist the evil that had engulfed it. But I was safe in an America filled with a spirit of complacency, isolationism and indifference. In my massive preoccupation with my own personal life, I was part of that grand and guilty indifference. Guilt and despair. Why had I left Europe and abandoned her? She never said this, but I did daily. Why was she not safe in Liechtenstein with my father as she might have been?

Bobby and I bring out the worst in each other. We only hang in there because we each are too afraid of the alternative. I have come to despise Bobby and I no longer believe he will change. He senses how far apart we have drawn and reverts to what first attracted me to him—his need of me. He cannot live without me; there is nothing else in his life but drudgery and disappointment; he has tried so hard. That makes two of us who tried. One cannot hold a marriage together by trying harder.

I feel stifled; my skin is nibbled away by daily irritations. I'm attracted to other men.

Bobby says if I leave him he will kill himself. I remember hearing that, standing in that shabby apartment with its view of a cement driveway, trying to gauge whether he means it or not. I'm killing myself, I think. "I will not accept responsibility for your life," I tell Bobby. "Not any longer."

He did not kill himself, but soon found another woman. He served in the Army as a medic, returned to Austria and became a doctor, married twice more, fathered three children and in the '50s died in a mountaineering accident.

On August 29, 1940, I wrote my mother from Miami, Florida. My opening sentence, urging her to leave France for Liechtenstein, had by then become a routine, a mantra.

It's a matter of life and death—I know what it means to you to live in Vaduz, but I know other things too and I tremble for your future. Please take this seriously. You could do worse than simply to survive. [Then my news.] The reason I'm writing from Miami is that Bobby and I have separated. I'm staying here a week to think it over, but it is over. I think it is essential that we live separately for at least a few months.

I returned to New York and quickly found a new job, in the garment district. The new job paid minimum wage, just enough to cover my food and carfare. Two weeks later I reported to my mother:

Bobby moved out the day after I arrived; he rented a little room and I'm alone with the ghostly apartment and the astonishing insight that it is I who cannot be alone.

Ili responded caringly, but she seemed to want me to stay in my marriage. "Remember the softer, gentler side of your being. You need much warmth, my child, even though you are always ready to deny that." She dreamed on of how she and I would live together in New York City in a studio, each working.

I waited to tell my father about my separation from Bobby until I had fully decided to carry it through. He responded at once in a way that seemed both supportive and cautious. He could not fully understand, but accepted our decision, trusting that it was not made lightly. He wanted me to think well of myself, so that others would think well of me. "You will grow through suffering. Head held high—your great happiness will come." The rest of his letter was more upsetting. The U.S. Consul in Switzerland was no longer giving visas to refugees in Switzerland in order to admit those in greater need in other European countries. The major need was to get Ili out of France and that could best be done by transferring her immigration application to the U.S. Consul in Nice. In the meantime he had again found a way of getting her into Switzerland, if she would only come.

Back to square one. This latest development meant that at the very time when I had separated from Bobby, I had to try and persuade his aunts to send off yet another set of affidavits to my mother, this time to Nice, with all the supporting income tax forms and endless notarized documents. It meant that we were in the grip of yet another bureaucracy and everything we had done up to now was wiped out.

There was a new tone of urgency in Ili's letters. She seemed determined now to come to America alone, leaving the Switzerland family in its safe haven. Her letters were more frequent than before, written in pencil in tiny lines that tumble all over the pages. Each letter repeated the impossible litany: Get new affidavits. Send letters of support to the Consul. Contact relief agencies. I heard it and I did not hear it. One cannot hear the desperate cries of the drowning when one is helplessly tied up on shore. I heard and I did not hear it. Moreover, the rest of her letters were glowing with happiness, full of high spirits, creativity, strength and a stubborn, irresistible vitality.

In October, as German troops entered Rumania and advanced toward Greece, she wrote about her philosophy of survival:

I feel at home in movement, flux. That is my terrain. A suitcase—a reflection of my bourgeois apartment. When I was fleeing [after the camp] I had my little hand luggage with your pictures inside. I called it "my country estate" . . . I feel cozy and safe in the waves of the ocean, no matter how large they are. The other day I fell asleep lying on my back in the water. On the other hand, I stumble crossing the street. To make decisions by way of my mind seems unnatural to me. I listen to my inner telephone . . . Blessed life, to have given me such clarity so late in life. I'm pure and blessed in not papering things over with false conventionalities. When you reduce your demands to zero, you become invulnerable, nothing hurts you. The recognition that life is one long solitary confinement becomes the basis for existence. Does it hurt? No, only occasionally . . .

The letter continues with six pages of instructions on what to do to get her to the U.S.A. and then:

I'm painting again . . . Make daily 5–6-hour walks with sketch pad in the magical, autumnal landscape of Provence—silver olives and palm trees, fat fig trees, mimosa, the incredible sky and ocean, pink squares of houses, sleepy villages . . . Alone or with my buddies, the painters—my student, a Hungarian, Rossi, an Italian mystic, a Latvian painter.

Her pride in what she had accomplished in her emigration spoke in each of these letters. She had created an island of culture and peace amidst the chaos of defeated France. She was surrounded, as always, by talented men and women who adored and admired her. Unlike me and under much harsher conditions, she had found a circle of support and friendship. But what was really happening was her relationship with the painter Rudolf Ray, which she had indicated to me in hints and oblique language for several months already. Her sudden decisiveness over coming to America must have been due to the fact that he had a valid immigration visa for the U.S.A. and was planning to depart shortly. Her letters, which abounded in precise details of her daily life, the food she ate, the flowers in her vase, the visits of friends, were totally bare of facts about this love affair, which I now know was profound and true and had the greatest impact on her work. I sensed, at the time, that she was withholding information from me, that she was not telling me the whole truth. In the complex tug of war and love between us that fact became an excuse for my not hearing the other appeal. Or hearing it only too well. The guilt was growing; the love was in denial.

[11]

I MET CARL LERNER six weeks after my marriage had ended—in fact, if not yet by law. Bobby and I had separated quite civilly. He moved out of the apartment and agreed to pay half of my rent. Once, he came back to get his things and we quarreled fiercely over five art books, our only assets. After that we resumed a friendly attitude toward each other.

I felt better living alone than I had for the past year and a half in my marriage. I kept up my activities in the refugee youth group and took on the job of education director. It was in that capacity that I became involved in writing a script for the celebration of German-American Day for Peace and Progress, an annual event that took place in Turner Hall in the Bronx and that brought together in a day of pageantry, music, dance, bratwursts and beer the unlikely alliance of progressive German-American trade unionists, old-time German immigrants and radical antifascist refugee youngsters.

A committee determined the content of the celebration—it was to be something highlighting the major progressive events in the history of German-Americans. Dutifully, I spent time researching in the public library and decided that the featured scenes would celebrate the defense of free speech by the colonial newspaper editor Peter Zenger; the arrival of the "forty-eighters" (survivors of the defeated German revolution of 1848); the establishment of the first German trade union local and of the Socialist Party in the U.S.A.; and a few other such events. I was given a budget of six hundred dollars—for supplies, costumes and the hiring of a director.

I called the New Theater League office, where, I had been told, one could find unemployed theatrical people willing to undertake such a job for the low honorarium we offered. I was told promptly that a man named Will Lee was just right for the job and would meet me at noon at the Seventh Avenue entrance to Macy's. When I went there on my lunch hour, Will Lee never showed up. On phoning the same office, I was told he had gotten a job, which may or may not have been so, but the league had another person with sterling qualifications willing to do the work. Even better, they claimed, as I could tell from his name, he was fluent in German. This time I spoke to the candidate myself and he assured me he would be easily identified—he wore a green tweed suit and a Tyrolean hat. That costume seemed to me to be over-doing the German bit, but it did make for easy identification. In fact, this was Carl's only suit at the time and the hat was a sort of a joke. He never wore hats.

Our meeting was unpropitious, for we both worried over who would pay for the tea and cookies we were consuming at a Chinese restaurant and most of our conversation consisted of sparring about money. He finally said he would want to see the script before committing himself to accepting such a pitiful honorarium. I thought he was quite greedy and not particularly impressive. The green suit was in bad taste; the pants were wrinkled around his ankles and the jacket sleeves were too long. He was short and his head was disproportionately large, but he did have a nice smile and seemed to have a pleasant enough personality. At any rate, he was the only candidate for the job. He called the next evening and said he had read the script and wanted to discuss it with me.

We met the following evening in a cafeteria and he came to the point at once. "The script is pretty bad and it will need a lot of work. I'll work on it with you if you want, but we have very little time."

"What's so bad about the script?"

He told me in excruciating detail, including all the grammatical and stylistic errors. He also praised what he found good, particularly the lyrics for several song numbers. He treated me with total seriousness as a colleague and co-worker, disregarding my raw amateur status and the fact that we had not yet agreed on his taking the job. His comments were sharp, knowledgeable and constructive. His intensity was engaging, his dark eyes glowed, his long thin hair kept falling into his forehead and we began working at once, improving the script line by line. We argued over differences and I made him explain his reasoning for every change, but I could see he knew more than I did about what would work on stage and what would not, and I accepted many of his suggestions. When a revision went well, his radiant smile lit up his keen, intelligent face and I wished we could stop working and talk a bit, but he was all business. We rewrote a good part of the script that first night, and in the end he agreed without much fuss to take on the job.

For the next six weeks we met nearly every night and part of each weekend, first for script revisions, then for rehearsals. I found the experience exhilarating and quickly realized that he was experienced, very talented and enormously effective as a director. He was deeply involved in the theater, having worked on some of the best productions of the Federal Theater. During the two years of his unemployment, after the Federal Theater closed, he worked with amateur theater groups in unions. His sensibilities in all of the arts were highly developed and he brought a lot more than simple craft knowledge to bear on his work. Out of nothing, in a bare room and with only a group of amateur actors, he created powerful dramatic moments. He patiently coaxed his actors and sometimes he bullied them, but always his concentration was on the product, on the play, the reality they were creating.

The amateur performers in our group listened respectfully to him, even though it turned out that he did not speak a word of German; the closest he came to it was speaking Yiddish, which was not exactly appropriate for this group. He worked people hard and took no excuses for sloppiness, lack of concentration or indifference. The pageant began to take shape, and I experienced the marvelous excitement of seeing words I had written come to life on a stage. Carl had informally appointed me as his assistant; during rehearsals we worked side by side.

One night we still needed to make script revisions and he invited me to come to his place for dinner. He lived in a walk-up in a tenement on Eighteenth Street with a handsome young man who was also unemployed, a writer and actor. The dinner menu would turn out to be the only thing Carl knew how to cook— shoulder lamb chops and salad and rice. I gathered that housekeeping was fitful and incompetent. As Carl was preparing the meal, I looked around the living room. All the walls were filled with original pictures, very good pictures, and there were some sculptures standing around, strong massive clay sculptures, mostly of people in groups. "Who is the artist?" I asked, thinking it would be Waldo, the housemate.

"My wife," said Carl from the kitchen.

I felt as though he had stabbed me and at that moment realized how much I liked him and how much I had taken for granted. "Where is she?" I managed to ask politely.

"Out," said Carl. Whereupon I began to praise the artwork and comment knowingly on the sculptures. Waldo came into the living room and, possibly responding to my stricken face, explained that Sylvia had moved out and that she and Carl had separated. I stopped chattering about the pictures. Waldo had to go out after dinner and left Carl and me working on the script, quite as usual. Finally I asked him, "Why didn't you tell me you were married? I told you about my marriage and separation."

"I don't want to talk about it," said Carl. I left shortly thereafter, embarrassed about the way I had shown my feelings. Why, after all, did he owe me any explanations about his private life?

Yet we could not drop the subject. Some time later he told me a little about his marriage and relationship of eight years and the way it had ended. She had, he said, taken up with a friend of theirs, a doctor, because he could better provide her with the security she needed to pursue her art. That was his story and his bitterness was palpable; he felt betrayed, which was understandable, but the betrayal was not only sexual; it was a betrayal of friendship and trust. I learned how important friendship and trust were in his scale of values; learning that resonated with my own needs. "When did all this happen?"

It turned out that she had walked out on him the very same week Bobby and I had broken up our marriage. "What a strange coincidence," I said, "it couldn't happen once in a million."

But he refused to see connections. "Thousands of couples split up every day," he commented glumly, persisting in his indifference to the hints of fate.

During the last week's rehearsals Carl and I sat in the back row of the hall watching the actors. He reached for my hand and we sat that way in the dark while the actors did their stuff and every so often he interrupted them with a comment. He did not let go of my hand. I felt calm and good with his hand in mine; nothing needed to be spoken.

One day during the last week his wife appeared at the rehearsal and sat in the hall. I recognized her from the picture in his apartment. I went over and introduced myself and commented on how much I had liked her pictures. We chatted quite pleasantly for a few minutes. She was shorter than I, very good looking, and I thought I might like her. Then I walked away and Carl and she talked, possibly quarreled, in a corner, and then she left. Carl came over to me, fury in his face and eyes. "Don't ever do that again," he said.

"What?"

"Don't start talking to her and having a relationship with her."

It occurred to me that he had no right to order me around and tell me what to do and that I should say so, and then it occurred to me that he cared what I did and I shut up and then I said, "I won't if it bothers you."

"It bothers me a lot."

"Good," I said and I grinned. And the smile came back to his face and everything was perfectly wonderful.

Two days before the performance I fell into a panic. Soon it would all be over; I would never see him again. I already knew then that I had fallen in love with him, but it all seemed utterly hopeless. He was obviously completely tied up in his struggle with his wife and had no room and no interest in any other relationship, especially not in something serious. But I felt I must see him again.

We had dinner together and spoke about nothing but the production and the work and I kept waiting for an opening, but nothing came. I pushed it, thanking him for the work we had done together, and he took it up on the level of a business-like discussion of what was wrong with the production and how it could have been made better. He was fending me off, clearly, and I felt more and more miserable. When we left the restaurant in downtown Manhattan he took me to the subway stop to Queens and said goodbye as though I were a business acquaintance and that was that. Then he went to his own subway.

I went home devastated and wrote him a long and angry letter about how rude and inconsiderate he was to send me home on the subway alone, as though I had not been traveling home on the subway alone each night for six weeks. On and on I wrote, and I mailed the letter first thing the next morning, feeling no better.

Dress rehearsal went badly, which was supposed to be a good sign, and not a personal word was spoken between us. I told myself that I blew it for good. "What comes after tomorrow?" I asked him, nevertheless.

"Oh, the usual. Unemployment and five-dollar-an-evening directing jobs with amateur groups." He stubbornly refused to respond. I said nothing.

"That was quite a letter you wrote me," he said. "I didn't mean to—"

"I just blew off steam," I interrupted.

"I'm not rude."

"No, of course not. Let's just forget it."

"I'm just very mixed up in my life. I need time." I felt all warm inside suddenly. He had heard me. It didn't matter anymore how long it took. It would happen, sooner or later.

The performance went well and everyone thought it was the best pageant they had seen in years and people complimented us and slapped our shoulders and thanked Carl for a great job well done and asked would he do it again next year. "Not on your life," he said, grinning his devastating grin.

We went away to the side of the stage and he put his arm on my shoulder. "I'll call you," he said.

Okay. Whenever.

"Day after tomorrow?"

Yes, yes, oh yes. I just nodded. "Will we meet in Queens this time?"

"If you'll take me home on the subway," he teased me. We had not yet kissed or touched, but it was all settled. Really, it was.

IT SEEMS UNLIKELY, but I have forgotten how we spent that first real date in some small cheap restaurant in Queens, what we talked about and how we arranged the dance of preliminaries that is so significant for lovers. I have forgotten what cautionary phrases we used to define our situation, how much or how little we promised each other and how tentative a platform we built upon which to stand together. But I can feel to this moment the deep inner certainty that spread through me and centered my being so that definitions did not matter at all. I felt right; I felt focused; I felt calm and immensely happy. Everything flowed from that and there was an absence of reasoned judgements, questioning and thrashing-about, an absence of the confusing tensions I had expressed in my awful letter. It all was as it needed to be.

I remember the absence of words between us, as though touch was everything, just the holding of hands, the warmth flowing from palm to palm straight into the body. I see him before me as I saw him that first night, in that mean, sparsely furnished little room in which I lived, where there was nothing of beauty to distract the eye. I was on the bed; the light was on and he stood before me naked. He was not beautiful to me; I noticed the disproportions in his body, the unevenness, the way he was flawed and I waited without anxiety to learn how he would bring himself to me, all of him, the way he was, which I already enveloped in my love and acceptance. He was not tall, not my ideal man, but he moved on his small feet with a grace that came quite unexpectedly and he embraced me with a strength I found surprising and quite overwhelming. We moved our bodies toward each other with assuredness as though there were no choices. I remember the exquisite surprise I felt at the delicacy of his lovemaking, at the way he waited for me and anticipated and needed no words or instructions and I remember feeling the giving over of myself to him as though we had been destined for that moment, knowing this was it forever. It was all so simple.

We awoke in each other's arms and I stroked his fine black hair and held his head against my shoulder. Later on I would plague him because he found it hard to tell me in words that he loved me, but then I had the wisdom of true love and needed nothing except that touch, that total trust.

Two nights later I moved my belongings into his room in his apartment and from that time on, for thirty-three years, we were never apart a night if we could help it. Our bodies had found wisdom. The friendship came later and the shared work persisted; whatever else happened between us, we never lost that passionate capacity for speaking to each other through our bodies.

TO FIND A NEW LOVE is always an overwhelming experience; it floods all aspects of daily existence and transforms each motion, each mundane event into something magic, a miracle transcending reality and comprehension. One wants to retreat from contact with other people and explore, intuit, taste every morsel of that enchanted Other into whom all energy flows. To find a new love and be certain that he is the "one," the right one, the only one forever, is an experience almost unbearable in its intensity; an enchantment, ecstatic. Our love was like that, but that was not the way it could express itself—not only did we lack the capacity for words or the trust in what was happening, we also were, each in different ways, hooked into difficult and harsh conditions of reality that had to be met. For that first year of our relationship we lived together in loving intimacy, but nothing was clear or settled except in our feelings and we dared not trust them. Carl was still emotionally preoccupied with his marriage and the psychic devastation caused by his wife's abandonment. Whatever complex reasons may have led to this break, he saw it only as a devastating betrayal. He was struggling for his very existence; he had not had a real job in two years and saw no prospect of one. He lived a miserable hand-to-mouth existence, which did nothing to bolster his self-confidence and his capacity for planning for the future. So he kept frantically busy looking for theater work and working with various amateur groups in the evenings. I labored at a strenuous, miserably paid job forty-eight hours a week, with little hope of improving my situation. For many months we lived simply for the moment, incapable of planning and afraid of making demands on each other's frail capacities for projecting a common future. And yet the miracle happened; our faith in each other began to build the way moss builds on barren ground and gradually there was a solid piece of earth out of which new life could grow.

I worked very hard at becoming an American. I tried to read the *New York Times* every day, although its headlines and condensed style made it virtually incomprehensible to me. I listened to the radio as much as I could and I tried to read American magazines. Shortly after I began to live with Carl I made a decision that had already been preformed by my writing in English—I would stay in America and become a citizen as soon as possible. This decision was the final straw for the young European politicos in my youth group—they practically read me out of their group for political treason. I would have despaired over that if it had not been for Carl, who said they were a bunch of infantile sectarians and forget them. He would introduce me to the true progressive America, where I would find my new home.

I wanted very much to be introduced to the true progressive America, having lived more than half of my life under dictatorships. In our sparse spare time Carl and I read poetry aloud to each other—Walt Whitman, Carl Sandburg, Langston Hughes. Carl talked a lot about American history to me. He had absorbed it the way I had absorbed the history of the Hapsburgs, by living in a city that was a historical monument. Philadelphia, where he had grown up, was that to Carl— the city where the new nation was born, the buildings and the streets where Benjamin Franklin and Tom Paine had walked. We read Tom Paine out loud, who seemed to us the precursor of the American revolutionary tradition. Resistance to tyranny, dedication to democracy—I saw a seamless connection between the revolutionaries who had risked their lives and sacred honor to end the tyranny of kings, and the heroic fighters against fascism in the European underground movements.

I was delighted to meet Carl's friends, most of them actors and writers who had worked for the Group Theater and the Federal Theater. Their stories of demonstrations, of struggles for funds and against censorship, their experiences organizing the unemployed during the Depression and giving theater performances in union halls, off the backs of trucks, in public parks, amazed and delighted me. Some of them had been part of the legendary first performance of Odets's *Waiting for Lefty*. Some of them had helped evicted tenants put the furniture back in their apartments; others had worked to organize unions. They were great people and they did good things. Their ability to work openly for progressive causes was something I could not simply take for granted. I kept thinking, as they told their anecdotes, how many years in jail they would have gotten in Austria for what they were doing here seemingly without penalty.

Carl was a Communist when I met him; he had integrated the ideals of a life dedicated to radical social change into his own way of living. Coming out of the political experiences of my life, I had no quarrel with that. I was a premature antifascist, as the latter-day term would designate me, and it seemed to me quite wonderful to have found someone whose commitment to politics was as strong and sincere as mine. Of course, I did not understand his political past and what experiences had pulled him in that direction, but I loved him and accepted him entirely as he was, and the political life was part of it.

As for me, I was pleased to be accepted by him and by his friends, but I was also terrified. The problem was that I was a noncitizen and that I had been badly scarred by my refugee experiences and by the way in which I had been grudgingly admitted to the U.S.A. I was afraid that merely by associating with Carl and his friends, by sharing his home, I was jeopardizing my chance of becoming an American citizen. I lived in a constant state of fear and it became a problem between Carl and me. I was afraid of his subscribing to the *Daily Worker;* I was afraid of the meetings he attended. Carl tried to reassure me that my "underground mentality" was quite inappropriate to the U.S.A. Here everyone had the right to their convictions; everyone had the right of free speech and association. I need have no fears. In retrospect, his statement sounds naive, considering the years of harassment and persecution that followed. Although I was prepared to accept his judgement on almost every subject, my pessimism about the world was by then too deeply ingrained in me to believe his assurances. I remained unconvinced and I joined no organizations; I attended no meetings; I signed no petitions. I was refugee-smart and he lived under the illusions of the freeborn American.

Being refugee-smart meant understanding exactly the difference between me and native-born Americans. I had learned it the hard way in the bad months of my unemployment when I had seemed to be outside of society, unable even to gain the smallest foothold. It was no accident that my first real job, as a candy store "saleslady," was in a store owned by Jewish refugees from Vienna. But they were rich refugees and they knew how to assimilate and become American bosses. The salesladies were not permitted to sit down, even if there were no customers in the store. My feet got permanently damaged from having to stand eight hours a day on high heels. Most disillusioning at all was the discovery I made when the daily deliveries from the candy factory were made to the store: everyone working in the factory was a Jewish refugee and they were all paid refugee wages—eight dollars a week, at a time when the minimum wage was twelve dollars a week. I wormed this information out of the frightened elderly man who daily delivered the candy. The office workers and the salesladies, who all were Gentiles (except for me, who had lied my way into that job) were paid minimum wage or above. I called the Labor Department and reported the violation of the

Minimum Wage Law to them. I insisted on anonymity for fear of being fired. The Labor Department inspectors came to the store and to the factory. I do not know what the outcome was for the factory workers, for I was fired that very day. The bosses figured out quickly that I was the only one of their employees capable of such a perfidious, treacherous action.

I hated the place anyway and I was glad to leave it. Fortunately I got a new job fairly quickly, although it only paid minimum wage. I now worked in the garment industry, for a wholesale buyer on Seventh Avenue and Thirty-fourth Street. I was a "follow-up girl," assigned to a loud-mouthed, gruff buyer named Rose. She placed orders with the factories for every kind of garment, underwear, hosiery, in job lots that were to be shipped to retailers all over the U.S.A. My job was to "follow up" and see that the orders were shipped on time or at least somewhere near the promised time. Each day I would get my day's assignment from Rose and, armed with copies of the orders, I would go from factory to factory trying to trace down the shipments. It was, by definition, an impossible job: the manufacturers would make empty promises to me or, if they were overdue and late, they'd throw me out of their place with threats to break my neck if I showed up again. When I reported such things to Rose, she would pick up the phone and holler and scream at them and then send me back three days later. I was terrified by the whole process at first, but I soon learned that the threats and the hollering were not to be taken too seriously and I began to stand my ground and sometimes even to holler back. "The *greene Kusine* is becoming a regular New Yorker," one of the wholesalers reported approvingly to Rose about me. She was so pleased, she yanked two skirts, three blouses and a dress from a sample rack and threw them at me, yelling: "Nu, if you're gonna be a New Yorker, get rid of your European *schmattes* and wear some real clothes." This kind of thing would have devastated me a year earlier; now I was actually proud of myself. I was holding my own in a rough world.

What I loved about that crazy job was my freedom to roam the streets of the garment center everyday, keep my own time, take a break when I wanted to, and get to know a lot of people. There were no fancy pretensions here; people fresh off the boat worked hard for low pay, but on the whole everyone was friendly. The good-natured banter, the cheerful stereotyping of everyone by everyone, the energy, vibrancy, even the fierceness of the competition intrigued me. I felt I was learning something about the real America.

I picked up some Yiddish that year, but in my spare time the acquisition of English was my main concern. Carl helped me a lot with that; he helped build my vocabulary, corrected my Germanic grammar and with endless patience and the skills of a voice coach helped me improve my pronunciation. During this first phase of his mentorship I fully depended on him; what he was doing for me and what I was doing to enter his world were all mixed up with falling in love and becoming a couple. But the political events in Europe and the fate of my immediate family were a constant counterweight, dragging me from hope to despair.

The westward march of the Soviet Union after the division of Poland continued with the invasion of Finland, which ended with the Finnish surrender in March 1940, the cession of Bessarabia and Bukovina by Rumania to Russia and the incorporation of the three Baltic states into the Soviet Union in August 1940. I believed then that all these westward moves of the Soviet Union were justifiable in the interest of securing the western Soviet borders and avoiding an attack on the Soviet Union by Hitler in alliance with the Western powers. In March 1940 the Vatican transmitted Hitler's "plan for peace" to the Western powers. Britain, France, Germany and Italy were to divide Europe into zones of interest and join in an anti-Bolshevik alliance. Germany would force all its Jews to emigrate to Palestine, Madagascar or Ethiopia. After twenty years the German colonies were to be restored. The Allies never agreed to this plan, but the threat of such an anti-Soviet alliance seemed real enough to me.

The Western nations' rejection of Hitler's grand plan made him decide to turn westward in the hope of conquering Great Britain with the same ease with which he had conquered most of Western Europe. From June 1940 on, Germany's naval warfare in the Atlantic and its air bombardments of Britain intensified and continued through the winter. In October of 1940 the Germans occupied Rumania. When Italy attacked Greece the same month, British troops landed in Greece and joined the battle there. Hitler's *Blitzkrieg* failed to break the British spirit and defenses and for the time being he abandoned plans for an invasion of Britain. In January 1941 Mussolini placed Italy under German control and Hitler followed up with an invasion of Bulgaria, Yugoslavia and Greece. Europe, as I had known it all my life, had ceased to exist. And war, worldwide war, now seemed inevitable.

The correspondence with my parents took its frustrating and ineffectual course and the tensions between us were now more palpable than they had ever been, despite our mutual best efforts. Each of them, *Vati,* Ili, Nora, stated in their letters in January and February 1941 that I appeared to have changed very much. I had sent them a photo and they commented on how thin I had become, how exhausted I looked. They ascribed it to a kind of willfulness on my part that made me overexert myself, to "Americanization," a change in values. "Don't ever lose your ethical world, your pure moral values," my mother advised me.

Father was better in health and spirits. Nora was now in a technical school in Lausanne, studying graphic art. Ili continued to share her seesaw of emotions with me. She wrote on January 30 that she lived happily only within her four walls. "The world frightens me." She was desperate for the additional affidavits she needed. "Do whatever is needed to get them for me." She had heard that there were efforts under way to rescue Jewish artists and writers; why didn't I try going to Washington to see if she could be helped? "So many others are leaving [Nice]; I'm often in despair. . ." Each of her letters contained these appeals as though her current condition were entirely due to my neglect, my insufficient efforts. She seemed unaware of what she was doing to me in constantly loading guilt on me. In the very next sentence she wrote cheerfully of her plans for her life in New York. "I will live with you at the beginning and live on nothing, I know how to do that." This kind of statement filled me with dread. I thought back to our weeks in Zurich, living on "nothing," and her trips to the fancy hotels. I did not believe she had changed in her attitude toward money and I feared what life would be like if and when she came here.

Yet, somehow, after these formulaic statements had been made, each letter conveyed something else, something genuine and exciting that touched me deeply. "Very important things are happening within me, I'm in the most feverish phase of my life, totally obsessed with my art, an entirely new life." She described several students who sought her out and were learning from her.

It seems to me as though my eyes have opened only just now. I see the model and I see the abstract connections, the space around the person and the surrounding air. It seems to me as though the emanation from the person I am painting were a sort of command and I follow it as a willing tool . . . There is a dynamic in my work, I think a strength, certainly honesty and courage—that is my material, that is what attracts me, that is what I have waited for . . . but I need to study more, to probe more deeply, to experience the light . . . My arm is sick and cannot rest—I work eight hours a day and then clean up . . . Is there such a thing as abstract art by women? Is there a woman who transcends everything and who . . . breaks through form—what's the use of all these questions; I'm drawn and I follow . . . It's the craziness of our current life that makes us uncertain. Down there on the naked earth and up there, in the realm of the spirit, there is serenity. There is no fear.

In March I was able to wire her that at last her American sponsors had sent the additional affidavits the American Consul in Nice had requested. She responded enthusiastically, but with a clear sense that the difficulties were not yet over. Due to the naval warfare in the Atlantic few passenger ships attempted the crossing. It would be very difficult to get transportation; she would have to go by way of South America. She also wrote in more detail about her new love, Ray. "Last week he had his boat ticket in hand. Everything was ready for his departure—and then his quota number was not ready and everything collapsed. It's enough to drive you crazy."

I could not respond to these letters, except quite briefly. My family was right, I was thin and exhausted. In fact I had been sick for months and had tried to deal with it as best I could without losing my job. I had not written to them about it.

I had for some time been feeling badly, constantly tired, and I had lost nearly twenty-five pounds over the last six months. I chain-smoked and from time to time had severe abdominal spasms. When they got so bad I would roll around on the floor crying, I finally decided to get medical advice. Bobby directed me to one of his colleagues, who recommended me to an ob/gyn specialist in a fancy Park Avenue office. He, in turn, promised to treat me for free, as a professional courtesy.

This generous professional courtesy arrangement made me trust this doctor, since he had no personal gain from treating me. I felt a little guilty at accepting it, since it was based on his assumption that I was Bobby's wife, which I was, but I was no longer living with him. But paupers can't be fussy in such matters; I unquestioningly accepted his diagnosis that I had infected fallopian tubes. I went dutifully twice a week for a rather painful treatment that after several months had not improved my condition. At length the doctor re-examined me and, with a grave expression, informed me I would have to have a hysterectomy. My ovaries were inflamed and enlarged; they had failed to respond to treatment and my entire abdomen was extremely tender. He talked about the possibility of appendicitis and the danger of a general abdominal infection and advised surgery as soon as possible. He had a consultation with Bobby as well, who later gravely explained the medical terms to me. It means I'll never have children, I said, trying to understand. I was just twenty and it did not look like I'd ever want children, still and all . . . The doctor was very kind and explained the surgery to me in a reassuring way. I had to consider the risk of a general abdominal infection . . . He would charge nothing for the surgery, professional courtesy, but the hospital would want three hundred and fifty dollars—in cash. Of course the amount was prohibitive. I did not have it. And then the recovery time, the loss of work—I probably would lose my job as well . . . Reluctantly and with great misgivings I wrote my father for help. I really did not want to burden him or ask for his money, but there seemed to be no way out. My father cabled back: "Am sending $50 now, but will send surgery money only after you have consulted Dr. B. from Vienna." In a long letter he also offered to pay my monthly wages, as long as I needed it, so I would have ample time for recuperation. In the same letter he wrote the long-awaited news: Ili was expecting to get her visa in the following week and had booked passage on a ship leaving Marseille on April 27 by way of Martinique. "It will be good," he wrote, "that she will be in New York in time to nurse you and take care of you."

I was in no condition to respond with anything but anxiety and apprehension to the news for which I had so long waited. I was living in the apartment Carl shared with Waldo, in a tiny bedroom that held little more than bed and dresser. Carl was unemployed. There was no way my mother could live with us. I was going to have major surgery and to have the medical care I needed I was forced to deal with Bobby, whom I would have just as soon not seen again at all. It was all too much.

One step at a time. I dutifully went to Dr. B., who was an old friend of my father's and had a great reputation as a diagnostician in Vienna. Dr. B. listened to my medical history and questioned me closely about my life and activities and about the other doctor's diagnosis. After giving me the most thorough examination I had ever had, he said: "Just as I thought. Whoever told you to have a hysterectomy should have his license revoked. You have acute nicotine poisoning and if you'll stop smoking you'll be fine in a few months."

I found it hard to believe that simple solution to all my problems. Dr. B. noticed my skepticism. "Tell you what," he said cheerfully. "You go home and stop smoking. Altogether. Not one cigarette. If you're not better in two months I'll treat you for free for the rest of your life."

That sounded convincing to me and I promised to give it a try. In fact, it worked miraculously—the spasms stopped, my appetite returned and I began to feel infinitely better within weeks. My father was delighted at the news and more than ever convinced of the superiority of the Vienna medical school over all others. All I could think was that poverty had saved me from unnecessary surgery.

While I was sick and expecting to have surgery I could not write to my mother. I told myself it was because I did not want to add to her worries, which certainly was true. But it also was because I knew she would not respond the way I needed her to respond. I could not trust her to be supportive, the way *Vati* was.

For several months she wrote only about her immigration situation. In April she wrote she expected to leave France for Martinique by May 15. "I shall be traveling with R. He does everything in order to help me." I remember reading this and thinking, *He* does everything to help me, while you, my own daughter, do nothing. What would life be like with her and her lover in New York City? She would try to take over my life the way she always had, only now I could no longer tolerate that. Would she ever accept that I now was an adult, with a life of my own? Even though I had waited for two years for the news of her coming, I now was terrified. The harsh tone of my response to her expressed my fears and my inability to deal with them forthrightly.

Early in May I wrote to her:

Your telegram that you have the visas arrived on my birthday, the best possible birthday gift . . . A few concrete questions—do you know that you can't live on art here anymore than in Europe? Are you ready to take other kind of work? Do you understand that such questions concern you and have to be answered without illusions? It is not "hard" of me to raise such questions, it is natural, the conditions are like that. Are you learning English? Are you ready to go away from Europe and to really come to America? The fewest refugees know how to do that and most of them are unhappy here. If anyone can do it, you can, you are smart and have enormous vitality. But you must know that there will be problems and they must be solved.

She answered: "How is it possible that your last letter to me is dated March 1. Child, you've never hurt me so badly before. You keep writing to *Vati* and telegraphing him . . . are you angry with me?" and a week later:

At last the letter from you for which I waited for two months . . . You punish me for some imaginary sin I have committed, Gerda. Your last letter was so distant . . . you seem to have forgotten everything . . . after nine weeks of silence to write me a letter in which I cannot feel you . . .

I answered coolly, doing as she did, focusing on myself. "Two of your letters arrived. I wrote two to three letters to you. Martinique is out. I read that in the papers here." As I read these lines now I am aware of their cruelty. Martinique is out. It meant that she was trapped again, that her hope of coming to America was crushed, but I could find no adequate words to express sympathy. I was leached out. I was preoccupied with myself:

> I feel like a new person . . . the pressures of the last two years seem to have lifted . . . Five weeks ago Bobby told me "You'll never have a normal relationship to people." Three weeks ago I was still crying into my pillow "Nobody loves me." Now, after one evening's acquaintance people tell me, everyone must love you, and they mean it . . .
>
> What a pair Carl and I are . . . We are always so preoccupied with looking behind us, we don't notice the timid new bonds that are forming. But the new keeps growing. I'm cynical; I say, fool, are you getting ready for another disappointment . . . Until the day comes when I just say, I want to get divorced. And he says, I saw my lawyer about my divorce yesterday . . . And since then it's all different. The doctor says I need rest. If *Vati* can send me the money he offered, I can go to Reno and get a divorce and rest.

Her answer brought more bad news. There was more delay. Her quota number would not be free until July. "All our friends are leaving, only R and I are still here. I will work in America and not be a burden on you."

JUNE 22, 1941—GERMAN TROOPS INVADE THE SOVIET UNION, ADVANCING RAPIDLY ALONG ITS EASTERN BORDERS.

Then, on the 24th of June, the latest devastating blow.
My mother wrote:

> For six months, actually three years, I've done nothing but prepare for my emigration and for three months I have had a definite promise of a visa— and now, today, a final NO. No more visas will be issued. The end . . . On June 4 I was informed that my quota (Hungarian) is up and all is well. Then a letter telling me my case is suspended and now: "no more visas." Now you have to start to help me. Your friend is an American, perhaps he can help you with this. Go to HIAS— [Then follow two pages of addresses, emigrant connections, etcetera.] Do you see that there is a fate? Within the general course of events, there is a personal fate . . . My beloved child, will I ever see you again?

What I had dreaded most ever since 1933 was actually happening—the war of fascism against the Soviet Union. Now, would the Western countries join Hitler? Would the great experiment of an alternative system to capitalism go down in defeat and destruction, the way most of the countries of Europe had gone down? Would the land of socialism and with it the hope of millions for a better future hold out in resistance? And just as I had most feared, the outbreak of that terrible conflict found my mother entrapped in Europe. Suddenly, I found my better voice again.

On June 27 I wrote: "I have been thinking of you a thousand times a day. Very worried and upset by the new ruling of the State Dept.—foreigners who have relatives within Germany or the occupied countries cannot be admitted to U.S. Fear of espionage. Do you still have relatives 'inside?'" I knew very well she still had relatives in German-occupied territory—the Czech branch of the family and her two sisters, Klari and Manci, in Holland. I listed the agencies I had contacted, HIAS, the National Council of Jewish Women, four or five individual friends. "I will do everything possible to bring you here." This was the old mantra again, now more useless than ever. But it needed to be said. All I could offer her was encouragement and hope. And then the letter changes, it becomes joyous, hopeful. Happiness speaks clearly through all the lines. "In one hour I'll be leaving N.Y. for Reno."

That was it. For a year now I had seesawed between hope and despair, I had hung on for bare survival; I had been sick and faced with major surgery. But all along the miracle had happened—my new love had steadied me as I steadied him. The future of which we both nearly despaired now seemed actual and true. We would leave the city and leave our troubles behind. Like the pioneers of old we would be going west, into a new life, into a joint future. We had not deliberated or talked about this; it had simply happened. I made up my mind one day that I must get divorced from Bobby. I met him, talked to him about it and got his agreement that he would pay his share of the expenses of going to Reno. On the very next day, without our having discussed it at all, Carl told me that Sylvia now wanted to get a divorce so she could marry that man, and he had agreed. She would pay the expense of the divorce.

It was really happening: we had both acted independently and moved away from our past. The practical problems were solved. We answered ads for ride-sharing and, after a few interviews, ended up with a nice young man, a social worker, with a good car. He and Carl would share the driving; we would each pay our own expenses.

THE TRIP WAS WONDERFUL. I was drunk with adventure, overwhelmed with the scale of the country, the vastness, the variety of landscape and views. Traversing the desert I felt fear and exhilaration—it seemed like a rite of passage. For once, the despair and gloom of Europe were banished. My letters to my parents from Reno are the happiest I have ever written; they were totally self-centered, bubbling over with my impressions and observations of the wondrous West. And for a few weeks in Reno, despite the anxiety we felt abut the war, we forced ourselves not to read the newspapers. We were on vacation; we were in love. Let the world spin without us. I felt as though I had jumped off a cliff and, miraculously, I was flying. America opened her arms to me and held me in her firm embrace. Carl and I would have a future.

[12]

WE VISITED HOLLYWOOD early in September 1941 on a whim and, literally, riding in the open back of a truck loaded with potatoes. We had already spent five weeks in Reno, Nevada, where we each awaited our divorces, which required nothing more from us than six weeks of residence.

Close to the end of our Reno stay, we started out one day on a local bike ride, found it boring, and felt we could indulge in a quick adventure. We decided to park our bikes, pack our toothbrushes and a change of clothing, and try hitchhiking west, seeing how far we would get. The truck drivers who picked us up, Bud and his mate, were headed for Los Angeles and, hearing we had friends in Hollywood, were so impressed by that fact that they drove us to the front door of our friends' house in the Hollywood hills before they delivered their load of potatoes to the Safeway store. They also offered us a ride back to Reno on Monday morning.

The friends we stayed with were New York actors from the Group Theater, who had a year earlier taken a chance on Hollywood and here they were, living in a shared house with other Group Theater people, an image of dazzling success. The house was gorgeous, on a hillside lavish with palms and rhododendron; their garden offered terraces, a tennis court and a swimming pool. On closer inspection they were living on hope and borrowed money, but they had already had brief jobs at fabulous Hollywood salaries and had agents and great expectations. That weekend they convinced us to join them as soon as our divorces were granted. They would stake us to bed and board until we could manage on our own. This, they assured us, was a place where talent was needed and well rewarded.

We listened to their dazzling talk, their tales of easy success, unbelievable earnings and creative challenges. I had left a job in New York paying twelve dollars a week; Carl had been unemployed for over two years. These people were talking six hundred a week . . .

We decided to take up our friends' offer and I wrote my boss in New York that I would not return. He wrote back, trying to induce me to change my mind with a generous offer he thought I could not refuse: thirteen dollars a week. Instead, we welcomed the kind offer by Bud, the trucker, to give us yet another lift to L.A. on the next of their weekly trips. The day came when we had our divorce decrees and, according to Reno tradition, threw our old wedding rings into the Truckee River. The next day we traveled to L.A., this time on top of a load of oranges.

Carl felt happy in Hollywood from the start and was certain he would make a career in film. We were with old and close friends of his and he quickly became part of their circle, their endless discussions, their schemes for getting contracts and launching various creative projects. I felt ill at ease among all these strangers and could not adjust to what I regarded as their bourgeois pretenses and Hollywood lifestyle. I only wanted to get a job and get out of there.

I started my job search the day after our arrival by walking down Hollywood Boulevard and asking in each shop or business if they had an opening. The first day I landed a job in a hat shop and I was promptly fired the next day for my obvious inexperience. Still, I had earned three dollars. Two days later I got a job in a dress shop, with the same result. It took me a week to land a job in the one trade in which I had some experience. I considered it a very good job—as candy saleslady at the Pig'n-Whistle at Hollywood and Vine. Forty-eight hours a week at eighteen dollars a week. A 50 percent wage increase over my New York job—not bad.

But it really was not enough to set up our own housekeeping, especially since it became quickly apparent that one had to have a car in L.A. in order to get and keep any kind of a job. So we invested our last cash in a Model A Ford. Now it was up to Carl to get a job and get us started on our independent life.

Unfortunately, he was looking only for film and theater jobs. His attitude was: If I take some shit job I don't want anyway, I'll never have time to look for the kind of job I do want. Talent must know how to wait. Meanwhile, we were very comfortable with his good friends, weren't we? Well, yes and no—he was and I was-n't, and it was during these weeks that seemed to have no end in sight that I began to wonder whether I had chosen a man who would never earn a living.

There were other problems. At first, it had felt good when he had worked with me on improving my pronunciation. I laughed even when he was outrageous and announced, not quite in jest, that he would not marry me until I could pronounce V and W correctly and until I permanently stopped smoking. In Reno that had seemed funny and I had spent a lot of time practicing "Mae West is wearing a vest," a good substitute for Eliza Doolittle's "The rain in Spain." It was not quite so funny after our divorces were final and we were living with his friends in Hollywood. Weeks went by and he neither got work nor made any move toward marriage. I had resumed smoking as soon as the symptoms from my nicotine poisoning had worn off and now I began smoking behind Carl's back and hiding my cigarette packs like a drunkard hides his bottles. Had I made a terrible mistake, after all?

I had to admit Carl worked hard at making contacts in the studios and try-ing to get an agent. Soon, he began to earn five dollars a script as an outside read-er and on weekends he brought home another few scripts for me to read as well and so we slowly amassed enough money to pay a month's rent somewhere. The outside reader system was a sweatshop operation in which part-timers were screening out scripts for the full-time script readers, who had regular studio jobs. The pay of five dollars for reading a script included writing a one- to two-page précis. One hoped, of course, that one's marvelous précis would so impress the studio personnel that one would be offered a full-time job.

Carl and I quarreled a lot during these weeks and I made no secret of my expectation that if I could work forty-eight hours on my feet for eighteen dollars, perhaps he could do the same. Finally, he did; he accepted a menial job at Technicolor on the print assembly line. He made what seemed to me a fabulous salary of sixty-five dollars a week—a small fortune on the strength of which we finally rented an apartment for thirty-five dollars a month and set up housekeep-ing on our own.

Having moved that far toward security and stability we moved to the next step quite easily: on October 6, 1941, we were married in a civil ceremony and celebrated by taking six of our friends for a dinner in Chinatown.

Our first apartment was on Franklin Avenue on the ground floor of an old-fashioned two-story stucco building. We had a living room facing the trunk of a huge tree, which made our room perpetually gloomy. At night, when the Murphy bed was pulled down from its frame on the wall opposite the window, it filled the room almost entirely. There was a tiny dark kitchen facing a wall, and a long narrow bathroom. What redeemed the apartment was a narrow garden in front, to which flowering hibiscus and azaleas lent an air of luxury.

Our Model A Ford ran nearly forty miles on a gallon, as near as I can remember. In the ensuing years of wartime gas rationing it proved to be a treasure that got us further on our gas rations than most people we knew. We each worked forty-eight hours a week and spent the half-day Saturday on joint housecleaning. Sundays we drove out of town—to the beaches, to our friends' palatial rented houses in the Hollywood hills, once or twice up to Mount Wilson and the alpine landscape I loved so much.

The news from Europe continued to be bad. I had written my mother with information about how to get a visa to Cuba, which was then the only country accepting European immigrants. Bobby's relatives had decided not to give me any more help with her immigration. They felt they had done what they could. I urged Ili to decide on the Cuba solution, but meanwhile to go to Vaduz and wait there for her visa. People were coming to the U.S.A. from Cuba; it might mean a wait, but she would be in safety. Certainly, France no longer was safe for her.

In October she wrote to me: "It is too late for Cuba, for this uncertain adventure. I don't have the strength for it." A week later, she had changed her mind. "This is a matter of life and death. Do everything, everything. I want to go to Cuba at once." A few days later she wrote again: "Everyone I know who was denied a visa in May already has theirs from Washington . . . Will you not go to Washington to help me?"

I did not know what to make of this, except that she continued to hold me responsible for what was happening to her. How could I go to Washington, and if I could, what would I do there? Her notions of my influence on the State Department were preposterous. I was as helpless as she was, but she did not want to accept that.

By November everything was, at last, decided. My mother wrote that her friend Ray had his visa in hand; he was leaving for the U.S.A. in three weeks. She would be going to Liechtenstein in December.

I now could understand why she had panicked in October. Her lover and only remaining support in Nice was finally leaving without her. This forced her decision to return to Liechtenstein and safety. No matter how badly she felt about it, I was relieved. She would have to deal with reality from here on out, the way all of us did.

In my next letter to my father, with a copy to Ili, I summarized the conditions for getting a visa to Cuba—it took somewhat over a thousand dollars as a bond guaranteeing that the immigrant would not become a public liability. And, at best, this would be only a temporary solution. In regard to her getting the U.S. visa, it now looked worse than ever. Aunt Ida, a cousin of my father's and my only actual relative in the United States, had refused outright to give any help to Ili alone. She might help with an affidavit for the whole family, but not for Ili. Aunt Ida was on my grandmother's side in the ancient warfare between Grandmama and my mother and her refusal was final. The only hope I saw was if my Uncle Richard would deposit a security bond for her in the U.S.A. and I would try to claim her as a relative on a preferential quota.

And so, despite all our efforts and endeavors, Ili returned to my father in December 1941. The letters she wrote in the following months were full of expressions of resignation and attempts at adjustment, but it did not work out. "I live in hopes of liberation," she wrote in one of her letters. I hardly knew how to reply, except in vague and cheerful generalities. I was worn out by the seesawing, the tug of war, the futile efforts that came to nothing. On my trip west I had made a decisive turning—toward selfishness, toward America, away from my obsessive identification with my mother.

I HAVE WRITTEN THIS ACCOUNT from the point of view I held then, in 1940–41. I truly did not understand why my mother had not earlier saved herself by going to Liechtenstein. She missed one opportunity after the other, while the noose tightened around her. It had been her decision in 1939 to go to France, no matter what the risk. She wanted to live in the country of Van Gogh and the Impressionists, to be free at last of family obligations, to be free to paint. It seemed to me then that she was stubbornly seeking short-range gratifications over long-range goals (to live her own lifestyle over saving her life). I was too young, too obtuse, too diffident to understand that the situation for her was quite different.

She had, for all her adult years, been trying to find herself and express her strong and liberated personality fully. She felt confined by her role as mother and bourgeois lady; she was frustrated in her marriage. As an artist, she had been a talented amateur all her life—in Nice she became a painter. She had to free herself from family and children before she could come to this stage. For her, emigration offered the one great opportunity of her life and she took it, consciously and with her eyes open. She spoke the truth in those rare moments when she stopped pretending that she was preparing to come to America. She wanted to stay in Nice, and if necessary to die there. She was happy there, as she had never been before, and she was working, as she had never worked before. The work she has left behind speaks clearly to that: it is the powerful, deeply moving work of a mature artist. After her death, when we collected her paintings, it turned out that indeed these hellish months, these short two years, had been the time of the flourishing of her art, a time of incredible productivity. She must have known, she surely knew that the end was coming and that her situation was hopeless and so she chose the manner in which to live out the remainder of her life. She chose freedom and creativity, at long last.

It is ironic that I could not understand her then, for part of my conflict with her over the past five years had been my disgust at what I saw as her conformity to propriety, her erratic attention to work, her squandering of her energies on unworthy friends, men who flattered her and betrayed her and needy women who hung on to her. I had wanted her to get a divorce, live alone and focus on her work. In my teenage wisdom I wanted her to fulfill herself my way.

That did not happen. The last time I saw her on the Riviera, she seemed to me to live out her old patterns. She had not changed; I concluded she never would. The sad, ill-fitted correspondence between us since my departure from Europe only reinforced my anxiety over the direction of her life—the same lack of focus, the same squandering of her energies, the same wavering in making choices, the same succession of worthless men around her.

Now, when more of the facts are in, I know that she did, indeed, find fulfillment in her life. The choices she made in Nice were rational and courageous. She found a meaningful love relationship, and she at last found focus in her work. Fifty years after her death her work has been "discovered" and honored with a one-woman show at the Jewish Museum in Vienna. Her belated quest as an artist has resulted in extraordinarily powerful and life-affirming work, created under the worst of circumstances. Had I been able to see it that way then, had she been able to acknowledge it that way then, our tragic parting would have had a redemptive effect on both of us. But that did not happen. Our relationship expressed itself falsely, in slanted versions of the truth, in half-truths and in suppressed anger. It dribbled away in the short time we had that might have been good time and then it was cut off by her illness. We were gagged and throttled.

A few months after coming out of Gurs, my mother began to show symptoms that at that time were ascribed simply to the effects of malnutrition and stress in the camp. She had episodes of temporary paralysis in her right hand and arm, and constant weakness in all her limbs. The symptoms were intermittent and during

1941, buoyed up by hope of her impending emigration, she functioned well. After her return to Liechtenstein, the symptoms recurred and worsened. She did not yet know it, but she was in the early stages of what was to be her terminal illness, multiple sclerosis.

I knew few of these facts at the time. My father and sister did not tell me until later the terrible details of her return or the severity of her condition. Meanwhile, I tried to cheer up my mother by writing about my new love, trying to give her a sense of my new happiness; I exaggerated the advances I had made since coming to Hollywood; I talked of plans for the future. But my mother was doomed and nothing could change that.

Survivor's guilt has become a cliche. What it feels like is something else. You build a wall around it; you pour cement into your heart; you dance on the grave. In fact, it's crippling, a fatal disease you carry with you as long as you live. It's more complex than guilt over having survived. It's guilt over having misunderstood, over having misjudged, over having been stuck in my absolutes while she set herself free in her own inimitable way.

Nothing I have ever written has been as hard to write as this account. My mother chose to pay for her art with her life. I still can't find the craft to transform this pain into something that can rebuild life. All I can do is state the bare outlines, and that's inadequate. Entirely inadequate.

DECEMBER 7, 1941. As the bombs fell on Pearl Harbor, the thin line of security, disengagement and precarious peace that separated the U.S.A. from Europe was torn to shreds. The sailors trapped on the sinking battleships, the civilian bodies lying in the rubble of the Pearl Harbor beach—now it was our war, our dead, our commitment. My preoccupation with the European battle lines was now reflected in the daily headlines. My private war had engulfed my new homeland, as it had engulfed my old home country. No longer split apart in my loyalties, I would finally belong—to the U.S. war effort, to the fight to end fascism.

That is what it meant to me, in a live and tangible way. The attack on Pearl Harbor was the beginning of the end of fascism—in the East as in the West. The end was inevitable; the grand coalition of the United States, France, Great Britain and the Soviet Union would inevitably prevail.

We were married just two months when the U.S. entered the war. It was a forgone conclusion that Carl would become a soldier—he wanted it and I wanted it,

even though we dreaded the thought of separation after such a short time together. I wished I could join the Armed Forces, but I realized that that was impossible
as a noncitizen. In France and Great Britain, with the outbreak of war, all foreigners had been arrested and sent to camps in remote places. This might happen
here too, and in my usual pessimistic way, I prepared myself for that possibility.

My own contributions to the war effort were seriously hampered by my being
categorized as an "enemy alien." President Roosevelt had signed a declaration
requiring the registration of "alien citizens of countries at war with us" in January
1942. It had the immediate effect of creating a new category of outsiders—those
holding an ethnicity similar to the current enemy. The next step was the infa-
mous order for the forced relocation and internment of all West-Coast Japanese.
That policy was purely racist, as can be seen from the fact that although the cat-
egorization of "enemy alien" included nationals of Germany and Italy, General
De Witt, in issuing the internment order for Japanese nationals and persons of
Japanese origin, told German- and Italian-Americans not to worry and to go
about their business. We were concerned about the cruel way in which the
deportation of the Japanese had been carried out—the resemblance to the expropriation of the Jews in Austria was to me striking, and the photos of long lines
of people of all ages, including babies and native-born Nisei, lining up in front
of barracks on the barren plains made me shudder. But it was wartime; nations
had to protect their security in wartime. Yet the categorizing of "alien citizens
of countries at war with us" ignored not only individual but also group differences: Japanese-born aliens were grouped together with their American-born
Nisei children, who were by virtue of that fact American citizens; immigrants
holding German citizenship were in no way distinguished from Jewish refugees
fleeing German Nazism, and Austrian Jews, even those who like myself had
never set foot in Germany but who had been forced to emigrate with a German
passport, were considered enemy aliens pure and simple. As such, I had been
registered and fingerprinted and was required to report to the local post office
once a month.

I found the policy outrageous, unfair and self-defeating, because it substituted nationality for political conviction. Devoted antifascists and Jewish refugees
were prevented from contributing to the war effort and were segregated out into
a suspicious category, while known pro-Nazi U.S. citizens, some of German origin and some not, were left free to do as they wished.

What particularly galled me about my characterization as an "enemy alien"
was the implicit acceptance of the *Anschluss* by the U.S. government, expressed

by the fact that no distinction of "enemy" status was made between Germans and Austrians. I stated my feelings, whenever I registered at the local post office, by insisting that I write the words "under protest" above my signature. The first time I did it I got into a horrendous argument with the postal clerk, who told me my action was illegal and might lead to prosecution. I explained I would welcome that, as it would give me a chance to properly protest this outrage. I was nothing if not principled and even then, I was already stubborn. After a while, they got to know me at the post office and let me do my futile little gesture without argument.

It would take a long period to educate the public in these political subtleties; meanwhile I might be next in line for the camps and the barracks.

LOS ANGELES, THE ENTIRE WEST COAST, learned to live with blackouts. The sneak attack on Pearl Harbor might occur again, this time on the continental coast, and L.A. was a natural target. Good citizens pasted black paper over their windows, lowered their shades, learned to travel and walk through darkened streets. I took a Red Cross lifesaving class, which was just about the only patriotic activity for which I was eligible. I tried to do war work in the factories, but that, too, was reserved for citizens.

Carl made a number of efforts to enlist. He was disqualified from the navy because he was nearsighted and too short; he could not meet the physical standards for the air force. Carl was not at all athletic, so he was not surprised at being turned down by the elite services. He expected to be drafted by the army in short order. Several of his friends who had already enlisted promised to get him into the Army's Signal Corps, where documentaries and war films were being made. If that failed, he would, because of his college degree, qualify for officer's training. Meanwhile, he decided to enter war work and was looking around for a training course.

I HAD BEGUN WRITING short stories in the spring, while we were still in New York. I sent them out to a list of magazines I considered a likely market, which I had drawn up in the public library. I was innocent and I had nerve and so I sent out my very first products to *Story Magazine*, the *New Yorker*, *Ladies' Home Journal*, the *Atlantic Monthly* and several prestigious small magazines. By the time we were settled in Hollywood I had four stories circulating—three about the occupation of

Austria by the Nazis and one my first effort at an American theme. The rejection letters, which came promptly, were not totally discouraging—several of them had little personal notes attached. "This story is very moving, and well written. The English is quite forceful, and the scene completely realistic," wrote the editor of *Direction.* "I'm sorry this story did not get all our votes for use in STORY," wrote Whit Burnett, the editor. I was beside myself with excitement. That meant it got some votes, didn't it ... Coming from the best short-story magazine in the U.S. this was hopeful indeed. I kept writing new stories and sending out the old ones.

Then, in August, just after we arrived in Hollywood, *The Clipper,* a small literary journal published by the League of American Writers, accepted my story "Prisoners" and it appeared in the September 1941 issue. This was the first story I had ever written. It dealt with my experiences in prison, which I ascribed to a fictional character. It was a strong story and still reads well today. Its publication confirmed my determination to be a professional writer. If my first story, written in a foreign language, could be published, then I could do it. All it needed was hard work and persistence.

Buoyed by my success, I sent packages of my stories to the story editors of all the major studios. Rejection letters followed promptly, and I decided I would first have to be published in magazines, then have the studios bid for my work.

Having a story appear in *The Clipper* meant that I got immediate feedback from some of the readers. By writing about my experience in Europe I acquired a sort of exalted status as a victim of fascism. I became a modest sort of celebrity in our small left-wing circle and people encouraged me to keep on writing. That heady first year in Hollywood, when early success and encouragement made me think I could actually earn a living as a writer, defined our marriage and our relationship and set it on its permanent course. We were lovers, comrades, good friends, but above all Carl and I were artistic collaborators.

At the League of American Writers' offices at Hollywood and Vine I attended various forums and discussion groups and joined a writers' workshop given by one of the league members, Viola Brothers Shore. In response to the teacher's questions about our motivation, life stories and self-evaluation, I answered with a two-and-a-half-page single-spaced critique of the workshop, the teacher, the questionnaire and the conduct of the class. I also offered this self-evaluation:

> I have a personality problem. I have a language problem. I have a problem
> of time and adjustment. I believe, that's all ... I am 21; I've lived under
> six different governments; I've been a student, a Nanny, a housemaid, a

research worker, a salesgirl, an office worker; I've worked in a factory and I've worked in hospitals; I've been in prison and I've gone to the opera twice a week. I've been married, divorced and am now married again. I've supported myself for the last three years. Four years ago I used to have a governess, because my father thought it was proper . . . My greatest weakness, I think, is a hangover from my childhood—my self-consciousness as far as people are concerned, my inferiority complexes, the false arrogance that I'm more capable because I've gone through more, the lack of understanding for the limitations of others. Also my absorption with whatever I'm doing at a particular time—my super concentration . . . I want to write honestly and write only about things I know. I want to write things that will make people more conscious, more honest and more antifascist. Also I'd like to get to know people better by writing about them.

My self-evaluation was right on target: I was unduly intense, super-serious, incapable of small talk or the kind of friendly gossip that holds acquaintances together. My perfectionism, insistence on antifascist commitment in word and deed and general "heaviness" as a person set me apart from others. Early in 1942 I joined a newly formed writers' workshop that sought to combine literary criticism and activist commitment. We alternately critiqued each other's novels and short stories and wrote leaflets and educational brochures for various good causes. I wrote leaflets and the text of a brochure for the Congressional campaign of a progressive Democratic candidate, Will Rogers Jr., in a folksy punchy style, and I was thrilled when the campaign committee actually printed my text. The candidate lost, unfortunately, but that did not dampen my enthusiasm for the effectiveness of my literary productions in "the real world." When our writers' workshop organized a small conference on the theme "The Pen Is Mightier Than the Sword," I participated enthusiastically. If my writing could serve my politics, then that was all the more reason why I could focus on becoming a writer.

Since the U.S.'s entry into the war I had begun to look for hospital work as an X-ray technician and at long last, in January of 1942, I was hired by a Catholic hospital in Pasadena. For me, this was the big break—for the first time I was going to work at a skilled job, making use of my professional training and earning forty dollars a week, which seemed like a fortune. The drawback was that I had a daily three-hour commute by bus to Pasadena and back, since I did not then have a driver's license. But I thought if I could stick it out for three months in that job, I would then be able to document one year's practical experience as an X-ray technician, counting my volunteer time in New York City, and that should be sufficient for me finally to secure a good job locally. I used the commuting time to read and even to write.

A few weeks later Carl signed up for a three-month training course to become a machinist, given by the U.S. Air Force. Since the course was given in Pasadena, near my place of work, we decided to move there, at least for the duration of Carl's course.

But Carl's training as a mechanic was as unsatisfying to him as had been his work on the assembly line at Technicolor. He just did not seem to be cut out for industrial work. But this time he tried hard to make a go of it. I still have the small and misshapen hammer that he brought home proudly, the first tool he had ever machined. He did not like the work and neither of us liked living in Pasadena, when all the action was in L.A. One day, on the way to class on his bicycle, Carl had an accident and broke his sternum and two ribs. This was sufficient excuse for dropping out of the training program and returning to Hollywood.

On the basis of his recent training, Carl had no trouble finding a war job as a machinist, but he had to work the graveyard shift, from 4 P.M. to midnight. We moved to a bright and airy apartment in a bungalow court. It had a balcony and felt like a tree house and, even though it had only one room, we considered it a great improvement over our first apartment. For the few months he held that job, we met each night at 1 A.M. for a meal and a quick chat and waited for weekends for a more normal schedule.

Then, in September 1942, our luck turned. The effects of the war on manpower were beginning to be felt; the country was at last moving out of the Depression and jobs were begging for workers. I was finally successful in getting a job as an X-ray technician in Los Angeles and gladly quit my job in Pasadena and with it the long hours of commuting. I worked for a radiologist who ran an outpatient clinic for the Southern Pacific Railroad. We did the routine chest X-rays for all workers and new employees, we did some work for ambulatory cases and we handled all the accident cases that did not require immediate surgery. Since the Southern Pacific Railroad was the main means of shipping war material to the embarkation ports on the West Coast, this was high-priority war work, the very thing I had been looking for. The only reason I was able to get this job, even though I was a resident alien, was that I worked for a private employer, not directly for the railroad. I worked in a downtown high-rise office building; I loved the location; I enjoyed my elegant quarters and my considerate and very professional boss. And I really loved my work.

Just a few weeks after I got my job, Carl got the break he had been waiting for—he was hired as an apprentice film editor at Columbia Pictures. Wartime manpower shortages were beginning to be felt in the motion picture industry and the old patronage system, whereby apprentice jobs in most of the skilled trades were reserved for male family members of union workers, could no longer be maintained. Jobs were made accessible to outsiders and talented people could advance more readily than before, when the medieval system of long apprenticeships and often lifelong status as journeyman (assistant editor) became unworkable due to labor shortages at a time of booming production. Carl advanced in one year from apprentice to assistant editor and thereafter his career was on a roll.

Housing was becoming very scarce in L.A., with tens of thousands of war workers and servicemen flocking into the city. In our new affluence, we looked for a larger apartment in the neighborhood and finally found one that suited us perfectly, quite near to our tree house apartment. This one was also in a *U*-shaped bungalow court with a beautiful green lawn in the center. Each unit was freestanding, a small cottage with a separate living room, bedroom, a good-sized kitchen and dinette and a full-sized bathroom. We were delighted with it and kept comparing it to the miserable housing one could get for such low rent in New York City. We were within walking distance of Griffith Park, one of the more elegant public parks in the city, and we often had our dinner as a picnic in the park. We signed a three-year lease that included a statement that we were childless and were not planning a family. We gave it no thought. The housing shortage allowed landlords to set all kinds of conditions for renting their places and restrictive covenants were still legal and widely used.

I HAVE STRUGGLED, over the years, to find a circle of belonging, a place or group in which I could be an insider. Perhaps this more than anything else has characterized my life since adolescence—always being an outsider, everywhere. At first I identified with the literary outsiders: Thomas Mann's Tonio Kroeger or Hanno Buddenbrook, Knut Hamsun's eternal wanderers and alienated strangers coming into a closely knit community and longing for acceptance, which was always denied. I associated it with being an artist—the creative genius forever doomed to alienation from his more commonplace fellowmen. In those days, and for many decades after, I could only think in terms of male heroes, since I never came across a female whose experiences spoke to mine. The women in fiction were strangely alien to me—now I understand that this was because they were figments of male invention, flat projections of male complementarity and need. They were not living creatures of the female kind.

What Carl gave me, from the very beginning of our relationship and throughout it, was a sense of belonging. He asked for faithful commitment on my part and, once he was certain of that, I felt I could be certain of his faithful commitment. We had our charmed circle of togetherness—we actually needed no one else, and although we each formed one or two solid friendships with persons of our own sex and had a number of long-lasting couple friendships, what mattered most to each of us was that we were coupled. In the best sense: two halves stronger together than each one alone. In the worst sense: each depended for inner security on what the other could provide. With such an arrangement one has no need to correct one's neurotic patterns and compulsions—one can survive with all one's faults.

Despite my deep pessimism and my various anxieties, I could not deny the miraculous transformations that had happened in my life. I had worked my way up to a professional job that gave me satisfaction. My Americanization progressed to the point where I finally gave away my beloved, indestructible and impossibly European blue tweed coat in favor of cheap and annually replaceable American ready-to-wear. I had settled down and was no longer a refugee, but a person soon to become an American.

ONE COULD HAVE TOLD THE STORY a number of ways:

By the time I was twenty-one I had been both rich and pampered and desperately poor. I had been in jail, my life in danger. I had been a hostage; I had been forcibly deported. I had been separated from my family and watched helplessly as many relatives were jailed, sent to concentration camps and killed. I had been exiled into a land I did not know and did not choose, where I knew only one person who had been my lover and now was my sponsor. I had been forced into marriage with him by bureaucratic pressure and the threat of deportation. I had married him, struggled to make a go of it and failed. I was divorced. With my fancy classical education I was equipped for no job; to survive I had to learn to lie about my qualifications and to bluff my way into poor jobs with long hours and terrible pay. I was undernourished, sick and trying desperately to rescue my mother from the nightmare of European war and advancing fascism. I was disenchanted with the young people with whom I had shared bed and board and political work and I had not a single friend.

OR ANOTHER VERSION:

After an economically sheltered childhood that was full of emotional turmoil, I had begun to define myself as a political being, an antifascist. I was terribly lucky in not being discovered as such, while I was jailed by the Nazis who wished to blackmail my father into signing away his property and his business. This was before the time of the more stringent anti-Semitic laws. I was incredibly lucky again in escaping six weeks of jail without lasting damage and in managing to escape Nazi-occupied Austria with my family. I found work when I needed it, always had a roof over my head and was the only one in my family able to immigrate to the U.S.A. I loved the country from the first day and adapted quickly to it. I went through a rough period of transition, marrying the friend I knew from Europe and discovering that this marriage was bad for both of us. I had the strength to leave him and to make it on my own. I began to write and my first two stories were printed in major magazines. I met the great love of my life and soon married him.

The first is a soap opera; yet every word in it is true. The second is a romance; just as true. In the first I am a victim; in the second a struggling heroine and finally a survivor.

ONE MIGHT TELL THE STORY yet another way:

I struggled out of an economically secure and emotionally ravaging childhood into self-reliance and alienation. I began writing at age sixteen and never stopped writing since. I met all kinds of challenges life placed in my path with a combination of luck, pluck and resilience. My good education helped me to adapt well; my good physical start in life helped me to survive a period of stress, physical deprivation and illness without serious damage; my strong political convictions gave me a perspective on everyday struggles that made it easier to cope with them. By the time I was twenty-one I had made the momentous decision to change my accidental immigrant status into a conscious choice—I would become a writer in the English language. And I succeeded and found early, quite spectacular and entirely short-lived recognition as a writer. And from alienation and social ineptitude I worked my way out to being able to hold a job, make a place for myself in various organized movements and build a marriage that lasted a lifetime.

I have been struggling all these years to arrive at a balance between these versions. Some days I see it one way, some days another. It depends on which side of my personality—the angry one or the heroic one—has the upper hand. In the end, it is usually the third version, the third mode that allows me to find some balance and to move on. That is, I remember who I am:

I am a writer. That's what really matters.

Ili (Ilona) Kronstein on her honeymoon, 1919.

Gerda as a baby, 1920.

Robert Kronstein with daughters Gerda *(left)* and Nora *(center)*, 1930. *Courtesy of Trude Fleischmann.*

Ili with Gerda, c. 1922.

Ili. *Courtesy of Trude Fleischmann.*

Gerda at sixteen. *Courtesy of Anita Dorfner.*

Gerda in Nice with her mother just before departing for the USA, 1939.

Gerda newly arrived in the USA.

Bobby Jensen in New York, 1939.

Nora, c. 1940.

Carl Lerner in Hollywood, 1941.

Carl and Gerda, 1941.

Gerda with Stephanie, 1946.

Gerda with Dan, 1947.

ABOVE: Gerda with Stephanie and Dan in front of their house in Los Angeles, 1948.

LEFT: Robert Kronstein, Gerda's father, with his second wife, Gretel.

ABOVE: Gerda in the late 1950s.
Courtesy of Maurice Constant.

Nora and Gerda, 1960s.

Carl and Gerda at her graduation, Columbia University, 1966.

Gerda in a new role, 1970s.

Gerda with daughter Stephanie and granddaughter Sophia, 1996.

Gerda with grandson Joshua Lapidus (Stephanie's son).

Gerda with son Dan and his sons Reed *(left)* and Clay.

Gerda at a speaking engagement in Vienna, Austria, 1995.

III

BECOMING
AN AMERICAN
RADICAL

[13]

T HE WAR YEARS, for us, were good years—if one could forget the horror of the war and its victims. We could not, nor did we want to—the war was our war and we wanted to be involved.

Now that Carl was working in the film industry, he no longer felt frustrated about not being able to volunteer for one of the armed services. Motion pictures were serving the war effort; whether he made them as a civilian or as a member of the Army's Signal Corps did not seem to make much difference.

Early in 1943 his draft call notice came. After a long day at the induction center, he was kept on after the other men had all been classified. He was again examined, this time by a radiologist and a heart specialist, and then was classified 4F— unfit for service due to a medical condition. He was advised to see a heart specialist as soon as possible.

We were both stunned. The army was notorious for taking the quick and the dead—people with longstanding medical problems found it difficult to get a 4F classification. What had they found in Carl?

The radiologist I worked for suggested that we do a chest X-ray and an EKG, free of charge. Carl came into my lab the next day and I did the procedures; the doctor was nice enough to read them at once. When he talked to us his face was grave. "You seem to have a serious heart problem, Mr. Lerner," he informed us. "Your heart is grossly enlarged and the EKG shows pathology. I suggest you take a sick leave and see a heart specialist." Was this a life-threatening condition, we asked him. He did not want to commit himself.

"If you were my patient," he said, "I'd put you on light activity, no stress, no physical exertion." But on the EKG report that he dictated it said "auricular fibrillation." I did know enough to know this was a most serious condition.

It took about a week before we could get an appointment with a specialist and during that week I sank to the bottom. All my fears, nurtured in tragic experience, all my pessimism and cynicism surfaced. I saw everything in the darkest possible light. He might be an invalid; he might die. I knew our love was too good to be true; I knew it couldn't last. Something terrible had happened and worse would come after . . .

Carl, as usual, was calm and steady under stress. Why not wait and see what the specialist says, he suggested. The army doctors were a random lot; they could make mistakes. As for Dr. L., he might have been influenced by the army doctors' negative appraisal. Anyway, a heart condition could mean all kinds of things . . . No, he did not believe it was some sort of bad fate pursuing me. He held me close to him and let me cry.

The heart specialist, after a long and thorough examination, had a simple explanation. Carl had no heart defect whatsoever; his heart was in perfect working order. What he did have was a congenital condition: his heart was slightly rotated on its axis in relation to the rest of the chest cavity; thus it appeared at an angle different from the norm, both in X-rays and EKGs, which led to the misdiagnosis of a heart enlargement. "Forget it," said the specialist. "Thank your lucky stars that you won't have to go overseas. Lead a normal life."

It was the kind of diagnosis after which one does not seek a second opinion. Carl accepted it and I was only too glad to believe it true. We had been reprieved; now life seemed sweeter and richer than ever. There *was* something special about our charmed relationship and maybe, just maybe, I could learn to be less cynical, less given to negative thinking.

OUR FRIENDS WERE SCATTERED among the different services. Jeff joined the navy and was shipped to the Pacific, where he saw a lot of action on an aircraft carrier. Dolph, a conscientious objector, enlisted in the Red Cross and was promptly posted on Guam, where he was in the thick of the fighting. John, a Lincoln Brigade veteran, had volunteered for the army, expecting to serve in Europe; instead he was stuck in the Nevada desert in a mine-detecting unit. His unit was full of reds, among them a number of veterans of the Spanish civil war. This could not be an accident. He sent desperate letters to everyone. "Help, they are trying to kill us here before we ever see any enemy soldiers." Phone calls to Congressmen, outraged petitions finally got him transferred and he served out the war in Europe with great distinction. The members of my refugee youth group in New York had all enlisted; they too had to fight for the right to fight. Many of them were sent to the South Pacific, despite or perhaps because of their European backgrounds. Bobby, too, enlisted in the army, was made a medic and served in the South Pacific. Only one of my European friends was appropriately placed—in the newly formed OSS. Blond and blue-eyed, though Jewish, this Austrian was parachuted inside Nazi Germany and served heroically behind the German lines. During most of the war I spent many hours each week writing them cheery letters from the home front, one of my self-imposed patriotic duties.

Everyday life changed as the country switched to a war economy. As more and more of the men were drafted and shipped overseas, the women took over their jobs. The move of women workers into "unusual occupations" was made rapidly and without too much resistance. War industries sprung up everywhere, especially in Southern California, where aircraft, shipping and weapons were made. War industries were put on a twenty-four-hour-a-day schedule, and *E* for Efficiency became the most important goal. Waitresses and secretaries found that, with only brief training, they could become assembly line workers and help the war effort. For many whose men were overseas, doing war work felt like being personally connected with their men. Former assembly line workers quickly moved into the more skilled mechanical trades. Housewives abandoned high heels, long flying hair, which might become entangled in machines, long fingernails and fancy clothing. Rosie the Riveter became the fashion model, and women, regardless of their ages and figures, proudly displayed their steel helmets, work goggles, heavy boots. Many mothers chose to work the graveyard shift so that they could be home with their children during the daytime hours. It was hard to get babysitters, and childcare, while suddenly much more widely available in the war industries, was still in inadequate supply.

In the bungalow court in which we lived, almost all the mothers were war workers, coming and going at all hours of the night and day and dragging their children to childcare centers in line with their work schedules. I remember one incident that was quite typical of the makeshift arrangements of women war workers.

I was awakened during the night by police lights blinking in my windows—it was 2 A.M. There were policemen in the yard and some of the neighbors had come out, as I had, watching what was going on. The cops were flashing their lights into the windows of one of the bungalows, then retreated in amazement and conferred with one another. I looked in on a rather startling scene: In one of the living rooms just like my own, two boys were happily playing. The floor was covered with flour, sugar, spaghetti and rice. The three year old was happily riding his kiddie car through the ankle-high mess, while his little brother was making piles of the novel play materials, tasting them and throwing them up in the air. The radio was blaring out country music, which is what had first alerted the neighbors and then the police. A neighbor explained to the cops that the children's mother was a shipyard worker on the graveyard shift and had left them sound asleep. She, the neighbor, was to keep an eye on them from 5:30 A.M. on, but apparently they had woken up and improvised. The other neighbors corroborated that the woman was a good and caring mother; her husband was a soldier in the Pacific theater. The woman was from the South and had no relatives in town. The cops decided to take no action; then several of the neighbor women went in to clean up the mess and put the children to bed. "But you tell her next time we'll take the children to Social Service," one of the policemen insisted.

"Don't you know there's a war on," one of the neighbor women said in outrage. The war workers' children learned to fend for themselves. Neighbors helped neighbors; strangers became friends.

AT LAST, IN JUNE 1943, my waiting period was over and I received notice that I now would be granted U.S. citizenship. This event provided the story of my registration as an "enemy alien" with a deeply ironic ending. When Carl and I went to the federal courthouse in downtown Los Angeles, where I would be sworn in as a citizen, I still could not quite believe that this was actually happening. I had already passed the required test about the Constitution and some aspects of U.S. history; now I lined up with hundreds of others in front of the door leading to the swearing-in ceremony. An official of the Immigration Service stood at the door with a clipboard in his hand and checked each name against his list. When my turn came, he asked me to stand aside. Carl rushed to my side and I whispered, "You see, it's not going to happen. They've found something to keep me out." I felt as I had four years ago when they pulled me out of the line on the ship in New York Harbor and told me I could not yet be admitted to the U.S., desperate, panicked, convinced my worst nightmares were true. Now, the official told me to report to a room on an upper floor. The clerk in that office looked over a file, which seemed to me ominously fat. He verified my name and address and then said in a puzzled tone: "Are you a German citizen?"

"I never was," I said angrily. "I am Austrian and Jewish, but I was forced to emigrate with a German passport. For some reason I've never understood, the U.S. government does not seem to recognize that that does not make me a German citizen."

"Well, you always registered as a German enemy alien," he said somewhat accusingly.

"Look again," I cried. "Surely you must have it in your record that I always registered 'under protest.'"

"I have that in the record and it looked puzzling to me. What did you protest?"

"The fact that I'm Austrian, Jewish, and not German, but I've been forced to register as an enemy alien."

He laughed and closed his folder. "Well, you can relax now. The U.S. government has just recognized that Austria was annexed by force and is considered an occupied country. So you never really were an enemy alien."

"What are you keeping me here for, then?"

"You can go downstairs and be sworn in," he said in a friendly tone. I did not wait for him to change his mind.

"Thank you." I rushed downstairs, joining the group of people waiting to be sworn in. And so, by government decree, I became deconstructed from my "enemy alien status" at the very last minute, and then, with a fervently spoken Oath of Allegiance, I at last became an American citizen.

"You see," said Carl, "it all worked out well." Always the optimist.

"By the skin of my teeth," I said.

Only a refugee, only a once-stateless person, can understand what that symbolic ceremony of naturalization meant. I have, in my long life, experienced all kinds of feelings of helplessness, fear, terror, insecurity. But nothing can compare to being cast outside the civil contract, outside the definition of the citizen. One still has life, but nothing more. One has neither residence, nor permanence, nor a voice that matters, nor the simple privileges that belong to others by right of birth. And so, to have the gift of citizenship granted at last was like being reborn.

I have always considered citizenship a serious obligation. I can say with some pride that since that day in 1943 I have never missed voting in any election and I have often actively participated in the process. I still, to this day, sing the national anthem with honest feeling. And I believe firmly that the U.S. Constitution with its Bill of Rights is the best model for democratic governance yet devised by human beings. I did not then nor do I now see any contradiction between a firm allegiance to this nation and its Constitution, and the belief that the social system, as it has evolved since the time of the foundation of the nation, needs improvement.

The big lie that would be inundating the country shortly after the end of the war, proclaimed from every newspaper page, in radio broadcasts and in every political forum from the State House to the Capitol, was that belief in socialism—in whatever form—was seditious and un-American. This lie was, of course, much older. It had been successfully used against the Knights of Labor and the American Federation of Labor (AFL) in its organizing days, against the victims of the Haymarket affair in 1886, against Wobblies in the early twentieth century and against left-wing radicals of every description during the Palmer raids of the 1920s. The right to dissent, that cherished pillar of the Bill of Rights, had been under attack ever since the Alien and Sedition Acts in Jefferson's administration. As I was becoming an American, I felt myself to be in line with an honorable tradition of American radicalism. In fact, the discovery of that radicalism, the peculiar American features of it, was an exciting and stimulating aspect of my experience of the war years.

My political beliefs were still very much grounded in the European radical tradition. I had studied Marxist texts in Europe; to me the Communist parties of Europe were the parties of heroes and heroines of the resistance. I believed that socialism was a long-range goal, attainable by democratic means, which would make life better for the vast majority of people. And the Soviet Union, as I then saw it, was, with the exception of Great Britain, the only country that was offering successful and sustained resistance to the advance of fascism. The incredible sacrifices of its citizens and of its armed forces during the German invasion gave hope to the world and reversed the tide of fascist victories. That very heroism of the Russian people seemed to give the lie to all those who had equated Soviet rule with fascist dictatorship. Oppressed people don't fight as the Russians did.

In 1943, millions of Americans saw the Soviet Union in this light. The Russians were our allies; they were bearing the brunt of the Nazi attack while we were preparing slowly, ever so slowly, for an invasion of Europe. It was not necessarily a sign of paranoia on the part of the American Left to see in this a desire by the government to let the Soviet Union become seriously weakened before committing U.S. troops to the contest.

Carl stage-managed an elaborate show at the Hollywood Bowl in support of opening up a second front in Europe, and was congratulated for his efforts by the Mayor of Los Angeles. For once, the advocacy of U.S.-Soviet friendship was a legitimate acceptable goal, not a sectarian pipe dream. My initiation into American radical politics started against this background.

Left-wing activity in Hollywood frequently took the form of fund-raising parties for one or another good cause. We attended these parties in the homes of our recently successful friends and there we mingled not only with long-term friends from the New Theater and the Group Theater, but with Hollywood stars and musicians. We heard Meade Lux Lewis play the piano, producing incredible runs of pearly notes with his stubby fingers. Earl Robinson, whose "Ballad for Americans" became the theme song of the 1944 Republican Party convention, played a preview of his new musical at a fund-raising party. Yip Harburg, then a rising star of musicals and film, entertained. And Zero Mostel, the New York comedian, had us in stitches with his "Senator Klaghorn" routine. The black sharecropper, Leadbelly, in overalls as though he had just come in off the cotton fields, appeared in the high-ceilinged living room with its unequalled panoramic view of the bay and sang his Southern blues. We loved it and enjoyed this rich cultural mix; still we were critical of our rich and successful friends. "Where they live, on a clear day you can see the class struggle" went a bon mot, mimicking the real-estate agents' claim about every Hollywood hill house, that on a clear day you could see Catalina Island from its living room windows. Too much of our friends' conversation consisted of name-dropping and self-aggrandizement. We were tired of always hearing of their latest acting or producing triumphs. Even as they were fund-raising for war victims, U.S.-Soviet friendship, racial integration and other excellent causes, they seemed to us to have "gone Hollywood."

"You can always tell when they've really made it," we joked. "It's when they start complaining about their domestic help and when they tell you about their psychiatrists."

Still, many of these successful Hollywood radicals were serious about their art and their social consciences. Many of them agonized about the corruption inherent in the studio production process. They wanted to be responsible for their work; they fiercely resented the producers' interference with their writing; they agonized over the gap between their scripts and what the public would see on the screen. In later years the question placed before the American public was whether the Communist screenwriters unduly influenced the American public with their "subversive ideas." To anyone knowing how the industry operated and how little control the individual screenwriter had over his or her product, the question is ludicrous. A number of our friends who had recently come from New York were constantly talking about returning there out of fear of losing their integrity by working under the Hollywood system. But it is easy to get used to fifteen-hundred-dollar-a-week salaries; much harder to give them up for an uncertain future and grand principles. Carl and I developed a workable philosophy, even though we were nowhere near the temptations of Hollywood fleshpots. Carl attempted to formulate a baseline for himself. "As long as I'm willing, at any time, to give up my job rather than do work I find wrong or evil, I can stay honest." With my munificent forty-five-dollar-a-week salary I was not subject to such temptations. But I agreed with him.

We experienced Hollywood differently than did the successful radical screenwriters, directors and actors. Ours was Hollywood, the company town, where craft people in a one-industry town tried to make a living and achieve some form of job security. The larger setting was Los Angeles, an open shop town, solidly Republican and politically and economically dominated by the Southern Pacific Railroad, the large growers, and the Hearst interests. Labor conditions in the film industry were outrageously bad when we first came to Hollywood. I remember the situation of our actor friends who lived in constant anxiety that they might miss the all-important telephone call from Central Casting, which might mean a day's or a week's work. "Central Casting only rings three times" was the ground rule. That meant that if the call was not answered before the fourth ring, the job would go to someone else. As a result, actors were tied to their fifty-foot extension cords as if to a lifeline. This was in the days before cellular phones.

Screenwriters were treated like exchangeable assembly workers by the studios. They were hired at weekly salaries that seemed fabulous to Depression-conditioned writers, but working conditions ranged from bad to intolerable. Screenwriters were each assigned a cubbyhole office on the studio lot; they had to be present all day and were expected to produce so many pages of script a day, as though writing were the same as operating a punch press or a lathe. Their written work was revised by other writers, edited, mutilated and distorted, as the studio saw fit, and it was not unusual to have three to four writers work on one script in succession. When on an assignment, writers and other "talent" workers labored unlimited hours and were on call during evenings and weekends without overtime pay. It took years of hard struggle by the Screen Actors Guild and the Screen Writers Guild to win better working conditions for their members. The battle for screen credits truly representative of the writers' contribution to the film script and for writers' property rights in their scripts, which included royalties for resales and, somewhat later, for TV rights, was fought for over a decade in the 1940s.

The union to which Carl belonged was the International Alliance of Theatrical and Stage Employees (IATSE). This union, servicing stagehands, backstage technicians and projectionists, had long been gangster-ridden and corrupt. In the late thirties and the early forties, during the period when the talent guilds in Hollywood consolidated their gains and won recognition, IATSE made sweetheart deals with the producers, provided strikebreakers and goons to break up picket lines and in general acted in the producers' interest. Representing manual craft workers, the IA had from its inception been organized along AFL craft union traditions and was able to offer its members far better and more secure working conditions than those of talent workers. Of course, the salaries of these craft workers represented only a small portion of the cost of production, while the demands of talent unions were far more costly to the producers and therefore were fiercely resisted. Because it included among its membership the screen projectionists, IA had enormous clout in the industry. The threat to pull the projectionists out on strike and thereby close movie theaters all around the nation, which would mean enormous financial losses for the producers, was therefore taken very much more seriously than a strike threat from the talent unions. Scripts could wait, and the studios always had massive backlogs of scripts ready for production, so that in the event of a writers' strike they could hold out for a long time without financial loss. But a strike by the IA would mean potential financial disaster, and the producers never allowed that to happen. In later years IATSE would use this power to enforce the blacklist on talent people whose political opinions were suspect.

FILM EDITORS WERE PART of the IATSE, whose president then was Roy Brewer. Carl joined the guild as soon as he was hired. IA followed the craft union principle of restricting membership (except for the sons of members) by charging very high initiation fees. Carl was earning less than eighty dollars a week as an apprentice editor when we had to pay off an initiation fee of several thousand dollars. But it was worth it, for membership in IA meant job security.

Carl soon learned that there was no democracy in his union and that membership meetings were called only to rubber-stamp decisions made by the union leadership. He worked quietly and patiently with a small group of progressive union members who were trying to democratize the union by offering an alternate slate in union elections. This was considered very threatening by the entrenched leadership; the progressives understood they were putting their own jobs in jeopardy.

Because of his membership in IA, a union in which very few progressive members survived for any length of time, Carl was in a Communist Party group of craft union members. I knew nothing about his activities in that group nor about its membership and I did not want to know about it. Mostly out of fear I did not join the party until years later. I did not really trust the fact that U.S.-Soviet friendship and cooperation meant the acceptance of the Communist Party as one among many legitimate parties in the U.S. political system. There were too many indications pointing in the other direction: the discrimination in the armed forces experienced by our friends who were veterans of the Abraham Lincoln Brigade; the continuation of the House Committee on Un-American Activities (subsequently HUAC), the so-called Dies Committee, named for its chairman, Martin Dies; and above all the passage in 1940 of the Alien Registration Act (Smith Act). The latter mandated the fingerprinting of all aliens, made it unlawful to advocate the overthrow of the U.S. government by force and violence, and made it unlawful to join any organizations that had such aims. I never in my life have believed in or advocated the violent overthrow of the government (nor did the Communist Party so advocate), but this kind of legislation implicitly defined all advocacy of socialism as treason. As it was designed to do, it had a chilling effect on any kind of radical dissent.

Thus, my "underground mentality" continued for far longer than I had expected it would. As I am recollecting this period of my life, I am struck by the fact that for most of my adult life governmental repression of radical dissent was an incontrovertible fact. I was fourteen years old when clerical fascism was instituted in Austria. I lived all my adolescence under fascism. Only during the war years in the U.S.A. did I experience a different climate. But because I was then characterized as an "enemy alien" I did not feel this democratic privilege extended to me, as indeed, by virtue of the Smith Act, it did not. Therefore, I continued living according to the underground principle that you ask no questions and know only what you need to know, for fear of betraying yourself and others under pressure.

WE FORMED SOME SOLID FRIENDSHIPS during those years. Most of them were with people Carl had known for years and who generously welcomed me into their circle. We were especially close to Jeff and Hope Corey, the Robisons and the Brodines. Jeff was an actor who had become quite successful in Hollywood when the war started and he enlisted in the navy. His beautiful wife, Hope, who looked very much like Ingrid Bergman, was left behind with her one-year-old daughter. We became adopted family and Carl tried his best to replace the absent father for Eve. I adored the sturdy little girl; being with her made me aware of how much I wanted to have a child, even though there were many good reasons why we were not ready for that big decision. I remember to this day how excited I was when Eve took her first tentative step, with Carl and I holding her outstretched hands.

David and Naomi Robison had two children already and a third on the way. Carl had known Naomi for years, from the New York theater. She was an actress then, and even during the war years and with three small children, she pursued her career. A petite dynamic woman with a mobile face and enormous amounts of focused energy, Naomi was always the center of community activity, of progressive politics, of a rich social life. David was equally gregarious, a very cultured man with broad interests. He came from a family of musicians, with a mother who was an accomplished pianist who saw to it that each of her children learned to play an instrument before age ten. She supplied each of her grandchildren with a Steinway piano at the appropriate time, explaining that there was no point learning music on a mediocre instrument. David had studied musicology in Vienna; he spoke fluent German and enjoyed reminiscing with me about Vienna. His first academic job had been in the music department of Fisk University, where he and Naomi had lived for four years. Their experiences as whites in a predominantly black university town fascinated me—I was deeply impressed with the way they carried their politics into daily life. David had a first-rate mind and loved good abstract talk, a passion I shared. He was restless and wanted a change—he had come to Hollywood to be a writer. Because of a rheumatic heart condition he was draft-exempt and soon began to work in radio. We formed a close "couple friendship" that held up over the decades of hard times and good. And for me, David was special—next to Carl he was my closest male friend. I regarded him as the brother I had not had and he, with his talented, close-knit, expressive Jewish family that certainly needed no addition, understood my deep longing for a close family and adopted us as part of theirs. Now that Naomi and David are long dead, my friendship continues with their children.

I met Virginia Brodine in the writers' workshop I had joined. She was working on a novel about four generations of women in her family, at the same time as I was working on my first novel. Her husband, Russell, was a bass fiddle play-er in the Los Angeles Symphony, a graduate of Curtis Institute. Virginia and Russell were from the state of Washington, the first native Westerners I had ever met—they were devoted trade unionists, Communists and activists in any num-ber of good causes, and they were the warmest, most honest and straightforward people. It seems to me we were never just acquaintances, but became friends at once in that passionate rush of recognition that happens when one meets a kindred soul. Virginia and I could not have been more different in background and upbringing. She came from a family that could trace its descent from Scotch-Irish in the twelfth century. She had had an exceedingly happy childhood, marred only by her mother's death when she was twelve; she was raised in a religious home. She was skillful at all household tasks, an excellent cook and baker, expert at making pies and canning fruits and vegetables, while my repertoire consisted of three dish-es. But we were very much alike in our aspirations as writers, both struggling with our first major work, both passionate stylists and fascinated with craft. We could talk for hours on end; we read and critiqued each other's work. During the war, we were both working full time, she as a journalist and I as an X-ray technician. Both of us struggled to find time for writing. It was a constant balancing act.

Virginia was, from the beginning of our friendship, part of my writing life and part of my Americanization. She had a vast knowledge of American history and literature, which she freely shared with me. We read the same books, argued about them, read each other's chapters as they took shape, and talked endlessly about our so very different childhoods. Virginia and Russell were "grassroots" people, always closely rooted in neighborhood, family and the workplace. Against their steady and firm anchoring in tradition, ethnicity and working-class culture, my newly acquired polish of Americanism seemed frail and inadequate. Virginia was one of the few people who ever mentored me, corrected me, straightened me out when I needed it, and in general acted like an older sister.

What particularly bound me to Virginia was her calm, her emotional stabil-ity. It was a quality I wanted very much to acquire. She was steady and deep; I was volatile, easily triggered, given to great enthusiasms and bouts of depression or anger. That despite all our differences I had made a friend of her I considered my good fortune.

After taking two short-story classes with Viola Brothers Shore, I had begun work on a novel. Like many first novels it was autobiographical, a fact encouraged by Shore. Her theme was "Write what you know." It took me decades before I understood that much of my writing was to find out what I know. In those days my views of art were simpler: I must write out of my own experience, because my experience carries a political lesson. If I wrote well enough, people would absorb that political lesson while being entertained. In my conscious effort to become an American writer, I gave up my German literary models—Thomas Mann, Knut Hamsun, Karl Kraus. I read all the O. Henry Award–winning short-story collections of the past decade, Hemingway, Dos Passos and Faulkner. Richard Wright's work struck me with elemental force—he spoke from the gut in a way I wished I could speak, but that seemed utterly unobtainable to me at that time. Carl and I read Carl Sandburg, Vachel Lindsay and Walt Whitman aloud to each other. The only German author I was not willing to give up was Bertolt Brecht, whose work on the emigration experience spoke to me directly and powerfully. I was determined that Carl must learn to appreciate Brecht as I did. I developed the ability to do simultaneous translation, reading in German and speaking in English, but I never did get Brecht's poetic quality right until much later, when I translated some of his work in earnest and with care, in writing.

I was struggling to acquire my new language as I struggled to "become" an American. I wanted both and I understood I needed one to become the other. It strikes me now that I might have done better to read more of the classics of English literature than to read only modern "relevant" authors, but I was looking for models for my own work, a political antifascist novel.

For my twentieth birthday Carl had given me an English dictionary; for my twenty-first I got *Roget's Thesaurus.* I absorbed vocabulary voraciously and collected "phrases" as though they were jewelry. I began to absorb the marvels of English syntax, the economy and expressiveness of short, declarative sentences as against the cumbersome, circuitous structure of German sentences. Like many self-taught persons, I wrote in a simple style because I lacked the knowledge of more sophisticated constructions. I acquired that knowledge much later and with it more subtlety in my writing, but that early, intuitive comprehension of the sharpness and incisiveness of Anglo-Saxon words and grammar has stayed with me.

Brecht wrote eloquently about the cost paid by the writer forced to abandon his language. I know whereof he speaks and it is not a minor matter. It goes to the depth of the soul, to the language of the unconscious. Many decades later, when I was in analysis, the crucial insights would always pop up in German, thus proving the very existence of the unconscious, since by then I never spoke it and hardly ever heard German spoken. In my early years in America, the markers of achievement were first the ability to think in English without translating; then that magical moment when I began to dream in English. It took me at least a decade before I could understand American jokes. To this day I cannot really tell a joke in English with any assurance of success.

As you think in translation or as you think in a language only dimly perceived, your work as a writer is the work of a sculptor using dull tools. There is a constant element of insecurity in every sentence written and there is self-doubt so fierce it works against the authorial voice. One cannot trust one's own voice and one needs to hear it affirmed before believing it. For this I needed Carl; for this I used him and submitted my most intimate product, my writing, to his judgement. Carl had encouraged my writing from the start; now artistic collaboration became an essential aspect of our marriage.

He read everything I wrote. As soon as I had "finished" a story, I would read it out loud to him and then he would read it silently, penciling in his comments and corrections. Then we would have a work session in which I usually accepted all his stylistic changes—I did not as yet have enough confidence in having a style of my own—although from the start I would fight him on grammatical changes. This is Germanic, he would say, and I would guiltily admit that it was and accept his change. But when it came to rules of English grammar I would argue with him. My linguistic ability was quite acute, due to my long years of apprenticeship and worship of Karl Kraus, the master of German style and language. Also, my eight years of Latin and my good French gave me an assurance well beyond my knowledge, when it came to the structure of language. After we checked out some grammatical rule, it usually turned out I was right, even though I did not necessarily even know the rule. I had a "feel" for language, an instinct I trusted from the beginning and that has never failed me. I guess this is one of the few gifts I have as a writer. "Meaning is to be found by tapping along the guiding rope of language," wrote Karl Kraus. I've done that and it has helped me become a bilingual writer.

When it came to content, characterizations, construction, Carl was an excellent critic, but I never took direction easily. We would argue fiercely and long and there were times when I insisted on doing it my way, even when he continued to disagree. But on the whole I was immensely grateful for his help. He, in turn, shared not only his writing—the drafts of screenplays, ideas for radio scripts and for dramatic presentations—with me, but also accepted my criticism, which most of the time had to do with characterization. We would argue about the psychology of our imagined characters as though they were intimate friends living with us. Later, when he was a successful film editor, he would discuss his editing and script problems with me in the same way. We agreed that my visual judgement was not as good as his, but that I was better at developing story line and characterization. Over the years, our collaboration took the shape of a number of joint screenplays, almost all of them unsuccessful, and constant mutual feedback on successful work. He had vastly more self-assurance in his work than I did and for decades he had success, while I was a failure. He was my mentor in politics, art, film and literature. I think without him I could not have progressed the way I did, but there was a cost to it, too, in that I did not experience directly the strengthening that comes with a sense of mastery. My sense of mastery, for years and years, was mediated through him. Just as I relied on him for the correct pronunciation of words, so I relied on him for verifying my style. And yet, underneath it all, I had the confidence, the assertive courage of the creative writer. But until the very last years of our life together I thought he was the greater talent, the true artist, while I was, at best, promising. When he died it took me well over a year to learn that I could write without him. I had seriously believed that I could not.

In 1943, my literary success seemed only a matter of time. I had acquired a literary agent, Frances Pyndick, at one of the two best talent agencies in the country. Miss Pyndick had accepted me on the strength of three short stories I had sent her. Within a short time she sold one of them to the best literary magazine in the country at the time, *Story: The Magazine of the Short Story.* My story "The Prisoner" appeared in the September–October 1943 issue. It was based on one of the war atrocity reports I had read in the newspapers, reprinted from the Soviet press. It concerned an episode when a guerilla group fought a German outpost on the Russian front. One of the guerillas captured turned out to be a woman, who was promptly raped and then shot by the Nazi soldiers. I told my story from the shifting points of view of four of the German soldiers involved in the incident and used it to explore the psychology of the killers. It was a good story and readers responded strongly to it. My agent thought my outline for the novel promising and began to market it as soon as I had written a few chapters.

During this period I attended several classes at the League of American Writers. One, which had a far greater impact on me than I realized at the time, was a course in American history given by John Howard Lawson. It was, in fact, my first course ever in American history. Lawson, later one of the Hollywood Ten, the unfriendly witnesses before HUAC who went to jail for their refusal to name names before the committee (technically for "contempt of Congress"), would be pilloried in the press and media as the "Communist cultural czar" of Hollywood. I knew him as a brilliant lecturer, a fine teacher, a man of broad learning. His course was a combination of what now would be called American studies—intellectual and social history, literature and film. It was lively, informative and, judging from my class notes and the syllabus, which I still have, offered a traditionally Progressive interpretation of history. Its most radical aspect was a heavy emphasis on the role of race and racism in U.S. history. What seems quite remarkable to me now was Lawson's matter-of-fact inclusion of sources by women and material about women. At the time I took the course, I did not realize what a truly unique feature this was and how untraditional compared to the then-current historiography. I enjoyed hearing about Anne Bradstreet, Margaret Brent, Sojourner Truth and Harriet Tubman. The discussion of the woman suffrage movement was linked to that of the labor movement—another unusual approach. Was it Marxist in content and attitude? Only insofar as awareness of race and sex discrimination was part of Marxist theory. As I look at the syllabus now and at my handwritten notes on the lectures, I find that this course could today be a standard American studies course in any good college. The only tendentious aspect of the course was Lawson's approach to creative writing. Here he followed the traditional Marxist line of his day—he downgraded any work he considered "formalistic" or "mystical" (Emily Dickinson, T. S. Eliot) and upgraded any work with easily accessible social significance (Whitman, Carl Sandburg). The style he favored was realism.

One of the students in the course was a tall, stooping old man, whose heavy head with its dark brows gave him an introspective, inward look. He seldom spoke, but was attentive to the lectures and sometimes interjected a few sentences to which Lawson paid respectful attention. This was Theodore Dreiser, one of the country's great novelists, who, late in life, joined the Communist Party. He was also, incidentally, one of the major exponents of realist writing. To have him in this class was, to me, just one more confirmation that the best minds in the U.S. were leftist radicals—a generalization I then firmly believed.

DURING THE WAR, communication with my family was difficult. Many letters were lost; others arrived four to five months after they were written. Telegrams were censured and so strictly regulated that they served only for emergency communication. The longer the gaps between letters, the more difficult it was to write back. For my father and my sister there was the additional burden that they felt they could not share the truth about my mother's condition with me, just because of the long intervals between letters. They felt that since most of the news was bad or inconclusive, sharing it with me would have imposed a terrible burden of pain on me, so they wrote little and in vague generalities. As a result, I did not know what was going on. My father explained it all to me eighteen months later, when the war was over and when the ugly reality of my mother's terminal illness was beyond doubt. I will set it down here not as I knew it then, but as it developed.

I had three letters from my mother between January and October 1943. In the first one, shortly after her arrival in Vaduz, she wrote optimistically and honestly about her difficulty adjusting to living with my father. In her next letter she wrote of her excessive weakness, her inability to walk a short distance without losing her balance. A few months after her arrival in Vaduz the same symptoms that had alarmed her in Nice recurred—paralysis and extreme weakness of the right arm and hand, weakness in the legs, dizziness and lack of balance. Vaduz has no hospital and Liechtenstein has no neurological specialist, so my father sent her to a clinic in Zurich, where the diagnosis was that she suffered from post-stress symptoms, the effects of malnutrition and general neurosis due to wartime stress. She was moved from one sanitorium to another and finally lodged in a mental hospital in Zurich, where she was given rest, something called "work-therapy" and large doses of cheerful admonition.

She wrote me letters from what she referred to as "the nuthouse" but they were censored by the doctor and she could not mail them until she was back in Vaduz. While she was in that hospital she wrote me the third letter that year. In it she said: "After a dark, mean night, battling demons, I got up early and stood in front of the mirror and made a self-portrait of my distorted face." (That self-portrait of my mother, in dark charcoal, a despairing, suffering woman, hangs in my study— terrifying and yet transcendent in its artistry.) Her letter continues: "I am learning to clean string beans and iron the laundry for two hours." This "therapy" was supposed to soothe her nerves. Other treatments, such as injections of various substances and hypnosis, proved unavailing. She returned to Vaduz in October, somewhat improved, and wrote me two letters, which reflected renewed optimism and the belief that her injured nerves would recover once the war was over.

In fact, her condition worsened within a few months and she had to suffer staying in several more hospitals. Every treatment failed and she began to have episodes of paralysis of the limbs and loss of speech. But her condition fluctuated and there were short periods of remission, some lasting several months, all of which reinforced the impression that this was a psychoneurotic illness. In 1944, after the invasion of Europe, all letters stopped.

I kept writing and my father and sister kept writing letters that did not arrive, and I'm sure my mother wrote many letters in her mind and in her heart. But in actuality we lived in a prison without walls, in a black pit of false facts and forced forgetting, which gradually became a sort of cocoon. What one does not know does not hurt. So goes the charitable explanation. I think otherwise. What one does not know hurts all the more—it becomes a slow, seeping poison, which tinges every happy moment with guilt and casts a fog over joy and hope. Ever since those years I have become a fanatic about truthful information, because I know how terrible the burden of being protected from pain can become.

Nevertheless, and still and always, life goes on. Europe and my family receded from my attention; the emotional calculus by which organisms survive functioned well. Just like becoming a practiced liar corrupts one's ability for true feeling, so becoming practiced at selective forgetting corrupts.

Politics became a great help in that process. Politics, like competitive sport, is always absorbing, intriguing, demanding, challenging. And there is also the added bonus of feeling one has served a greater good by all this strenuous effort.

I became active in the 1944 election and volunteered as a precinct captain for the Democratic Party in the neighborhood in which I lived. This area had been solidly Republican for decades and the challenge was to carry it for Franklin Delano Roosevelt. I was in charge of thirteen blocks and found two people in each block who took responsibility for canvassing in that area. We did purely Jimmy Higgins work: the distribution of election literature to each household, which was combined with personal contact with the household wherever possible; then, just prior to election day, the covering of each household with Democratic sample ballots and a leaflet urging voter participation. Finally, we visited each Democratic household again, in person or by phone, on election day, to get out the vote. It was strictly routine organizational work. I had a full-time job and could do the work only in the evenings and on weekends.

Most of my canvassers were women, full-time housewives and mothers. When I went into the Democratic Party headquarters to pick up literature, the volunteers were mostly women, but the staff members were men. Later, when I had contact with the District Committee, I noticed the same pattern. I would see it over and over again in succeeding election campaigns, in California and in New York. This knowledge of practical gender politics was something I later brought with me into my work when I became a historian.

The activity was very important to me. I had never voted in my life and to be able to be an active participant in the process was part of my Americanization.

Seeing to it that my territory was adequately covered by volunteer canvassers, trying to hold each of these canvassers to her task and checking up on her performance, was entirely new to me. I discovered that I enjoyed this kind of work and was good at it. I also enjoyed getting to know my neighbors well. By the end of the campaign I knew many of the voters by name and knew a little something of their lives. When in the end we carried the district for FDR, I felt as though I owned a share of the government.

CARL AND I HAD for some time considered having children. Our relationship had grown in love and friendship and, in principle, we both wanted children and had agreed on that before we got married. But as fascism spread across Europe and the war engulfed more and more of the world, it seemed irresponsible to put a child in such a world. The future was uncertain; our economic position had only just recently been somewhat above poverty level. We had no house of our own; we had a tiny cheap car and we had to face the fact that Carl's trade union activity put him in constant jeopardy. Also, he realized that if the war were to end, his job would probably go to a veteran. All of this spoke in favor of waiting.

But early in 1943 the war was taking a favorable turn. The Russians had turned back the German army at Stalingrad in February and went on the offensive along their entire front; the Allies invaded Italy in July and slowly fought their way up the peninsula. At the Teheran Conference (November 1943), the Allied invasion of Europe was coordinated militarily and politically by Roosevelt, Churchill and Stalin. On the 6th of June, 1944, the long-delayed Allied invasion of Europe signaled the final phase of the war, in which Germany would at last be besieged on two fronts. The end of the war was in sight, and the unity of the Allies for the postwar period seemed assured. The world, once again, looked like a hopeful place.

I got pregnant in May 1944 and decided at once to quit my X-ray job to protect the baby from possible radiation. I quickly got an office job in Hollywood with a fancy job title and better pay than I had earned. I did not mention the fact that I was pregnant, thinking I might not be hired if I did. I became "assistant business agent" of the Screen Publicists Guild, one of the more progressive Hollywood unions. Despite the nice title I was simply the typist, file clerk and girl Friday to the business agent of the union. He was a newspaperman of the old school, smoked a big stinking cigar, wore his hat in his office, put his feet on his desk and swore into the telephone. He had the old newspaperman's working hours—he arrived at the office at 4:30 or 5 P.M., just as I was leaving, and worked till 11 P.M. or later. As a result of this schedule, we had very little contact with each other, which was fine with me, since he seemed to regard female "assistants" as a necessary evil to be tolerated but not indulged.

So I ran my own show all day, answered phone calls, gave information to the union members who had questions, kept the books and tried to learn something about Hollywood unionism. I wrote the letters the business agent dictated into a Dictaphone and kept in touch with him as needed during the day, which enabled him to keep his favorite hours.

Mostly, though, I was happily preoccupied with my baby. After the first three months, when I could hardly hold any food down, I had a thoroughly uneventful pregnancy. I felt well; in fact I had never felt better in my life. Carl was sweet and solicitous; our married friends offered much-needed advice and, best of all, Virginia was pregnant three months ahead of me and I was able to help her with her baby after the birth. This gave me a little experience and a glimpse of what I might expect. My own life, so rich in so many experiences, had not included any knowledge of small children and none of babies.

Pregnancy made me not only fat and glowing with health, but pleasantly relaxed and lazy. For the first time in my life I would enjoy just sitting down and watching the flowers grow or watching children play in the park. I felt entitled to letting myself enjoy a sort of contemplative stupor.

I quit my job shortly after Christmas. My boss had never mentioned anything about my pregnancy, which I ascribed to his awkwardness with women. When I told him I was quitting, he said, somewhat outraged: "What's the matter? Aren't we treating you right?"

"I'm going to have a baby," I said over my protruding belly.

"Well, dammit, I didn't notice," he grumbled, genuinely surprised. He offered me the job back after the baby came, but I declined. I wanted to stay home with the baby, at least for the first year.

Stephanie Jean was born in February 1944 after difficult and very protracted labor. She was a beautiful baby and could always be distinguished from all the other babies in the nursery by being constantly in motion, waving her arms and legs. When we brought her home she continued bright and alert and wonderful, but she was a bad sleeper and I was a nervous mother. This caused a real problem for us.

The bungalow court where we lived did not have any tenants with children. The lease we had signed stipulated childlessness. As soon as my pregnancy became noticeable, the manager informed me that we would have to move, since "they did not permit children." In wartime Los Angeles with a horrendous housing shortage the prospect of moving was a disaster. We asked around a bit and found that we could not actually be evicted for having a baby and so we just ignored the manager.

When the baby cried at night—not an unusual event in the lives of most babies—the manager came to us in great agitation and said that the other tenants were complaining and that the child constituted an intolerable nuisance. The phrase was telling, because one could get evicted for "being a nuisance." As a result, we did everything we could to keep the baby from crying at night—feeding her frequently, walking around with her, rocking her—and pretty soon we had a baby totally conditioned to having a fine social time at night and sleeping mostly during the daytime.

In our small apartment with its single bedroom this routine meant both of us were up most of the night and Carl was so exhausted he fell asleep in the projection room at work. Finally, I consulted the pediatrician and he said the only thing to do was to break the baby of the habit by letting her cry and not picking her up. She was nearly six months old when we finally resorted to this draconian treatment. It took three nights, and then she decided to sleep at night after all.

The manager was highly displeased and tried to reinforce her threats by more direct action. When I put the baby out in the garden in front of my door, she would set the sprinkler in such a way that the baby would get soaked. We had to threaten a lawsuit to get her to stop harassing us. We stayed another year and a half in that place; we had no more success in finding another place to live than did thousands of war workers and soldiers' wives and children.

That first year, taking care of Stephanie and having some free time for writing, I was very happy. The war was coming to an end; I still hoped that soon I could go to Europe and see my parents. Carl's career was going well; he had recently been advanced to assistant editor and he was working on big films in the major studios.

Then, on April 12, 1945, the news came on the radio that President Roosevelt had died suddenly in Warm Springs, Georgia. I remember that moment. Tears came to my eyes and it seemed as though I just had lost a father, a protector. I picked up Stephanie and hugged her against my shoulder; then I ran outside, hoping to see some of the neighbors I knew, hoping to be told it wasn't true, it was all a mistake. Other people had apparently had the same instinct; some stood in the doorways, crying; others ran outside saying, Did you hear? Did you hear?

Seeing me crying, the baby began to whimper. I hugged her tight. "Don't worry, sweetie, things will be all right . . ."

But I did not believe it. I knew what the world had lost that day would not come back. The promise of victory in the war was now soured and stained—an epoch had ended, in my life as well as in the life of the nation.

[14]

WITH STEPHANIE'S BIRTH I entered a new stage of my life. Political activist, writer, wife, immigrant—all these aspects of my being had somehow to be squeezed into eighteen waking hours, expressed in thought and action. Motherhood took over, pushing everything else into the background. My uncertainty about my capacity for motherhood was compounded by inexperience. Like all new mothers, I was impressed above all by the baby's frailty, the delicacy of her limbs, the softness of her skull, her fragile bones. I thought she would break easily; I feared anything I did wrong would mark her for life. I had no mother, grandmother, sister or cousin to guide me through those early months.

Dr. Spock always at the ready, I was a great follower of instructions. Then, I got a hold of a copy of the Women's Bureau pamphlet on baby and childcare and the old-fashioned commonsense approach of that publication made me question some of Dr. Spock's wisdom. With the resurgence of skepticism, my mind began to function again and I decided that childcare advice, like everything else, needed to be tested in practice and evaluated in the light of one's own experience and needs.

No, I was not going to make the mistakes of my parents: my children would be raised by Carl and me, not by hired strangers. They would not be rigidly scheduled and disciplined; they would be seen and heard and listened to. Their creativity would be fostered and encouraged. What I had not counted on was twenty-four-hour service for the baby, the long sleepless nights, the never-ending demands. But my baby taught me that she was a lot sturdier than I thought she was. When she rolled over against a hard surface and screamed pitifully, she recovered in a second when I held her close. She taught me to relax and let her explore and stop overprotecting her. When she began to crawl and then stand, her excitement at discovery and at her own competence was so compelling, I stopped setting too many boundaries. She taught me to watch and learn, to read her body language and signals. Since she loved the outdoors, I spent many hours walking her in her carriage and later in her stroller, enjoying the way she saw the world. Being a mother was a great experience and most of the time I loved it.

Stephanie was a beautiful, engaging baby, very lively, very joyful and outgoing. What I had not expected of motherhood was that it would help me break out of my sense of isolation. As a mother of a small baby I was no longer myself, that prickly, aloof personality marked by destiny—I was just a woman with a baby, akin to any other mother. It was easy to make small talk about babies; it was easy to find common ground. From that time forward, wherever I might be in the world, I could always find access to other women by showing them a picture of one of my children, or in later years, one of my grandchildren. Most likely, they would reciprocate, and from then on the conversation would flow.

What made these first years of my being a full-time housewife much easier was my friendship with Virginia. Her little girl Cynthia was three months older than Stephanie and the two were fast friends. Virginia and I had joined a writers' workshop made up of four women. We were all working on first novels, reading each other's chapters in turn and offering our reactions and encouragement. We all became close friends and treasured our monthly sessions.

Virginia and I decided that we would have to organize things better if we wanted to take care of our children and continue to work as writers, so we set up a collaborative housekeeping arrangement, which served us both very well. For two days each week we spent the whole day together at one home or the other and shared our work. Then for the rest of the week, the constantly repeating chores at home did not seem quite so arduous. "The first thing you have to learn if you want to be a writer," Virginia explained, "you have to be a sloppy housekeeper. Just do everything well once a week and then let it go. A little dust won't kill you." Good advice, which I found hard to take.

Russell, who as a musician worked afternoons and nights, was home and helped out a lot during the mornings. Russell and I would pile into his old jalopy and we would spend a morning doing the week's shopping for both families at the farmers' market and the wholesale fish and meat market downtown, while Virginia minded the girls at home. Mondays, Virginia and I would bake for both families, enough to last us a week—pies, cookies, cakes and muffins. Meanwhile Russell would prepare some fabulous Swedish dish and all of us would have dinner together. The same routine was followed on Thursdays, but then Virginia and I would share the job we both hated the most—laundry and ironing. During these domestic jobs, we would talk about our writing, recite poetry, argue about current political issues and, later, do our neighborhood organizational work. It was a marvelous solution for us as young mothers and as writers, one that turned housework into fun and kept our minds active even while we were doing routine domestic chores. I also, incidentally, learned all the necessary household skills from Virginia and improved my cooking by learning from Russell. And it was great for the children.

Things looked good for us in 1945. Carl was making steady progress in his career. After *Cover Girl* with Rita Hayworth, he worked on *The Jolson Story*. Carl loved the industry—apparently his years of theater experience showed in the quality of his work. He had advanced more rapidly from apprentice editor to assistant than could have been expected. He worked long but not unreasonable hours, except for the last weeks of editing, when there was overtime and weekend work. Good pay, but bad hours. If only he could stay on at Columbia for a few more feature films we could get out of debt and begin to save some money.

We were on a high at the end of the war with Germany—tyranny was defeated, the thousand-year *Reich* of the Nazis was in ruins, the Japanese were nearly defeated and now we would build a new world based on democratic ideals and humanitarian principles. It seemed possible, easier than it had been to win the war.

For a short time, there was a delirious richness. Springtime: having a loving marriage, trusted friends, a baby to grow into a better world. Anything was possible. And then it shattered, it turned to ashes.

For me, the cold war started when President Harry S. Truman made the decision to use the A-bomb on August 6 and 9, 1945, which destroyed the cities of Hiroshima and Nagasaki. The horror of those events went beyond anything I had ever experienced. It turned the moral compass; it opened up vistas of a new world of terror and fear. When, during the Spanish civil war, a German plane manned by Franco's airmen had bombed the peaceful market square of one Spanish village, Guernica, and killed a dozen or so people, the civilized world recoiled in outrage. When, in retaliation for an attack by partisans on their occupation troops, the Germans destroyed the village of Lidice in the former Czechoslovakia, this appeared to a horrified world as a shocking example of Nazi barbarity. The bombing of London with its high toll of killed and wounded civilians was equally condemned as a tactic that violated all rules of warfare among civilized people.

The concept that an American President, the leader of a democratic country that had just won a war against German fascism, would make a calculus of saving the lives of U.S. soldiers in exchange for killing a hundred and sixty thousand Japanese civilians was close to the "reasoning" of the Nazi regime and its concept of the superiority of the German "race." Leaving quite aside the highly debatable question of whether these bombings in any way shortened the war, what they did signify was that the leaders of the U.S. recognized no moral limits to the means used for gaining victory. This, to me, seemed to be the kind of thinking that had made fascism possible. The acceptance of the American public and the press of the Hiroshima bombing as morally justifiable seemed very close to the reaction of the "good Germans" to Hitler—expediency, conformity, silent acquiescence to evil. I was stunned and outraged. Now I, as an American, was part of a country that could justify the mass killings of civilian populations during wartime.

The weeks and months following the bombings, the slowly emerging additional information, the fierce conflict of interpretations of the events, made the situation only worse. If, as the Truman administration claimed, the bombing of Hiroshima had been designed to show the Japanese that further resistance was useless, because of the power of atomic weapons in U.S. hands, why had the U.S. not first used the weapon on some uninhabited island, accompanied by a solemn warning to the Japanese? And why, after the Hiroshima bombing, had it bombed Nagasaki without first offering an ultimatum to the enemy and a warning of further atom bomb attacks? If it was true that the Japanese were already, prior to the Hiroshima bombing, proceeding with negotiations toward peace, why unleash this horror at all? The explanation offered by the Nobel Prize–winning British scientist P. M. S. Blackwell in his book *Fear, War and the Bomb* and later taken up by the U.S. physicist Philip Morrison, that these bombings had been, in fact, motivated by a desire to curtail Russian influence in ending the Pacific war and that they therefore were the opening moves in the next war, that of the U.S.A. against the Soviet Union, carried a great deal of plausibility.

I began working for the peace movement as a result of the Hiroshima bombing. It seemed to me nothing else I could do would have much importance as long as the threat of atomic warfare remained an actuality. The enormous destructiveness of the new weapons must never be used again, anywhere in the world, for any reason whatever. I signed every peace and anti-nuclear development petition I could find and circulated them as well. Later, I joined SANE and other peace groups. I can honestly say that my peace activities had nothing whatever to do with my attitude of support for the Soviet Union; in fact, after the Soviets exploded their first atomic weapons, I felt they were as much of a threat to world peace as was the U.S. I was motivated by a simple and primitive sense of danger to my own child and the world's children, and by the emotional resonance of my experiences with the coming of fascism.

August 6, 1945, marked an end to the short period in which I had begun to feel a sense of belonging and a hope for stability in my new country. After Hiroshima, I would, once again, live in opposition to government policy, wary of official pronouncements.

In 1946, labor unrest, pent up after the years of no-strike pledges during the war, broke out all over the nation. The National Association of Manufacturers took the lead in an effort to halt wage increases and to reverse New Deal labor legislation. The Chamber of Commerce advocated a federal loyalty oath program and the investigation of Communist influence in the media. Both recommendations would soon be enacted as law by the Democratic administration and carried out in practice.

The first sign of the shifting climate was a law passed before U.S. entry into the war. Ostensibly designed to control potentially disloyal aliens, the Omnibus Alien Registration Act of 1940, commonly known as the Smith Act, contained a section that gave the government the right to persecute people for the opinions they held. It was first used in an unsuccessful attempt to deport the West-Coast labor leader Harry Bridges, and it was used during the war to prosecute twenty-nine members of the Trotskyist Socialist Workers Party of Minneapolis-St. Paul. Although the Communists and the progressives they influenced were very active in defense of Harry Bridges, they did nothing to protest the indictments against the Trotskyists, with whom they had long-standing political differences. This fact weakened their potential for a principled defense of free speech rights when, in 1947, the Smith Act was used to indict 145 Communist leaders, resulting in 108 convictions for "sedition."

But these events lay in the future. In March 1946, Winston Churchill spoke in Fulton, Missouri, with President Truman beside him, warning of the "expansive tendencies" of the Soviet Union. "An iron curtain has descended across the continent," he asserted, indicating a decisive shift away from the wartime alliance with Russia toward a policy of containment. In Hollywood, these as-yet subtle shifts in foreign policy were reflected in labor relations and in government investigations of the motion picture industry. Such investigations were not new and, because of the public's interest in the movies, always provided welcome publicity for aspiring politicians. As early as 1940, HUAC, headed by Representative Martin Dies, found the motion picture industry to be "a hotbed of Communism." But producers and the leaders of the writers and actors guilds did not, in 1940, cooperate with HUAC and the committee did not reappear in Hollywood for four years.

In 1941 workers at the Disney Studios, led by Herb Sorrell, who had helped to organize the Screen Cartoonists Guild and whose ambition it was to bring honest, rank-and file unionism to Hollywood, struck the company. Disney Studios had long been a stronghold of paternalism and was notorious for bad working conditions. The Disney strike succeeded and Walt Disney, in an ad in *Variety,* accused Communist agitators of bringing about this situation.

But two consecutive investigations of alleged "red" influence on the motion picture industry by a committee of the California legislature brought no startling revelations.

Next, in 1941, came an investigation of the content of motion pictures by the Senate Subcommittee on War Propaganda, sponsored by prominent isolationist Senator Burton K. Wheeler, who accused the film industry of a propaganda campaign designed to lead America into war. The committee's investigation of twenty-five feature films was met by staunch resistance from the producers and the guild, got bad press and had to be abandoned by the committee. With the Soviet Union as our wartime ally, the red-baiting business was, for a brief interlude, in retreat.

With the end of the war and the changed political climate, attacks on Hollywood "subversives" were used effectively to legitimize union-busting by the studios. The showdown came over a jurisdictional dispute between the IATSE and the producers on one side, and the progressive unions, united in the newly formed Conference of Studio Unions (CSU), on the other. CSU, under the leadership of Herb Sorrell, had been organized after the Disney Strike. Uniting screen office employees, film technicians, machinists and painters, it gradually built up a membership of ten thousand in the crafts field, posing a serious threat to the corrupt, gangster-ridden IATSE with its sixteen-thousand members. CSU was dedicated to rank-and-file trade unionism and the producers considered it anathema. Early in 1945 the producers refused to recognize a request of the set directors' local to change their affiliation from IATSE to CSU. An appeal to the War Labor Board upheld the legality of that request, but the producers again refused to accept it. CSU was forced into a jurisdictional strike that both sides believed would be decisive for the future of labor relations in the industry.

The strike dragged on for seven months and in September 1945 the IATSE International President issued a charter to the strikebreakers. This led CSU to call for mass picket lines in front of Warner Brothers' studios. On October 5 local police, studio police and L.A. County sheriffs broke up the picket line with tear gas and fire hoses deployed from the studio rooftops and cleared a path for IATSE strikebreakers.

The violence outraged the film community. A group of film people not directly involved in the strike volunteered to surround the studio entrance as observers. They carried cameras and promised to document and publicize any violence that might occur. This somewhat dimmed the enthusiasm of the studio heads for teargassing their striking employees and for the next two days mass picket lines succeeded in halting production at Warner Brothers. But the calm did not last.

On October 10, 1945, a large contingent of police, sheriff's deputies and studio police paraded in front of Warner Brothers, some armed with rifles. When the picket lines formed, the U.S. flag was raised over the studio at 6:30 A.M. and the national anthem was played. This was the prearranged signal for an attack by police, again using tear gas, some brandishing guns. This time, they arrested over six hundred pickets, herded them on to studio stages and spent all day fingerprinting and booking them.

Carl was an observer on that day and came home angry and distraught. "They're out to destroy CSU and break the progressive unions," he said, "and they don't care who gets hurt." It upset him terribly that there was no sign of solidarity from the unions not affiliated with CSU. He had gone to work after his stint as observer that morning and told his co-workers what had happened, but people were afraid to do anything.

"Probably they don't see any threat to themselves."

"I feel rotten I can't go on that picket line myself," Carl complained. It struck me that he was taking a considerable risk anyway, openly supporting a strike in which his union was sending in strikebreakers and granting them union affiliation.

The next day there were two thousand strikers on the Warner Brothers picket line. All was peaceful and then a caravan of AFL machinists carrying a flag and giving V for Victory signs arrived to join the picket line in sympathy. Labor solidarity was real, even if the Hollywood unions could not seem to get mobilized.

The next day pickets appeared in front of RKO-Pathé, Technicolor, Universal and Columbia. At Universal, five hundred IATSE members refused to cross the picket lines. At Columbia, the writers and a few others walked out when they saw the pickets. Carl was among those who refused to cross the picket lines.

That night IATSE members were phoned by the union and told that IATSE was involved in a jurisdictional dispute with CSU and that, as IA members, they were ordered to cross the picket line in support of their union. What's more, because their union had signed a no-strike pledge in the contract, they were legally bound to cross the line. Carl was busy all night calling other union brothers and trying to persuade them not to cross the line. He argued that the producers were out to destroy all unions. If they succeeded with CSU, the other unions would be next. He had never in his life crossed a picket line and would not do so now. No contract clause could bind him to expose himself to physical violence in crossing the line. That argument had been used by the writers as they walked out in sympathy and was, he felt, a good answer to the IA's appeal to a no-strike clause.

I don't know how well he succeeded with other IATSE members, but the next day production was halted at all the major studios. There followed three more days of violence at Warner Brothers; then the Screen Writers Guild joined the strike. On October 22 negotiations started and three days later the strike was settled, a total victory for CSU. They won reinstatement for all the strikers, recognition of their right to represent the set designers and the settlement of all jurisdictional disputes within thirty days.

Carl returned to work when production resumed, but his action had once and for all brought him to the attention of the IATSE leadership. His business agent indicated that his support of CSU would not be forgotten and there, for the time being, the matter rested. We felt great about this victory and thought the risk he had taken entirely worthwhile. We could not know that this CSU strike was in fact the last victory progressive unionists would see in Hollywood for decades to come.

Carl was then an assistant editor and earned around eighty dollars a week, but brought home less after deductions. From the many years of unemployment we still had some debts and we were still paying the hospital and doctor for Stephanie's birth. He was unemployed from January to August 1946 and during that period we had to make do on his thirty-five-dollar-a-week unemployment insurance check. Fortunately, I had learned how to live a good life in relative poverty. We took advantage of all the wonderful free events available: picnics in the parks and on the beaches, free playgrounds, library story hours and lectures. We drove out of town to farm stands for cheap fruit and canned and pickled and preserved. We bought at rummage sales and at the Salvation Army. There were fire department fairs and clowns in the zoo and museum trips and public concerts. Then, and in the many months of unemployment he experienced in the following years, when we had to live on unemployment insurance, we went into debt for the doctor, we postponed going to the dentist, we did our own repairs and some bartering with friends. I learned to sew (never well), to paint walls and furniture and to finish woodwork. The fact that at last I could be competent with my hands and do all that was needed to keep a family comfortable gave me real pride. The years of living in strained circumstances gave me an unexpected sense of freedom; I knew how to get by, no matter what.

The studios took their defeat in this strike seriously. They had not lost their determination to wipe out CSU, to curb the Screen Writers Guild and to win back the Screen Actors Guild for conservatives. If violence and strike breaking did not work, there were other ways of achieving their ends.

TELLING ALL OF THIS in retrospect, when the outcomes are known, distorts the actuality of the lived experience. This was true in my personal as well as my political life. The two have always been so closely connected it is hard for me to separate them out in retrospect. The hope that Carl could make a career in Hollywood and that we could expect some economic security was dimmed when he lost his job at Columbia in favor of a returning war veteran. In the fall he finally found a job at Star Pictures, an independent company, followed by a few weeks at Republic, where he worked as a montage editor. Then he got a job on a feature film at RKO. In short, he took whatever job he could get, waiting for the break that would land him a permanent studio job. But everything was insecure. Between jobs there were weeks, even months of unemployment. Finally, late in 1946, he was hired as an assistant editor at Samuel Goldwyn Pictures, where he worked on *The Secret Life of Walter Mitty* and *The Best Years of Our Lives*. Again, things looked up for us and we had great hopes.

After the war in Europe had ended, mail again came promptly, bringing terrible news. My mother's illness had at last been diagnosed correctly: she had multiple sclerosis and there was no hope of a cure. On the contrary, her condition had been deteriorating for some time and was expected to continue to worsen. The disease sometimes allowed for periods of remission, but since all the medication given to her had not brought any results, the doctors held out no hope. At long last, my father and Nora wrote me in detail about the horrors of the past years, the false leads, the wrong diagnoses. They had decided to withhold the truth from my mother and they kept assuring her that "soon" she would get better. They felt she needed, above all, to have hope, but the few pitiful lines she dictated to her nurses to send to me showed that their approach was not working. She wrote like a trapped person, desolate and victimized. All I could hear out of her barren words was incomprehension, a desperate struggle for resignation and dignity. Once in a while, her old spirits flared up. "The woman I live with," she wrote after her transfer to a private nursing home,

> is old. She coughs, she groans, she smells and she spits when she talks. Her hands are never quite clean and she uses my face cloth to wash my body. Still, I like her; she is a good soul—how appreciative I've become . . . My right hand and both feet are paralyzed. When I try to take a step, I fall and so I've given up and stay in bed all day.

This was the last letter I ever received from her that sounded like her and showed any kind of spirit. Months later my father wrote that she was taking Russian lessons. Her mind was clear; only her body had ceased to function. Of all the illnesses she might have had, this seemed to me the most cruel. For a person of her vivaciousness, her restlessness, her constant need for interaction with others, paralysis was the cruelest possible state. I saw her before me, see her still, lying flat on her back, staring up at the blank ceiling, unable to move anything but her head and her eyelids (that stage went on for two years). How cruel that she was denied the positive knowledge that her illness was terminal. At least that would have given her a chance to settle with death, even to look upon it as a release.

Yet, I cannot fault my sister and my father for their decision. What they had suffered in that terrible period of uncertainty and then, perhaps even worse, in that period of watching her die so slowly was now at last becoming clear to me. Nora, finished with schooling and eager to embark upon her own life, was staying on in a sort of limbo, in order to be with Ili as much as possible. My father, struggling bravely to make a living despite his own serious health problems, was investing a good part of his earnings to keeping Ili in comfortable and dignified surroundings. He had, by then, already fallen in love with another woman, but he postponed any plans for marriage until after my mother's death. I did not know that at the time, but as I look at it now in the knowledge of what came after, his actions then seem quite heroic. After the kind of marriage he had had, after the complexities and tensions between himself and Ili, and especially after the way she had treated him during the period of exile, no one could have blamed him for divorcing her at this stage and marrying the woman with whom he was truly happy. But he was a man who lived by his own old-fashioned code of honor, and he was the best friend Ili ever had. The way I see it now, marriage was hard for both of them, but in a mysterious, an inexplicable way, they were each other's true love.

During this period I was torn with conflicting emotions and doubts as to where my duty lay. I wrote to my father that I wanted to come to see my mother again before she died, but I could see no way of taking my baby with me, considering the difficult travel conditions at the end of the war. Also, we had no money for the fare. I also worried; what would be the effect on Ili? Would my inevitable departure after a short visit be so wrenching that my visit would do more harm than good?

Vati answered without hesitation that I should not come. Mother's state was so bad that any kind of excitement might have disastrous consequences. I accepted that decision then, even though I do not accept it now. Whenever we say that the terminally ill must be protected from undue excitement, we are simply expressing our own fears and guilt, nothing else. No one knows what kind of "excitement" would occur and how this psychic effect would impact on the sick body. I have trained myself in many long years not to play the "if only" game. It leads nowhere and is a waste of energy. Still, knowing what I know today I can say without hesitation that my life would have been easier had I gone to see my mother before she died. The undercurrent of pain and guilt has never left me, no matter how rich and challenging my life has been in the here and now.

NEVERTHELESS, DAILY LIFE CONTINUED with great intensity. In my election district we set our sights high for the fall elections of 1946. The focus was on the House of Representatives race, where an unknown lawyer, Richard Nixon, was running on the Republican ticket against the incumbent liberal Democrat, Jerry Voorhis. Again, I mobilized the canvassers in my thirteen precincts. We thought it would be easy going for Jerry Voorhis. Instead, we found ourselves in one of the dirtiest campaigns in U.S. history. Nixon had hired Murray Chotiner, who would serve him in later campaigns with "dirty tricks." This was his tryout.

Nixon accused Jerry Voorhis of being a tool of the CIO's Political Action Committee, even though Voorhis had no PAC endorsement in that campaign. He had had some PAC money in previous campaigns, but Nixon did not bother with such fine points. He accused Voorhis of having Communist support, even though Communists had denounced Voorhis for his recent endorsement of Truman's foreign policy.

Nixon's technique was to make grand accusations, provide little proof and keep his opponent on the defensive. In this he succeeded brilliantly. He hammered away at Voorhis, depicting him as a tool of extremists. He published a long list of Voorhis's votes in which his position coincided with that of the CIO. Before Voorhis could answer these accusations, Nixon published a list of votes in which Voorhis had voted the same way as Congressman Vito Marcantonio, then the single radical voice in the House. Guilt by association was introduced in that first campaign and handled expertly by the young Richard Nixon. The campaign workers in the district were told of Democratic voters receiving anonymous phone calls in which the caller warned them that Jerry Voorhis was a Communist. The real dirty trick came late in the campaign.

According to California law, a candidate could file in both parties, and both candidates had cross-filed. To make clear to the voters which were the party-endorsed candidates, each party customarily handed out its own list, on which all the candidates endorsed by the party were listed and which the voters could take into the election booth with them. The day before the election our district was flooded with fake Democratic ballots—they listed all the Democratic candidates correctly except for Representative—in that column they listed the Republican candidate Nixon, as though he were one of the endorsed Democrats. We had, that same day, distributed our official ballots; now the voters found themselves with two nearly look-alike, conflicting ballots. By the time the Democrats found out what had happened, it was too late to do anything. This trick alone did not account for the outcome, but it was the beginning of an era in U.S. politics when cynical manipulation of the voters by a variety of dirty tricks became an accepted fact of elections. By the skillful use of red-baiting and unscrupulous smear tactics Richard Nixon won 56 percent of the vote, beginning his career in a style that would later advance him to the presidency and down the road to Watergate.

I had not been able to be very active toward the end of the campaign, because our housing situation had become so pressing that I needed to devote all my time to finding a new apartment for us. Hundreds of thousands of war workers, who had come to California during the war, had decided to settle in the state. So had thousands of returning veterans. Housing was extremely scarce and with the lifting of wartime restrictions, rents soared. Discrimination by race and ethnicity was rampant and there was open discrimination against young couples with children. We were caught right in that nightmare, because our landlady's campaign to get rid of us had not abated. I spent months looking for another place to rent. One of the worst incidents that happened is still fresh in my memory.

I followed an ad for an apartment rental, wheeling Stephanie in her stroller. To my delight the landlady seemed to like children—she oohed and aahed over beautiful, fair, blue-eyed Stephanie with her engaging smile. I found the place acceptable, if not ideal, and the price only somewhat above what we had expected to pay. I assured the landlady that I wanted to take the apartment, but I thought my husband should see it before I signed the lease. She agreed to hold it until that evening.

We went right over after Carl came home from work. When the landlady opened the door, she could not disguise her dismay. "Is that really your little girl?" she asked Carl, looking from his black hair and dark eyes to the little blue-eyed girl with her fair pigtails.

"Certainly," said he.

She would not even let us come into the apartment again.

"I'm sorry," she said, "I rented it this afternoon to a couple without children." And she slammed the door in our faces.

I did not even "get it" right away. What was that?

"Race or religion," Carl said matter-of-factly. "I look too dark to suit her. Anti-Semitism."

No ... I had to come to California to experience the kind of personal anti-Semitism that I, thanks to my fair skin and blue eyes, had been able to avoid in Nazi Austria. "Has this happened to you before?" I asked my husband.

He laughed. "You led a sheltered life, didn't you? Of course. Where I grew up in Philadelphia I could not walk on the other side of the street without getting beaten up by Italian kids. And in back of the house the turf belonged to the black kids."

"So?"

"The Jewish kids walked to school in bunches, for protection. You got beaten up sometimes; you fought back sometimes. You learned to stay on your side of the street."

With that context in mind, I continued my search for housing and finally, in the fall of 1946, I lucked out. We found a one-bedroom apartment at an affordable price in a Jewish neighborhood. We would live upstairs, above the landlady, who was widowed and living with her old father. They liked children, and best of all, they had a beautiful fenced backyard that we could use. We signed a year's lease and the landlady said there would be no problem about renewing it, if we were "good tenants."

We loved the new apartment; our upstairs windows gave us a view of the garden and the tops of the trees. Another good feature was that we had friendly next-door neighbors. Lillian's boys were near Stephanie's age and she had friends and playmates and two yards in which they could play. Lillian and I soon became good friends. Carl and I felt greatly relieved to have a friendly landlord and a good housing situation, at last.

Sometime late that year I joined the Communist Party. It was not, at the time, a major step or a difficult decision. Later, red-baiting and witch-hunting would make of the act of "joining" or "leaving" the CP a momentous decision with not inconsiderable consequences. The fact is that I can neither remember exactly when I joined nor where and when I first attended a branch meeting. All it meant at the time was an added number of meetings each week and the obligation to read not only the *People's World,* but the CP's theoretical organ, *Political Affairs.* The latter was generally an unpleasant task, for the articles were written in turgid prose full of cliches and usually dealt with obscure theoretical questions that had no bearing on the neighborhood work I was doing.

What was important to me then about joining the Communist Party was that I believed I was joining a strong international movement for progress and social justice. I had no particular love for the Soviet Union, although the heroism of its people during the war had impressed me as a sign that there was indeed a vibrant experiment in social reconstruction going on in that country. After Hiroshima and Churchill's "iron curtain" speech it seemed inevitable that sooner or later the capitalist nations would again unite against the Soviet Union, as they had in the period just after the Bolshevik revolution. As it had been essential to defend democracy in Spain, so it seemed essential to defend and maintain the existence of the socialist experiment in the Soviet Union. Just in this way, in the late eighteenth century, European radicals had looked on the great "experiment" of the American Revolution as the hope of humankind. Tom Paine vigorously supported the idea of popular democracy and an end to the privileges of aristocracy and royalty, which in his day had seemed as radical as was the idea of socialism in the beginning of the twentieth century. The radical Scotswoman Frances Wright came to America in 1821 and wrote a glowing account of the workings of democracy, which she saw as the hoped-for alternative to the class privileges and injustices of British and European societies.

At present, we have all but forgotten the radical origins of democratic society in the United States. After fifty years of the cold war and internal red-baiting witch hunts, one is expected to explain why reasonable persons of good will, social conscience and patriotism could ever have worked for radical alternatives to the capitalist system. All I can say is that fifty years ago it seemed a reasonable choice to make.

But why the uncritical defense of the Soviet Union, why the blindness to all the evils of their system, which now are so clearly revealed fifty years later? I wanted the Soviet Union to be a successful experiment in socialist democracy and so I checked my critical faculties when it came to that subject, and instead accepted what I wanted to hear on faith. It is easy to see now, with hindsight, that that was a serious mistake, but it was not so easy to see it then. My attitude toward the Soviet Union was never an important aspect of my decision about becoming a Communist. What was important to me were the issues close at hand—the struggle to unionize Southern California, the fight against racism, the resistance to nuclear weapons and war. The price of hamburger, the availability of decent housing, adequate low-cost childcare—these were my issues. The Communists I knew were stronger, more consistent fighters for these issues than other people I knew. I was proud to become part of a collectivity that I believed would make my country more just, more democratic.

[15]

IN 1946 I BECAME INVOLVED in grassroots organizational work that, in retrospect, seems to have been the best experience of its kind I ever had. I became active in the Congress of American Women, helped to form its Los Angeles chapter and for a short time became a local and national leader in that organization.

Shortly after the end of World War II the founding convention of the Women's International Democratic Federation (WIDF) met in Paris, attended by women from forty countries who claimed to represent 81 million women. WIDF's aims were the advancement of the rights of women, protection of children, world peace and democracy. The last phrase embodied an understanding that the continuation of the wartime antifascist alliance between the Soviet Union and the Western democracies was essential to the maintenance of peace. The fact that from the outset there were Communists and non-Communists active in the organization seemed ideally expressive of that aim. Although the U.S. press from the inception of the organization labeled it "Communist-dominated" and accused it of following the Soviet party line, this was not obvious to me at the time. And if it had been, it would have made no difference. I was fully convinced that the maintenance of world peace required coexistence with the Soviet Union and cooperation with Communists.

The thirteen American delegates to the WIDF founding convention came from diverse backgrounds, ranging from housewives and professional women to union leaders, teachers and creative artists.[1] They and others founded Congress of American Women (CAW), the U.S. branch of WIDF, in March 1946. Dr. Gene Weltfish was the first President of its national board, which set up three commissions to carry forward its program: Peace and Democracy; Protection of Children and Education; and Rights of Women.[2] The organization encompassed all the issues I found worth working for and I was delighted to be able to help in establishing a Los Angeles chapter.

Our founding meeting on October 26, 1946, was celebrated with the performance of a cantata called "Women Are Dangerous," written by my friend Virginia Brodine, with music by Fred Warren, directed by Carl Lerner. True to her profound interest in the history of American women, Virginia wrote of the lives of nineteenth-century feminists, and of the achievements of union women in the twentieth century. Looking back on it now, it seems that my interest in the history of American women and my future career as a historian date from this period and the ways in which CAW consistently incorporated women's history in its work. This concern with the history of women gave CAW a unique position among women's organizations of the 1950s.

Together with my neighbor and friend Lillian I founded a neighborhood branch in Hollywood and also served on the city-wide Executive Committee. Our first local activity was to take part in the meat boycotts. In 1946, when the Office of Price Administration (OPA), which had supervised wartime price controls, was abolished, food prices went out of sight. I remember a dramatic increase in the main staple of our diet, hamburger meat, which during the war had sold for fifty-five cents a pound and now went up to a dollar twenty-five. The reaction of housewives was first to change their menus and then to begin a campaign for lower prices.

1. Among these delegates were Muriel Draper; Gene Weltfish, a Columbia University anthropologist who had worked with Franz Boas; Florence Eldrige March, the actress; a WAC sergeant from California; Henrietta Buckmaster, a writer; the Communist leader Elizabeth Gurley Flynn; and three African-American delegates, Dr. Charlotte Hawkins Brown, the noted educator and President of Palmer Memorial Institute in Sedalia, North Carolina; Thelma Dale, representing the National Negro Congress; and Vivian Carter Mason.

2. CAW Vice Presidents represented a left-dominated interracial coalition: Muriel Draper; Mary Jane Melish, a minister's wife; Rose Wortis; Eleanor Gimbel; June Gordon, the President of the Emma Lazarus Federation of the International Workers Order, a Jewish fraternal organization; Dr. Charlotte Hawkins Brown; and Mrs. Gifford Pinchot, wife of the former Governor of Pennsylvania. Notable among board members were Nora Stanton Blatch Barney, the granddaughter of Elizabeth Cady Stanton; the feminist writer Susan B. Anthony II; and Jeanette Stern Turner.

We picketed the local supermarket a few hours each day, putting homemade signs on our baby strollers. The response was excellent. Many shoppers turned away from the market and each day there were a few who joined our picket lines. Union auxiliaries and CAW chapters in the midwest and the east sparked similar campaigns. A few months later meat prices went down.

Another issue on which our CAW club was active was childcare. With the end of the war the childcare centers connected with war industry and supported with federal funds had been quickly discontinued. But the need for childcare was as great as ever. We wrote letters to the newspapers, petitioned our representatives and, in 1947, organized a cooperative playgroup to take care of our most urgent needs. The women who organized this group were full-time housewives and mothers; we spent all our days in the company of small children and felt we needed a few hours off each week in order to survive. Six mothers formed a playgroup that operated quite simply: each morning two mothers took care of all the children in one of our apartments or in the playground. We did this from nine to twelve and took the children home for lunch. That way, without much overhead and extra trouble, each mother had two mornings off each week, which seemed like freedom.

Similar self-help coops sprang up in many places. After a few years, the work and pressure generated by groups such as ours and by the childcare coalition resulted in a pre-kindergarten program being established in the Los Angeles public schools.

From its inception the Los Angeles CAW chapter, like the national organization, was interracial. Black women were part of its leadership at every level and we struggled constantly with finding better methods of working across race lines. Unlike in any other group or organization in which I ever worked, white women in CAW did not assume that we had all the answers and that black women had nothing to teach us. Quite the contrary. But we did not get to that stance easily; we started with the usual white supremacist assumptions.

In order to tell this story I am here condensing the events of three years into one narrative. For me, working with black women in the organization brought a harsh realization right at the beginning of our work. I had always considered myself firmly opposed to racism and entirely free of the unconscious racism with which white Americans grew into adulthood. The only black person I had ever seen before coming to the U.S.A. was a black boy a few years older than myself, who was born in Vienna and spoke beautiful Viennese dialect. Johnny was the idol of all the teenage girls at the swimming pool where we hung out all summer, and since I was too young I never had a chance even to speak to him. He seemed to me very attractive, interesting and out of reach. After I came to New York, during my training as an X-ray technician, I had worked with black doctors, nurses and patients without any self-consciousness.

The incident that shook my complacency occurred in the summer of 1946, before the founding of the Los Angeles chapter of CAW. A small group of women had been meeting for a few weeks to do preparatory work. One of the black women from the south side was Mabel Gray, a community and church leader whose organizational experience far exceeded that of the rest of us. On one occasion the meeting was to be at my apartment. We were then still living in the apartment court whose landlady was trying to evict us. I remember that a few days before the scheduled meeting it occurred to me that the landlady might object to having a black woman come to our place in the evening. The landlady's bungalow was straight across from us and she could see everyone coming and going without leaving her living room. I realized that this might be just the kind of incident she had been waiting for to justify our eviction. I momentarily panicked and considered canceling the meeting with some excuse. But then I realized that if I did such a thing, I would be taking part in an act of racist discrimination. So I did nothing and the meeting took place and the landlady was not heard from on the subject. The fact that I could have experienced anxiety, even panic, simply because a black woman I greatly respected was going to visit my house made me aware that I was not immune from racism.

Mabel Gray and Myrtle Pitts, another black woman, regularly met with us as members of the Executive Board of the L.A. chapter. They spoke only rarely and they did not offer what the rest of us most wanted them to offer—suggestions for how we might work more closely with the black community. Once Mabel briefly mentioned a church supper in her neighborhood that was being given for the benefit of a childcare program and invited us all to come. At our next meeting she reported briefly on the event and noted regretfully that no one from our group had been able to attend. We each had our individual good excuse.

I remember that on several occasions some of us white women talked about how difficult it was to work with black women. We thought Mabel was overextended; she belonged to at least twelve organizations, some of which we judged to be politically insignificant, like the fraternal orders, and we considered her activism in several churches excessive. We were strong on making judgements and weak on knowledge of the reality of life in the black community. We also thought Myrtle might be shy and that this was why she so seldom took part in our endless discussions.

After about a year of this, in the late spring, Mabel Gray made a short speech in our meeting. She told us of a raffle being given by one of the fraternal organizations to which she belonged. The profits were going to be used to send black children to summer camp. The tickets were a dollar each and she had brought enough raffle books for all of us. Her remarks were greeted with silence until Bea, our one trade union member, asked for one raffle book.

"There are nice prizes for the winners," Mabel said pleasantly. "A TV set and several radios."

"It's not that," someone finally said. "It's the idea of it—we're not a charitable organization."

"And I doubt that we should be," I chimed in, someone explaining the obvious. "We're working for social change, for decent schools and summer camps for all children. If we start doing specific actions like this, we'll get diverted from our main purpose, which is political."

Mabel Gray turned toward me, but she spoke to all of us, with a tone of authority and with a force of anger we had never seen in her before. "My children can't wait," she said. "They need to go to camp this summer. That's the issue now."

The discussion stopped with that and we took on another important topic. Afterwards, several of us, myself included, got our raffle books. After Mable and Myrtle left our meeting—they traveled together to their part of town—Bea said: "That was shameful. We did this all wrong. It's a wonder Mabel keeps coming back here, the way we handle her issues."

The discussion that ensued was all about principles of organization, political strategy, the difference between strategy and tactics. Bea listened for a while, then cut through all our arguments. "If you want to organize people, you've got to organize them where they are. You've got to listen to their issues and respect their judgement. I might want to organize a union on broad, general principles, but if what's needed in the place is a water fountain or a clean toilet, then that's the issue. And that's what you organize around."

Virginia chimed in from her experience in organizing domestic workers in Seattle. Gradually, we all began to reconsider. For my part, I sold all of my raffle tickets honestly, even though at first I had considered simply giving Mabel my own money for the whole book.

At the next meeting Mabel thanked us quite formally for the fine job we had done for the children. After that she participated much more actively in our discussions. And not long after that Myrtle offered to have a meeting of our group at her home.

We all carpooled to the south side, feeling perhaps a little smug about our undertaking such a long ride, until it dawned on at least some of us that Mabel and Myrtle were taking that long ride every time they came to the meeting in our neighborhood. We were surprised to find Myrtle living in a large, comfortably furnished old house she and her husband owned. We were greeted with more lavish refreshments than were usually served at our meetings—everything we were offered was home-baked and Myrtle, our reticent, "shy" Myrtle, was an outgoing, gracious hostess, talkative, informative, and ever alert for her guests' comfort. After that evening, we rotated the location of our meetings fairly among us and something subtle but quite important changed in our relationship to Mabel and Myrtle.

After the raffle episode, they not only became participants in our meetings, but they brought their community issues and causes into our organization with the expectation that we would find time and energy for these issues. And we did. If we did right, Mabel taught us how "to appreciate and recognize." If we did wrong, she would straighten us out. In the course of several years of working together we became friends. When I left Los Angeles in 1949, Myrtle Pitts gave a huge farewell party for me at her home, as always with plentiful homemade food.

Much later, when I was already an academic and was working to organize a conference on housework, which involved white academics, black domestic workers and white working-class housewives, mostly Italian and Polish housewives, the lessons of the raffle ticket incident served me well. We learned that if we truly wanted participation by the nonacademic women, we would have to meet in their neighborhood, their homes. So we planned the conference, which was sponsored by Sarah Lawrence College, on 125th Street in Harlem. And we listened when the Polish women told us they were sick of the skimpy refreshments—wine and cheese—that were offered at our meetings. "Come to our neighborhood and we'll show you how we entertain." We did and they did and those of us who had not learned it earlier learned then that for many women sharing food is more than a polite requirement to be met with minimal effort—it is a way of becoming a neighbor, maybe even a friend.

I met many women like Mabel Gray and Myrtle Pitts when I began to study and research African-American women's history—strong, patient women who belonged to many organizations and managed somehow to be active in all of them, who took collective responsibility for the welfare of the community's children and who were always ready to find practical solutions for immediate needs.

I recognized them at once, as I came across traces of their existence and their work in organizational records, old newspapers and letters. I found them because I knew they would be there. This was at a time when Women's History as a field did not yet exist and the possibility of tracing a history of black women seemed unthinkable. I knew they were there, because I had known them, worked with them and learned from them.

CAW nationally was active on foreign policy issues, especially in protests against nuclear weapons. Annually, on March 8, CAW celebrated International Woman's Day. One time they staged an event in Seneca Falls, New York: reading the 1848 Declaration of Sentiments out loud in the presence of Susan B. Anthony II, the grand-niece of the suffrage leader, and of the grandson of Frederick Douglass, the African-American who had been at the Seneca Falls convention. To celebrate International Woman's Day CAW selected some historical incident that was closest to its own interests and in this way our organizational work and our construction of women's history were linked organically. In Los Angeles, our March 8 meetings would end with the singing of "Bread and Roses," the song of the strikers in the Lawrence mill strike of 1912. One of the CAW organizational affiliates was the Emma Lazarus Division (ELD) of the International Workers Order, a fraternal organization that provided health and life insurance for its members. The ELD was strong on Jewish women's history and celebrated the story of the heroic struggles of the New York textile workers for their right to organize. Remembering women of the past and celebrating their achievements, we felt better about the kind of work we were doing day by day.

Our work in CAW had led a number of us who were CP members to be critical of the party's attitude toward women's political struggle. As we organized women in the neighborhoods we found that our work was not regarded with the same respect and interest in the CP as was that of people working in trade unions or political mass organizations. The progressive press, especially the *Daily People's World,* reported on women's organizational activities only when trade union women were involved. While there had been an article in the *People's World* on the founding meeting of CAW in California, that was the last report on our activities in more than a year. Meanwhile, the "human interest" page to which "women's interests" were relegated offered its readers household hints, recipes and, nearly daily, some cheesecake picture of a scantily clad woman. There were a few patronizingly stupid columns addressed to housewives. The only women featured in stories were European or Soviet women. The sole exceptions were three columns on U.S. women's history by Virginia in successive issues of the paper. Apparently similar complaints were being raised on the East Coast. We saw a sudden opportunity when Virginia was asked to form a Women's Commission, which was to make recommendations to the leadership on work among women. Virginia asked Bea, one of our most active CAW women, and me to be on the commission. There were six of us in all and we had some exciting meetings, mapping out a women's agenda for the party.

All of us had read a pamphlet by Mary Inman, which challenged traditional Marxist doctrine on the "woman question," namely, that women's emancipation would come when women became part of the paid labor force. This doctrine held that the struggle for equal pay, equal opportunities and equal advancement for working women was a worthwhile "aspect" of the struggle for the advancement of the working class. Working women were urged to organize in trade unions or auxiliaries; their role was that of helpmates in the social struggle. The song "There Once Was a Union Maid" said it all. The union maid was unafraid on the picket line; she hated scabs and resisted strikebreaking goons; the song celebrated her nerve and daring. In the end she was advised to "marry a man who's a union man and join the ladies' auxiliary." We on the Women's Commission did not think this was great radical politics for women.

According to traditional Marxist theory housewives were problematical as to their class consciousness; they often were unreliable allies of radical men. They were usually grouped with peasants and intellectuals as a potentially conservative drag line on the forward march of proletarian men. Women's equality was a stated goal of all Marxist movements, but the way women's issues were treated, one got the clear message that what women did was marginal to the struggle, unless they excelled at doing it the way men did. The great and celebrated heroines— La Pasionaria, Mother Bloor, Elizabeth Gurley Flynn, Clara Lemlich—did not organize housewives; they organized female factory workers, women's auxiliaries or men.

Mary Inman asserted in her article that housewives were exploited workers and should be organized as such. She gave a sophisticated analysis of the way unpaid housework was structured into the capitalist economy and served the interest of the employers. She argued that if women did not do their daily maintenance work and childcare, employers would have to provide workers with such services. She cited mining camps as examples of bosses providing domestic services where no women were available to render them. She showed how not only employers and the state, but individual men benefited from the housewives' unpaid labor and she called for organizing housewives and an end to sexism.

The article was far more radical on the subject than anything that had appeared before, and it was promptly shot down by the highest level of party leadership in New York. In a scathing attack the author was accused of right-wing deviation and bourgeois tendencies. Our Women's Commission thought the Inman article deserved a better hearing and wider discussion and we used some of its arguments to bolster our contention that organizing housewives was as important as organizing working women. In our report we stressed the importance of working for childcare centers, for health care and for peace. We asked that the party publications, and especially the daily press, report women's issues with more seriousness and concern. We particularly wanted the stereotyped "housewives issues" and the cheesecake pictures to be removed from the paper. We asked that the party as a whole undertake a campaign against sexism within its ranks. What we asked for was a well-rounded, advanced feminist program, which we expected to be discussed and acted upon. We were thanked for our effort, and we assumed the statement would make its way up through organizational channels. It did go as far as the state leadership, for some months later we were told that the issues we had raised were "premature" and that nothing further would be done about them at this time. The party did however appoint a Women's Commission at the national level, headed by Claudia Jones, a dynamic West Indian woman, and there were some signs that political issues of concern to women were being given more attention. By then Virginia had moved out of the state and the Women's Commission had been disbanded. Nationally, the party was heavily under attack, with its leadership under Smith Act indictments. Survival issues clearly had higher priority than the fight against sexism and for a women's agenda.

I do not remember any more details about this episode, but I do remember that I felt disappointed and ill used. Still, the way I saw it then, we were all living under a sort of siege, and one could not expect to make many advances in inner-party democracy at that time.

At any rate, problems and changes in my own life absorbed my energy in that year, about which I will write below. In the fall of 1948 I traveled to Europe to meet my family. During my stay there, the third World Congress of the WIDF was meeting in Budapest. Since I was scheduled to be nearby in Vienna around that time, I offered to attend the Congress, if I could get at least a part of my expenses paid. I was appointed by California CAW to represent the organization as part of the American delegation. The California CAW chapter raised two hundred dollars toward my expenses, with the understanding that on my return I would do some public speaking on my experiences.

THE WIDF CONGRESS lasted four days and was attended by thousands of delegates from around the world. It met in the House of Parliament and was treated with pomp and circumstance by the Hungarian government. We were welcomed at the railroad station by women with bouquets of flowers. Schoolchildren lined the streets, waving flags and peace signs. In the Parliament building, which had been heavily damaged during the war, red, white and green bunting camouflaged the repair work. Women in blue uniforms, members of the Hungarian Women's Federation, formed an honor guard and served as ushers and guides. The speaker's stand was set against a background of a huge WIDF insignia, a map of the world with the peace dove flying across it. As the hall filled with the various delegations from all over the world, many of them in their national costumes, it looked like a United Nations of women. It is hard to communicate fifty-three years later, in a world so totally changed in its perspective and outlook, how awesome and moving this scene appeared to me. I had spent a week in Vienna before coming to Budapest, and had been horrified at the ubiquitous signs of war devastation in that city. Both Vienna and Budapest had been under siege at the end of the war. After their successful defense of Stalingrad, Russian troops in their final offensive push entered Hungary in October 1944. German troops tried to stop the Russian encirclement of Budapest, but failed, and the city surrendered to the Russians in February 1945. In April the Russian armies moved toward Vienna, which surrendered after a brief siege. In Vienna, three years after the war's end, most of the bombed buildings had been fenced off from sight, but the rubble had not been removed. Some apartment buildings, sliced in half as though cut by a ragged knife, still stood, baring their innards to the winds. I was horrified at the way Vienna looked and at the fact that seemingly very little had been done to repair the damage. It was palpably and impressively different in Budapest, where bomb and artillery damage had been more extensive than in Vienna. Here, rehabilitation and rebuilding were well under way, at least in the downtown district. The rubble had been cleared away, so that bomb sites were simply empty lots, and many new structures had been erected.

There, as in Vienna, the people looked shabby and war-worn. As various groups of European women during the Congress spoke about their lives and experiences, the suffering, devastation and personal cost of the war came alive. As we gathered for the opening session in that great hall, women of fifty-six nations, all so visibly different and yet all working for world peace and nuclear disarmament, sisterhood seemed real and tangible. We might not be able to communicate across barriers of language and custom, but we smiled as our eyes met, we hugged and found other ways of expressing good will.

Our U.S. delegation consisted of thirty women, most of whom were strangers to me.[3] We had a very bad moment when, during the opening session, a group marched into the room that, at first glance, seemed to be U.S. infantrymen. Looking at them more closely, we realized they were women wearing U.S. Army uniforms or parts of these uniforms. They carried a flag and were greeted with tumultuous applause as representing the women of the socialist Greek partisans. The clothes they wore, the translator explained, had been won in battle off Greek government soldiers who had gotten them from the U.S. Army, which trained and equipped them. For most of us Americans, the Greek civil war was a distant and confusing issue, part of what the U.S. press referred to as the endless civil wars in the Balkans. Greek partisans, together with Yugoslav partisans, had fought bravely for their independence during the years of German occupation. At the war's end, the royal government was restored to Greece and with it the repressive ruling elite that had governed before the war. Left-wing Greek partisans, still organized and armed, refused to recognize the restored government and fought on, in a civil war that foreshadowed and actually launched the cold war. The U.S. and the Western allies supported the royalist government, while the Yugoslavs helped the partisans with arms and supplies. President Truman, already alarmed by the Russian's imposition of Soviet-type governments in the newly liberated countries of the Eastern bloc, such as Czechoslovakia and Roumania, decided on a show of strength in regard to Greece. He proclaimed the "Truman Doctrine," which made it a policy of the U.S. to "support free peoples who are resisting attempted subjugation by armed minorities or outside pressures." Scaring the U.S. Congress with the prospect of Soviet expansion, he secured a $400 million aid package for Greece and Turkey. Here, in the shape of Greek partisan women wearing U.S. Army uniforms, we could see one form this aid had taken. Although CAW had opposed the U.S. government's intervention in the Greek civil war, we in the U.S. delegation felt personally uncomfortable and guilty confronted with these women.

Later on during the conference I made it a point, as did some of the other Americans, to meet the partisan women and speak to them. They clearly did not hold us responsible for the actions of our government and were friendly toward us, probably as a matter of policy. They assured us that the uniforms had been taken off Greek royalists; there were no American troops in Greece. We pledged

3. From the notes I kept and from my failing memory I can reconstruct some but not all members of the delegation: Muriel Draper, Gene Weltfish, Ella Winter, Agnes Vukcevics, Marie Reed Haug, Minnie Golden, Ann Devonich, Frances Smith, Stella Allen, Hazel Johnson, Helen Phillips, Nora Stanton Barney and myself.

to each other to work for peace, whatever that may have meant to either of us. I have a picture of one of our delegates dancing with one of the Greek partisans. The moral high ground I had been accustomed to taking as a victim of fascism was shattered. Now I belonged to those whom others regarded as their oppressors. Sisterhood was no longer innocent, but had become infinitely complex.

The deliberations of the Congress produced a lot of formal speeches, which after a while seemed more rhetorical than substantive. Yet I found the reports from the various delegates as to the activities of women in their countries fascinating. The scope and range of these activities were enormously impressive, even as the reports spoke of much discrimination, poverty and misery among women and children throughout the world. The fact that women were organizing and uniting seemed hopeful. I made use of my knowledge of some European languages to get personal stories from a number of the delegates. I spoke to a Hungarian Jewish woman who said she owed her life to the Russian army; to a peasant woman who described the prewar school conditions in Hungary, where for most of the working people four years of schooling was considered adequate. She spoke with enormous pride of the fact that Hungary now had free public schools for all children up to age sixteen. The Hungarian Women's Federation had arranged for members of the various delegations to visit schools, factories and childcare centers. I visited a middle school and a nursery school and wrote down my impressions the same day. I still have what I then wrote; it says in part:

> I made an unofficial, unannounced visit to a small nursery school run by the Hungarian Women's Federation in a suburb. There were 25 children enrolled, the staff consisting of three teachers, a cook and a laundress. The school is free of charge or low-cost to all neighborhood children, from infants to age 5. It is open from 6 A.M. to 6 P.M. daily and Saturday. Each child receives a complete set of clean clothes daily, which are laundered at the school, saving the mothers a lot of work. The babies get a prepared bottle of infant formula to take home for the night. A physician daily visits the schools and examines each child. Other than the scarcity of toys, the school compared favorably with the average private nursery school in the U.S.

The school visits and the many personal contacts I made gave me a very favorable impression of social conditions in Hungary. I was, however, somewhat disturbed by the official proclamations and resolutions that began to emerge from the

Congress. A speech made in English on the first day by one of the U.S. delegates was reported in the official Congress newspaper in an English version that sounded as though it had been issued from *Pravda*. It bore little resemblance to the actual speech and it used phrases no American English speaker would use. The tendency toward homogenizing and omissions, if not outright distortions, surfaced elsewhere, too. In preparation for the final day of the Congress our delegation held a meeting. The final resolution truly disturbed us. It was full of pro-Soviet rhetoric, speaking of "the glorious heroism of the Soviet people, the unwavering fight for peace of its great leader, Joseph Stalin," etcetera, while it condemned and castigated U.S. foreign policy without qualification. It made no distinction between a particular government policy, any past record and the existence of internal opposition. After some discussion, we all agreed that we could not accept this draft and that we would not be able to take it back to our country the way it was. We labored over changes and amendments and delegated the women who had been elected to the executive committees of the Congress to negotiate these changes for us. We also spoke to delegates of several other Western democratic countries, such as the delegates from Sweden, who felt as we did. They added their protest to ours.

An emergency meeting was called late at night, to which the chair of the Executive Committee, the Russian Nina Popova, came in person. She was pleasant enough at first and listened without expression to our arguments. We explained that the language in which these resolutions were written would make them totally unacceptable to women in the U.S.A. We suggested that an international Congress should put resolutions in a more neutral frame of reference and above all should stress positive work for peace, rather than condemning one country for all the political tensions in the world. Popova accepted a few minor changes, but was adamant in refusing our argument. This was the text that had been accepted by a majority of the Executive Committee; it could not be tailored to fit the needs of particular delegations. And that was that. We were dismayed and dispirited. Even the open Communists among us found it difficult to defend her tone and absolute refusal to pay attention to our concerns. What were our choices?

We could demand to be heard by the entire Executive Committee or make an issue out of it at the final session of the Congress. This would surely hit the press and put us in the position of having to attack the Russians at an international peace conference. It was an option none of us liked.

We could on our return home publicly state our opposition to the wording of the resolutions, but this would only add fuel to the red-baiting of the WIDF in the U.S. press and give aid and comfort to those who sought to tar all peace activities as Communist. All the positive messages we brought home from the Congress would be wiped out by us thus offering proof of "Communist domination" of the organization. As always in polarized political situations, closing the ranks seemed the easier of two bad choices. We decided, without any formal vote, that we would downplay the resolution in the U.S. and stress other good features of the Congress.

The incident left a bad taste in my mouth, but I reasoned that the difficulties faced at home by U.S. progressives in defending international attacks on the foreign policy of the U.S. government could not be a consideration for people who were victimized by that foreign policy. The Greek partisan women had every right to protest U.S. intervention in their civil war, whether this sounded good to U.S. women or not. Probably, Popova's attitude reflected Russian bitterness at the disproportionate sacrifices their country had made in the antifascist war. Twenty million Russians had died in that conflict; they had every right to consider themselves the defenders of peace and democracy. It is interesting to me today, that I never questioned why the Russian view should be decisive at this gathering, nor why Popova alone should be making decisions for the Executive Committee. Rather, I tried to find good reasons to excuse what had happened. This is the closest I ever came in my life to being "used" for the good of the Communist cause.

When I returned to California I gave six talks to small groups of women, reporting on the Congress. I described my personal contacts, my impressions of the city and the country, my visits to the schools. I did not read the Congress resolutions, nor did I report on the unpleasant incident regarding them. This is not one of the things I'm proud of in my life. I closed ranks; I put on blinders. I opted for international sisterhood and the contradictions be damned.

Another incident happened in Budapest that at the time disturbed me a lot more and which I handled badly. One of my mother's Budapest cousins had survived the war and several German concentration camps. Ruth had been liberated by the Russians and had gone to Czechoslovakia, trying to recover her health, but then she had recently moved back to Budapest. My sister, who by then lived in England, was in contact with her and had helped her financially. When my sister heard I was going to Budapest, she gave me Ruth's address and urged me to visit her. Reluctantly, I did so one afternoon. My reluctance was due to the fact I did not know her and I was terrified at meeting a person who had survived the worst of the Nazi hell. I really did not want eyewitness descriptions. That was part of it, and not a very nice part, but my real reluctance was due to having heard through Nora that Ruth had had horrible experiences *after* the war. She was, I had been told, a thoroughly unpolitical person, and I sensed, before I ever saw her, that she would be the person to upset my certainties. Her credentials as to suffering were impeccable, surely greater than my own. I determined to listen to her with an open mind.

I was taken to the street address by one of the women guides who helped us at the Congress. Ruth lived in a small rented room in an old-fashioned middle-class apartment. It was sparsely furnished; I noticed a few books on a shelf above the bed. She looked to be about forty, but the camps had made her gaunt and haggard. Still, she was vivacious and very gracious. She had been a teacher of French and English before the war and she offered to speak English with me, but I preferred her German. She said she was so very glad to see me; I looked much like my mother.

This was not true, I knew, and it struck me as a sign of sentimentality. I hastened to explain why I was in Budapest.

"I know," she said. "If you weren't an American, I would not have let you come to visit me. They would make trouble for you. But as an American, I'm sure they won't bother you."

"Trouble?" I said. "I have no idea what you mean. We are treated like honored guests here. And why should visiting you—?"

"They spy on you here; they watch every step you take. I'm on their list because I've applied to emigrate. Nora is trying to get me into England. All I want is to get out of here. They're all anti-Semites here."

I told her of the Jewish woman I had talked to, of the sympathetic remarks made by several other Hungarian women. The government has made anti-Semitism a crime, I protested.

"That's all propaganda. The reality is different." She told me her story from the time she had come out of the camp, how she had arrived in Prague emaciated, without warm clothes, penniless. The government had given her a small allotment, but she was twice evicted from her room when the landlords found out she was Jewish. She told me one incident of anti-Semitism after the other—all perpetrated not by Germans, but by Czechs. As a Hungarian citizen she had been able to return to Budapest, hoping things would be better here, but she ran into hatred and anti-Semitism here as well. "The Hungarians were allies of Hitler, as you may remember. They're anti-Semites from way back." Her dark eyes flashed; her thin hands nervously fiddled with her cigarette.

I felt truly sorry for her. Obviously, the horrible experiences in the camp, about which she did not want to speak, had made her paranoid, probably half crazy. I thought of the warm, hospitable women of the Hungarian Women's Federation. Surely, if she made any effort, these women would be glad to befriend her. I tried talking to her about this.

Ruth looked at me with an odd expression of mockery and contempt. "You believe all that," she said. "Did you like the flowers they gave you, the parade, the people lining the street?"

I admitted I did.

"They can get the school kids to skip school and commandeer them out with their teachers to stand in the street for hours, waving their little flags. The women you saw had to go on their own time, without pay."

"Of course," I cried, "they wanted to welcome us."

"Or lose their jobs," she said bitterly. "Nobody volunteers—they have to work too hard and spend hours standing in line for food, they don't volunteer."

What she said seemed preposterous to me and I ascribed it to her general despondent state. Probably one who had suffered as she had could not appreciate the enormous positive effort at rebuilding going on all around her.

She did not pursue the matter and I soon left. The encounter had gone about as badly as I had suspected it would. I explained to my Hungarian escort that this was a relative of my mother's I had visited and told her a little about the woman's hard life.

"They all get nice pensions," the woman said. "Better than the soldiers. All the Jews."

The way Ruth lived it did not look to me as though she was getting a "nice pension," but I did not pursue that matter either. Ruth managed to get to England a few months later by accepting a position as a domestic worker. My sister regularly supplied her with clothes, books and money and often urged me to contribute to her support. Quite apart from the fact that I could not afford to do it at that time, I would not have done it could I have afforded it. I considered her a reactionary and never mind that she was my mother's cousin.

I am appalled at my behavior then and ashamed of it. Not so much that I disbelieved everything she said and discredited her, because what she told me did not fit into my political world view, but that I closed my heart to her humanity and suffering. As I am working on this memoir, I began with the conviction that in my many years as a Communist I never did anything of which I am ashamed now. That is true, with this exception. But this exception cannot be dismissed lightly. I had compromised with wrong, silencing my doubts by denial. It is strange how going down that road is not a matter of making major decisions. It's just a matter of silencing one's own conscience, of denying one's own experience. Lying to oneself is the worst of all sins, because one can then no longer trust one's own judgement. Just one incident, just one little step.

As always, I could trust reactionary politicians to put me back into focus. On my return home I read newspaper accounts of the WIDF Congress that treated the U.S. delegates as pathetic women who, in their desire to work for peace, had been duped into participating in the Kremlin's attack on America.

Six months after my return home we moved to New York City and I not only joined a local chapter of CAW, but I also became a member of its national board. Our main activity during 1949 was circulating the Stockholm peace appeal, which demanded an end to all nuclear armament in the world. The government and all the media denounced the Stockholm Appeal as a tool of Communist propaganda.

In October 1949 the House Un-American Committee launched an investigation of CAW. The committee's stated purpose was to warn naive American women against joining a group that sought to weaken and disarm American democracy. During the HUAC hearings the resolutions passed at the Budapest Congress were cited as examples of the organization's subversive nature. The committee particularly focused its attack on the two CAW members most identified with the old feminist movement. Susan B. Anthony II and Nora Stanton Barney. As a member of the Budapest delegation, Barney had, in an interview, favorably compared the freedom of Hungarian non-Communists with the increasing restrictions on the freedom of American Communists. This remark was read into HUAC's record, branding her as subversive. Susan B. Anthony II was charged by informers with membership in left-wing organizations and with having once published an article in the *Daily Worker*.

Under all these attacks and because of being on the Attorney General's list of subversive organizations, CAW began to lose membership. People were simply afraid to belong to such a stigmatized group. Still, the local work continued. CAW issued a peace calendar, to which I contributed two poems, but which is mainly remarkable for celebrating American women's history on each of its pages.

Because of the subversive label, our tax exemption as an organization was threatened. The final blow was struck when in 1950 the Justice Department formally demanded that the organization register as an agent of a foreign government. The implication was that CAW was representing the Soviet government.

It was obvious that we could not comply with this bit of chicanery. We never had any connection to the Soviet government; our only "crime" was our affiliation with WIDF, a legal organization representing millions of women the world over. After long and very painful discussions, the board decided that we would give up our affiliation with WIDF. We announced that fact and so informed the Justice Department. But the order to register was not rescinded.

To comply was impossible, because it would have meant admitting to a lie, namely that it was "subversive" to belong to organizations in which Communists were active. The essence of working for peace after World War II meant coexistence, the coexistence of Communist and capitalist nations, and cooperation among them. What we were asked to do was to abandon that goal and this we could not do.

We might have refused and fought the Justice Department order in court. We considered this at length, but recent history had shown that much larger and stronger organizations that had been placed on the Attorney General's subversive list had not succeeded in winning their cases. We would have had to concentrate on nothing but raising money and fighting legal battles and our active leaders might still have been liable for long jail terms if we lost our fight. We decided to disband instead.

It was a bitter decision and it was a decisive defeat. Ours was the only women's organization since the 1930s that had attempted to link feminist goals to the work for peace. None of us who sat on the national CAW board and made the decision to disband knew about the similar situation in 1925 in which the women's peace movement had been under attack because of its international affiliations. Jane Addams, Emily Balch Green and Cary Chapman Catt had been smeared by the "red network" charge and accused of traitorous activities. They had lost respectability and membership under the smear attacks. Their international ties were severed; their appeal to American women was undermined and what suffered the most was the sustained organizational work for world peace.

Now, twenty-five years later, the same pattern was repeated. Only we, who now were the targets, thought the attack on us was unique to our time and unprecedented.

All of us were frightened and felt humiliated. I remember an evening when I searched my house for papers, reports, publications and correspondence pertaining to CAW. I made a pile of all I could find and then, as I had done after the Nazi occupation of Austria, I burned it in the fireplace. The connection between these two events was quite sharp in my mind. There is something truly terrible in watching a book burn; it is even worse to set it on fire. For me, the fact I was doing this, out of fear and to protect myself and my family, became a symbol of repression and defeat. Once again, my underground psychology took over.

The years of work in CAW were my best political experience. I am proud of the work we did, proud of the impulse that guided us, and secure in knowing it was for the good of America, even though the majority of the country had fallen under the spell of cold war witch-hunting. As for burning the papers, I should not have done that. Obviously, many others did the same, for it has been inordinately difficult for historians to retrace the history of the organization for lack of documentation.[4] It has even been difficult for me to verify my memories of the events I have described. The U.S. government destroyed Congress of American Women for no other reason than that we were an effective voice of opposition to cold war policies. Their intent was to cow dissenting Americans by making them fearful. I should not have burned books and papers, because in doing so I helped to perpetuate that fear. And what is worse, I helped to destroy memory.

4. See "Congress of American Women" by Amy Swerdlow in *Encyclopedia of the American Left,* ed. Mari Jo Buhle, Paul Buhle and Dan Georgakas (New York: Garland Publishing Co., 1990), 161–62. See also Amy Swerdlow, *Women Strike for Peace: Traditional Motherhood and Radical Politics in the 1960s* (Chicago: University of Chicago Press, 1993), chap. 2.

IV

IN THE EYE
OF THE STORM

[16]

THE YEARS 1947–49 sit like huge black boulders in my brain, refusing to give way. They block out detail, hide remembrances and stifle memory, the way rock obscures light. I have struggled to get past them, to consider them in their actuality, to sort out events and feelings so as to reconstruct "what happened" with some sense of proportion, but nothing works. To say they were extraordinarily painful is to omit the many happy times, the generally hopeful personal life, the joy of infants and the wonder of living with children. Objectively seen, other years of my life were probably worse, and yet it is these years that have proven most resistant to memory.

It is by now common wisdom that deeply traumatized people, when faced with new trauma, relive the old with increased intensity and horror. Perhaps that is my case. Perhaps, in order to survive those years and do what needed to be done to protect my children, my family, I had to repress the pain, the trauma, the fears, and did that so thoroughly it cannot now be undone. I can get at it from the outside, so to speak, as though I were telling stories about another person, not myself. The only person who might be able to restore my memory is Carl, and he is long dead.

Far worse for me than all the real problems of those years was what is now referred to as McCarthyism, which from my point of view looked and felt like a reprise of the coming of fascism.

The political events fitted a certain pattern, especially if one had experienced it before. First came the shift in policy after FDR's death—the commitment of the U.S. government and its allies to a cold war against the Soviet Union, which might at any time have turned into a real nuclear war. The legitimation of red-baiting through Truman's loyalty order was followed by HUAC investigations in Hollywood and the collapse of the liberal middle in the face of right-wing attacks on free speech, freedom of association and the basic principles of unionism. The *"Gleichschaltung"* of the media followed a pattern that to me was instantly recognizable—anything left of center was suspect and defined as "Communist." That word now carried the weight of instant condemnation—it had become the word for deviance and treason. Like the word *"Jude"* in Nazified Austria it brought instant reprisal without the possibility of discussion or explanation.

Then began the time of betrayals, denunciations, the casting off of friendships and trust. Here is where my mind gets stuck—I remember it all and yet I recall nothing.

Looking back on this more than fifty years later I think I was probably overreacting and unduly pessimistic. I had no idea of American history, no sense of the strengths of the country in the face of its excesses of violence and intolerance, nor of its long democratic tradition. I could not then, as I could now, make an argument for the fact that "it can't happen here." I thought it could and it did, and while that judgement was objectively wrong, it was appropriate for me and my own experience.

THE YEAR 1947 BEGAN PLEASANTLY. After it had become clear to my father that I could not travel to Europe with or without Stephanie, he made the decision to visit us in Hollywood. It was, for a man with his serious heart condition, quite a dangerous trip. He came by boat to New York City, and then expected to travel to California by train. After arriving in New York in January 1947 in a raging blizzard and being stranded for hours on the cold pier unable to find a cab in the storm, he spent three nights sick in a hotel room in New York. Then came the long and strenuous train ride across America—on doctor's orders he could not risk flying at high altitudes in planes, which were then not pressurized. When he finally arrived at the Los Angeles train station, I had trouble recognizing him. He was haggard, at least fifty pounds thinner than when I had last seen him eleven years ago, and his eyes had a haunted and desperate look. But then he saw the three of us, and his face lit up with a wonderful smile, and I knew all would be well between us, better than it had ever been. And so it was.

He instantly fell in love with his granddaughter and she had eyes only for this utterly adoring admirer, who held on to her hand wherever she was. *Vati* and Carl liked each other from the beginning; they shared easy laughter and joy in living. In the few weeks of my father's visit, he and I overcame the years of our mental and psychological separation. We accepted each other, made up for lost years, and were able to communicate with each other on a new level of understanding. We still had profound differences in regard to politics and our views of the world, but my father could see me in a new light, as a happy wife, a housewife, a good mother—for him these were the important values and he had all but despaired of ever seeing them in me. I was still shaken by his frail condition, the look of sickness in his face and in his body—the dominant father of my adolescence now stood before me as an old man. Yet we found that middle ground between us and I will forever be grateful that life gave me that chance.

He paid for the stress of the trip with a serious setback in his health, and spent several weeks in the hospital on his return, but he never regretted taking the trip. And he was totally delighted when I wrote him in March that I was expecting a baby in October.

MARCH 21, 1947—BY EXECUTIVE ORDER, PRESIDENT TRUMAN ORDERS LOYALTY CHECKS FOR ALL FEDERAL EMPLOYEES. Standard for dismissal was "reasonable grounds . . . for belief that the person involved is disloyal to the government of the U.S.," as evidenced by the person's affiliation with any group deemed "subversive" or "totalitarian" by the Attorney General.

The beginning of my second pregnancy was much easier than the first one; I had little discomfort and nausea and felt quite energetic. But two blows to our hopes followed swiftly, one upon the other. Our nice landlady had decided to sell the house and the new owner sent us an eviction notice on the grounds that he wanted to use our apartment for a member of his family. This was one of the few legal grounds under which tenants could then be evicted. The technicality was that our one-year lease, which was up on October 1, would not be renewed. The prospect of being homeless a few weeks before the expected birth of the baby was bad enough. But the housing situation had only worsened in the past year and I knew that the search for another apartment would be most difficult. I began following leads right away and it was as bad as I had feared. Even with my pregnancy not yet noticeable, landlords took one look at charming two-year-old

Stephanie beside me and declined to rent to us. With a very tight housing market landlords had the right to refuse tenants with young children.

The second blow was Carl's persistent unemployment. Being a freelance editor in Hollywood was always difficult, since the big studios had stable crews and only rarely put on freelancers. Carl was just beginning to build up some contacts with the independents, but nothing seemed to pay off.

He was unemployed from February to July 1946 and then worked on two unmemorable low-budget productions as assistant editor for an independent producer. Finally, just a few months before the birth of the baby, he had a break. He was hired as editor-in-charge on Howard Hawks's *Red River* for the last months of editing. He was the third and final editor to work on this picture, two others having been replaced. This was his first chance to work as an editor, not as an assistant, and on a great picture.

JUNE 23, 1947—THE TAFT–HARTLEY ACT PASSES OVER PRESIDENTIAL VETO. It banned the closed shop, required unions to keep a sixty-day cooling-off period before striking, outlawed union contributions to political campaigns and required union leaders to swear that they were not members of the Communist Party.

The passage of this law seemed catastrophic to us, an ominous turn away from the pro-union labor policies that had governed politics ever since the New Deal. We had no illusions about its implications, and saw it, as it proved to be, as the opening gun in an assault on hard-won union rights. But in my own life, politics had to recede behind the personal.

In June, in my fifth month of pregnancy, I had an intestinal infection that quickly escalated into toxemia. In what appeared to be hard labor, I was rushed to the hospital by ambulance and for twenty-four hours the baby's life and my own hung in the balance. Antibiotics saved our lives. It took a week in the hospital to bring my kidney infection under control. The rest of the pregnancy was marked by fatigue, a lot of discomfort and constant worry that I might have another such episode and a premature delivery. The "total rest" the doctor prescribed was an impossible goal, but I did discipline myself not to pick up anything heavier than a teakettle. That meant that Stephanie, at age two, had to learn to become very independent. We got her little step-stools and she managed to climb up to the sink and to the toilet, get in and out of the bathtub without help and in general to be quite self-sufficient. She took it as a challenge, and did quite well with it, but I worried all the time about it harming her psychologically. As far as I can tell it did not. Carl pitched in and helped me with carrying groceries, housecleaning and Stephanie's care, as best as he could.

We were unable to find a rental apartment and by late in August we decided to buy a house. We found a beautiful old wood-frame house with a nice fenced yard in a somewhat run-down district near Chavez Ravine. It was on the border of an area largely inhabited by Mexican-Americans. An elementary school was within walking distance and we fell in love with the place at once. We needed two thousand dollars as a down payment and all we had was five hundred. But we managed to borrow small sums from family and friends and were able to make that down payment. With Carl again working on a feature film, our credit was much improved and we were able to secure a good second mortgage. The monthly mortgage and insurance payments were really above our means, but we found a young writer friend who needed a place to live and he promised to pay regularly and in advance in exchange for a large room, half bath and separate entrance. We did not have enough furniture to furnish anything but the kitchen and one bedroom, and lived for months with orange crates and bookshelves made of plywood boards and bricks. Garage sales yielded some fine living room pieces. We had an informal exchange system for children's toys, clothing and supplies going among a group of friends, so that everything was passed around and nobody lacked for anything. By the middle of September we were in the new house, delighted with the space, the privacy, the shady porch.

The last four weeks of my pregnancy I was in really bad shape—I could not comfortably lie down, sit or stand. The baby had dropped very early and I was totally clumsy, with lower back problems, aching legs and feet. The only comfortable position for me was to sit cross-legged on the floor. I gave myself a pleasant goal until the end of the pregnancy: I would plant a privet hedge along the fence on both sides of our property. I bought a hundred seedling plants and, daily, edging myself along on a foam rubber pad in my cross-legged position, I planted a half a dozen. The project was finished, but the baby refused to come. The due date passed; I could feel the baby's head with my fingers, and still he refused to arrive. "No baby is ever late," my kind doctor said. "It just means we figured wrong. Babies get born when they are ready."

After my difficult delivery with Stephanie I had become disillusioned with the team of male obstetricians I had then used and had searched for another obstetrician. Dr. Louise Light came highly recommended by several of my friends and so I went to her for the second pregnancy. I felt amply repaid for my confidence in her when she saved my life and the baby's in the toxemia episode. I trusted her completely, for in that crisis she had shown herself as reliable, capable and accessible.

After the long and difficult pregnancy, baby Dan was born quickly, within a few hours of the first labor pains. He was large and seemed perfectly healthy, but he had a bright red forceps mark on his forehead. The mark was shaped like a W turned sideways and when I saw it, I was certain it would remain there for life. The doctor and nurses all assured me it would be gone in three days, but I refused to believe them and cried uncontrollably. My baby was marked . . . All the tension, worry and uncertainty of the past months flowed into the tears I could not stop until three days later, when the mark, as predicted by the experts, disappeared. The baby was fine, he was beautiful, he was calm and contented. When we brought him home, his sister, taking one disappointed look at him, declared: "He looks like a red monkey and I hate him." Everything was quite normal and ordinary.

The house was quiet, with tall ceilings and many windows. The bedroom windows were covered by lush poinsettia bushes, their floppy wide leaves tapping against the windowpanes. I remember lying in bed, which was just two mattresses on top of each other on the floor, an orange crate by the bedside to hold lamp and books and clock, the baby in my arms, Stephanie playing on the floor beside the bed, feeling soothed and safe. The baby's head was covered with thin dark brown strands of hair; his wide forehead was smooth and pink; he slept serenely. He had survived so much turmoil and assault even before he was born and emerged calm and perfect. My terrors and fears, the harsh reality of our lives had not damaged him. The promise of his courage and his vitality strengthened me as though he were still connected with me through blood and sinew. I felt a deep peace.

But baby Dan, after his serene first six weeks, launched us on a period of constant crisis. He began to spit up after each feeding, to the point where he did not hold any food at all. We experimented for a few days, under doctor's orders, with changing his formula, but nothing worked. A test finally showed that he was allergic to cow's milk. Today there are many formulas available for such children, but in that period it was difficult to find good cow's milk substitutes. Finally, Carl found a place in the San Fernando Valley where they sold goat's milk and he drove there each day after work to pick up the day's supply. I was instructed by the doctor to boil this milk for fifteen minutes while constantly stirring, and then to strain it into sterilized bottles. That routine added an hour's work to my day, but it seemed to placate Dan's sensitive stomach. By the end of the second month he was beginning to gain weight and to sleep through the night. But then Stephanie came down with the chicken pox and he soon followed. Barely recovered, both got the measles. It was not until spring, when the baby was six months old, that we finally had a period of normalcy, without sickness.

Once he was in good health, Danny was an even-tempered baby who charmed everyone with his big grin. Stephanie quickly became very motherly and protective with him. We had enrolled her in a childcare center, together with Virginia's daughter, which finally gave me some hours of relatively free time, with only the baby to watch. I used it for writing and doing political work.

The work on my novel was taking much longer than I expected, mostly because of my still inadequate command of the English language. I rewrote the novel seven times in all, until I transformed the text from a series of translations to an original work in English. It would take me nearly twelve years to finish it. I did my writing after the children were asleep. Around 9 P.M. I would drink three cups of strong tea and work for two or three hours. The work progressed, but excruciatingly slowly.

Meanwhile, the situation in Hollywood had deteriorated. HUAC had been conducting hearings on Communist influence in the motion picture industry since March 1947. The committee claimed to have a legislative purpose, but no laws ever resulted from its hearings. In earlier HUAC investigations of the content of motion pictures the committee had been unable to find any objectionable evidence, except for *Song of Russia,* a film celebrating the wartime U.S.-Soviet alliance, which HUAC interpreted as signs of "Communist" influence. The producers had been firm in their opposition to HUAC proceedings. In October 1947 HUAC held public hearings in Washington, D.C., for which it had issued forty-three subpoenas and summoned nineteen witnesses. The issuing of many more subpoenas than the number of witnesses actually called had a predictably intimidating effect. Each of those subpoenaed had to define his position and try, if possible, to avoid appearing at all. It was an intimidation designed to produce "friendly witnesses," which certainly succeeded. Of the nineteen witnesses called, sixteen were writers. At the October hearings the committee first called the "friendly witnesses," that is, witnesses who agreed with the committee's assumption that the motion picture industry was infiltrated by Communists and that this represented a serious danger to the republic. Jack Warner, president of Warner Brothers, assured the committee of his support and named twelve people as Communists, several of them among those already subpoenaed. The other "friendly witnesses," stars like Robert Taylor, Ronald Reagan, Gary Cooper and George Murphy, set the proper tone by naming twenty-nine names and assuring the committee of their full cooperation.

In response the Committee for the First Amendment, a newly formed group of liberals and progressives opposed to HUAC, presented a petition for redress of grievances to the House of Representatives. Among the signers were prominent film stars like Lauren Bacall, Humphrey Bogart, John Huston, Gene Kelly and Danny Kaye. Mindful of their previous success in stopping legislative inquiries into the content of motion pictures, the producers pledged to resist all efforts at censorship and above all, to resist "badgering" by political committees. Eric Johnston, representing the motion picture industry, was expected to take that position at the public hearings. Representatives of the Committee for the First Amendment attended the Washington hearings, hoping to bolster Johnston's position.

But Johnston was not called upon until later. The first of the "unfriendly witnesses" before HUAC, John Howard Lawson, was met by rules of procedure that would become standard for subsequent hearings. Denied an opportunity to read a prepared statement or to explain his political views, Lawson was gaveled down repeatedly by Chairman Thomas, and responded assertively to what he considered an infringement of his First Amendment rights. He was followed on the stand by Louis Russell, a former FBI agent and now HUAC investigator, who presented a Communist Party registration card issued in 1944 for Lawson. HUAC members then voted to hold the witness "in contempt of Congress" for refusing to answer questions about his alleged CP membership, a crime that carried a one-year jail sentence.

Lawson's testimony created bad publicity for the "unfriendly witnesses." The media stressed his shouting and truculence, and professed bewilderment as to why he and the other nine witnesses who followed him did not simply explain their political affiliation openly and be done with it. While several of the "Hollywood Ten" used a low-key approach and tried to present their political views in prepared statements, only one of them was permitted to enter his own explanation of his beliefs into the record. Because they relied on their First Amendment rights, they could not evade HUAC's formulized trap, which brought them jail sentences not for any overt act they had committed nor for any actual ideas they had advocated, but for the carefully constructed crime of "contempt of Congress." The contempt citations were upheld by an overwhelming majority vote in the House and confirmed by all the courts to which they appealed. The "Hollywood Ten" were jailed in June 1950.

If one believed that the First Amendment of the Constitution guaranteed the rights of each citizen to be protected from prosecution due to his or her political beliefs, then one could not, even under threat of prison, abandon that right by answering the committee's questions as to one's political affiliation. One could not concede HUAC's right to ask such questions. The Hollywood Ten believed the law was on their side. And in October 1947 they believed the majority of the film industry, including the producers, were on their side. On October 18, Eric Johnston, speaking as president of the Motion Picture Association, denied any rumor that the producers planned to institute a blacklist and denounced such a rumor as a libel on him.

But the HUAC hearings inspired a public outcry against Communists in the film industry. The American Legion threatened to boycott any film on which an alleged Communist had worked. On November 24, 1947, the three major organizations of motion picture producers met at the Waldorf Astoria Hotel in New York City to see what could be done by way of damage control. After two days of deliberations Eric Johnston announced their decision: they would not continue to employ any of the Hollywood Ten

until such time as he is acquitted or has purged himself of contempt and declares under oath that he is not a Communist ... We will not knowingly employ a Communist or a member of any party or group which advocates the overthrow of the Government of the United States by force or by any illegal constitutional methods.

The blacklist was on.

As legal appeals wound their way through the courts, it became clear that the courts would not contradict prevailing popular opinion. HUAC's right to question witnesses as to their political affiliation was upheld. As a result, subsequent "unfriendly witnesses" had only the Fifth Amendment for their protection. But here too, entrapment threatened. If one did not take the Fifth on the first question asked, one had presumably waived one's right to take it at all. As soon as witnesses had answered to their names and addresses, they were asked for their union or party affiliation. "Are you now or have you ever been a member of the Communist Party?" "Are you now or have you ever been a member of the Screen Writers Guild?" If they answered yes, they would then immediately be asked to identify others who were CP or union members. If they refused, they were cited with contempt of Congress. This meant, in effect, that a witness could not afford, even if he wanted to, to testify as to his political affiliation unless he was also pre-pared to "name names."

The Fifth Amendment to the Constitution was designed to give protection against self-incrimination to the innocent as well as to the guilty. In the cold war atmosphere anyone using the amendment was presumed to be guilty and would be blacklisted.

Later, several famous personalities—Lillian Hellman, Pete Seeger—success-fully used a First Amendment defense, but that was in the years when McCarthyism was already in retreat and had lost its appeal. In 1948 the inquisi-tion machinery still worked like clockwork.

The Hollywood HUAC hearings and the huge publicity they produced were highly effective in turning "Communists" into outlawed monsters in the public mind. These hearings also set the pattern for the concept of "guilt-by-association," by labeling certain unions as "Communist-dominated" and, therefore by associa-tion, "subversive." Today, many historians agree that one of the results of the HUAC hearings was to curb the strength of progressive Hollywood unions, such as the Screen Actors and Screen Writers Guilds. The inquisitors' secondary aim was not so much to affect the content of motion pictures as to capture the minds of the American public and to make witch-hunting respectable. In both respects the committee certainly succeeded.

Fifty years later, documents secured under the Freedom of Information Act have shown that at the time of the Hollywood HUAC hearings the FBI had in its hand the entire membership list of the California CP, given to them by an informer who had been the CP membership director. Thus, there was no need for the "naming of names" in order to expose infiltration of the industry. The names were already known. As Victor Navasky has convincingly argued, what was insti-tuted in these hearings was a "shaming ritual" that served to create a new cate-gory of deviant outsider, "the Fifth Amendment Communist."[1]

Dalton Trumbo, one of the Hollywood Ten, characterized the period bril-liantly as "the Time of the Toad," a period in which the nation denies its tradi-tion and aims "to destroy any heretical minority which asserts toad-meat not to be the delicacy which governmental edict declares it. The triple heralds of the Time of the Toad are the loyalty oath, the compulsory revelation of faith and the secret police." He described the effect of several years of such policies, the hound-ing of actors, teachers, artists, writers and civil servants,

1. Victor Navasky, *Naming Names* (New York: Viking, 1980), chap. 10.

and nothing, really, done about it, no cry in the streets that murder was afoot, nothing at all to be heard except a few cranks and do-gooders howling in vain to the rising wind. Colleagues, friends, fellow workers stepped softly into the jobs of the damned, and the hole which their disappearance left in the fabric of community life was scarcely noticed except when one of them killed himself or required commitment.[2]

Trumbo's description is apt, but late in 1947 the full extent of what was coming was still not clearly visible.

The events I have here described occurred at a time when our family could not deal with anything but babies, sickness and daily domestic crises. Still, we were deeply affected by the political developments around us. Several of the Hollywood Ten were men we knew and respected; we had friends and acquaintances among the second group of "unfriendly witnesses." As the "naming of names" began, it was clear we could, any day, be among those "named" or subpoenaed. What position would we take, in that case?

The story of the Hollywood Ten has been told many times since and they have become the symbol of the blacklist. While they certainly deserve their place in history and while their defense of First Amendment rights should be celebrated, they were not typical of those victimized by the blacklist. Most of them were highly successful writers, with long Hollywood careers and some wealth and savings. On the other hand, most of the people who would fall victim to the blacklist were "little people." The blacklisted writers could attempt to sell scripts under pseudonyms; they could write for other media, but blacklisted actors, teachers and civil servants were thrown out of their professions for good.

One of our friends, the actor Al Hammer, had been part of a team of four nightclub performers, The Reviewers, who had come to Hollywood together and had won studio jobs. Now, called before HUAC, Adolph Green and Betty Comden became informers and moved on to steady engagements and brilliant careers. The fourth in the group, Judy Holliday, was grey-listed. Al Hammer, an uncooperative witness, was blacklisted. He had a wife and two small children, who were friends of our children. The family struggled to survive, lost their house and finally moved out of Hollywood altogether. He was one of those who never made a comeback in Hollywood or on the stage in New York.

---

2. Dalton Trumbo, *The Time of the Toad: A Study of Inquisition in America and Two Related Pamphlets* (New York: Harper & Row, 1972), 3–4, 146.

Fear became our daily companion. A strange car pulling up near our house, a man emerging from it, made the heart race and the knees grow weak. The sub-poena servers liked to come around at mealtimes, or quite early in the morning. Each morning, you peeked out from behind the window screens to see if they were there. Friends told stories, all of them bad. The FBI followed the wives of those subpoenaed; two men in regular cars would be parked near the school entrance as the wife picked up the children. They would knock at your door: two men in business suits, flashing their badges. "We'd just like to talk to you for a few minutes, ma'am," they would say in their clipped, rehearsed voices.

"I have nothing to talk to you about" was the only answer that worked, but it would make them follow you for days, questioning your neighbors, your employer, your friends. Neighbors would avoid you; others, friendly, would warn you what was up. "You're wanted by the FBI."

Those were the stories. The chilling effect truly worked, like slow corrosive poison. We lived in fear, we ate it; we slept in fear, with nightmares of violence and useless resistance. Kafka was right—all those accused are guilty. We had com-mitted no crime, violated no law. We worked and paid our taxes; we cut our lawn and put the garbage out on time. We were good neighbors and by all normal stan-dards we were good citizens. We voted regularly and in all off-year elections.

You began to wonder about yourself. Maybe you were avoiding the FBI inter-view because of your cowardice, your secret knowledge that, pressed hard enough, you would answer with whatever they wanted to hear: the names of your friends, their version of your political life, your redefinition of yourself as having been naive, duped or coerced or betrayed, just so you could save your own skin, your job, your children. You hunkered down, trying to stay calm and do the daily work that needed to be done, waiting for the next blow.

Ever since the Truman loyalty program for federal employees, anti-Communism had become mainstream politics. At the core of all the various loy-alty programs that would spring up and flourish in the coming years was the belief that adherence to Communism meant disloyalty to the U.S.A. The rea-soning was that future conflict between the U.S. and the Soviet Union was inevitable; Communists would, in that case, individually have to choose between their loyalty to one or another power; they would inevitably choose loyalty to the Soviet Union over loyalty to their own country—therefore, in anticipation of this inevitable future dilemma, Communists presented a "clear and present dan-ger" to the security of the U.S. Every part of this chain of thought was specula-tive and flawed. The Soviet Union had just emerged from the bloodiest conflict in its history as a staunch ally of the U.S.A., having lost 22 million people in that conflict. It was in no way a sensible prediction that the Soviet Union would launch a war against the U.S.A. On the other hand, for purposes of the cold war, in which one of the main aims of both sides was to restrict the other's zone of influence in the world and to expand its own, it was desirable to constantly stress the likelihood of such a future war. Those committed to cold war assumptions cast U.S. Communists as traitors and spies in order to stifle dissent.

The same big lie had been used by European fascists to advance their causes. Mussolini, Hitler and Franco had come to power claiming to rescue the nation from the threat of Bolshevism. In 1947–48, as I saw the HUAC investigations in Hollywood proceed, the European parallel was vivid in my mind. Today we speak of the chilling effect of these witch hunts on left-wing opposition, and we conflate a great many events under the name of McCarthyism. But the events I am describing here antedated the coming into public consciousness of Senator McCarthy by three years. And the persecutions, the rhetorical stoking of hatred against people who were described in stereotypes as deviants and outcasts, the scapegoating and witch-hunting took place under the leadership of a Democratic President, in the trade unions, in academe and in every state and local government. Senator McCarthy is being given undeserved credit for a broad and deep movement that he neither spawned nor controlled and that thrived despite his excessive and flamboyant style.

In the next few years, the mass media would be flooded with the stereotype of the treacherous unpatriotic Communist who posed a threat to every decent citizen. The flip-flops of the CPUSA, following the Soviet party line, were used effectively to lend credence to these stereotypes. But the people I worked with and knew in the CP did not fit any of these characterizations, nor did the work we did have anything to do with the horror world of treason and conspiracy the media and the politicians created like magicians.

Here is what we actually did:

Since we had moved into our house, I had become affiliated with a party neighborhood club. We met each Tuesday night at different people's houses. We were four or five housewives, mothers of young children, a middle-aged couple, a single young man. The most important work the women in our club did was in Congress of American Women. It was during this period that we organized and participated in the meat boycotts, the picket lines in front of grocery stores for lower food prices. The political work could be done easily with the children in tow.

The party group also did "educational" work—that is, we read the *Daily Worker* and *Political Affairs.* It was the job of the education director, a position I held for a time, to digest the heavy-duty theoretical articles, put them into teachable form and try to get a discussion going. From time to time we made suggestions as a group on how to improve the form and content of *Political Affairs,* but such criticism never seemed to reach the proper ears.

During this period the party was convulsed by its campaign to eradicate racism from its ranks. The campaign was based on thoroughly laudable good intentions; its ostensible aim was to reverse the trend whereby Blacks were recruited into the party, but they left it in short order. Its secondary laudable aim was to equip party members better to fight the pervasive racism in the general society. The inner party discussions of U.S. racism, its forms, its insidious nature, its pervasiveness were quite helpful in raising everyone's consciousness. I remember feeling proud about being in an organization that was seriously dedicated to the fight against racism. But on the whole the campaign degenerated into guilt-tripping, personal attacks and even the scapegoating of some members. Public mea culpas by white members at "self-criticism" sessions were the order of the day. An atmosphere developed in which it was impossible to criticize a black person for any reason whatsoever. Fortunately, in my neighborhood branch the campaign never took on such destructive dimensions, but it was troubling nevertheless that the best of intentions produced division and bad feelings. What it did NOT produce was an increase in black membership. (As we now know, many of the black party recruits were FBI agents. One of the side effects of this campaign was that they could carry out their role undisturbed, because the atmosphere in the party did not make it possible to question the actions of any person of color.)

Early in 1948 I became active in Henry Wallace's third-party campaign. Henry Wallace had been Secretary of Agriculture under President Roosevelt and FDR's Vice President from 1941 to 45. An outspoken advocate for labor and civil rights, he was considered too liberal and was replaced as vice-presidential candidate by Harry Truman in 1944. On Truman's succession to the presidency, Wallace was appointed Secretary of Commerce, but his public opposition to Truman's hard-line policy against the Soviet Union led to his dismissal from the Cabinet. Long a favorite with labor and Blacks, Wallace became a controversial figure. In the 1948 election he ran against Truman as a third-party candidate. He was excoriated in the press when he declared that, if elected, he would see to it that every child in the world would have a quart of milk a day. This was turned into "A quart of milk for every Hottentot"—a utopian goal for which the candidate was roundly ridiculed.

The Independent Progressive Party (IPP) campaign went into high gear in California in January 1948 with the goal of collecting three hundred thousand signatures in the state to put the party on the ballot. Once again, I returned to door-to-door canvassing, this time with two children in tow. It was not hard to secure signatures; all the canvassers reported a lot of voter dissatisfaction with Truman. Our hopes for Wallace were high—nothing less than a reversal of domestic and foreign policy, which we hoped would result from either his victory or a sizable showing in the election. IPP was placed on the ballot with many more than the needed signatures. Through the writers' workshop I got involved in the production of a slide show for candidate Wallace, for which I wrote the script. The show was performed at neighborhood meetings and fund-raising parties in homes. I attended a large campaign rally for Wallace in downtown Los Angeles and cheered myself hoarse for the handsome, elegant candidate, who seemed to me to embody the best of American Progressivism.

During these months I was equally active in educating people about the horrible case of Mrs. Rosa Lee Ingram and her two teenage boys and trying to raise funds in her defense. Mrs. Ingram was a black Georgia sharecropper, trying to support her thirteen children on a small piece of land. She had for some time been harassed by her white neighbor, who one day advanced upon her, rifle in hand, when she tried to stop him from shooting her farm animals, which he claimed had strayed on his land. She grabbed the rifle, whereupon he beat her bloody with a knife handle. Two of her boys—Lee, thirteen years old, and Wallace, fifteen—rushed to their mother's defense. In the ensuing scuffle, the white neighbor died from a blow to the head. An all-white jury quickly condemned the mother and the two boys to death, ignoring their pleas of self-defense. On an appeal, which was handled by the NAACP, the sentence was commuted to life imprisonment. After a worldwide amnesty campaign the Ingrams were finally released from prison in 1959.

All of this added up to a lot of political activity for a mother of a toddler and a new baby. It meant not enough sleep and the constant juggling of conflicting activities, but it also made it easier to adjust to full-time motherhood. My daily life was washing diapers and sterilizing bottles, wiping noses and nursing sick children, but it was also full of politics and involvement in the larger world. Being in the party gave one a sense of participation in the major events of the time. "The party keeps your conscience on the alert," Carl used to say. I think he was right, except that it also excluded from your conscience or even consciousness anything that might interfere with your blind faith in the party and in the Soviet Union. Sometimes now, with a far wider perspective, I refer to how I felt then by saying with a slight sneer, "I was saving the world." Later, when I studied the radical abolitionists and their fight against slavery, I instantly recognized the mindset. "Saving the world" gives one a sense of purpose and the satisfaction of contributing to a greater good. It energizes; it gives one courage in adversity. Today, in this much more cynical and disenchanted world, I struggle with keeping some such sense of a greater good, a larger purpose. But it must be constrained by retaining critical judgement.

Like a skilled juggler, I was keeping a lot of balls in the air.

THEN, IN APRIL 1948, my mother died in Switzerland. She had suffered so long that her death felt like a release, for her and for us who loved her. I could not leave my two small children to go to her funeral, even if I had had the money to pay for the fare, which I did not. So I told myself and so it was. I wept, I grieved at a long distance, but the daily life and the children absorbed me to such a degree that dealing with complex issues of grief and guilt was impossible.

Decades later, in a deep emotional crisis after the death of my husband, I began to comprehend the cost of having displaced and repressed my emotions after my mother's death. The ghosts of that past were haunting me like demons and only years of work in analysis helped me finally to come to terms with my feelings. I never saw my mother after I left her in France before the war. I never helped her through her terminal illness. I did not go to her funeral.

A few months after my mother's death, my father let me know that he now felt free to marry the woman he had loved for many years. Their wedding would take place in Vaduz in September and he was inviting me and my entire family to come and celebrate with them. I felt happy about his decision and excited at the prospect of being at such an event with my old and my new families. Since Carl had finished working on his last picture, *Red River,* we felt a little less pressed financially. Things looked good for him and he expected to get some work over the summer. We decided to accept my father's invitation and began to make travel plans for September.

But things turned out differently than we expected. Carl did not find work over the summer, even though he tried hard. As we had the previous year, we went back on unemployment insurance and the family lived on thirty-five dollars a week. It was harder now, with the added expenses for the new baby and the mortgage payments on the house. Our renter, Larry, also lost his job sometime during that summer and fell behind in his rent payments, which put us into a financial crisis. We had no margin to play with. Larry came through, a few weeks late, and we managed, but it made us realize how precarious our financial situation was.

During that summer there was an internal struggle going on in the IATSE, with a progressive slate trying to unseat Roy Brewer. Carl was part of the small group of IA members working for a change in union leadership. I don't remember the details, but there was one union meeting at which Brewer flew into a rage at something Carl said. Pointing his finger at him, he said: "I've got my eye on you. You'll never work in a studio again." I know this incident only secondhand from Carl telling me about it, and it seemed then so preposterous that we both chose to simply disregard it as an outburst of bad temper on the part of an intemperate man. We could not believe that such a raw threat of reprisal was anything more than empty bluster. We did not know our man and had no inkling of his power.

All this, again, is in retrospect. The blacklist was, in 1947, not yet fully established and Brewer was simply a red-hunting union leader trying to scare his own members into toeing the line. There is nothing I can prove or document. But it is a fact that after this incident Carl, for one reason or another, could not get a job at a big studio in Hollywood. The pattern became clear to us after he had been twice promised a job as assistant editor only to be refused the job a few days later.

Four weeks before our planned trip to Europe, Carl landed a job with an independent studio. It was a B picture with few redeeming features, but it would mean three months of solid employment. After that difficult summer, it was too good an opportunity to miss. He took the job and persuaded me to make the trip to Europe alone with the children.

Traveling in postwar Europe with a three-year-old and a nearly one-year-old who did not yet walk was a test of endurance and physical strength. But it was all made worthwhile by experiencing the delight my father and his new wife took in his grandchildren. I liked Gretel enormously and for the first time in my life saw my father truly happy. She was a warm, kind person, pretty and traditionally feminine, whose life revolved around husband and home. She gave my father what he had never had—a wife totally focused on making him feel loved and appreciated. I was very happy to see this development and to have her as my children's grandmother.

It was during this European trip that I made my side trip, first to Vienna and then to Budapest for the WILDF Congress. I was gone just two weeks, with my children well taken care of, but still I missed them terribly. But the trip was very meaningful for me in other ways. I wrote to Carl from Vienna:

Oh, darling, my first day in Vienna . . . How to get it all down? I started remembering at once, on the train, every mountain, every road. It got worse in Vienna proper. Right at first: the destruction, the shabbiness and sordidness of the city come as a bad shock. Like seeing someone you've loved disfigured and horribly old. Most of the real beauty of the place is buried under layers of rubbish and soot. Yet, I've forgotten nothing. The closeness I feel for this place is something very real; it comes back with the onrush of language, the inflection, the pride of being taken for a Viennese everywhere. In spite of all, it's like coming home.

Of those I knew few are left. Even in the street, the faces you see, there is a pointed absence of Jewish faces. Even so, the town has got me in its clutches already.

All during the trip I was working on various schemes to launch a film production in Austria and get Carl to come and live there. My father was delighted at the idea, but in the end nothing came of it.

Soon after we returned to Hollywood in January 1949 Carl's job was finished. We had been able to pay off our debts and save a little money. If, as we expected, his having worked on *Red River,* a major picture, would lead to some other good job offers, we could look forward to a more secure period. Altogether, this was a happy period for me. My time in Europe had helped me to come to some kind of closure with my childhood. I saw my father in a new light and now had a solid, loving relationship with him. Going through my mother's papers, letters and artwork made her death more real and acceptable. And despite my initial enthusiasm for the city, my short time in Vienna had firmed up my conviction that I had left that place for good.

Our marriage had reached that level of trust and mutual acceptance that made it feel like a solid foundation. I had proven to myself that I could be a competent, loving, full-time mother. And the other aspects of my being, the political activist and the writer, had also been incorporated in my life. I felt in balance and, at last, I felt at peace.

That period of serenity did not last long. Again, Carl was getting job offers that mysteriously vanished after a few days. Finally, a kindly soul tipped him off that there was some sort of "trouble" connected with him and that it looked as though he could not be employed in Hollywood. That tip-off made us realize how serious Roy Brewer's threat had been. This man truly seemed to have the power to prevent a union member whom he wanted to punish from getting work in the film industry.

A few years later, this power was to be openly used and finally institutionalized. It was Roy Brewer who would become the most powerful man in the Hollywood blacklisting racket. It was Roy Brewer to whom accused "reds" would go humbly, hat in hand, to find out by what terms they might again work in their profession. Brewer screened them, negotiated with their lawyers and imposed the terms of their penance. Usually they would have to "name names" and then make some sort of public statement about their own guilt, how they had been "duped" and seduced and misled. All this, again, is in retrospect. At the time when this happened to Carl, Brewer's power seemed preposterous and outrageous. But it was real, and we were helpless against it.

One of Carl's friends, a film producer, had started making TV films in New York and assured Carl he would give him work. On the strength of this promise we decided that Carl should return to New York to see if he could build a career in TV and film there.

As it turned out, his being blacklisted so early in the game proved to be a blessing in disguise. Had he stayed in Hollywood, Carl certainly would have been hauled before HUAC and his career would have ended with his refusal to name names. The blacklisting machinery of the entertainment industry would never develop on the East Coast to the same deadly precision as it had in Hollywood. Carl was able to build an outstanding career in the world of New York filmmaking, which was, in the early 1950s, just beginning to develop as an alternative to Hollywood.

We did not, of course, have an inkling of this when he left for New York early in 1949. All we knew was that our dreams and hopes of the past eight years had been shattered. All his talent and hard work had ended in a void. Once again, with just a few hundred dollars in reserve, but now with two children to support, we would have to start from scratch.

[17]

POLITICAL EVENTS followed one upon the other like hammer blows:

MARCH 1949—ALGER HISS, A STATE DEPARTMENT OFFICIAL, IS ACCUSED OF ESPIONAGE BY WHITAKER CHAMBERS. Since the statute of limitations has run out, Hiss is being tried for perjury.

JULY 8, 1949—PERJURY TRIAL OF ALGER HISS ENDS IN A HUNG JURY.

SEPTEMBER 23, 1949—RUSSIA EXPLODES A NUCLEAR BOMB. President Truman orders U.S. development of a hydrogen bomb.

OCTOBER 1949—THE CHINESE RED ARMY HAS CONQUERED ALL OF MAINLAND CHINA AND HAS PROCLAIMED A REPUBLIC. In the U.S., the China lobby blames the State Department for "losing China."

In the trial of the top leadership of the Communist Party, defendants are accused of conspiracy to teach and advocate the violent overthrow of the government. Thirteen undercover FBI agents testify in the trial. When none of the defendants can be shown to have advocated violence, Louis Budenz, a former Communist, testifies that they used "Aesopian language" to mean the opposite of what they were saying.

OCTOBER 14—THE TRIAL OF COMMUNIST PARTY LEADERS ENDS IN THEIR CONVICTION.

NOVEMBER 1949—THE SECOND TRIAL OF ALGER HISS BEGINS.

The rantings of paid informers and stool pigeons, stale with empty repetitions and bizarre scenarios, had jumped to the front pages, become lead stories for the evening news, the subject matter of feature movies and TV shows. Perjured witnesses in repeated trials, Philbrick, Bentley, Crouch and Matusow, had become national heroes, their paranoid dramas elevated to gospel truths.

WITH THE EXPLOSION of the Russian atomic bomb, America's monopoly of atomic weapons had ended and with it America's age of security. The Communist victory in China was seen as part of a worldwide Communist advance that ultimately threatened American democracy, both ideologically and militarily. It was inconceivable to the American public and politicians that Russia could have developed the atomic bomb by its own efforts. It was equally inconceivable that the "fall of China" could have occurred without the conspiratorial aid of traitors in the U.S. government. Thus proving the existence of a "Communist conspiracy" was essential to upholding the ideology upon which the cold war rested.

The reasoning was simple: all American Communists and their sympathizers and defenders were involved in an evil conspiracy to overthrow democratic government. One could tell who they were by some simple signs: advocacy of world peace and international cooperation, militant trade unionism, and ideas of communitarianism and social justice. If they had ever worked for American-Soviet friendship, against atomic and nuclear weapons, for international cooperation, against racial injustice in the U.S., then they were tainted. Guilt by association was an accepted fact. If they acted like Communists, were related to Communists, knew some Communists, failed to denounce Communists, then they were Communists.

And Communists had become the devil, the witches, the traitors. The Smith Act trials, the hearings before the various investigative committees—HUAC, the MacCarran Committee, the anti-subversive committees in each state—all told the same story over and over again. One big lie.

Walking through the streets of Vienna, my hometown, seeing the swastikas everywhere—in the lapels of pedestrians, in the shop windows, on the flags flying from all the houses—you felt disembodied, emptied of yourself. This was before the obligatory wearing of the Jewish star, but an absence is as strong a sign as a presence. People glanced at you as you passed by and they noticed the ABSENCE, the swastika that was not there, the sign not carried before you as protection, and they knew. You were not one of them; you were the Other. On street corners, on walls near schools and churches and bus stops, were the wall newspapers, the Nazi propaganda sheets changed each day. *Der Stürmer* with its horrible cartoons: ugly old Jews in kaftans and stiff hats, hook-nosed with bulging lips, assaulting some blonde girl or dragging sacks of hoarded gold—figures of a distorted imagination that revived centuries-old stereotypes. You passed them by, trying to see them and not to see them and you thought, but nobody looks like that, I don't look like that, no Jew ever looked liked that, entirely missing the point. Of course no one ever looked like that, but the idea was to fix the image in the mind of the beholder until he could superimpose it on reality. Until the image substituted for reality. It worked, oh how well it worked . . .

Graffiti on the walls: BUY ARYAN; *JUDA VERRECKE.* The latter translates "Croak, Jews," but that is not really accurate, for that would be *JUDEN VERRECKET.* But it says *JUDA* and that is a nonexistent word, a newly minted word for a nonexistent entity, the entire Jewish community, not the real community but an imagined caricature of a worldwide community, that constituted by the anti-Semitic hoax, *The Protocols of the Wise Men of Zion. JUDA* is the community of Jewish conspiracy, invented centuries ago by Czarist anti-Semites in Russia to justify their persecution of Jews. When it appeared as graffiti on doors and walls it brought to life old myths of blood guilt, of Jews draining the blood of Christian children to bake into their *Mazzoth,* of ritual murder and the desecration of the host. It made the *Stürmer* caricature a substitute for the Jewish doctor one knew, for the Jewish neighbor with whom one had lived in peace for generations, for the Jewish classmate. Instead, the horror image took over and one no longer saw the actual person, known or unknown. When that happened, Auschwitz and the final solution were made possible.

Now I walked through American streets, pushing the stroller with my baby in it, my toddler walking beside me, and the headlines screaming at me from the newsstands seemed exactly as they had been then. Now the Communist was the devil incarnate, the outcast, the deviant. The brave men and women who resisted the Inquisition, who tried to read their prepared statements to the investigating committees to put their true belief, the record of their lives and activities into the hearing records and who were gavelled down, ruled out of order, silenced and cited for contempt—they were blowing into the wind, throwing sand into the storm, bailing out the ocean with a spoon.

Escape, we had dreamed in Vienna. America . . . Now I was in America and there was no escape.

The witch-hunting and blacklisting system was built on old foundations. Like the slave system, like the medieval witch hunts, like fascism, it flourished by instilling fear and by letting the imagination of the victims work its self-destructive course. One did not need to imprison or kill large numbers of people—all one needed to do was to set an example with a few, and the fear this example created in other potential victims was sufficient to insure the falling in line of thousands of others. The Hollywood Ten, the first group of writers faced with jail sentences, were still appealing their convictions in the courts, but hundreds of others who were candidates for persecution by the Inquisition decided then and there that they would "cooperate" and name names in order not to face such a fate themselves. And tens of thousands more decided that it was safest not to protest what was going on, not to make any kind of waves, not to call attention to oneself. And so the witch-hunters stood center-stage, ostensibly unopposed, and *Gleichschaltung*—the imposition of political conformity—dominated the land. And those few of us who did not fall into line experienced an alienation so profound that we often thought we must be going mad.

I knew so many of them—those subpoenaed, those dodging subpoenas, those in exile. The ones who had named names and those who had made silent deals. The seventy-nine blacklisted people I knew in Hollywood included seventeen informers. If I were to add the names of those I knew in New York City and elsewhere who were blacklisted—the teachers, government workers, university professors, musicians, writers, journalists and artists—the list would go well over a hundred.

There is a historian's way of looking at such numbers. Perhaps three to four thousand people in Hollywood were blacklisted; at least two to three thousand were grey-listed. The numbers cannot be accurately computed, because in addition to those subpoenaed and hauled before the various investigating committees and those listed by FBI and the L.A. police department, there were those listed on "unofficial" rosters such as "Red Channels" and by various private keepers of lists. Measured against the population figures in the census, or measured against the total population of the U.S.A., the number of those affected by or involved in the Hollywood blacklist was not large. Since most of the targets were writers, they were not the best-known celebrity figures.

But if one looks on Hollywood as an industrial company town the figures are more significant. From the point of view of the progressive craft unions and

guilds, nearly the entire leadership of these organizations was effectively paralyzed or destroyed.

Seen in a more personal way, from within our own lives, the figures were devastating. If from within a circle of friends and acquaintances one could list over a
hundred people subject to blacklisting and persecution, the figures took on the
aspect of a major disaster. When one of my friends is dying of cancer and another is diagnosed with a less virulent form of it while a third is waiting out her five
years of recovery, that seems like a lot of blows, an epidemic of illnesses. In the
case of the blacklist, all our friends and most of our acquaintances were involved.
Our doctor, dentist, lawyer were involved. The members of the organizations to
which we belonged and in which we were active were involved. Most of the
organizations were, in the course of a few years, proscribed or put out of business.

Living with insecurity of this kind is like camping out on a rock face on a
windswept plateau. You surround yourself with pebbles and call it home.

Sometimes, thinking back on these times, I wonder how we lived through it
at all. How we dressed and fed the children, took out the garbage, shopped,
talked to the neighbors, did our jobs. Drowning in lies, suffocating in betrayal,
denied a chance to defend ourselves and always waiting for the next hammer
blow. How did we survive it?

Now, so many decades later and with so much abstract wisdom, I can write
long essays about the social construction of deviant outgroups, about the social use
of stereotypes to maintain the maldistribution of resources. But in my bones there
is this knowledge of what it is like when what you are is taken from you and distorted and denied, held up for shame, ridicule and contempt and you are gagged
and bound and cannot say or do anything. Just, somehow, ride out the storm.

Hitler's thousand-year *Reich* lasted twelve years; Congressman J. Parnell
Thomas, chairman of HUAC, ended up in jail convicted of corruption; Joseph
McCarthy's reign of terror lasted less than four years; even the endless horror of
the Vietnam War came to an end. The Soviet Union collapsed from within,
defeated by a system of police terror and thought control that made it impossible
to correct errors and crimes committed by cliques in power.

The wonderful strength of democracy lies in its openness, its flexibility, its
potential for correcting errors and crimes committed by those in power. Even in
the worst years those who refused to go along with the mass hysteria, those who
persisted in blowing against the wind, could survive. Persecuted, harassed,
hounded—yet they were not sent to Siberian labor camps or mental institutions.
In Europe, in Latin-American totalitarian regimes, the period of repression we

then experienced would have led to the establishment of fascism. But the long tradition of democracy, the safeguards of the Bill of Rights, the checks and balances upheld by an independent judiciary prevented the worst from happening in the U.S.A. Thus, that feeble band of resisters could hold out until their voices could again be heard.

CARL DEPARTED FOR NEW YORK sometime in February 1949 and quickly found work on two independent films, but the work lasted only a few weeks each time, and what he earned was just enough to support us during this period. The TV series to be shot at a New York City studio, on which he had been promised a job, was postponed. He felt he should stay on a while longer, but we decided to wait on making a permanent move until he had a secure job.

The months of separation were hard on us and hard on the children. Our correspondence during these months was filled with practical survival questions. Where would we live; how much of a rent commitment could we make; should we rent or sell our L.A. house? In each letter I tried to give an account to Carl of the children's activities, but on rereading these accounts now, it is obvious to me that I was near the breaking point in dealing with them during their father's absence. They were both "acting up" and doing the most mischief possible. Stephanie was angry with me most of the time, accusing me of all kinds of sins of neglect. She went around quoting "my Daddy" continually and showed her resentment of everything I did. Clearly, in her mind, I was the culprit. Fortunately, she was still going to Childhouse, the nursery school where she had spent a happy time the year before. That gave her some continuity and security. Dan showed his discomfort by being very dependent on me, hanging on to my skirt, screaming if he lost sight of me for even a minute. He had frequent episodes of diarrhea and upset stomach, and woke up at night with nightmares. Clearly, the uncertainty of our situation and my tensions were upsetting them; they needed individual attention, organized activities with other children. They needed their Daddy.

Carl's nerves were frazzled, his letters were a long list of complaints and, as I never tired of writing to him, he did not answer my practical questions. How he could have answered questions that demanded financial and lifestyle decisions while he was sleeping on a living room couch in the apartment of friends and trying to rescue his career from the shambles left by being grey-listed is hard to figure out now. The letters were frustrating to us both.

I don't know exactly what made me rally myself to write the letter I am here reprinting, but I must have sensed the danger to our marriage, for this letter is quite different from all the other hasty and irritated notes and daily activity logs we were then exchanging.

Darling,

The steady and steadfast warmth of your love comes to me in your letters—it is the core, the deep singing root of my life. It is knowing you are far away and still being able to function, with an ache deep inside me for wanting you, but nevertheless being able to function and without ever a doubt of you—it is this I feel more strongly, more beautifully than anything I have ever experienced. It is becoming a better person through you and because of you, and finding the same process in you—different rhythms perhaps, over the years, but the same direction. It is knowing your sentence in every word you write, knowing your thought in every sentence and the whole of you in this turmoil; this harsh, beastly struggle, seeing you come through unscathed and growing with the demands made upon you: gentle, because you see the whole as well as the detail, hard and solid because you can love and have a stake in the fight.

In all this mad uncertainty, in this shattered world where you get so used to danger you no longer notice it, in all the enervating tug and pull of our struggle for existence, I have found a quiet certainty, very close to peace. It is because of the children and their incessant need of me, because of their beautiful growing bodies, their agile, growing minds, because of their immature powers and the ever-widening boundaries of their horizons, it is because I have been thrown upon their company as my sole distraction that I have discovered the enjoyment of the moment, even apart from you. This is something we have always found together, forgetting and deep true joy. But I never knew it could carry over, become part of heart and mind as long as life lasts.

In the stamping, gleeful body of that less than two-year-old boy we carried and fretted over is a wonderful message, a deep truth, of frailty, of the sturdiness of growth, a glorious hymn to change. Today, this minute, this is how he is and in this very moment we know how he was yesterday in the crib and before that. And in him too is us—what we were and what we are becoming. And that four-year-old, talking of long long ago when she was a tiny tiny baby that played in a playpen. So immature and yet so wise . . . Sometimes they are so beautiful they bring tears to my eyes.

I wish I had the words, the talent, the endurance to set these moments down, set us down and our times, and speak of that tiny particle of our experience that mirrors all the world, all creation. And speak about our love that keeps on growing, taking in the children, friends, comrades, life.

I guess I have finally written you a love letter, after all.

This letter stands alone among dozens of others that fret and worry and complain.

Meanwhile in New York Carl was working very hard on several film projects, while at the same time looking for work as an assistant editor. That way, if one project did not pan out, there was hope another would. That's how it went in the independent film business—lots of unpaid ventures, lots of creative effort and then some things would pan out years later, but most would not. It was not for the lazy or the faint of heart.

The long separation was wearing us down. Carl had re-established contact with our old friends, four or five couples with young children and several childless couples. Their warmth and helpfulness promised to make our transition easier. So, with nothing more to go on than Carl's temporary jobs, we decided to make the permanent move to New York sometime before the start of school. But first I had to sell our house and possessions.

Fortunately, Carl had a lucky break in July—he was offered a job as an editor on a B picture. It was not the kind of work he really wanted to do, but the chance to move from assistant editor to editor was important for his career, the pay was two hundred dollars a week, a little over union scale, and the job would last several months. In our current situation two hundred dollars a week was a fortune. A few weeks later, having sold most of the furnishings of our L.A. house, I rented it. A year later, we managed to sell the house without making a penny on it, just enough to cover the closing costs and the outstanding mortgage. Considering our precarious financial situation, we considered ourselves lucky to get away without being in debt.

WE MOVED TO NEW YORK CITY late in August and, for a few weeks, stayed in the apartment of friends in Jackson Heights. I spent each day apartment hunting and, early in September, just before the start of school, we found a suitable place, an upstairs apartment in a two-family home in Astoria, Queens. The land-lord and his family lived downstairs; there was a small backyard and the street, which unfortunately ended in a huge gas tank belonging to the Con Ed power company, seemed fairly quiet. The main attractions of the place were its cheap rent and the fact that the landlord and his wife said they liked children. We signed a two-year lease and began to assemble our usual assortment of Goodwill and garage-sale furniture. Stephanie started kindergarten in P.S. 122.

I liked the fact that we were close to the school and playground and within easy walking distance of the main shopping street, with its large variety of ethnic food stores. Italians, Greeks, Germans, French, African-Americans, West Indians and Jews all mixed in easy proximity and the street life was as lively as that in a Mediterranean city.

Our landlord, Tony, and his wife, Maggie, seemed to be a typical Italian working-class family. They had a little business, selling homemade hero sandwiches with thick Italian sauce and meatballs off a truck at construction sites. They had to get up at 5 A.M. and Tony would go to the site early while Maggie waited to send the kids off to school and then joined him. There was another round of sales at lunchtime. The couple went home by 2:30 and Maggie immediately set about the time-consuming task of making her sauces and meatballs for the next day. Then she would do her housework and shopping, while her husband made various improvements around the house and garden or went out for a beer with his buddies. Maggie's father, a retired construction worker, also lived in their home and helped with the business. There were times when Tony left town for a few days; then the old man would run the sales from the truck.

Their ten-year-old daughter, Peaches, had her mother's pale, stringy hair and watery eyes. She turned out to be a problem to us from the beginning. She mercilessly teased Stephanie, "borrowed" her toys and never returned them, and generally acted unpleasantly. The little boy, almost five years younger, was a thin, quiet child who had a subdued, frightened look about him. He seemed terrified of all grown-ups except for his grandfather, whom he followed around like a puppy. An abused child or merely a child disciplined harshly in a family that considered such discipline valid and right? Peaches was the obvious family favorite and, in her parents' view, could do no wrong.

Tony was exceedingly friendly and outgoing, but he could be a bit of a busy-body. We had trouble getting a phone—there was a long waiting list for new phones and we were told it might take months to get one. When Tony heard of this, he offered to connect our phone right away. How was he going to do that? Carl wanted to know. "Just leave it to me," said Tony. After some prodding he explained he would simply tap into the line and nobody would be the worse off. Nobody would know. When Carl politely refused, Tony shrugged his shoulders. "Do it your own way, then."

We had bought a secondhand car in New Jersey and were waiting for our license plates to come in the mail. Meanwhile we parked the car in the street in front of the house. One day, I happened to look out the window just as a city tow truck was hooking up our car to tow it away. I ran downstairs and protested. The tow truck operator said they had had a complaint from the landlord that a stolen car was sitting in front of his house. I produced our sales contract and convinced the guy that there had been some mistake. In the evening, Carl and I went downstairs to find out what Tony had had in mind, calling the police on us.

He was outraged. "Why didn't you tell me you had a car with no license plates sitting in front of the house? How was I supposed to know it's yours?"

"Well, why do you call the cops for a thing like that? What business is it of yours in the first place?"

"I'm not gonna have strange cars in front of my property," Tony said with real feeling. "It's my property, that's what."

"Well, my car is my property," Carl said with equal feeling. "I rent here, I have a right to park in front of the house."

"Wanna have a cup of coffee," Maggie offered, trying to smooth things over. "I just baked this coffee cake."

So we settled down for coffee and cake and let the matter go. But we tried to stay clear of the downstairs landlord, as best we could.

Maggie dressed like Alice in *The Honeymooners*—house dresses, a bib apron with ruffles and flat, comfortable shoes. It made sense, considering the heavy work she was doing all day. We noticed that, unlike us, the couple never went out of an evening, not even on Sundays. For relaxation, they mostly sat in front of the TV or on plastic chairs out in the backyard.

There was a finished basement with a washing machine and a dryer. As part of our rental agreement, I could use it one day a week to do my laundry. As I did, I noticed that the basement was nicely finished and carpeted and had a row of closets along each wall. A nice setup for storage, I thought. Once, when I came downstairs, one of the closet doors was open and, to my surprise, there were three full-length mink coats hanging inside. Mink coats for Maggie? Just then, she came downstairs from the outside, unloading one of the heavy steel pots in which she carried her sauce. "What're you doin' down here? You ain't supposed to be here on a Tuesday."

"I was looking for something I left in the dryer," I explained.

She started yelling, even as she slammed the closet door shut. "I don't want you coming down here snooping around . . ." Obviously, I wasn't supposed to see the mink coats.

The mystery was soon explained. After Thanksgiving, there were banner headlines in all the newspapers about a Mafia-dominated money-laundering ring that had been busted by the police. Among the eighteen men arrested was our landlord, Tony. He was charged, specifically, with passing stolen thousand-dollar bills in Detroit. The FBI took full credit, having had the homes and places of business of the arrested men under twenty-four-hour surveillance for the past six months. This was great news for us . . . Here we had been under the illusion that in moving to New York we would make it harder for the subpoena servers to find us. And by chance we had been living in an apartment under twenty-four-hour FBI surveillance. But who could have known that . . . We took some comfort from the fact that there had been no subpoena served on Carl, despite his easy accessibility. Maybe this meant we were safe, for the time being.

I went downstairs to see Maggie. "I'm sorry to hear about Tony," I began. "You must be so upset. And with the holidays, too."

"Oh, he'll be home by Christmas. Nothing to worry about," she said cheerfully. Apparently, this kind of thing had happened before.

And Tony was out a week before Christmas on huge bail. Just as cheerful, combative and law-and-order-minded as ever. The Mafia took care of its own. Later, he served a few months of a long sentence, while his wife and her father carried on the hero-sandwich business. That business was not just a front for his illegal activities, but a real business in which the family's hard labor and sweat was invested.

Our brush with the Mafia and the totally efficient FBI was unnerving. We felt we had innocently placed ourselves in a more exposed situation than was good for us. What if the FBI came around to ask about us and questioned Tony and Maggie? Surely they would turn us in, just to curry favor for themselves. We considered moving, but gave up the idea when we analyzed the situation more fully. The main damage, if any, had already been done. If the house was still under surveillance, whoever watched it would notice where we were moving, so there was little to gain by it. In a way, we would be better off staying, only we had to get along with our criminal landlord.

"What a joke," Carl said. "The real gangsters have this cozy setup and people like us are hounded and kept from making a living." It was a lesson in social realities.

As it happened, we also benefited indirectly from the Mafia, as did all the inhabitants of Astoria. At that time the two big Mafia families, the Bonannos and the Genoveses, had all kinds of family businesses in Astoria, where many of them had grown up. Liquor stores, drug stores, trucking companies and the Mafia's Mamas were living in Astoria. The Mafia's Mamas were small Italian widows, all dressed in lifelong black, who pushed their shopping carts around the stores on Broadway, looking for the best, the freshest vegetables and the nicest cuts of meat. They were favored by the butchers and grocers and would get immediate and polite attention as they made their daily rounds. And each Sunday, in front of the small frame houses, each with its fig tree and statue of the Madonna in the yard, the black Mafia stretch limos would line up and spend the day—the Mafiosi were visiting their Mamas. The Mamas could have lived in nice houses in the suburbs, which their sons would have gladly furnished for them, but they did not want to leave their neighborhood any more than they wanted to give up their black widow dresses. And as a result, Astoria was a district virtually free of street crime, one of the safest districts in New York City. The Mafia took care of the Mamas and, incidentally, all of us in the district, which would much later be known as "the Archie Bunker district," lived in relative security.

AUGUST 1949—THE AUDIENCE AT A CONCERT BY THE BLACK SINGER PAUL ROBESON IN PEEKSKILL, NEW YORK, was prevented from entering the premises by a noisy and violent crowd of legionnaires, veterans and citizens outraged by what they considered Robeson's "unpatriotic" statements.

A second concert was held at Peekskill. When the crowd drove home on a two-lane road lined by protesters, they were attacked with baseball bats, bricks and other missiles, while local police turned their backs on the scene. A hundred and fifty people were hurt.

Stephanie's first year in kindergarten went quite well. Her school day was short, only three hours, and she had a kind teacher. We had enrolled Dan in a private nursery school, which did him a world of good and gave me a few hours each day in which I could write. I was still working on that novel, but I also tried to do articles and short stories. With all my disciplined effort and hard work, my literary career had ground to a halt before it had actually started. I tried to keep working and not think about that. A stint of translating the lyrics of German folksongs for a record company gave me some pleasure, a few hundred dollars, and even a byline on the record jacket.

I had joined the PTA at Stephanie's school, because I was concerned with the poor physical condition of the building. The hallways and bathrooms were dirty; several of the sinks and toilets were stopped up and perpetually "out of order." The Principal of the school was a fussy, unpleasant man past retirement age. The rumor was that he would retire by the end of the year. When several PTA mothers came to talk to him about the condition of the school plant, he brushed us off with generalities and promised to ask "downtown" for funds for repairs. I was not then familiar with the Byzantine structure of the New York City Board of Education and did not know that conditions in our school were not exceptional but average. The buildings were old and overcrowded, but what particularly plagued the system was that the superintendents in each school, the men in charge of plant maintenance, were considered private contractors, each doing his own hiring and subcontracting. The scandalous state of corruption and graft that such a system fostered would be revealed in subsequent years in the press and the media, but such revelations did not necessarily lead to improvements. I also learned later that conditions in each school reflected the financial resources of the parents. In our white, working-class district, the schools were poor and poorly maintained.

Shortly after the PTA complaints, parents were informed by way of a memo from the Principal that "for the safety of the students" the building would be closed to "outsiders" during school hours. Parents who had appointments with teachers or other personnel might enter with a pass, but otherwise they were to wait for their children outside the school.

It took quite a while before the PTA members were willing to see any connection between these regulations and our previous lobbying for better plant maintenance. This was an old-fashioned PTA whose members saw their function mostly as supplying volunteers for bake sales and school trips. They did not like to question authority. There were a few women in the group who felt as I did, that the Principal's regulations were offensive and most likely illegal, and should be protested.

After a year of working in the PTA I was appointed to chair a newly formed Child Study Committee. Our small committee organized a series of monthly discussion meetings on topics relating to parenting and to parent-teacher relations. The committee decided not to rely on outside "experts"; instead, for each meeting, three mothers would do some advance reading of a study or discussion outline and act as discussion leaders. We also started collecting a reference library of child study books and articles and provided lists of free educational and entertainment events for children in our city.

The Child Study meetings proved quite popular and the opportunity to discuss school issues freely helped the mothers gain a sense of authority. Through the active lobbying efforts of the PTA and a campaign of protests to the Board of Education and to public officials, the long overdue repairs of our school plant were scheduled to begin in February 1951. This tangible effect of organizational action encouraged the mothers to become more involved in the school itself, especially since our success seemed to annoy our Principal. He perceived the greater organizational involvement of the mothers as a threat to his authority, which, in fact, it gradually became.

The triggering incident occurred in the year Stephanie was in first grade, 1950–51. One of the boys in her class came home from school quite upset and said he had been punished unfairly for something he had not done. The punishment was administered by a group of older boys, who lined up in the gym and paddled him as he was made to run a gauntlet. The boy had bruises on his legs and buttocks and his mother was angry enough to go to the Principal the next day. He denied any such thing had happened and suggested the boy had probably fallen in the hall. But this mother did not give in so easily and began to tell her story to the other mothers. Before long, similar stories came out and several children reported matter-of-factly about the punishment run in the gym, which they had either seen or heard about.

No wonder the Principal did not want mothers freely wandering around in the school . . . The matter came up in the PTA and we had a long and involved struggle, first to convince the mothers that they had a right to protest and be given real answers, and then to decide that the practice had to stop. Many of the women were not strongly inclined against physical punishment by teachers; they thought discipline in the school was a good thing, as long as the children learned their lessons. The Principal not only stood pat, he lied and began to slander the women who protested.

Authoritarianism in P.S. 122 . . . Marine Corps discipline in the first grade . . . It seemed in line with the political trends in the country as a whole. Just as we mothers in P.S. 122 had to be "authorized" in order to visit our children's public school, so was "loyalty," certified by an oath, the new requirement for being allowed to hold a job. Unions purged their "subversive" members; universities purged their faculties; mass organizations purged their ranks. States established

"Red squads" and Un-American Activities Committees, elevating witch-hunting to a national pastime.

In 1948 the Attorney General had made public a list of seventy-eight organizations he defined as Communist front groups. By 1950 the list included 110 organizations. The list included not only radical but most liberal causes, especially those having to do with the struggle against racism. The Inquisition had the force of a hurricane, the intensity of avalanches triggering new avalanches.

But we could resist the tyranny in P.S. 122 and we could choose to remove our children from further exposure to it. We decided to leave Astoria and move somewhere out of town, within commuting distance. Also, our relationship with our gangster-landlord continued to be highly unpleasant. Carl tried to talk to Tony about letting us move before our lease was up.

"You can leave anytime you want," Tony replied. "I'll keep the last month's rent and the security payment."

"What for? You can rent the place the next week."

"Because you signed a contract and I don't break no contract," said our law-abiding gangster.

We could not afford to lose nearly eight hundred dollars, so we had to stay on. I continued to be active in the PTA and finally found allies willing to fight the Principal and the Board of Ed. A committee of mothers went to protest the conditions at P.S. 122 at the Board of Education in "downtown" Brooklyn. We got weeks of runaround and promises, but the beating of children at the school stopped. We demanded the removal of the Principal, or at least an official investigation, but we got nowhere with that. Our small victory, which seemed quite large at the time, encouraged other mothers to become more active in the PTA. In the following year the slate of PTA officers elected were all women who had taken part in the protest action, and, finally, the Principal announced his retirement. Democracy, it seemed, still worked on a local scale.

But the hammer blows continued:

JANUARY 21, 1950—ALGER HISS CONVICTED OF PERJURY. The implication is that he spied for Russia in the 1930s.

FEBRUARY 3, 1950—THE PHYSICIST KLAUS FUCHS IS ARRESTED IN BRITAIN AS A SOVIET SPY AND CONVICTED IN MARCH. His arrest leads to the arrest in the U.S. of David Greenglass, Ethel and Julius Rosenberg, Morton Sobell and Harry Gold, all accused of conspiracy to commit espionage.

FEBRUARY 9, 1950—SENATOR MCCARTHY CLAIMS TO "HAVE A LIST" OF 205 CP
MEMBERS WORKING IN THE STATE DEPARTMENT. The next day he revises
this claim to fifty-seven "card-carrying" Communists.

HUAC INVESTIGATES J. ROBERT OPPENHEIMER, A NUCLEAR PHYSICIST
WHOSE BROTHER, FRANK, HAD BEEN A CP MEMBER UNTIL 1941.

JUNE 27, 1950—AFTER NORTH KOREA INVADED SOUTH KOREA ON JUNE 25,
PRESIDENT TRUMAN, WITH UNITED NATIONS SUPPORT, SENT U.S. FORCES IN
AID OF SOUTH KOREA. The U.N. "police action" involved the United States
in a full-fledged war that ended only in July 1953.

SEPTEMBER 25, 1950—MCCARRAN INTERNAL SECURITY ACT PASSED OVER
PRESIDENT TRUMAN'S VETO. It specified: (1) The Communist Party is a
clear and present danger, although membership in the CP is not a crime,
(2) officers of "front organizations" must register with the Attorney
General and (3) a Subversive Activities Control Board (SACB) would
decide which organizations were covered as front organizations under the
act. It barred individual CP members from defense jobs and from holding passports, tightened espionage laws and denied entrance to the country to aliens who had ever been members of a totalitarian organization.
It also mandated the detention of "likely" spies and saboteurs, in case an
internal-security emergency were to be declared by the President.

NOVEMBER 1950—SACB DECIDES CP MUST REGISTER UNDER THE MCCARRAN
ACT.

My organizational work during these years was entirely community-centered.
As educational director of the PTA I regularly reported on United Nations activities for children, a focus that made me immediately suspect as a radical in my conservative community. I remember a mean-spirited, ugly controversy in the PTA
that burst out when I suggested we should make an effort, as part of the PTA's
Halloween activities, to help the world's needy children by collecting money for
UNICEF. This was seen by many of our members as an effort to "politicize"
Halloween. My motion was not only defeated but the PTA also voted henceforth
not to get any reports on United Nations activities.

I also became more and more involved in activities for peace. I canvassed door-
to-door with the Stockholm Appeal against nuclear weapons. The papers and the
government, in a variety of official pronouncements, had cast the Stockholm Appeal

as a subversive document. Circulating it was equated with being "subversive" and yet many people signed it gladly. Of course there were those who slammed the door in your face, but on the whole the response was surprisingly good.

I joined a peace committee in Astoria and in the course of the Korean War helped to organize women's peace committees in Jackson Heights, Kew Gardens, Astoria and later Peekskill. I gave talks to such committees on U.N. activities and on work for world peace and against atomic weapons. I went on various peace demonstrations and lobbied at the United Nations. In that year I also served as a national board member of the Congress of American Women in its final year.

"Mommy, we have to bring something to school for show and tell time," Stephanie announced one day. "But please don't wrap it in the paper we read."

"Why not?"

She hesitated, clearly embarrassed. "The children will make fun of me and call me names."

"What paper that we read don't you want me to use?" Could she have noticed the *National Guardian, In Fact,* the *Daily Worker?* We kept those in our bedroom, in a separate pile.

"The *New York Times.*"

"The *New York Times?* What's wrong with THAT?"

My six-year-old had already been properly indoctrinated in the current political climate. "Nobody in my class reads that. Just us."

"Well, what do they read?"

She knew that, too. "The *Daily News.*"

I was not going to buy the *Daily News,* even to please my child. So we compromised by wrapping her package in brown paper. Those were the kind of times we were living in. Thought control and conformity fully internalized, even in the first grade.

FINALLY, PEACHES WENT TOO FAR. Mail was missing out of our mailbox and after observing her for a while, we concluded that she was going through our mail and throwing letters and checks away randomly. This time we both went downstairs to complain and after repeated denials, Peaches finally admitted she'd been through our mail "just twice" to see who was writing to us all the time. We were getting so much mail . . .

The parents, in their usual fashion, tried to make light of it, but Carl was furious. "I'm not going to stand for this. Interfering with the mail is a federal offense," he said, looking straight at Tony, who was out on parole. "You better get your kid to stop this. If it ever happens again, I'm going to the cops."

"So what? You trying to scare me?"

Back upstairs, I wanted to know what the hell Carl was doing. "Are you trying to get Tony sore at us, so we have more trouble?"

"No. But it's possible he put Peaches up to this and is already spying on us."

I hadn't thought of that. "Well, if he is, what was the point of further antagonizing him?"

"It's the only language he understands. I bet you, he'll stop and so will Peaches."

Carl was right. Peaches was on her best behavior from then on and Tony seemed to try to be pleasant. A few weeks later he offered Carl a friendly way out of our impasse. "I thought it over—if you guys want to move out, I'll let you break the lease. I don't need your money."

And so we moved out three months before the expiration of our lease, getting our deposits back and parting with Tony and Maggie on civil terms.

About six months later, as we were eating dinner, Carl got a phone call from Tony.

"How ya doin'? Everything all right? Well, I just want you to know the FBI is asking for you. They came snooping around here, wanting to know why you moved and where you are."

"What did you tell them?"

"Nothing. I don't give information to the bastards. But you better get out of town. Lay low somewhere."

"Well, thanks a lot, Tony. That was real nice of you."

"I don't give a shit about politics. I just don't like the bastards snooping around."

So, with a little help from a Mafia underling, Carl avoided a subpoena by staying away from home for a few weeks. You never know who your friend in need is going to be.

We found a summer rental on a farm near Peekskill, New York, and moved there as soon as school was out. We lived in a simple cabin whose main features were its cheap rent and a screened porch overlooking fields where cows were grazing. We spent a wonderful summer there. Every morning the children and I drove Carl to the train station; every evening we picked him up. We decided to try for a winter rental in the general area and, before long, we found it. People who own summer houses within commuting distance of New York are eager to rent them cheaply during the winter season in order to avoid damage to houses standing empty in the cold. We signed a September-to-June lease for a comfortable house on Furnace Dock Road on nearly an acre of wooded land.

The children were ecstatic at the idea of living year-round in the country. Before long, a dog, Buddy, joined our household. He was a mixture of German shepherd and collie, a gentle and reliable creature who guarded the children as though they were sheep. I enrolled Stephanie in the public school in Peekskill, which was a great improvement over P.S. 122 in Astoria. We enrolled Danny in a fine private nursery school in Croton.

Our social life centered on the progressive community of artists, writers and film people in Croton-on-Hudson. It was an old, well-established community of homeowners, enriched in season by summer people who commuted to New York City. I quickly made friends there and became active in the local peace committee. It felt very good in these times of persecution and controversy to be among like-minded people. This was a luxury we had not often enjoyed.

The move was a blessing for the children and me and made our lives much easier than they had been in the city. I loved country living: the twenty-five-minute daily commute to the railroad station along wooded country roads, the long rambles in the woods with the children, lazy brooks and hidden ponds, and deer coming into the yard for feeding. With so many talented creative people in Croton, there was a rich cultural life that also served a political purpose. Blacklisted writers, musicians, teachers and artists rode a cultural lecture circuit in the homes of sympathetic people, where they could tell their stories, present their work and net perhaps thirty dollars for an evening, enough to feed themselves and their families for a week. This cultural network, organized mostly by women in each neighborhood, was an important way of helping the victims of the witch hunts and of offering resistance by keeping progressive ideas alive. The importance of this network in the creation and maintenance of folk music through hootenannies has been recognized by historians, but that has not been the case for the cultural resistance movement in other fields. Blacklisting and terror not only deprived creative people of their livelihoods, it also demoralized them and made them unable to continue their productive lives. This small-scale cultural resistance movement, happening quietly and without fanfare in many communities, helped such people to maintain their morale, break out of their isolation and continue their work.

Even in the worst of times, with a little bit of luck, one could live like that, in pleasant surroundings, with congenial friends, one or two steps removed from the hunters and the haunters. I loved living in the country and would have liked nothing better than to stay there forever. But the burden of it all was on Carl.

He never was an outdoors person and living in the woods held no special attraction for him. The commute added three hours to his workday. Since he now had begun to edit features, his workday often ended only at 9 or 10 P.M. and at that hour commuter trains ran at one-hour intervals. In effect, he saw the children only in the car on the way to the station and on weekends. He found that too high a price to pay and I had to agree with him. The children missed him and I missed him. We also missed our old friends in the city and their children who had become friends for our children. Lastly, there was a political consideration, although we did not argue it explicitly. We were too far removed from struggle, too comfortable, too isolated. We felt guilty about that, even though we could easily muster arguments against such feelings. One might think we'd already paid the price for whatever interval of peace we had allowed ourselves. Yet the feeling persisted. We decided that by September 1953 we would be moving back to the city, where transportation for him was easier.

Our experience with country living had one good result: it encouraged us to take the risky step, given our still precarious financial situation, of going massively into debt to buy a house.

[18]

WE COULD NOT AFFORD MANHATTAN. The subway lines to the Bronx and to Brooklyn were ancient, the cars dirty and decrepit. The trains to Queens were newer, ran more frequently and seemed less crowded. We had friends in Queens and liked some of the neighborhoods. We decided to search in an old neighborhood in Queens, and we were determined to live in a racially mixed neighborhood. We had strong feelings about that, after our year in an all-white community with nearly all-white schools. We wanted our children to mix naturally and on a daily basis with children of color so that they would grow up as free from prejudices as possible. That narrowed our choice considerably. There were a number of racially integrated apartment-house projects in Queens, several of them middle income, but when it came to houses the racial boundaries were firmly drawn.

The two major areas where African-Americans lived were Jamaica, a concentration of low-income projects and low-income tenants, and the upper- and middle-class black community in St. Albans, which clustered around the huge Veterans Administration Hospital. We looked on the fringes of the St. Albans community and soon found a few streets we liked, mostly because they had rows of old trees. The streets were all white, a typical working-class neighborhood of modest homes, all at least twenty years old, but two blocks away there were black homeowners and we figured the children would be going to the same school. There were quite a few houses for sale on these streets. We soon found a house that seemed to fit our needs as to size and that seemed suitable as to price. After we had made an offer and put a small deposit down, the real-estate agent, a pleasant young woman, told us with an air of painful concern that she had to be honest with us, we seemed such a nice couple and she wouldn't want us to be disappointed later ... In good conscience, she had to tell us that a black family had just bought a house on the street behind us, in fact THE house directly behind us. So, if we moved, we would have black neighbors ... Of course, she said, you have a backyard fence and your street is okay—

We assured her the prospect of having black neighbors was not unpleasant to us. In fact, we were looking forward to it.

The young woman was obviously relieved that she was not going to lose a sale. Nothing further was said on the subject and we bought the house. We realized that had we looked for a house five or six blocks away, we might have saved two to three thousand dollars on the sale price. Contrary to common mythology, when Blacks moved into a neighborhood the real-estate prices did not fall; they rose. Real-estate agents advised the white sellers to raise their prices so that only "the better kind" of Blacks would move into the neighborhood. The kind of "warning" our real-estate agent had given us would usually scare off potential white buyers. Sellers and real-estate agents reaped the benefit. We were, in effect, paying "black prices."

The house itself lacked charm or individuality, but it was solid and in good repair. A poor imitation of imitation-Tudor row houses in the more genteel sections of the borough, it stood flat-chested and stolid behind a tiny plot of front lawn. Separated from its neighbors by a narrow cement driveway, at the end of which a small wooden garage provided space for just one car, the house offered respectability without privacy. Six steps leading up to the front door and six steps leading down from the kitchen into the tiny backyard offered room for neighborly "stoop-sitting" and little else. From the front stoop one could observe the comings and goings of neighbors, their careful lawn-mowing of their postage-stamp front lawns, their hedge-trimming, their car-washing. Inside, the rooms were good-sized and airy, even though our living room was always dark. The upstairs bedrooms looked out on the treetops, which meant a lot to me, but compared to our great old house in L.A. and the wonderful house in the woods we had just left, this was a come-down. It was simply that it was a house we could afford even if things should get worse financially. And that was our main concern in those days.

In the fall of 1952 we moved in. Stephanie entered second grade and Dan kindergarten in the nearby public school. I walked them to school and picked them up and I drove Carl to the subway. In that sense, it was a great improvement, since he could spend more time at home during the children's waking hours.

The people on the street were postal clerks and government employees, men and women working in the Veterans Hospital, a few craft workers, a bus driver. The neighbors on our right were an elderly couple, unfriendly and resentful of having neighbors with small children. We were barely on speaking terms with them during our entire stay there. The neighbors on our left were a couple about our age with three boys, ages nine, seven and five. The father was a carpenter working for a construction company, the mother a full-time housewife. They were Catholics, but sent their children to public school. We were quite different in education, lifestyle and political convictions, but we were good neighbors. The boys next door were playmates for our children and their mother and I helped each other out with child-minding, babysitting and shopping.

I made it my business to introduce myself to the neighbor in the back. The Prices had two daughters, one of them Stephanie's age, the other younger, and since their mother, too, walked them to school and picked them up, it was easy to move from a neighborly acquaintance to inviting the girls to play in our house and inviting the mother to share a cup of coffee. Sarah Price was a highly educated woman, a high-school music teacher whose ambition was to make a career as an opera singer. She had a great voice, a fine stage presence and coffee-colored skin, but she was labeled a "Negro" and that, in the 1950s, made an operatic career an unlikely dream. She sang in church concerts and gave voice lessons.

Before long we organized an interracial playgroup, which included the two Price girls and two Indian girls, originally from Calcutta; the boys next door; the four Hartmann children (white, Jewish) and Billy, a science whiz kid without social skills. The playgroup was an informal child-minding club for the mothers, who could take turns leaving their children once a week under the care of the other mothers. It was also a group designed to break down cultural and racial barriers. We celebrated each child's birthday, then Christmas, Chanukka, Easter and Passover, and we learned about Indian holidays and ate Indian food. Such superficial multicultural exchanges have become much more common in recent decades and are now part of the experience of many children in schools. At the time we did this, such contacts were unusual.

Shortly after we moved in, we noticed that several houses on our block and in the neighboring streets had FOR SALE signs. This development turned out to be part of a well-organized campaign by real-estate agents to turn our neighborhood into a black neighborhood. Several times a week, real-estate agents would knock on our door to inquire whether we wanted to put up our house for sale. When we said no, they explained, in the same bereaved tone our own real-estate saleswoman had used, that they simply wished to let us know that "colored people" had begun to move into the neighborhood—just one street away, as a matter of fact—and that this would undoubtedly decrease the value of our property. We would be well advised to sell, as soon as possible.

These forays were followed up by stronger tactics. Real-estate agents would appear at your door with a black couple in tow to show them your house. When told that the house was not on the market, they would profusely apologize for "the error" and move on down the street. A few weeks of this and the FOR SALE signs went up.

This kind of campaign was known as "block-busting," and it apparently worked well to "turn" neighborhoods. The white working-class families who had put their entire cash reserves into their homes were truly panicked at the prospect of losing their real-estate investments. Even if they would not have had any objections to living on an interracial street, the fear of economic loss convinced them to sell and move. When two or three houses on a block had been sold to African-Americans, the street would be "red-lined" in the banking and real-estate community; that is, it would be treated as a "black" street. House prices would go up and mortgages would become more expensive, presumably to compensate the lender for a more risk-prone population. People living in "red-lined" neighborhoods would pay higher car and medical insurance rates and find it difficult to get credit. All of this based on racist myths—that any influx of non-white people meant lower real-estate prices, more crime and drugs and a deterioration of public schools. Block-busting and red-lining were practices the banking and real-estate companies denounced publicly, but which flourished unchecked. Nobody admitted to doing it, but it was done in neighborhood after neighborhood. And in a way, the dire predictions of the realtors turned into a self-fulfilling prophecy. Because real-estate prices were so much higher for African-Americans and mortgages for them were so much more expensive, many families could afford a house only by sharing with relatives. Thus, one-family houses were often occupied by extended families or by several families, with both parents working in order to be able to afford their home. This meant that children were often unsupervised after school hours and more conspicuous on the streets, a fact that, even if such children did not get into any trouble, fed racist myths and beliefs.

AFTER A LITTLE CHECKING AROUND with neighborhood organizations and churches, I found out that there was a sort of resistance movement in effect, which had been able to win a few victories in the past. We joined in this effort, in which I was quite active.

We went door to door to speak to our neighbors. When I told people that we had just moved into the neighborhood, they were impressed, because it refuted the real-estate agents' claim that no whites would move in. Our main argument was that we could keep the neighborhood as it was and welcome the few black families that were moving into it if we did not give in to panic-selling. Sometimes we went from door to door, white and black together, and introduced the old neighbors to their new neighbor. People were usually quite friendly when we did this, but it is hard to tell how much impact we had. People who responded to our appeal were asked to refuse to talk to real-estate agents. We put signs in our front windows that read WE LOVE OUR HOME AND OUR NEIGHBORS. THIS HOUSE IS NOT FOR SALE. After several months of our resistance campaign about half of the houses on our street had our signs and the real-estate agents stopped coming to the door. If we did not stop the block-busting, at least we slowed it down.

We made great efforts in the PTA to welcome the new black neighbors and to make the PTA an organization in which ethnic and racial differences were celebrated. Our luncheon meetings always featured varied ethnic foods and our school parades and celebrations were quite inclusive.

Still, the onward march of racist real-estate practices could not be stopped. I know of no white family that moved into my neighborhood after we did. A good way to chart the racial change in home ownership is to look at the children's class pictures, year after year. The year after we moved in, there were a handful of black children in each class. Four years later, there were a handful of white children amidst all the black faces.

The new black neighbors on our street were economically more advantaged than the white residents. They were predominantly middle class and certainly better educated than the people they replaced. They were "house-proud" and outdid each other in home improvements and neatness of front gardens. Their cars were distinctly better and higher priced than was customary on the street, and they spent as much time as their neighbors washing and polishing them. In short, by all definitions of white standards, they were "good" neighbors. Ironically, our family was censured more by the black neighbors than by the white. We were not known for great neatness of front lawn or house, and our car, an aged Chevrolet, was distinctly inferior to those of the neighbors. And yet Carl claimed to be working in TV and motion pictures . . . This upset a set of stereotypes held by our black neighbors, namely that all people working in the media must be rich and status-proud. We were asked direct and pointed questions about this by some of our new neighbors and I'm not sure our answers were satisfactory. I think several of them thought of us as some sort of "hippies" and remained cool and formal in their contacts with us. Trying to break down cultural stereotypes is always an ambiguous undertaking. One of the things I learned by living in an interracial community is that hierarchies and prejudices against those who are "different" exist among all groups, not only among whites.

Our white neighbors on the right, the elderly couple, responded to our appeal to stay and put an appropriate sign on the door. I understand they stayed for years, until they were the only white family on the block. They did not become much friendlier toward us or anyone else with children, but give credit where credit is due.

Our new African-American neighbor, four houses down the street, bought an expensive snow blower. He drove a Buick and put shutters on all the front windows of his house, transforming it into the best house on the block. He was an accountant, and when it snowed, he made it a point to clear the entire sidewalk on his side of the street with his snow blower. We were all obliged to him, but he would not visit with the Lerners. Probably because of the Chevy.

Sarah and I had become close friends. We shared our interest in music, in education, in books. Now her husband's mother had come for a visit and was staying for a month. She was from South Carolina and Sarah introduced her to me as a leader in the state's NAACP. I knew that meant she was a person at great risk in her hometown and Sarah confirmed that. I was eager to get to know her, but she was distinctly cool to me when we first met. About a week later, after she had been at our playgroup meeting and had once visited, quite formally, at my house, I sat at Sarah's kitchen table, drinking coffee with her and Sarah. Suddenly she faced me with the authority of a schoolteacher over a pupil, an older woman over the young.

"How come you folks moved in here, after the neighborhood turned?" she asked sternly.

"We wanted our children to be raised in an interracial community."

She didn't buy it. "That sounds too good to be true."

"Just the same, that's the reason."

"Are you Commies?" she asked.

"I don't ask how you vote."

"Republican. Baptist. NAACP. Sorry," she said, "that was out of line. I've been called a Commie many times, myself."

"Well, we have that in common. But maybe you'd understand better if I say, it's because we're Jewish. And I, in particular, am a refugee from Hitler."

"Yeah. Sarah told me that. I'm sorry to hear it. I haven't had much contact with Jewish people. So I can't understand—"

"You've lived in the Jim Crow South. You've been excluded from public rest rooms, restaurants, trains. Segregated because of race. Well, after Hitler came, Jews in Vienna were not only excluded from schools, public places, parks, but fired from their jobs, imprisoned without cause, many sent to concentration camps. And as you know, six million were killed, deliberately, men, women and children. So to me, any kind of discrimination is evil. I can't stand it. I want my children free of it."

"I can believe that," she said, for the first time with real warmth.

I felt I had passed the test. That such a test should be necessary at all I found not surprising. For fifty years after World War II, whenever I met a German or an Austrian old enough to have been an adult during that time, I needed to know what they were doing THEN and, more or less overtly, I would give them a similar test. Suffering oppression does not make you into an open, trusting person.

After that, during the years we lived in the neighborhood, Sarah's mother-in-law accepted me as a family friend.

MY LITERARY "CAREER" seemed to have ended before it had actually begun. My novel *No Farewell* was finally finished in 1951 and sent out to fifteen publishers, all of whom rejected it; most of them did so with high praise. The general sense was that the theme of the coming of fascism had been treated in fiction many times before in the past ten years and was a dead subject.

Considering the fact that I had worked twelve years on this book, rewriting it over and over again, as I was improving my knowledge of English, I was bitterly disappointed to learn that all I had achieved was wrong timing. My agent gave up on it and for a while so did I. Still, I decided to send it to publishers in Austria, where it was accepted, translated into German and published in 1955. It sold out three editions in the first year and was very well received by the critics. The irony that my attempt at making myself into an American writer had backfired and caused the fruit of this long labor to be published first in a German translation did not raise my spirits. As soon as the English version was finished and while it was still circulating on the market, I began to write short stories. Several of these were sent out by my agent and received similar kinds of rejection. Most editors praised my ability as a writer and refused to publish my material.

But I am stubborn, if nothing else, and I am a writer, so I had to continue to try. Before long, I was at work on another novel. This time I selected an American theme, one that I thought would not soon be out of date. My novel dealt with the struggle for housing integration in New York City and was based on an actual case I knew intimately, in which a white family had taken a black family into their apartment in order to help them secure housing in an all-white co-op. A similar struggle for housing integration had taken place in New York City's Stuyvesant Town apartments. What interested me most was the reaction of the black and white families to this temporary close association and the playing out of race relations between them.

Off and on, during the years of writing the second novel, I also produced more short-range, more political writing. Soon after coming to New York I had become acquainted with the poet Eve Merriam, who later became a close friend. She and I collaborated on a dramatic revue, *Singing of Women.* We jointly conceived the framework and general tone of the piece; she wrote most of the lyrics and I wrote the straight text.

Our revue would revive some important moments in the past of American women. We put the historical scenes into the context of a quarrel between a contemporary couple over what were their appropriate roles in marriage. As I reread the single worn, typewritten copy of this work that has survived in my possession, I'm struck by the aptness of our selection of the historical material, by the sharpness of our feminist critique (the piece was written in 1950!) and by the limitations of our understanding, which cast solutions always within the Marxist framework of the "woman question." We dramatized scenes of colonial women forcing a greedy merchant to lower his prices; a slave rescue by Quaker women; a strike at the Lowell textile mills; the first Woman's Rights Convention; Sojourner Truth's speech at Akron, Ohio; the later woman suffrage movement; some union women's struggles. The second act was a dramatization of then-current women's issues— unequal pay, race discrimination, the threat of war. We understood women's oppression to come from capitalism ("the boss"), from the remnants of sexism in otherwise supportive males, and, above all, we presented a glorious vision of male-female, black and white cooperation in the greater cause of unionism and peace. The musical sounds naive today, yet its very existence is significant. Like the work of Congress of American Women, it represents the radical, old Left strain of feminism that would later resurface in the modern women's movement as one of its long-unacknowledged sources. We knew about sexism and class and race and we knew about women's history, long before the revival of modern feminism. I'm proud of having been part of that knowledge and having brought some of it into my later work.

Under the sponsorship of the New York Committee for the Arts, Sciences and Professions, *Singing of Women* was staged and performed at the Cherry Lane Theater in Greenwich Village for three nights running. It was well received by the audience, but for lack of funds did not survive.

I did other political writing in this period. The format of the musical revue, with speaking chorus, a balladeer and some short dramatic skits based on historical material, all of which we had used in *Singing of Women,* was well suited for providing entertainment at a large meeting. It was suitable for performance by amateurs and served both political and educational purposes. In 1954 I wrote the text for such a "dramatic presentation" for a concert and meeting of the Emma Lazarus Federation of Jewish Women's Clubs, which had formerly been affiliated with the International Workers Order. The latter was a fraternal association of ethnically based workers' clubs, mainly providing insurance and death benefit payments for its members. Like Congress of American Women, it had been placed on the Attorney General's list of subversive organizations in 1951 and was eventually forced to dissolve. The concert was staged under the direction of Alice Childress, an African-American actress and writer, at the Brooklyn Academy of Music, with the participation of both amateur and professional musicians, dancers and actors. The piece was titled *Bread and Roses Too,* echoing the slogan of the 1909 New York City garment workers, and it was billed as a celebration of "300 Years of Jewish Life in America." Rereading it now I am again struck by the well-documented and well-researched historical material I managed to assemble, by the inclusion of several female heroines and by the general tone of optimism and uplift.

APRIL 1951—DASHIELL HAMMETT GETS SIX-MONTH PRISON TERM FOR REFUSING TO NAME THE CONTRIBUTORS TO THE CIVIL RIGHTS CONGRESS BAIL FUND.

APRIL 1951—SCREEN DIRECTORS GUILD MAKES ALL ITS MEMBERS TAKE LOYALTY OATHS.

1951—HUAC, UNDER NEW CHAIR, JOHN WOOD, RESUMES THE HOLLYWOOD HEARINGS. One hundred and ten subpoenaed for these hearings, among them Larry Parks, Gale Sondergaard, Howard DaSilva, Richard Collins, Waldo Salt, Paul Jarrico and Robert Lees. Of 110 called, fifty-eight admit CP membership. Martin Berkeley names 155 names.

SOME WITNESSES BEFORE HUAC ATTEMPT TO USE THE "SLIGHTLY DIMINISHED FIFTH" TO TESTIFY ABOUT THEIR OWN PASTS, BUT NOBODY ELSE'S.

THE ACTOR LARRY PARKS BEGS THE COMMITTEE NOT TO FORCE HIM TO DO WHAT HE ENDS UP DOING: NAME TEN NAMES.

MARTIN BERKELEY, RICHARD COLLINS, LUCILLE BALL, EDWARD G. ROBINSON, STERLING HAYDEN, LEON TOWNSEND AND ELIA KAZAN NAME NAMES IN ORDER NOT TO LOSE THEIR CAREERS.

1952—THIRTY STATES ENACT LOYALTY OATHS FOR TEACHERS.

When progressive organizations no longer could organize public rallies, I wrote pamphlets for the Civil Rights Congress and undertook an assignment for the American Committee for the Protection of the Foreign Born (ACPFB). Both of these organizations were on the list of "Communist front" organizations that the Attorney General had proscribed. Under the Internal Security Act of 1950 no member of such an organization could hold government office, work in a defense plant or "apply for, use or attempt to use a passport." This was just for starters. The same act also contained the "Kilgore Concentration Camp provisions," which called for the arrest and detention of any individual about whom there is "reasonable ground to believe that such person will probably engage in, or probably will conspire with others to engage in an act of espionage or sabotage." The same act specified numerous regulations for the detention and deportation of any alien suspected of being a Communist or of being "affiliated with any organization required to register under this Act." The vagueness of the definition of the suspect person, who could be denied a passport and be sent to a detention camp, was truly alarming. No longer was it necessary to prove that a person had committed a crime or was planning to commit a crime; all that was needed was reasonable ground to *believe* that this person would *probably* conspire with others, etcetera. Due process was ignored; evidence to be tested in open court was declared unnecessary by this act of Congress; the cornerstone of the

American judiciary system—the presumption of innocence until one was proven guilty—went out the window. When the Japanese were put into detention centers during World War II, citizenship rights were disregarded; veterans' status was not taken into account. Ethnicity and race were the only considerations. Now, the net was cast much wider, making a far broader group of persons liable to be turned into social outcasts.

DECEMBER 31, 1951—U.S. BUILDS DETENTION CAMPS FOR REDS, IN CASE WE GO TO WAR WITH RUSSIA . . . Federal prisoners are already at work . . . on three installations with a combined capacity of more than 3,000 persons . . . The project is under the supervision of James V. Bennett, director of the Federal Bureau of Prisons. *(New York Post)*

Once again, I found myself among the social pariahs. It was not dissimilar to the state of existence I had experienced in Vienna after the *Anschluss*. One lived in constant anxiety, as though under a suspended sword, waiting for the blade to fall. Curiously, that alertness to danger was transformed into a kind of daring, the courage of those without hope, who feel free of normal constraints since they have nothing to lose. One lived intensely, moment to moment.

For me, this meant working hard for whatever progressive organizations still existed. The ACPFB struggled to raise funds for the legal defense of hundreds of long-time residents who were facing deportation proceedings. A number of naturalized citizens were facing denaturalization to be followed by deportation. All of those targeted were left-wing radicals. Of 206 noncitizens whom the committee was trying to defend, fifty-five had lived between forty and fifty years in the U.S., eighty-seven between thirty and forty years, thirty-eight between twenty and thirty years. Most of them were workers who had been active in trade unions; many of them had earlier been denied citizenship because of their union activities. The largest group of them (139) was between the ages of fifty and seventy. Most of them had American-born dependents. In short, hundreds of elderly men and women who had for decades lived and worked in the U.S.A. sought citizenship papers and were denied them, served in the armed forces and raised American children were now declared to be pariahs and were to be deported.

The committee tried to humanize the plight of the accused by issuing pamphlets about individual cases and getting people interested in their defense. I researched the cases of several among this group and wrote pamphlets about them. Here are excerpts from one I found among my papers.

She is 68 years old now and the fruits of her long life are there for everyone to see—five daughters, six grandchildren, two great-grandchildren, all American native-born citizens, except for the one daughter she brought with her as an infant when she came here in 1906.

Her hands lie in her lap, gnarled and bent from hard labor . . . She reasonably might expect to sit quietly in the fall of her life and watch her children and grandchildren grow up around her. But that is not the way it is to be for Marie Kratochvil . . .

They came early one morning, two men and a woman, and arrested Marie Kratochvil and took her to jail and the charge was "belonging to a party" from 1917 to 1918, which party was said to have been the direct predecessor of the Communist Party. And it did not matter that between 1917 and 1918 Marie Kratochvil had five little girls on her hands to feed and clothe and school and that from early morning to late at night she earned her living washing clothes by hand, at 75 cents for a big basket. It is hard to see how in those years Marie Kratochvil could have done anything besides keeping body and soul together nor how anything she might conceivably have done then could today, in 1952, threaten the security and peace of this nation and so disturb the Department of Justice as to necessitate her arrest and deportation . . .

Deportation—what would it mean to Marie Kratochvil? One day, she would be placed on a boat and the tickets for her trip would be paid for by the taxpayer. Her five daughters and their husbands, the six American-born grandchildren who have learned about the Bill of Rights in school, and the two little great-grandchildren would stand at the pier and wave goodbye. The ship would leave the harbor and the police and the army, the navy and the air force, and yes, the mighty Senate and the House would be safe once more and the republic secure. And Marie Kratochvil would land someplace where she had not been in 45 years and put her old bones into some strange bed and strangers would stand around her and wonder at American justice.

This must not and cannot be the way it will end. Marie Kratochvil is everybody's grandmother—and her old age must be with us, with her children, in the land of her life's labor.

I wrote several such pamphlets; I wrote them with true feeling. I identified with each and every one of these potential deportees. There but for the grace of

God go I . . . Deportation, to me, was the ultimate horror. Worse than jail, worse than unjust persecution. To be taken away from the land in which one had lived and worked for decades, to be severed forever from one's family and friends, to be torn, as a mother, from husband and children—there was nothing worse. I had experienced it once before, but then I was young, and my investment in time and place was relatively short. Now, I felt, with my roots sunk so deeply into family and community, I could not survive it. We each have our special nightmare horror and this was mine. Fighting it with my writing was a form of resistance and of healing.

AND THEN THERE WAS the Rosenberg case.

Each generation experiences an event that for the young people is politically life-defining. For Europeans of my day, it was the Spanish civil war. For Americans of the same generation it was the Depression and for some it was the Sacco-Vanzetti case. For later generations it would be the Freedom March in Selma, Alabama, or the Kent State shooting. Such events become, for some contemporaries, larger than life, metaphoric by encompassing social relations and realities with which they must deal. Such events force people to make political decisions, to take a stand, to engage.

Of all the injustices and persecutions that had been experienced by left-wing radicals since 1948, the Rosenberg case had this special significance. There was, first of all, the dramatic aspect of family conflict and tragedy.

David Greenglass, Ethel Rosenberg's younger brother, served as a machinist in the army during the war and was stationed at the Los Alamos atomic project. Julius Rosenberg, Ethel's husband, was employed at the U.S. Signal Corps but lost his job in 1945 when he was charged with being a Communist, a charge he denied. A failed business venture of Julius Rosenberg and David Greenglass after the end of the war caused much animosity between the Greenglass and Rosenberg families.

In June 1950 David Greenglass was arrested by the FBI. He confessed to stealing atomic secrets for the Russians and implicated Julius Rosenberg. Ruth, David Greenglass's wife, admitted her own guilt and charged both Rosenbergs with complicity. In July Julius Rosenberg was arrested on the charge of having recruited David Greenglass into a Russian spy ring. In August Ethel Rosenberg was arrested. The couple's two children, Michael (age seven) and Robert (age three), stayed with Mrs. Greenglass, their maternal grandmother, for a few days and were then sent to a city welfare shelter, where they stayed for nearly a year.

In August 1950, indictments were handed down, accusing the Rosenbergs, David and Ruth Greenglass, Anatoli Yakovlev (a departed Soviet consular official) and Harry Gold with conspiracy to transmit atomic secrets to the Soviet Union. In October 1950, a second indictment was returned, adding Morton Sobell, a classmate of Julius's from City College, as coconspirator. Sobell had moved to Mexico after the Rosenberg's arrest and was seized there and returned to the U.S.A. by FBI agents. David Greenglass pleaded guilty to the indictment; his wife Ruth, who had admitted her guilt, was never indicted or tried.

In January 1951 a third indictment was returned indicating incriminating evidence against Julius by one Max Elitcher, another of his former City College classmates. Elitcher had faced a perjury charge for denying CP membership in applying for a government job when the FBI questioned him about Rosenberg. He signed a statement that Julius had twice asked him to spy for the Soviet Union. The perjury charges against Elitcher were never pressed.

On March 6, 1951, the trial of Ethel and Julius Rosenberg and Morton Sobell began before Judge Irving R. Kaufman in New York. The case of David Greenglass was severed, since he had pleaded guilty. During the period of indictment and trial, the Greenglass family sided with David and rallied to his and Ruth's defense. They used most of their contacts with Ethel to urge her to plead guilty.

The trial in March 1951 lasted three weeks. Both Rosenbergs and Sobell pleaded not guilty to the charge. No documents linking the Rosenbergs with espionage were introduced; they were questioned at length about their political beliefs and referred to as Communists by Judge Kaufman. After eight hours of jury deliberation, the Rosenbergs and Sobell were found guilty as charged of "conspiracy to commit espionage." On April 5, 1951, Julius and Ethel Rosenberg were sentenced to death, Morton Sobell was sentenced to thirty years in prison and David Greenglass to fifteen years in prison.

The extreme severity of the sentences seemed savage even to those who believed the Rosenbergs guilty. They had NOT been convicted of any act of espionage but of "conspiracy to commit," a vague charge that made conviction much easier for the prosecution than conviction on actual acts. Conspiracy convictions abound in the history of the labor and radical movements in the U.S. and have often been used to jail innocent people. The alleged "conspiracy" had taken place not in wartime, but in peace. No civilian had ever been executed in the U.S.A. for either spying or treason. In World War II thirty German-Americans were arrested and tried for conspiracy to set up a Nazi-type government; their case was dismissed. A pro-Nazi tavern keeper who sheltered escaped Nazi war prisoners was sentenced to death, but the sentence was commuted to life imprisonment. Five Americans convicted for treason for broadcasting propaganda for the enemy during wartime (including Tokyo Rose and Axis Sally) got prison sentences. Even military men who switched over to the enemy after capture received life sentences, not death.

The fact that the main evidence the government produced was that of David and Ruth Greenglass, both of whom were themselves under severe jeopardy and turned state's witness, made their evidence seem tainted. The leniency in sentencing shown David Greenglass and the fact that Ruth Greenglass was never tried at all was seen as a reward for their providing the kind of evidence the government needed to convict the Rosenbergs. At the time of the sentencing, many people believed that the convictions would be overturned on appeal.

Many Jews believed the Rosenbergs were treated so harshly because they were Jews. The government seemed aware that that impression might prevail and selected both a Jewish prosecutor and a Jewish judge. In fact, the Jewish community reacted in two polarized ways. The large majority believed the Rosenbergs were guilty and represented a threat to Jewish reputation and existence, which could only be wiped out by their being severely punished. A small minority believed the Rosenbergs were innocent.

I experienced the case with profound empathy, with dread and terror. How typical my reaction was of Jewish radicals in general I do not know. I saw the case as an exact parallel to the Reichstag trial of Dimitroff. In his case the German Nazi Party, which had just gained power legally but with a narrow majority, needed above all to prove itself as the defender of law, order and stability. It needed a showcase trial that would prove to the German public that the German Communists represented a clear and present danger to the nation (by an effort to bomb the Reichstag, the seat of government) and that they were part of an international conspiracy. The actual defendant in that case was a mentally retarded Dutch citizen, Van der Lubbe, who after extreme pressure admitted to having set the fire. The international conspiracy was to be proven by showing that Georgi Dimitroff, a Bulgarian Communist, had instigated Van der Lubbe's act. Van der Lubbe was found guilty and condemned to die, but Dimitroff succeeded in proving his innocence and in showing up the Nazi conspiracy. Historians have since proven that Van der Lubbe did not set the fire and that the whole case was a frame-up.

Since 1948, the hundreds of investigations of Communists and left-wing radicals by police, FBI and congressional and state committees had yet to produce a single overt act of "force and violence" against the U.S. government or any of its agencies. The thousands of house searches and monitored phone calls had not produced a rifle, a bomb, an arsenal of any kind except books, articles and pamphlets that expressed ideas and by that very fact stood under the protection of the First Amendment. The government needed a case of espionage to show that all its efforts and expenditures, all the violations of the civil rights of persons of radical convictions, could be justified because of an actual threat to the security of the state. What the government needed and wanted most of all was the testimony of one or more admitted Communists that they had engaged in espionage. This fact was clearly demonstrated by the several offers to the Rosenbergs to "talk" in exchange for a life sentence. Just as the victims of the blacklist could "clear" themselves by naming others to be persecuted, so the carrot of surviving for the sake of their children was dangled before the Rosenbergs, while the stick of the death penalty provided force.

JUNE 20, 1953—ROSENBERGS DIED WITH LIPS SEALED; COULD HAVE LIVED IF THEY TALKED. United Press reported . . . telephone lines were open from Sing Sing [prison] to [Attorney General] Brownell's Washington office and the President was available to issue the necessary executive order that would have stopped the execution had the A-spies elected to tell the truth. (*Long Island Daily Press*)

The description of the pair as "A-spies" is typical. The article also described their crime as "delivering to Soviet Russia the secrets of the atomic bomb," an overt act of which they were neither accused nor convicted. This kind of distortion in the press and the media revealed the function the Rosenberg case was supposed to perform—to show, to prove what all the previous persecutions and hearings had been unable to prove, that Communists were traitors and spies. Especially Jewish ones. Had they "talked," the way the informers in Hollywood talked under pressure, the witch-hunters would have gained legitimacy for their endeavors and authority to keep the witch hunt going.

But it was the case of Morton Sobell that particularly affected me. His connection with Julius Rosenberg had been of the most tenuous kind. Yet, when the Rosenbergs were arrested, he and his wife and children left the country, ostensibly to take a vacation in Mexico. The government, the media and the jurors ultimately interpreted this panicky reaction as an admission of guilt, just as the use of the Fifth Amendment by witnesses before HUAC was taken as an admission of guilt.

But when there is hysteria in the country, when people are dragged before inquisitorial committees because of their associations and beliefs, is it not possible that innocent persons might panic and run? Many of those facing the blacklist had done just that. Yet, on the flimsiest of evidence, Sobell was found guilty of "conspiracy to commit etcetera" and sentenced to thirty years in prison. Any citizen with a radical background could be as easily drawn into this dragnet on the testimony of an informer trying to save his own skin.

When there is so much reason to fear injustice and attack, some run, some freeze. I've always opted to swim into the wave as it comes crashing towards me, in the hope I can swim through it before it throws me. I was very active in defense of the Rosenbergs.

In recent years, with new sources becoming available, there have been several studies re-evaluating the Rosenberg case. None have been definitive; most have cast doubt on the severity of the punishment. Many people formerly active in their defense now believe that Julius was indeed guilty of espionage, but that Ethel Rosenberg was entirely innocent of it and that the government knew this before they were executed. Evidence from Russian files and documents is directly conflicting—some say they were not spies, others that they were, while a third says only Julius. In retrospect the charge by Judge Kaufman that "they were responsible for the deaths of tens of thousands in the Korean war," made to explain the death sentence, seems more and more preposterous. Many nuclear scientists have now questioned the assumption that there WAS an atomic secret at all and that, if there was one, it was possible to transmit it through "spies" who had inadequate scientific training.

I have read much of the recently uncovered evidence and struggled with the question of the Rosenbergs' guilt or innocence. The trial evidence for Julius's guilt consists entirely of testimony by witnesses who had a self-interest in cooperating with the prosecution. Even at that, the evidence presented in court could never have convicted him of "espionage." The only way a conviction could be obtained was through the course followed, namely to accuse him and all others even peripherally connected with him of "conspiracy." To convict a person of espionage the government needs the testimony of two witnesses for each overt act. But in a trial for conspiracy, hearsay evidence is admissible and each conspirator is held fully accountable for the acts of others, as though he had committed them. The state, the prosecution, counted on the climate of the day to obtain a conviction on the flimsy evidence they had. They counted on the fact that media publicity would disregard the fine points and dub the Rosenbergs "atom spies," so that in the public eye what they were convicted of was "espionage." The prosecution's judgement prevailed.

I am still convinced of the Rosenbergs' innocence—Ethel's, because there was not a shred of evidence against her except the self-serving recollections of the Greenglasses. I believe in Julius's innocence because, if he had been a spy, he would have recanted and named names. There is no single case history in the cold war when actual spies, once confronted with evidence against them and faced with the prospect of decades in jail, did not admit their guilt. Everyone who has read the Rosenbergs' letters and studied their case, regardless of whether they think of them as innocent or guilty, has acknowledged their deep love of their children and their concern for them. Julius's love and dependency on Ethel has been noted even by the prosecution and by J. Edgar Hoover, who counted on it to secure a confession. Offers by the government to both Rosenbergs of a deal to save their lives are on record to the last hours before their execution. If Julius had been guilty, the knowledge that he could save his wife's life and give his children at least a halfway normal childhood would have prevailed. At the very least he would have tried to strike a deal, confess in order to win the promised clemency toward Ethel, and then refuse to name others. Such a deal might have finally been refused by the prosecution, but it was never offered by the Rosenbergs. I believe the reason it was never discussed by them was that they were innocent.

I WAS AT THE DEATH VIGIL in Union Square the night of the executions. Two days later, I went to the Rosenbergs' funeral in Brooklyn, together with nearly ten thousand people who stood behind police barricades listening to the service. It was a hot day; still, thousands marched on foot from the chapel, following the hearses at least part way. Seven thousand cars followed as cortege. I remember the stillness of that walk, the sobbing, the solemnity of the marchers. I have no personal recollection of the service in the funeral home, but I vividly remember the graveside service. The family group was small—Julius's mother, Sophie Rosenberg, his brother and two sisters, the rabbi in his prayer shawl, members of the Rosenberg Defense Committee, Dr. W.E.B. Du Bois. Several hundred people stood around the gravesite. The Rosenberg children were not present, but to the mourners they were constantly present, as they had been through the months and years of the struggle to save their parents' lives. I felt as though I had lost a member of my own family. There were police everywhere, in uniform and in plain clothes, surrounding the gravesite, the mourners. And all through it, while the service proceeded, there was the roar of a police helicopter and one from the *Daily News* circling low over the graves, their noise so great one could not hear the words of the service. Vultures . . . It was the final indignity. I cried at that gravesite—for the dead, for their children, for the victims of persecution, for myself. The acrid taste of defeat and fear hung over the scene. Who would be next?

THE WORST OF WHAT HAPPENED to me in personal terms during those years happened when I was driving my children to music school one afternoon. Dan was studying the violin; Stephanie was getting piano lessons. As always the children were noisy and rambunctious in the back seat so I turned on the radio, hoping to soothe them with the hit parade tunes they so cherished. But I had turned on a newscast, a report on the latest hearing of HUAC in Hollywood. The committee, having exhausted its supply of suspected reds in the film community, was then focusing on Los Angeles doctors, lawyers and teachers. The hearings had gone on for some time.

"Dr. Louise Light, a physician, admitted that she had for a time been a member of the Communist Party and, in secret session, named . . . persons she knew to be Communists."

I pulled the car to the side of the road and sat there, stunned. My own doctor, the woman who had saved my life and that of my child, had become an informer . . . Nothing that happened before or after hit me quite as hard.

Later, I learned the full story. Dr. Light was married to Max Silver, a man who had been membership secretary of the L.A. CP for some years. He was on the list of those to be indicted in the next round of Smith Act prosecutions. If those went as the Smith Act trials in New York City had, he would face five years in jail. Dr. Light made a deal to protect her husband from this fate and named a large group—all of her patients. They knew who I was when they came to me, she explained. Well, I for one didn't know anything about her private life or who her husband was. I was told she was a good and caring doctor, and so she was. She went further and named a dentist to whom she had referred patients. How could she know if any of her patients were CP members? Presumably her husband must have told her or else, like many of the informers, she simply named people at random to curry favor. Her husband was never indicted under the Smith Act.

Doctor-client privilege, I was thinking. Trust your doctor—and she'll turn you over to the Inquisition.

"Mom, what's the matter? Why you upset?" the children insisted.

Because faith has been broken and honor is dead. Because the poison of the witch hunters has spread all over and trust and friendship are corrupted.

"It's nothing," I said and moved the car back into traffic. "Something flew into my eye and I wanted to get it out. We'll be at the music school soon."

Above all, I prayed, let me be strong enough to keep dailiness going. Let me save these children from troubled waters.

[19]

T HINKING BACK ON THOSE YEARS, 1953 to 1956, I remember an
incredible amount of activity, some of it ordinary in a family with
school-age children, most of it chosen. Carl and I were determined to
give our children a normal life, when our own lives were far from normal. Part of
that effort was a great investment of my time in child-centered activities—PTA,
playgroup, school trips, music lessons, activities around birthdays, holidays, vaca-
tions. Partly out of economic necessity and partly because I believed it made for
a good family life, I cooked and baked and served all the family's meals. Carl's
erratic employment schedule did not permit us regularly to eat dinner together,
but we did so whenever we could. I often served three dinners—one for the children at their usual time, one for myself when I finally grew tired of waiting for
Carl and then his dinner, when he came home after working late.

Like many other radical parents in those times, we tried to shield our children from our fears and anxieties. Both of us felt strongly that children should
not be coerced to adopt their parents' political convictions. We each had spent
many years rebelling against our own parents' values and we were firmly convinced that we must do things differently from our parents. A basic principle of
our marriage was that we would not lie to each other and we would not lie to our
children. We also would not engage them in activities that were contrary to our
own values and priorities. On this score we did badly, not intentionally, but from

ineptness. For example, we never made any effort to teach the children how to play baseball, even though we watched the game on TV. I saw to it that both children learned to swim and I fought with Carl and finally won him over to the idea that we must take up family camping, so that the children could have a direct experience in nature. Dan later became an avid basketball player. This was a sport I liked and had taken up myself in Vienna, yet neither Carl nor I made it a point to attend the high-school basketball games in which Dan was playing. This was, as I now know, a very bad mistake and one that Dan has often chided us for with considerable and understandable bitterness.

What parents intend to transmit to their children and what children pick up from their parents are different matters. We believed strongly that playing with war toys would train children to accept violence as acceptable. So there was a strict policy of no guns in our house; no play guns either. While we were living in St. Albans I watched from the kitchen window as Dan and one of the neighbor boys were playing. Dan was about seven years old at the time. The boys had acquired two long sticks, which they were using as guns.

"Bang, bang, you're dead."

"Poof, I got you."

They got tired of running, falling, jumping up, running and falling again, and were on their way to the house, probably to get cookies and juice.

"Let's put the guns in the garage," Dan called out. "My Mom doesn't want guns in the house." So they put the sticks in the back of the garage and trooped in for their refreshments.

My pacifist upbringing had obviously failed. On the other hand, the lesson in parents' values had definitely taken.

It was a little more complicated when it came to politics. When the children were very young, I used to take them on picket lines and canvassing in their stroller, but once they were older, I tried not to involve them in my political work. It felt coercive to me to do that. When we left Hollywood, we told the children that Daddy had lost his job and was getting work in New York, but we did not attempt to explain the blacklist. On the whole, we thought the less they knew, the less they would be burdened. We did, however, instruct them not to talk to strangers, not to answer questions about their family put to them by strangers, not to discuss in school what was said at our dinner table. We tried not to talk about frightening events when the children were present. But in a time of persecution, it is hard to avoid upsetting news, if you are among the group being persecuted. Our friends David and Naomi Robison, a writer and an actress, had been among those subpoenaed by HUAC in Los Angeles. Their children watched on TV as both of their parents were pilloried as subversives and traitors. After a futile effort to make a living in Hollywood as blacklisted "Commies," the Robisons moved their family to Westchester County, New York, where David's mother had a farm. They thought it would provide a less stressful environment for their three children and enable the family to survive financially. We often visited the farm and our children were close friends of the Robison children. There was no way we could shield them completely from the reality of the blacklist.

We could try to be reassuring and point out that the blacklisted people who were our friends were surviving well (a gross exaggeration) and taking good care of their children. But we could do nothing against the fear and anxiety our children experienced in those years. Fifty years later I have tried to find out how they remember these times and they tell me they always felt they lived under some shadow, some unknown dread. There was a great secret in the family that they felt, but it was something about which they could not talk to us. Stephanie remembers the Rosenberg case clearly as making her afraid that we, her parents, might be taken away and killed. So, just as in the case of pacifism, we failed to protect our children, even as we thought to protect them.

Just in this way, it has turned out, many children of holocaust survivors report that their parents never talked about the horrors they lived through. The parents tried to protect the children from nightmarish knowledge, but the children experienced a hidden dread, a great secret, a sense of disharmony between themselves and their parents.

The schools, the media, the politicians certainly did not try to protect the children from knowledge of the cold war, a possible nuclear war and the kind of thinking that casts half the world as the Other, the enemy to be destroyed. School newspapers and assigned readings all reflected cold war beliefs.

In school, the children were issued metal dog tags with their names, addresses, telephone numbers and serial numbers on them. They were instructed to wear them day and night, "in case of nuclear attack." Parents were instructed to tell the children this was for their safety, in case they got lost. The children were not fooled. "It's metal," they explained, "so it won't burn in a bomb attack." This was St. Albans, Queens, New York, U.S.A.—the madmen had taken over the asylum and were issuing edifying bulletins of instruction. We took off the dog tags, sent letters to school explaining our opposition to this foolish and insane set of bureaucratic orders. We would not allow our children to be frightened to death about imaginary war dangers, nor did we believe that in the actual event of a nuclear attack any teachers or parents would be around to collect these dog tags and the children attached to them.

"All the children wear these tags," Stephanie wailed, feeling once again forced into isolation and marginality.

"We don't have to do what everyone else does, if it is not right," we explained. We had to hurt our child in the short run to protect her in the long run. There was no way you could make a good choice in a situation like this.

The children were subjected to regular "air raid drills." They were ordered to crouch under their desks, shielding their eyes and faces with their hands. This, they were told, would protect them from injury in case of an air raid. Even as obdurate a bureaucracy as that of the N.Y.C. Board of Education must have known by 1953 that wooden desktops would not protect anyone from air attack nor would hands shielding eyes protect children in case of nuclear war. The cruel hoax being perpetrated on a whole generation of children was designed solely to accustom them and their parents to the inevitability of war. The frantic media drive to get people to build private air raid shelters in their backyards and to store food and medicine for "emergencies" was of the same order. Our pitifully small neighborhood peace groups, made up mostly of outraged mothers, distributed reprints from the *Journal of Atomic Scientists* that showed a twenty-five-mile radius of destruction from a nuclear bomb hit, the kind of destruction visited upon Hiroshima and Nagasaki. Peace is the only answer, we insisted, and our government branded us as subversives for doing so.

Looking back from the distance of five decades, I still think that those who fought against nuclear armament, for coexistence and for peaceful conflict resolutions were better defenders of children's interests than were those who acquiesced to cold war ideology and domestic conformity. At the very least, we taught our children how to think independently, how to stand up for their convictions, how to resist conformity.

My activity level continued at a frenetic pace. I edited, for some time, a newsletter of the peace committees in Queens, collected information, wrote copy and finally mimeographed the text and mailed it out. I took part in delegations and lobbying efforts at the United Nations. I attended endless fund-raising events for the embattled good causes of the Left. In 1954 I wrote a friend:

> I'm working on the new book, editing the old one, keeping house, fend-
> ing off summer guests, cooking three squares a day, doing the laundry
> and cleaning as usual, driving Carl to and from the train, keeping up my

end of peace activities and trying to catch up with some of the reading that's been piling up for months.

This was written from a summer vacation. During the school year I organized and chaired a legislative committee for a PTA that had never had such a politically oriented activity. I attended PTA meetings, peace committee meetings, party club meetings, committee meetings of various embattled organizations. When and how I did all this I cannot recall, but I have enough leaflets, announcements of meetings, petitions and other written evidence left in my files to know that I did it. It strikes me now, looking back on all that feverish activity, that whatever intrinsic value it may or may not have had, it was a way of holding fear and despair at bay. When things are out of control, one can be paralyzed and withdraw from reality or one can fight a dozen small battles over local issues just to survive, to keep one's sanity, to keep some vestiges of resistance alive.

Even after the coming of fascism, in the face of deportation and jail, you make the beds, you cook the meals, you do the dishes. You try to resist, to the best of your ability.

In the fall of 1952 I decided to go back to work in the medical field. Both children were in school until 3 P.M. and I was able to work out after-school care for them with members of my interracial playgroup and with babysitters. After a false start as a medical assistant to a doctor in private practice, I found just what I wanted in a group practice office. I was hired to be of all-around service to the twelve doctors in the group—to type medical reports and to do electrocardiograms, diathermy and short-wave treatments. After a short while I became the special assistant of the internist, a highly capable young doctor who took splendid care of his patients and did interesting research. He became our family doctor and friend, and later helped me to kick my smoking habit, for which I am eternally grateful.

I enjoyed working, but the juggling act required to keep home and children cared for was very stressful. In May 1953 Carl and I sat down and figured out what my actual earnings had been since September. Once we deducted the essential expenses that I had incurred due to working—babysitters, carfare, clothing, beauty parlor once a week—it turned out I had been netting approximately twelve dollars a week. This seemed entirely counterproductive, and we both agreed I should quit my job, which I did at the end of the school year.

Carl's employment situation had been steadily improving. He worked for TV and did some independent films for businesses. These jobs paid quite well and compensated for the intervening periods of unemployment. But there was still a great feeling of uncertainty, since there was no carry-over from one job to the other. To gain some more reliable, steady income, Carl started teaching classes at night at the New York Film Institute, the predominant film training center, and later at the New York University Film Department. He taught editing and was a popular and effective teacher whose courses were always oversubscribed. To this day, I sometimes hear from his former students who have made great careers in the film business. He gave the first course ever given in the U.S.A. on Ingmar Bergman, the Swedish filmmaker, whose work he greatly admired.

Carl never was happy doing merely commercial work; he always wanted to do work that had some social significance. "In between jobs," as the unemployment periods were euphemistically dubbed, he would prepare projects, often made on a shoestring, which provided entertainment with positive social values. His documentary work sustained his spirits during the most difficult periods. At last, in 1954, he was hired as editor of the TV series *The Doctor,* which provided some longer-range employment. The major turn in his employment status did not occur until 1956, when he edited a feature film, *Patterns,* for United Artists. After that came the prize-winning documentary *On the Bowery* and the film classic *Twelve Angry Men.* By the end of 1957 Carl was securely established as the foremost film editor in New York City and from that period on he mostly worked on feature films. Of course, all of this stability was fragile, since a subpoena to a HUAC hearing would instantly put him on the blacklist. But at least, in New York, the union blacklist did not function against him and his talent and energy could help him to make a career. He remained steadfast throughout in his convictions. "The only way I can see myself in this business," he said to me in his usual quiet manner, "making big money while other people are blacklisted, is if I am at any time ready to give it all up rather than become a stool pigeon. As long as I know I can do that, I can make a career." And so he did. I have always admired him for it.

MY FATHER, who had recovered from two severe heart attacks, had continued in deteriorating health. He was still running his business in Liechtenstein and had even begun to build up his pharmaceutical business again, but it was all too strenuous for him. He was very happy in his second marriage with Gretel, although they had to live on a very modest income. He delighted in the pictures and anecdotes of the children I sent him, and we were planning another visit to see him. But this was not to be. He had another heart attack and died on November 18, 1953.

I took his death very hard, because I now knew I had wronged him for many years. I was very happy that we had been able to work through that during our last two visits with one another. We had missed so much; the good times together had been so few. And the joyful old age that he had earned with his responsible, good life, his caring for his family, the incredibly loyal friendship that he gave my mother, this good old age never came for him. I only valued him truly when it was too late. He was a kind, an honorable man, and much of what is good and decent in me, I owe to him. I was able to express that to him once while he was still alive, but it was not enough. It never is enough, after death cuts off all possibilities. Our unfinished business with the dead continues for the rest of our lives.

When one suffers a great loss, it helps to have young children; they pull you out of grief and contemplation of the past. "Don't cry, Mommy." Their fat little arms wrapped around my neck, they insisted on their needs, their rights to an untroubled existence.

IN 1954, I STARTED on a new organizational venture, which would occupy much of my time and energy in the next two years. Ever since the early 1950s, artists and writers of left or liberal leanings had felt the effect of the blacklist. Publishers were careful to avoid printing anything that might make them subject to the charge of pro-Communism. "Controversial" topics were taboo, as were topics pertaining to working people, unions, or racial problems. Galleries closed their spaces to left-wing artists; writers of repute no longer could get their books published. As was to be expected, the general climate of self-censorship and repression fell hardest on the unknown artists and writers, those just beginning their careers.

Blacklisted people had fought back by organizing a sort of semi-underground cultural movement, which inspired a few writers to organize a publishing project along similar lines. The moving forces in this organization were Henry and Dorothy Kraus. Henry had been educational director of the United Auto Workers union during World War II and Dorothy had been very active in the union in various functions. They both were blacklisted during the purging of the unions in the early fifties. They had moved to New York, where Dorothy continued an earlier interest in collecting antiques by dealing in imported art works. Henry, who accompanied her on shopping trips to Europe, gradually became more and more involved in the study of medieval art. He trained himself in art history and later would uncover a hitherto neglected medieval art object, namely the misericords in churches. These were underseat ledges against which the clergy could rest while standing during the long hours of prayer. When unfolded, these ledges revealed vivid wood sculptures on their undersides. Since the subject matter of such sculptures could not be sacred—considering the physical purpose they served—they were decorated universally with secular illustrations. Henry Kraus discovered a vast new source for medieval social history and became world famous for his several books on the subject. Late in life, he would be honored by being awarded a MacArthur "genius" fellowship.

I had known the Krauses for years from L.A. and Dorothy and I had worked together in Congress of American Women. Now, in 1954, Henry organized a small group of people to form a cooperative publishing house, Associated Authors. The idea was that we would publish several manuscripts independently, by advertising the availability of these books and trying to get subscribers to pay in advance for them. The money would be put in escrow and when we had collected enough to pay publishing costs, we would ship the book to the subscribers. If we did not get enough advance orders within a given period, we would refund the subscriptions. The operation would be entirely nonprofit, except that the authors would receive a small royalty. We would do extensive mailings to lists of progressive people and to the authors' friends. The authors would organize readings of their work in order to promote the books and collect the necessary funds for publishing.

It was a simple idea and we soon learned that we had illustrious company in the past. A number of great American writers, among them Mark Twain, had self-published their writings by subscription. Walt Whitman found no publisher for *Leaves of Grass* and decided to publish the book himself. He set the type by hand in a friend's print shop and in 1855 printed a thousand copies, of which very few were sold. Inspired by such examples, our little group set up shop, late in 1953.

Since we had no capital, the six partners assessed themselves for current expenses, such as stationary, a P. O. box and a bank account. All of us worked on organizing potential readers. We enlisted Angus Cameron, formerly editor-in-chief of Little Brown, now head of Cameron & Kahn Publishers, to help select the manuscripts we wanted to publish. As soon as we announced the project, dozens of applicants sent us their manuscripts. Three were selected: Bernard Mandel's *Labor: Free and Slave,* a historical study of the effect of slavery on labor in the

North; Estolv Ward's "The Piecard," a novel of trade union struggles in the New Deal era, and my novel *No Farewell,* which was announced as "a novel of young love and family conflict in prewar Vienna." A fourth manuscript by Lars Lawrence was slated to come after these three had been published.

We spent the summer months soliciting the endorsements of well-known writers, assembling a mailing list, sending out our first announcement and organizing readings for our authors. In our first mailing we described each book and invited the reader to accept our special prepublication price of $2.50 per book. "Not only will you save money," we exhorted the reader, "you will also have the satisfaction of knowing that your faith in decent, honest writing has brought a worthwhile, humanist book to life." Since the mailing list we used was made up of our friends, co-workers and comrades, this appeal, mixing thrift with idealism, was sure to win.

We had figured out that we needed to sell 1400 books in advance in order to pay for publication. It was slow work. Bernie Mandel was most successful in sending out several hundred promotional folders, then following up with a personal letter and often a visit. Estolv Ward reported that he and his wife had sent out four hundred personal letters with brochures, plus an additional three hundred brochures distributed without accompanying letters. I, on the other hand, relied mostly on "soirees." In the summer of 1954 I reported on some of these to the other authors:

> Last week I had a highly successful lecture in the country. The reason for the success was that I was teamed up with Yuri Suhl, who very generously donated his talents and name to support our venture. This drew in a crowd much greater than I could have hoped to attract. If we could get a few more name writers to help us out in this way, we might not only get more publicity, but also help to demonstrate that writers of some standing share a sense of responsibility toward young writers and humanist literature . . .
>
> People often tell me that they enjoyed my reading-out-loud, despite the fact they are not used to being read to, in fact though they didn't like the idea at first. I think doing more of this may change people's attitude. I, for one, find it extremely stimulating as a writer to be in direct personal contact with my audience.

But the effort required to make the necessary advance sales was high. In another letter I reported on the darker side of our venture:

The evening in Parkway Village was a flop, because it fell on a 95 degree night with 83 percent humidity. Had eight people there, most of whom had already ordered, sold two books and gave out two order books.

Another soiree was a flop. The people in Woodside houses invited thirty couples, got twenty-one acceptances and two people showed up. Very discouraging.

But I persisted, as did the other authors. I spoke to a group of the American Labor Party, to a house meeting in Croton, another in Levittown. It was a grueling, labor-intensive effort, and it succeeded. We were able first to publish Bernard Mandel's book, then mine. We never did get enough advance sales for Estolv Ward's book, and the organization collapsed from its members' exhaustion as soon as we had sold the books we had published.

And yet, we had accomplished something—we had brought two books to life that otherwise would have been unborn and with it, we had saved their authors. Bernard Mandel continued as a scholarly author and my future life as a writer was made possible by the remarkable response to my novel. Not only the gratifying feedback I received at the readings, but also an astonishing set of good reviews encouraged me to think of myself as a professional writer and to continue writing. We sold 2500 copies of *No Farewell,* which is a respectable number for a first novel by an unknown writer. Amazingly, it got a fine, though brief review in the *New Yorker,* which meant a lot to me.

The most important result of the two years spent in publishing and promoting the book was the experience I gained as a public speaker. Two decades later, when I became a successful academic and scholarly writer going on book tours and being interviewed on radio and TV, I discovered that I loved lecturing and promoting my books in public readings. Over and over again, meeting my readers at book signings and after lectures, I would get that wonderful sense of power as a writer that comes from knowing there are people out there, actual living human beings, who love and understand my work. I would feel a connectedness, an affinity with them, and a sense of achievement in being able to speak to them and to their lives. When women come up to me and say, as they often do, "You said what I always knew," I feel justified and worthy, honored in a more profound way than by all the ceremonial honors I have received. It all began then, so long ago, in that hot summer and the long winters of trying to prove that humanist writing and grassroots organizing could keep hope alive.

WHEN YOU HIKE up a high mountain, carrying your backpack, near exhaustion from the long trek behind you, there comes a moment when you see the barren peak in front of you and it seems so near that you can discern every crevice, every outcropping of rock. Usually, you stand on a high plateau and the peak rises up sharply above you. You try to discover where access might be possible and it all seems easy, so temptingly close. But experience tells you that now you are faced with the hardest part of the ascent and that it will take hours of strenuous work to scale that last height. Then a wind comes up, or it might be snow, the kind of weather high peaks create around themselves. Breathing is harder and the load feels double its weight.

It is then that you take one small laborious step after the other, and you force your mind away from the goal. You look at the narrow trail just ahead of your feet; and, to conserve energy, you try to control your breathing and restrict your movements to those absolutely necessary. One foot at a time, and as you ascend, the summit vanishes from view, since now you have become part of that summit. This is the time when you must focus on your feet and nothing else. Forget the goal, forget the possibility of failure, forget the sweat running down your back, forget the pain of your pack. Every summit is climbed one step at a time, thousands of repetitions, thousands of seemingly hopeless movements. This is the time when the mind forces the body to do more than it can, when you struggle against gravity and wind, against hopelessness and despair. One step after the other, that's the only way to conquer a high mountain peak.

So it was in the years 1953 to 1956. One step at a time, only there was no conquered peak at the end, no glorious view, no inspiring vista. Just the knowledge that one was still upright, still breathing and undefeated. One had survived.

[20]

E VER SINCE WE HAD LEFT HOLLYWOOD, our affiliation with the party was quite loose. Blacklisted people were dropped from participation in party activities; it was assumed they were being followed by the FBI and would therefore only endanger anyone with whom they were in contact. That distancing, at the time, suited us fine, for Carl and I had each in our own way experienced disillusionment, a slow eroding of trust. Had cold-war hysteria not taken such extreme forms we would have left the party years earlier than we did, for reasons of our own dissatisfaction. But one was held by the long habit of self-discipline and by the belief that one's choices, at this period, were to stay in, with whatever misgivings one had, or to become an informer. There seemed to be no middle ground.

I ask myself now why there had seemed to be no middle ground. The CP in the late 1950s was embattled, enfeebled, infiltrated by police and FBI agents. To leave at such a time seemed to be the rankest opportunism—rats leaving the sinking ship. People who left were denounced and ostracized by their former comrades on one side and were under enormous pressure from the other side to inform on them. This was, certainly for the blacklisted people, the prize extracted of them, if they wished to be accepted in mainstream society.

Many former Communists have, in their memoirs and retrospective narratives, stressed the failure of the human element in the Communist movement.

That charge certainly had some truth to it, which every party member experienced at one time or another. It was particularly evident in branch meetings. Branches based on common activities, such as those in a particular trade union or mass organization, worked well because the members had a common goal and purpose. Where that was lacking, branch meetings were often embarrassingly competitive bragging sessions, in which each person vied with the others for credit, acclaim or even status. Who had made the most contacts and sold the most papers? Who had "built a base" in a mass organization? Far from being support groups, these meetings could turn destructive.

I think there were more than the ordinary human failings involved in this. I have worked in many groups formed in voluntary association, and most of them were held together by the members' common goals and objectives. Usually, one or more persons took on dominant roles. People tend to accept such dominance, if the "leader" can maintain authority by superior achievement towards the common goal. In such voluntary groups there is silent, common agreement to avoid too much intimacy, too much intrusion into the private affairs of the members. Boundaries are set and the possibilities for harming individuals are more limited. In the party, there were unspoken assumptions about the relationship of the group to the individual that were bound to produce bad results for at least some members. The party group, ideally, was supposed to be a beloved community, a group of comrades dedicated to working for a goal far larger than that of their own ambitions. It was supposed to be a place where people became better than they were, where they learned to turn away from the selfishness, individualism and competitiveness of the larger society. The ideal of collective wisdom and selfless dedication to the common good had brought most of us into the movement. We hoped and expected to have it strengthened in our party work. I think the fact that most party members did not experience that growth and support, that feeling of being part of a loving community, was the greatest failing of the movement. I hesitate to make generalizations here, since obviously those who stayed on through thick and thin and years of persecution did, in fact, experience community. And so did I, for a number of years. But it faded, it eroded, it wore thin.

In my work in Congress of American Women I had seen true democratic community at work. The local chapters were made up of women who truly cared for one another, who saw themselves first as neighbors, then as friends and as political activists only for a part of their lives. In each CAW meeting, whatever else was on our agenda, we talked about children, about schools, about the price of groceries. I had experienced that before in some party neighborhood branches, but in the later years that kind of spirit seemed rare. Instead, a judgmental attitude prevailed. Did this one or that one slacken in their party work? Was this one or that one too involved in mass work and not sufficiently interested in selling the party line to others? Was there evidence of hidden racism in one or another person? Self-criticism and collective criticism sessions were held in some such cases, and they were inevitably destructive. People might, under such pressure, admit to this or that transgression, but they felt hurt in doing so and resentful in ways that would come out on other occasions. It was these resentments that led many to leave the party disillusioned and angry.

There is no question in my mind but that the infiltration of FBI and police spies into the party apparatus tended to aggravate these destructive tendencies. On the one hand, many sincere members tended to always look over their shoulder for evidence of behavior that could lead to the unmasking of some infiltrator or police spy. This made for paranoid behavior all around. On the other hand, these FBI people often built their credentials by acting super-militant, outdoing everyone in zeal and especially in their condemnation of any "deviance." In such an atmosphere it was difficult for trust and comradeship to flourish.

Carl and I had spent several years only loosely affiliated after we came to New York. Finally, I joined a writer's branch, which met in downtown New York, far from my own community. Since I was by then organizationally involved with Associated Authors, this seemed like a good solution. None of the people in Associated Authors were in this group; all of its members were established writers, more successful than I. This should not have mattered, one way or the other. I had been in writers' workshops before and some of them had been very helpful and supportive. But this particular group could never quite decide whether we were a writers' workshop and support group or a party branch dedicated to political work only.

We combined both functions, which sounded fine in theory, but did not work well in practice. Some of us were actively writing, others were not. The latter tended to focus their energies on criticizing the work of those writing, which led to resentment. And since we clearly were also a political unit, the criticism tended to focus not on artistic questions, but on content, on political correctness. I had not experienced this earlier in all my years in the party, where despite the heavy cultural debates, the individual writer was left fairly free to write what she pleased and was not criticized until the work was published. I was then working on my novel "Start a Stone," which was quite political in content, with its theme of racial integration in housing. In view of the generally negative attitude of publishers toward this book, I felt very vulnerable and did not take well to criticism. I remember feeling outrage and anger at the discouragement coming at me from this group. Since they were people older and more experienced than myself, I humbly took whatever they dished out. But I remember one meeting, which took place in my own apartment, when I fought back and showed my anger and resentment of the way they were treating me. That night I decided to get out of that group, once and for all. And so I did.

FEBRUARY 1956—SOVIET PREMIER NIKITA KHRUSHCHEV DENOUNCES STALIN'S CRIMES.

NOVEMBER 4, 1956—THE HUNGARIAN REVOLT IS CRUSHED BY THE SOVIET ARMY.

NOVEMBER 6, 1956—PRESIDENT EISENHOWER IS RE-ELECTED, DEFEATING ADLAI STEVENSON.

Khrushchev's revelations, as printed in the pages of the *New York Times,* had a devastating effect on what remained of the American Communist Party. For the first time, the party press stopped automatically apologizing for and justifying Soviet policy and opened its pages to genuine debate. In May 1956 the party leadership called for sixty days of open debate prior to the next party convention.

John Gates, the editor of the *Daily Worker,* took a strong and well-defined position. In essence he argued for an American Communist Party based entirely on American interests, democratically constructed and governed. He wanted open debate in the paper and at all party meetings in which everyone could air their grievances and in which people could work for genuine reform within the party. Unlike the party leadership, which had reprinted Khrushchev's devastating list of atrocities in the *Daily Worker* and then commented on it by referring to "errors," Gates acknowledged "serious mistakes." He even questioned the infallibility of Leninist doctrine. A large part of the CP leadership greeted his stand as though it were total betrayal. Soon there was a sharp, no-holds-barred debate.

We watched this debate with a mixture of hope and cynicism. Now that the *Daily Worker* was publishing its readers' comments without censoring them, the paper became more readable and interesting. The many grievances, which had for so long remained unmentionable, now burst in the open. The three major teachers of the Jefferson School, Howard Selsam, David Goldway and Doxey Wilkerson, gave a thorough analysis of their own mistakes. The school had too long tolerated a doctrinaire Marxism; it had discouraged true dissent and had paid too little attention to socialist scholars outside of the CP. It had failed to represent a Marxist viewpoint in mainstream public debates and it had been lax in upholding its own educational standards.

Other readers pilloried the party's lack of democracy and the arrogance of its leadership. "We are not a vanguard," one reader wrote. Others confirmed his judgement. "Working people do not listen to us and we have failed to speak in a language they can accept." Some readers called on the national leadership to go back to work in shops and communities, so they could learn what it means to be in touch with working people.

Others answered in the familiar tones of the past, speaking of "right-wing deviations" and lack of Marxist understanding. Members of the national committee took part in the debate with articles that recycled every cliche of the past. When it became clear that this debate would end with the victory of the party faction represented by William Z. Foster and Gus Hall, the most doctrinaire Stalinists, and that the reforms proposed by John Gates would not be given a chance, Carl and I left the party.

HUAC, the FBI informers and all redbaiters have an obsession with "crucial" dates. "When did you join? When did you leave?" As usual, they are asking the wrong questions. I cannot remember either date and no threat of dire consequences can make me remember it. What I do remember is the slow process at either end of this road taken, the slow growth in convictions and courage it took me to join an embattled underground movement, which promised persecution but also offered hope; the slow process of disenchantment and disillusionment that caused me to leave it and, finally, the years it took me to think my way out, not of one political movement only, but out of Marxism, the theory.

ALTOGETHER, 1956 WAS A BAD YEAR for me. The novel was circulating among publishers, but generated only negative responses and considerable criticism. Stephanie was entering her teenage years with spirited resistance against parental control. Theoretically, I had been prepared for that and considered it a necessary phase in her development toward independence, but practically I found it hard to take. Dan, too, at age nine, had developed interests and activities of his own. At times it seemed to me the children needed me only to provide food, shelter and clean clothes. Worse yet, I had developed a chronic health problem, a uterine cyst, which caused me to suffer from severe cramps and bleeding for several weeks each month. The male gynecologist who had discovered the condition informed me cheerfully that we were dealing "with a race between the tumor and the menopause." What he meant by this inappropriate metaphor was that there was hope that by the onset of menopause the tumor, which was benign, would shrink of its own accord and no surgery would be necessary. His jocular tone and metaphor made me think of the race between the tortoise and the hare; it also made me decide to get a different gynecologist. The woman doctor I found confirmed the diagnosis but without the jokes. She thought, considering my age, one might hope that the onset of menopause would come early and we might be able to avoid surgery. Meanwhile I felt weak, irritable and often in pain for weeks at a time. In 1958 my hemorrhages got so serious that I decided on surgery anyway, and so that problem was resolved.

It seemed that Carl and I were moving in very different trajectories. His career was finally advancing steadily. He went from one good feature film to another, from one great director to a better one. I rejoiced with him and enjoyed the benefits of his steady income and his growing reputation. But I seemed to be moving in a downward spiral, contributing little but negative news, aches and pains and disappointments. It was a time of stress in our marriage; we were out of synch with each other.

Almost instinctively, reaching back to a mode of cooperation that had always worked for us, Carl found a solution for our problem. We had both been watching the news of the emerging civil rights movement with avid interest. The Montgomery bus boycott, the struggle for school integration in the South were enormously moving to us and evoked our sympathy. We donated money to the NAACP and often considered what more we might do to help. We discussed going south and actively participating in the struggle, but we felt that if we were arrested, which was a contingency for which one had to be prepared, we would harm the cause more than help it. Here was the final, bitter irony: the CP had become so isolated, so discredited, that even one's past association with it would make a person harm any cause he or she would support. The inspiring and courageous struggle for dignity and equality in the South, for which we had hoped and worked for so many years, had no place for people like us. None of this was said quite so explicitly at the time, but we were both aware of it and it added to our confusion and disillusionment.

But then, early in 1957, an opportunity opened up for us to contribute to the struggle for justice in the South and in a way that would allow both of us to be involved in a joint project.

On April 5, 1957, representatives of seventy-five African-American organizations meeting in Washington issued a call for a "Prayer Pilgrimage for Freedom" to Washington, D.C., to be held on the third anniversary of the U.S. Supreme Court decisions ending segregation in public schools. The organizers expected fifty thousand people to participate. A leaflet stated that the purpose of the event would be "1) To demonstrate the unity of the Negro community behind the civil rights demands before Congress. 2) To show support of the Supreme Court's decision. 3) To protest the terrible intimidation and terror under which colored people live."[1]

The call for the Prayer Pilgrimage was issued by Rev. Martin Luther King, Jr. of the Montgomery Improvement Association and his co-chairmen, Roy Wilkins, President of the NAACP, and A. Philip Randolph, Vice President of the AFL-CIO and President of the Brotherhood of Sleeping Car Porters. The main work of organizing this event fell to Bayard Rustin, Ella Baker, and Stanley Levison. This unlikely trio—Bayard Rustin, a homosexual black pacifist and socialist; Ella Baker, the foremost black organizer of her time and longtime NAACP activist and Stanley Levison, a liberal white attorney and fundraiser—had a year earlier founded a group called In Friendship in New York City for the purpose of supporting the Montgomery bus boycott. After the victory in Montgomery, Rustin had proposed the formation of a national black activist mass movement with Rev. King at its head. With the help of Baker and Levison, the Southern Christian Leadership Conference (SCLC) was born in February 1957, composed largely of black clergymen. The organization had a more activist stance than NAACP and was perceived as an upstart competitor by NAACP leaders. Much of the tension between the two leaders was based on Wilkins's perception that Rev. King, organizationally inexperienced and yet catapulted into national prominence as a result of the Montgomery bus boycott, represented a new and threatening style of Negro leadership. The animosity between the two men was palpable and Rustin, Baker and Levison had their work cut out in preventing flare-ups and in mediating differences.

It was, I believe, Stanley Levison, who served as liaison to the media and PR people, who approached Carl with the idea of filming this event.

Carl eagerly accepted. It was understood that the sponsoring organizations were not providing any funds for this film project, which would therefore be

---

1. Call for March on Washington, May 1957, unsigned, part of FBI confidential file, in author's possession. I use the word "Negro" as it was used in the primary sources of the time.

entirely a volunteer enterprise. Carl managed to get thirty filmmakers in the various crafts and specialties to volunteer their services, pay their own way to Washington and promise to work for the duration of the project. Later he recruited some thirty more, who worked on the technical end of the production. These were all progressives, active unionists, many of them experienced documentary film makers, who were delighted to have a chance to contribute to the civil rights struggle. We held several fund-raising parties to finance the project. Carl put me on as writer and production assistant. It meant we could once again do what we liked best: work together on a project we believed in.

In order to get a feel and basic understanding of the organization, the planning and the leadership, I spent six fascinating weeks in the Prayer Pilgrimage headquarters in Manhattan. My desk was next to Bayard Rustin's and I had a chance to see this fine organizer at work. His elegant appearance and manner lent style to whatever he was doing. I was greatly impressed with his ability to connect with people and to handle stressful problems with seeming ease. He was witty, and in that dingy office with its poor lighting, worn desks and hard chairs he seemed to be having a good time. I tried to make myself as useful as possible, answering phones and fielding inquiries, while taking notes and trying to develop an approach to a script.

It was evident to all participants that this was going to be a historic event. Nothing of this scale and scope had ever been undertaken by African-Americans. The first March on Washington had been organized by A. Philip Randolph to take place July 1, 1941, in order to compel President Franklin Delano Roosevelt to end race discrimination in munitions factories. The prospect of such an event evoked fears in the nation's capital and brought to mind memories of the bonus marchers during the Great Depression. Under pressure to avoid possible violence, FDR issued an Executive Order banning all discrimination in defense industries and government employment, and Randolph canceled the march. Baker and Rustin, well aware of this history, were careful to avoid any parallels. The event was not a "March on Washington," but a "Prayer Pilgrimage." In a staff memo, signed by them and Stanley Levison prior to the organization of a National Committee they stressed that the pilgrimage was to "demonstrate in action the spiritual quality ... of the Negro's struggle for freedom and equality." Participants were to adhere to nonviolence. It was essential that the pilgrimage demonstrate "the greatest sense of unity and urgency in the Negro community." The unity of the three leaders of the Prayer Pilgrimage was considered of the essence and was to be prominently displayed to the public. The political aims were to safeguard the rights of Negroes in the South, to urge the passage of civil rights bills pending in the Congress, to protest the harassment of the NAACP in the South, to encourage the drive to register Negroes to vote and lastly to proclaim "the need for federal action to secure for Negroes the franchise."

They suggested a carefully balanced assignment of tasks for the co-chairmen: Mr. Randolph to act as chairman of a planning conference to be held in Washington in early April, Rev. King to outline the purpose and plans for the Prayer Pilgrimage and the NAACP and the Brotherhood of Sleeping Car Porters to each provide a staff person for the organizing committee. Baker presumably already served as staff person representing NAACP. It was also suggested that "a clergyman acceptable to the major church forces be one of the top staff people." They planned, as soon as possible to open an office in Washington charged with handling fund raising and local arrangements.[2]

The steps outlined in the memo were essentially followed. True to the organizers' intentions, the preparation for the pilgrimage translated into a lot of local activity. One progress report from national headquarters can give a sense of the scope and nature of the preparations:

Harry Belafonte, Jackie Robinson and Sidney Poitier were leading a delegation of media personalities to Washington.

Boston was sending a large delegation of NAACP and trade union members in buses and cars.

From Los Angeles, California, Rev. Maurice Dawkins sent a big delegation by chartered planes and buses. One busload of forty ministers will leave seven days ahead and be traced across the country by news reports, radio and TV.

Chicago—Chairman Willoughby Abner reports at least one thousand people were coming in buses, planes, trains and cars . . .

Simultaneous mass meetings and prayer services would be held in cities across the country at noon on Saturday, May 11, to spur participation in the Prayer Pilgrimage. Such meetings were held in New York City, Chicago, Detroit, Los Angeles, Atlanta, Montgomery, Richmond, Philadelphia and Baltimore . . .

---

2. The memo is in the author's possession. All quotes are from it.

The preparations in Washington were equally detailed and precise. NAACP and twenty-five churches would act as reception centers for the delegates arriving from out of town. Most centers provided a light snack at reasonable cost. Special appeals were made to black trade union and youth leaders to send delegations. Rallies, parties for delegates, posters in local schools, libraries and stores, and publicity on a local level were planned and organized from New York headquarters.

I observed all this activity and expert organizing technique from close up. From my experience in local organizing involving African-Americans I already had a respectful appreciation for their organizing abilities. Living in the black community had taught me to see some of the aspects of black life generally hidden from whites: the enormous amount of creative energy and talent present among any group of African-Americans that did not respond to white initiative, but immediately sprang into action when motivated by black leadership. My education was now continuing as I watched two master organizers at work.

Carl had arrived at a working agreement with the three co-chairmen, which gave our film unit the official stamp of approval. The letter he wrote is still in my possession. It reads, in part:

> Our purpose is to produce a documentary that can be used by the three co-chairmen to further the cause of human relations in the United States.
>
> . . . The film, when finished, becomes the sole property of the co-chairmen of the Prayer Pilgrimage Committee. It is their sole responsibility to handle it as they see fit. Once the film is finished, we relinquish all claim to its use.
>
> . . . We shall submit the script to the three co-chairmen for their suggestions, changes, in emphasis and final approval.
>
> Further, we agree that the co-chairmen have the right to take out of the film any parts that they feel tend to make it less effective for the uses to which they wish to put it.
>
> It is understood that whether or not the film is used, revised, or discarded at your sole option, you are not responsible for any cost whatsoever, since the offering of this material is a contribution to the committee. In return, our only requirement is the closest co-operation of the co-chairmen in order to present you with an effective film.

I regret that I have no memory of how this remarkably generous document was negotiated. In afterthought it is clear that it was unwise of Carl to relinquish all claims and rights to the film and especially to specify the right of the three co-chairmen to revise or discard the film. That much idealism was uncalled for.

After the signing of this document we received ID cards for the film people and had full access to all the events and participants. Carl and I felt that the film had, above all, to document the enthusiasm and determination of a broad variety of the pilgrims. In true documentary style we would interview as many people as possible and use their own words as part of the script. We had to do the interviews mostly on the day of the event itself.

I do not recall any problems with the organizers regarding the film except that we were repeatedly told that the three leaders had to be featured by giving each strictly "equal time." While we agreed to do so, this point became a source of contention in the editing and cutting stage.

The day of the event gave us perfect weather. The film crew had come a day early and we had scouted locations and roughly determined where the cameras would be placed. Several teams, each with a cameraman and a soundman, would be stationed at the various locations where the buses would arrive. They would film the arrival and randomly select some people for interviews. Other teams would cover the arrival at the Lincoln Memorial. Still others would cover celebrities whom we knew we wanted to interview. I had furnished each team with a few questions to ask: we wanted a little background about the person; we wanted to know what made them come and what they expected to result from this event. Because the cameramen we had were experienced documentary filmmakers, we knew we would get great "special" shots: a baby carried in a backpack; an old woman walking with a cane; a veteran in uniform in his wheelchair.

Later, official police count would tell us that "only" twenty thousand people came to the Prayer Pilgrimage, but for us, from the platform, it was a thrilling sight. No one had ever before seen so many African-Americans gathered in Washington. The police called it the most orderly crowd they had ever handled.[3] The peaceful black crowd, most dressed in their Sunday best, patiently gathering in this grand location, with a sprinkling of white faces throughout, was stunning to behold. Unlike the protest actions on school and lunch counter desegregation, there were no hostile white crowds to be seen, no hate-filled screaming protesters. It seemed as though, for once, the Sunday-quiet city of Washington had been turned over to the black pilgrims in recognition of their dignity and power. When

3. As cited in the *Chicago Defender,* May 25, 1957, p.1. The following account is based on my memories, the Prayer Pilgrimage Film and accounts in the *Chicago Defender* as well as the *Washington Post,* May 18, 1957.

the hushed crowd responded to the opening prayer and later, when it resonated to the gospel singing of Mahalia Jackson, it seemed to all present that it was possible that the dream might come true: democracy could work and right the wrongs suffered for so long by one tenth of the country's people. It seemed that peaceful prayer and demonstration could and would work wonders.

We opened our film with shots of people walking from the railroad station to the street, to background music of the "Negro National Anthem."

NARRATION: This is the day; this is it. The pilgrims are coming to Washington to stand up for rights and freedom.

{Image: Rev. Kilgore} REV. KILGORE: Through the years the church has given hope and leadership.

{Image: Rosa Parks, inside a church.}

{Image: Anonymous woman} ANONYMOUS WOMAN: We are tired of being second-class citizens. We have come from all over the nation to tell our leaders to pass civil rights legislation now.

{Brief speeches by Ted Brown, labor leader, speaking of black and white unity; Harry Belafonte; and Hulan Jack, Borough President of Manhattan.}

{Image: Bayard Rustin} BAYARD RUSTIN (speaking of the principles of nonviolence): The man who believes in nonviolence is prepared to be harmed, but not to harm. This is what we mean by saying not one hair of one white man's head is going to be harmed in our struggle.

{Images of mob scenes around school desegregation and of black children bravely making their way through threatening white crowds.}

{Image: A. Philip Randolph} A. PHILIP RANDOLPH: We have come to demonstrate the unity of the Negro people . . . to tell white supremacists to keep their evil hands off the NAACP.

{Image: James and Theresa Gordon, two young children from Clay, Kentucky, who defied angry mobs to go to an integrated school, laying a wreath at the foot of the Lincoln Memorial.}

ROY WILKINS: We are here because of the forces of darkness of this world, ignorance, prejudice and hatred . . . We have been given not bread but a stone. States have set up laws against the NAACP . . . We are in warfare for our rights.

{Images: "Colored Waiting Room"; "Colored Water Fountain"; KKK parading through town.}

{Closeup image: Black woman} BLACK WOMAN FROM TALLAHASSEE, FLORIDA: They bombed our church. But we have had no violence.

{Closeup image, Mahalia Jackson} MAHALIA JACKSON: I been 'buked and I been scorned, Oh Lord . . .

NARRATION: We are perplexed, but not in despair . . . We are cast down, but not destroyed. We are marching and nothing will stop us.

{Images of the Montgomery bus boycott; people walking. Rosa Parks closeup.}

NARRATION: They walked on weary feet till their cause was won . . .

{Closeup image, Rev. Martin Luther King, alternating with shots from his point of view into the audience.}

REV. KING: Our most urgent request to the President of the United States and every member of Congress is to give us the right to vote. (Audience: Yes.) Give us the ballot and we will no longer worry the federal government about our basic rights. Give us the ballot (Yes) and we will no longer plead to the federal government for passage of an anti-lynching law; we will by the power of our vote write the law on the statute books of the South (All right) and bring an end to the dastardly acts of the hooded perpetrators of violence. (Laughter) Give us the ballot (Give us the ballot) and we will transform the salient misdeed of bloodthirsty mobs (Yeah) into the calculated good deeds of ordinary citizens . . . Give us the ballot (Yeah) and we will place judges on the benches of the South who will do justly and love mercy . . . (Yeah) Give us the ballot (Yes) and we will quietly and nonviolently, without rancor or bitterness, implement the Supreme Court's decision of May 17, 1954. (That's right.)

{Long shot, as audience rises in standing ovation, waving placards and flags. Images of crowd filing out in orderly procession.}

NARRATION: We have come to claim our rights as citizens of this land. We have come to bear witness that all men are brothers. Walking, singing, praying, we are headed for freedom.

{Images of children in the crowd; image of a white boy and a black girl sitting on the lawn.}

NARRATION: Let us live together in freedom; let us walk together in love.

{Music up and over.}

So ended our film, on an upbeat note of hope and goodness. So ended the pilgrimage, as its organizers had hoped, peacefully and with dignity. By nightfall the pilgrims had left town, many of them filled with a new spirit of hope and with a sense that the tactic of nonviolent resistance to evil might actually be effective. Above all, march participants had found a new leader—young, vigorous, fearless and inspiring.

Despite the best efforts of the organizers to be evenhanded in the allotment of speaking time and in publicity, there was no way one could equate the impact of the three speakers. All three spoke well and with conviction, but only Rev. King set the crowd on fire. It was the first of Rev. King's speeches delivered to a national audience and its effect was electrifying. His deep, resonant voice, which would soon become familiar to most Americans, his poetic metaphors and his superb command of all the conventions of Baptist pulpit oratory were here displayed to an audience of tens of thousands, who visibly vibrated in response to his incantations. Press reports in both the mainstream white press and in the African-American press featured his speech as the outstanding event of the day and declared him the new leader of American Negroes. The Prayer Pilgrimage, which had originally and always been the inspired idea of A. Philip Randolph, launched, as Roy Wilkins had feared, the newly formed Southern Christian Leadership Conference under the leadership of Rev. King into national prominence. Bayard Rustin, Stanley Levison and Ella Baker had organized the SCLC for this very purpose. Ella Baker, dissatisfied with the disdain for women in leadership that she perceived and experienced in this ministerial association, would soon move on to becoming the chief sponsor of the Student Nonviolent Coordinating Committee (SNCC). Bayard Rustin and Levison stayed on to become Rev. King's closest advisors and consultants until his death. Rustin would be the chief organizer of the 1964 March on Washington, for which the Prayer Pilgrimage had been a kind of preparation, but which soon eclipsed it in public memory and in the record of historians.

The Prayer Pilgrimage did not noticeably affect the passage of a civil rights bill in Congress; in fact, politicians hardly recognized its existence. But it prepared the ground among African-Americans for the leadership of Rev. King and for the tactics of nonviolence.

Our group of filmmakers soon disbanded, except for the few who continued to work on post-production tasks, such as editing film and sound. We all felt exhilarated to have been part of this event and spoke in hopeful terms about the potential impact of the film in acquainting larger audiences with what had happened that day in Washington.

As is often the case with low-budget ventures, we soon ran out of money. On November 20, 1957, Carl sent the following letter to the three co-chairmen, Bayard Rustin, Ella Baker and Henry Lee Moon of the NAACP:

Since March 17 of this year a number of professional film people under my direction have been working steadily toward the completion of the Prayer Pilgrimage film. I am happy to be able to report that we have finished the major part of the job, including film editing and script, and have what we believe is a very exciting and unusual film . . . [He offered to arrange a screening for all interested.]

All of this labor has been donated, as were the services, facilities and much expensive equipment from numerous motion picture business organizations. By conservative estimate, this film, if commercially produced, would cost $30,000. So far we have spent in the neighborhood of $3,000 to make it. This sum has mostly been expended in such absolutes as film raw stock, laboratory processing and sound studio charges. All of this money was raised by the motion picture people themselves . . . The following remains to be done: final narration to be recorded, music and sound effects to be purchased and added, stock library footage to be laid in and final re-recording and printing to be done. Our schedule calls for . . . delivery to you of a [final] print before the first of the year.

In the final stages of production commercial facilities must be used and paid for. It will take $1500 now to complete the film . . . We have exhausted our resources . . . We are now asking for financial help from the three co-chairmen and their organizations . . . A single, well-promoted New York City premiere would more than recoup the relatively small amount we need now.

The response and enthusiasm of film people on behalf of this project has been truly remarkable and inspiring. I trust you will be pleased with the result of our efforts.

A. Philip Randolph answered on November 26 and thanked Carl and his co-workers for "a magnificent labor of love done in behalf of the cause of civil rights." However, he regretted that the Brotherhood of Sleeping Car Porters had "no funds to apply to such a purpose although we are deeply appreciative of the project and believe it a most creative and constructive job." He suggested that Carl get in touch with the other two sponsoring organizations and, if they had no ready funds available, he promised to help them raise such funds.[4]

Rev. King did not get around to answering Carl's appeal until December 17, 1957, when he assured him that he had read his letter "with scrutinizing care." SCLC's budget was small and could not be disbursed without the administrative committee's approval, which committee would not meet for three weeks. He would be glad to take up the matter with this committee when it met again.

I do not have the answer from NAACP in my files and I do not remember how the fifteen hundred dollars was finally raised. But I know that the film was finished and that we turned a copy over to Bayard Rustin. Carl meticulously kept all the bills, no matter how small, and I rather think he would have kept and cherished a letter from the three co-chairmen referring to receipt of the film. There is no such letter in the files and it may well be that it was received and lost. I know the premiere showing of the film took place under NAACP sponsorship on the anniversary of the Prayer Pilgrimage. I do not remember attending this event nor do I have any record of our being invited.

What I do know is that after this premiere, the film vanished. We never saw any evidence of its being used for fund-raising or educational purposes. Bayard Rustin did not answer our phone calls. Inquiries to the NAACP also remained unanswered.

This, to us, was a puzzling and upsetting result of our "labor of love." Even Stanley Levison could not offer any plausible explanation. He was vague and elusive. If the film had simply been lost or misplaced and the organizations found it embarrassing to admit it, this fact should have been easily obtained by Levison. If the co-chairmen singly or as a group were dissatisfied with the film, they could have edited it and used it anyway, as Carl's generous contract with them permitted them to do. Considering the various instances of jealousy and competitiveness among them we thought that perhaps one or the other had felt slighted by the way we treated them on screen and that the film had been shelved to avoid further con-

4. Quotes are both from letters to Carl Lerner, in the author's possession.

flict. This was a possible explanation, but it was also very disappointing, if true.

"It feels like being blacklisted all over again," Carl said once.

"Paranoia will get you nowhere," I responded cheerfully.

But the idea stayed with us and seemed more plausible the more our efforts at getting an explanation were rebuffed. With hindsight it seemed quite likely. Red-baiting played a great role in the jockeying for leadership of the African-American community. Randolph was a staunch anti-Communist from way back and had once even barred Rustin from assuming a public leadership role in the coalition because of rumors of Rustin's early flirtation with the Young Communist League. Rev. King seemed equally touchy on the subject and in a pre-pilgrimage news conference stressed that the Prayer Pilgrimage did not permit the participation of groups like the Communist Party and the Ku Klux Klan. With what we now know of the close FBI surveillance of Rev. King, which included taps on all his telephones, it is conceivable that he was warned, through third parties, not to utilize a film made by Communists or their sympathizers. Rustin, too, could have been put under such pressure.

Finally, there is the ambiguous role of Stanley Levison, whom the FBI accused of being "influenced by Communists," but who managed throughout all the smears to stay close to Rev. King. He had brought us into the project; it was hard to understand why he would not help us find out who was killing this film.

The co-chairmen and the organizers of this event were eager for the broadest possible publicity. They had been handed, free of charge, a means of publicity and fund-raising that would have cost them tens of thousands of dollars to produce and one that they individually praised. And yet, they never used it and all copies vanished. Finally, we gave up on the whole thing and tried to forget it.

Thirty years later, in my capacity as a professional historian, I finally was able to track down the film through the courtesy and generosity of Professor Clayborne Carson, the editor of the M. L. King papers, who unearthed what appears to be a pirated commercial copy of the film, now spliced together with another speech of Rev. King on a VCR. If it had not been for that copy I would not have been able to piece together this account, for the paper trail in my files proved inadequate.

Carl and I drew a moral from this event; whether we made it explicit or not I do not remember. We felt it illuminated the ironic position in which we found ourselves: after being harassed and persecuted by the government and the film industry because of our convictions, we were now considered unacceptable even by the leadership of the civil rights movement for being too radical.

We were unimportant people, compared with such outstanding radical African-American leaders as Paul Robeson and Dr. W.E.B. DuBois, who were similarly treated as embarrassing allies by the fledgling movement. Red-baiting, the casting out of those defined as "deviant outsiders," worked like a charm to split and weaken the movements for social change.

As for ourselves, we would have to find other means of acting on our beliefs.

[21]

I N 1958 I WAS ABOUT AS LOW as I had ever been. My health was bad; my
political work seemed to have failed. The loss of the Prayer Pilgrimage film
was then not quite evident in its full dimensions, but it was clear that the
film was not being used as had been intended. The betrayal of socialism by the
Soviet Union and the collapse of the Communist movement by repression and by
the weight of its own faults and mistakes was something that I could not then
appraise coolly and comprehend intellectually. It felt more like the deaths of several family members and friends, all at once and due to a major catastrophe. One
tried to bear it; one tried somehow to survive it; one hunkered down.

Normally, this might have been a time for introspection, for personal writing, for self-examination. But, as it happened, my writing career seemed to collapse at the very time when it might have saved me. The second novel was clearly unsalable. Associated Authors had flared up, succeeded briefly, then died. I
seemed to have lost my confidence as a writer; I was totally blocked.

A year or so later, I took the unprecedented step of pouring out my problem
to a writer I greatly admired but who was not personally known to me. Lillian
Smith had written an article in the *Saturday Review* in which she had urged writers to make a deep social commitment. I responded to it by sending her a very
personal letter. I described my unpublishable novel and wrote: "Commitment is
not enough. I am blocked as an artist, deprived of any audience ... How can a

writer breathe and grow, deprived of criticism, deprived of the reader to whom he must speak?"

Amazingly, Lillian Smith answered with a long and sympathetic letter.[1] She wrote: "The artist must have a sense of vocation, a sense of being 'called' to his work . . . he must listen when he is told to 'make a new thing' . . . He must make this 'new thing' out of his own personal experience of life."

In my response to this letter I spoke of the writer's loneliness, the pain out of which "something new" is formed. I suggested that in her case, every line of her work spoke of rootedness. "It is different with me," I asserted. "I'm one of the uprooted." And I continued with an impassioned outcry that described my crisis and my despair more accurately than I had been able to define it even to myself.

It takes a certain amount of presumption to choose to be a writer. To hear that inner call, to perfect oneself as an instrument, to persist. It is daring and painful and glorious. If one succeeds, if one can be heard, then there is affirmation. But if one is blocked, out of tune? Must one go on? Should one? Is it not arrogating to oneself a rightness of judgement as against the judgement of others? Failure is never pleasant, but it is something the creative artist must surmount. But for me failure sets into motion the whole pattern of rejection and uprooting. I feel that perhaps I have not been able to overcome all the barriers my particular situation imposed, that perhaps I simply speak for no one. And if that should be the case, how can I go on? Or, to put it more sharply, by what right do I persist in going on?

This was the crux of the matter. I had considered myself a writer since the age of sixteen. I felt I had come to the end of the road; for the first time in my life I seriously considered giving up writing.

Lillian Smith, then battling cancer, was too sick to answer my second letter, but she asked her friend and companion, Paula Snelling, to advise me of that fact. Perhaps it was that generous gesture of an accomplished and famous writer that saved me. Perhaps it was just my stubborn vitality. But sometime in 1958, with my health improving, I decided to take some academic courses and I decided to find a new mode of writing—I would write a historical novel.

---

1. For the full text of Lillian Smith's letter to me, see *How Am I to Be Heard? Letters of Lillian Smith*, ed. Margaret Rose Gladney (Chapel Hill: University of North Carolina Press, 1993), 266–67.

The course I chose to take at the New School for Social Research, an institution that specialized in refugee professors and adult learners, was somewhat quixotic. It was a course in English grammar, taught by a Yugoslav professor with a horrendous accent. Carl, who always had admired my proficiency in grammar, thought I was finally really out of my mind. He was not impressed with my lame explanation that I still felt unsure about certain points of grammar and wanted to improve this. The course actually was quite good and satisfied my need for certainty. The next course I chose was English poetry of the seventeenth and eighteenth centuries.

The historical novel on which I decided to work told the story of Angelina and Sarah Grimké, daughters of a Southern plantation owner, who become agents for antislavery and women's rights. I set to work and actually wrote eight chapters of a fictionalized biography, but I was not satisfied with my work. The discrepancy between the historical sources pertaining to the sisters and my ability to interpret them became increasingly clear to me, even as I added some history courses to my study. I decided that I needed formal training as a historian to do justice to this story, discarded the eight chapters and started all over again on a proper historical biography of Sarah and Angelina Grimké.

I enrolled at the New School, where I earned my B.A. in four years of part-time study; then I earned my M.A. and Ph.D. at Columbia University in three more years, with the Grimké biography as my dissertation. While still an undergraduate, I offered my first course in Women's History at the New School in 1963; I taught it again in 1964. Thus, my career as a historian began almost by accident; I thought of it as a way of acquiring a skill necessary to my writing. But history as a subject grabbed me and never let me go and before long, when I realized that what I wanted to do was to create and promote the history of women, I put all my energy, passion and talent into becoming a good historian. I knew that as a pioneer in a neglected or nonexistent field I could succeed only through excellence. This meant learning the best of what traditional history training had to offer. I did that; I loved it; and then I went on to challenge it and change it.

Whatever influence on the field I had came not only through my research and writing, but also through my organizational work. I have participated as an activist and, at times, a leader in the struggle of professional women for equal access and equal opportunity in the academic establishment, and I have helped to advance Women's Studies and see it grow as a widely accepted scholarly discipline. I have become an "insider" in academia, even though my work and my position have long been either at the frontier or at the margin, depending on the beholder's viewpoint.

The years since 1957 have been extraordinarily rich in struggles and victories, in exhilarating experiments and discoveries, in friendships and cooperation in the building of a new field of scholarship. Above all, they have at last given me that "beloved community," women struggling for their equal place in the academy and in the content of academic knowledge. It is, despite all the stresses of "differences," an international community engaged in a work of enormous significance: women, so long defined only as man's "Other," are defining *themselves* and entering as equals upon the field of cultural and symbolic redefinition.

Yet my own life has retained the pattern of sharp breaks and fissures, the constant struggles with new beginnings. In 1973, when Carl died after a long and terrible illness, I had to relearn how to live and work alone after thirty-three years of shared work and living. In 1980, at the age of sixty, I moved to a state in which I did no know a single person to start a Ph.D. program in Women's History at the University of Wisconsin—Madison. Twenty years later, after nine years of "retirement" during which my lecturing and writing continued at the usual pace, I am engaged in yet another transition. Faced now with somewhat limited mobility, I spend the winters in Durham, North Carolina, close to Stephanie and her family. Another new beginning with the usual challenges. I take a somewhat ironic pride in the fact that at age seventy-nine, I began to teach again, part time, at Duke University. How fortunate that at long last I found an occupation that constantly renews me and gives me strength.

People who have only known me in these past decades inevitably regard me as successful, privileged and "strong," as though these characteristics were lifelong, inborn or given. I know better, and that is another reason why I wrote this book about struggles, mistakes, detours and searches for direction.

I end this autobiography in 1958, the year that marked the major transitions in my life: from outsider to insider, from writer to historian, from activist to theoretician. Even as I write this, I realize these distinctions are not apt. They still reflect my earlier consciousness, one of absolutes, one of exclusive choices. The fact is that I combine all these elements of my life, and I think I have finally found the wholeness that embraces contradictions, the holistic view of life that accepts multiplicity and diversity, a view that no longer demands a rigid framework of certainties.

As I look back in 2001, when Communism in Europe has long ago collapsed of its own errors and crimes, it is quite difficult to face my own political journey with honesty and understanding. Before undertaking to write this autobiography I felt that my political development was quite comprehensible and had followed logically out of my own personal history and the times and events out of which I came. Despite all the decades of the cold war and its propaganda, despite the incessant barrage of anti-Communist revelations of conspiracies and deceits, I never felt that I personally had anything to apologize for. My convictions were sincere and derived from my own experience as an antifascist, as a Jew, as an unskilled immigrant worker, as a woman. My own activities and those of the people I knew intimately were solid grassroots activities for usually excellent causes, often at times when such causes were highly unpopular and when there were heavy disincentives for pursuing them. I mean such causes as peace and nuclear disarmament during and after the Korean and Vietnam Wars, race integration and the rights of minorities, trade union and community organizing. The rank and file Communists I knew similarly came to their convictions and to their party activities on the basis of their own life experiences, especially during the Depression. They were the first to work for racial integration in sports, for unemployment insurance, for trade union rights, for nuclear disarmament. During the cold war years, they were denounced as dupes and tools of a foreign power, accused of evil intentions; their motives were distorted and their goals were misrepresented.

The obscene conformity of the fifties and the rush of people to establish their own respectability by denouncing former friends and co-workers as Communists at a time when such denunciation meant loss of work and reputation seemed to me so much like the conformity of the "good Germans" that I saw no other choice but resistance. When blacklists existed and when there was a prison sentence on unpopular opinions, I chose to be on the side of the attacked rather than that of the attackers. Such resistance demanded not only considerable courage, but also a firm belief system that did not entertain doubts or admit troublesome information that might undermine it. Had I written this account twenty years ago, I would have focused on the rightness of my position and on explaining to the post-Vietnam generation that the Old Left has been unduly maligned and its achievements have been forgotten. That still seems partially true to me, but now everything has become far more complex and disturbing.

I write to find out what I know. What I now know is different from what I knew then.

Then, I could have said, in true good conscience, that in all my years as a Communist I rarely personally did anything of which I am ashamed, nor did I know others of whose actions I am ashamed. The latter part of the sentence is no longer true and neither can I say the former with the kind of assurance with which I would have said it for a large part of my life.

For even if all my own actions and those of the people I worked with had been without reproach, there still remains the stubborn fact that we were part of and supported a system whose "errors" and atrocities we refused to see and admit, in the face of contradictory evidence. Had I known in 1939 of the secret Stalin-Hitler agreement on the partition of Poland, which was part of the Nazi-Soviet Non-Aggression Pact, I would never have gone along with it. That sounds nice and reasonable; the only thing wrong with it is that it does not answer this question: why did I disregard all the information published in the New York Times *and other papers accessible to me, which made the charge that there were secret agreements to the Non-Aggression Pact, which served to disillusion many pro-Communists at that time? I remember very little about that period in my life, but I do remember heatedly defending Stalin's right to protect the Soviet Union against invasion, to gain time. Munich and its betrayal of antifascism loomed as a major precedent in my mind. Much later, when I read Harrison Salisbury's devastating account of Stalin's betrayal of his own people, of the unpreparedness of Russian troops for self-defense, of the tens of thousands of needless losses in the early weeks of the German invasion, I still disregarded it and refused to see it as part of a larger picture. Now, with the publication by the Russian government of the map of partition, I cannot evade my own complicity in studied ignorance. I hesitate to say I was duped; I'd rather say I believed what I wanted and needed to believe, as I clung to the certainty of my fixed paradigm.*

As a historian, I have often studied that phenomenon in others: the true believers of Garrisonian abolitionism quarreling with their former allies over minute points of difference and espousing ever more radical beliefs the fewer supporters they could muster; the various splinter groups of Social Democracy fighting one another with more vigor and heat than they could muster for any other cause; the Woman's Party, in an age of victorious reform feminism, becoming more and more isolated and more and more reactionary, paranoid and defensive in its isolation.

I have striven to lead a conscious, an examined life and to practice what I preach. It now appears that, nevertheless, I failed in many ways, for I fell uncritically for lies I should have been able to penetrate and perceive as such. Like all true believers, I believed as I did because I needed to believe: in a utopian vision of the future, in the possibility of human perfectibility, in idealism and heroism. And I still need that belief, even if the particular vision I had embraced has turned to ashes.

I have called myself a post-Marxist for several decades and I came to that stance as soon as I became a feminist. Ever since the late 1950s I believed that the so-called errors of Communist leadership in the Soviet Union were structural and built into the very fabric of Marxist doctrine. Basically, I came to the conclusion that Marxist thought was in error in

regard to race and ethnicity in its insistence that class subsumed these categories. As for gen-
der, Marxist thought, while giving lip service to the "woman question" (the very phrase
positing it as a marginal problematic interfering with a larger concern), was unable to com-
prehend or improve the situation of women, because it marginalized them and reduced patri-
archal dominance to economic dominance. Its analysis never went further than that of bour-
geois liberalism in regard to women's rights, leaving women's emancipation entirely out of
consideration. And the Bolshevik concept of the "dictatorship of the proletariat," which
automatically destroyed the basis of voluntary grassroots organization of all kinds, made
the destruction of autonomous women's organizations inevitable. Without these, women's
emancipation and even women's rights are unattainable.

I thought my way out of Marxism the same way I had found my way into it—by rea-
soning and by relying on my own experience. My attitude toward the Soviet Union had lit-
tle to do with it. Like many persons of the Old Left I retained my class analysis and my
deep commitment to racial equality, which I brought into my understanding of Women's
History at a time when such ideas were new to most of the young women then building this
new discipline. I never was actively involved in the Marxist-feminist debate and effort,
although I know some of the best minds among feminists were deeply involved in it. I was
simply out of synch with it—what they were newly discovering and embracing I had long
known and then left behind. So my outsider status continued, even into the new paradigm
and movement.

On balance, I think whatever contributions as a feminist theoretician and thinker I have
been able to make derive from my life experience, including my life as a Communist, my
experience of persecution and, above all, my life as a grassroots organizer. My work as a
women's historian has been noted for taking race and class into consideration as early as
1966. That comes directly out of my life and my experience. I could never have written and
edited Black Women in White America: A Documentary History *(1972), the first*
historical work to document the existence of a history of African-American women, if it had
not been for my experiences in Congress of American Women, in the interracial housing
struggles in Astoria, in living in an interracial community.[2] The style and method of my
teaching, the practical extension of my academic knowledge through community outreach, of
which the Summer Institute in Women's History for Leaders of Women's Organizations
(1979) was perhaps the best expression, came directly out of my organizational work. I
have to face the reality that in all the years of my life as an American radical I influenced

2. Gerda Lerner, ed., *Black Women in White America: A Documentary History* (New York: Pantheon, 1972).

very few people and changed society very little. By contrast, the 1979 institute took as its class project making Women's History Month a national annual event. The project succeeded and has been annually renewed ever since with a presidential proclamation. It helped to create one of the biggest grassroots history movements in the country, which affected and involved tens of thousands of people. Earlier, when I helped to initiate a project that would identify Women's History sources in U.S. archives, a project that after four years of work resulted in the publication of Women's History Sources: A Guide to Archives and Manuscript Collections in the United States *(1979), I had hoped that this project would make sources on women more easily accessible to scholars.[3] It did that, but in fact it revolutionized the way U.S. archives catalogued and classified their holdings on women and proved to the scholarly community that primary sources on the history of women were available in every community in the United States. I think my ability to identify crucial issues that have large-scale impact comes directly out of my years of working on lost causes. One learns from one's mistakes.*

The various projects I have worked on in past decades were all group projects and collective endeavors. The fact that, despite my antisocial upbringing, I could work successfully with women much younger than myself who came from various backgrounds quite different than my own speaks to the positive impact my radical political life had on my character development. It is easy in the glow of official recognition and acclaim to forget one's radical roots. It would probably be safer to keep silence. Even now, as a write these words, I am afraid. The kind of fear I have lived with since the age of fourteen does not vanish in the periods of comfort and acceptance. It is always there, ready to flare up with the slightest draft.

I do not want to live with it anymore. I want to be honest with my readers, my students and my colleagues, honest about who I am, who I was and how I got to be who I am. I neither regret nor disown my political past. Sometimes I think that what I was finally able to learn from my father is to take life as it is, with its lies and corruption and illusions, take it and try to survive without doing harm to others. This I have done, though perhaps not as well as I might have.

Yet in a deeper sense I have always made that basic leap from human frailty into a nonexistent security of order. As if the utopian vision were becoming reality; as if I were not an outsider; as if I could, by willing it, make life and the world meaningful. We know we must die; we know the world is bad; we know we are corruptible, and yet we act as if it were not so. And as we act, we actually are in the process of changing ourselves and those around us. We are making a future.

---

3. Andrea Hinding, ed., *Women's History Sources: A Guide to Archives and Manuscript Collections in the United States*, 2 vols. (New York: R. R. Bowker, 1979).

After a forest fire rages over a mountainside, leaving everything black and charred and life-less, there is a time when life, even the promise of life, seems to have vanished from that desolate landscape. And then, first with green shoots, then red flowers, the fireweed comes out of the barren ground, insisting on survival, pushing its persistent roots under the ashes of destruction. Soon, the black and rocky landscape is punctured by patches of small red growth, which will spread and make soil, make space for hope and future transformation.

Acting just as if fireweed could make a forest.

THANKS

This work has been a long time in the making, several sections of it having been written as long as forty years ago. Most of it is the product of the past seven years, a period following my professional retirement.

The decision to write an autobiography of this sort takes more nerve than jumping off a cliff into cold water. Unlike the academic writer, the autobiographer is sustained neither by grants nor by the sobering weight of dozens of pages of endnotes that testify to years of effort and verifiable facts. The autobiographer is quite alone out there, much like the writer of fiction. In this book I have combined literary techniques with those of the historian, but the literary mode has predominated. For me, returning to the writer's way of seeing life has been a welcome and joyous end of a long journey.

My sister, Nora Kronstein-Rosen, has shared her own memories with me and helped me to stay cognizant of the limitations of memory by pointing out many instances when her version of events differs from mine. Our wrestling separately with a past unique to each of us has kept us engaged in a constant process of reinterpretation and reevaluation that has been challenging and stimulating. I am thankful that, although we are physically as far apart as ever, we have finally come to a place of rest and common understanding.

My friends and colleagues Steven Feierman, Sandra Barnes, Joyce Antler, Elizabeth Minnich, Steve Stern and Amy Swerdlow, and my daughter, Stephanie Lerner, read the entire manuscript. Mary Lou Munts read early chapters. These readers offered honest and insightful criticism, encouragement and, most importantly, support for the validity of the enterprise whenever I doubted it and faltered. Their belief that what I had to tell was worth hearing supported and sustained me during difficult periods. I am profoundly thankful to them not only for their help with this book but for the intellectual stimulation and sustaining love and friendship they have given me over many years.

The two readers for Temple University Press, Mari Jo Buhle and Susan Porter Benson, offered valuable criticism that improved my final editing. Their enthusiastic response helped this book come to life, for which I greatly thank them.

My agent, Frances Goldin, never wavered in her faith in the author and her work, and invested her great knowledge and energy in making the book get into print. I warmly thank her for it and feel privileged to have come to know her so late in life.

I am equally privileged in having found in Janet Francendese of Temple University Press an editor whose understanding comments greatly helped me in revising. She read the manuscript twice, in different versions; her professional knowledge and her faith in this work have made our collaboration unusually pleasant for me. Thanks and thanks again.

Janet Benton has been a most efficient and rigorous copy editor. Her dedication to precision and clarity have been pleasantly balanced by her willingness to adapt to occasional peculiarities of my style. I have learned much from her and appreciate her skill and patience, with thanks.

I am also thankful for the fine professional work of Nancy Berliner and Janet Greenwood of Berliner, Inc., and of Gary Kramer and Ann-Marie Anderson of Temple University Press.

Over these seven years, the interest other friends and colleagues expressed in this project was a lifeline for me. The historical understanding, the political wisdom and the intellectual support they gave empowered me and kept me going. Thank you, Gerhardt Botz, Helga Embacher, Estelle B. Freedman, Paula Giddings, Linda Gordon, Jacquelyn Dowd Hall, Darlene Clark Hine, Bonnie Johnson, Linda Kerber, Alice Kessler-Harris, Bob Korstad, Ann Lane, Judy Walzer Leavitt and Lewis Leavitt, Lawrence and Cornelia Levine, Albert Lichtblau, Florencia Mallon, Nellie McKay, Ruth Rosen, Kathryn Kish Sklar, Annie Topham and Susan Traverso. The splendid work of Larry Ceplair on the Hollywood blacklist has influenced my work and sustained my interpretation.

A number of friends whose lives and thoughts influenced my writing are no longer living. I hope they will live on in memory and in this work: Virginia Brodine, Kay Clarenbach, Merle Curti, Liz Karlin, Henry Kraus, Eve Merriam, George Mosse, David and Naomi Robison, Viola Brothers Shore. And always, Carl Lerner.

Those who lived through persecution and hardship, who stood their ground, who shared their stories and memories with me, who challenged my way of looking at their story—they are my sources, my inspiration. I thank them for their generosity and trust and, above all, for the kinds of lives they led.

I HAVE BEEN A WRITER far longer than I have been an academic. Now I have come full circle: it feels good to acknowledge and practice both parts of my being. I trust the readers of my academic work will follow me into this expansion and exploration. I could not have come to this without the support of my friends and the love and support of my children, Stephanie and Dan; their spouses, Todd and Elizabeth; and my grandchildren, Joshua and Sophia, Clay and Reed.

The feminist community of scholars and activists, for all its conflicts, tensions and contradictions, has been home and grounding for me—truly a beloved community. I offer it this work, as my form of offering thanks.

Gerda Lerner
Madison, Wisconsin
February 2002